DIVINE COUNCILS IN THE AFTERLIFE

THE FLIPSIDE COURT

By Richard Martini

Michelangelo: The Last Judgment

DIVINE COUNCILS IN THE AFTERLIFE:

THE FLIPSIDE COURT

BY RICHARD MARTINI

Copyright 2022 © by Richard Martini

All Rights Reserved. No part of this book may be reproduced by any mechanical, photographic, or electronic process, other than for "fair use" as brief quotations embodied in articles and review without prior written permission of the publisher.

The author of this book does not dispense medical advice or prescribe the use of any technique as a form of treatment for physical or medical problems without the advice of a physician, either directly or indirectly. The intent of the author is only to offer information of a general nature to help you in your quest for emotional and spiritual well-being. In the event you use any of the information in this book for yourself, which is your constitutional right, the author and the publisher assume no responsibility for your actions.

Cover design: Michelangelo's "Last Judgement." As a young man Michelangelo was adopted by the poet Lorenzo De Medici, made a member of his Platonic Academy in Florence. Years later, after the Pazzi Conspiracy and Lorenzo's brother Giuliano was murdered in the Duomo of Florence, at the behest of the Vatican, the son of Lorenzo became Pope Leo X and hired Michelangelo to paint the Sistine Chapel.

In terms of the "Last judgment" it's when people report they have a life review. Medium Jennifer Shaffer and I have interviewed Michelangelo, Lorenzo, Giuliano and Botticelli in our books "Backstage Pass to the Flipside." While I won't say it was "divinely inspired" to use his artwork on the cover for this book, I did seek out his permission. *Signore Buonarroti approvato.*

Certain Names and identifying characteristics have been changed. Interviews have been edited for time and context.

Homina Publishing PO Box 248, Santa Monica, CA 90406
www.hominapublishing.com

CHAPTERS

FOREWORD: CURIA POST VITA – *FLIPSIDE COURT*
INTRODUCTION:
PICTURE YOURSELF IN A BOAT ON A RIVER
CHAPTER ONE: *A SHIFT IN CONSCIOUSNESS* **– KELLY**
CHAPTER TWO: KEN
CHAPTER THREE: KIKI
CHAPTER FOUR: DAVID
CHAPTER FIVE: ELOISE
CHAPTER SIX: JULIET
CHAPTER SEVEN: MIMI
CHAPTER EIGHT: RONNIE
CHAPTER NINE: GIANNI
CHAPTER TEN: THE NEUROSCIENTISTS –
AKILA WEERASEKERA, PHD
CHAPTER ELEVEN: *DR. CARLO, PHD*
CHAPTER TWELVE:
OTHER COUNCIL DISCUSSIONS **- ANDREW**
CHAPTER THIRTEEN: REVEREND WILL
CHAPTER FOURTEEN: MIRELLA
CHAPTER FIFTEEN: LILIAN
CHAPTER SIXTEEN: MICHAEL THE DIRECTOR
CHAPTER SEVENTEEN: *RANDOM COUNCIL VISITS –*
 MAO FROM CHINA
CHAPTER EIGHTEEN: CATHY
CHAPTER NINETEEN: SIMON
CHAPTER TWENTY: STORY TELLERS SKIP AND JANE
CHAPTER TWENTY-ONE:
A COMPENDIUM OF COUNCILS – PART ONE
CHAPTER TWENTY-TWO:
A COMPENDIUM OF COUNCILS - PART TWO
CHAPTER TWENTY-THREE:
A COMPENDIUM OF COUNCILS – PART THREE
CHAPTER TWENTY-FOUR:
A COMPENDIUM OF COUNCILS - PART FOUR
SUMMA THEOLOGIAE MORALIS
AUTHOR'S BIO AND THANKS

FOREWORD: *CURIA POST VITA* – AFTERLIFE COURT

Everyone's welcome in court. Just feels like we're not.

"There is a higher court than courts of justice and that is the court of conscience. It supersedes all other courts." *Mahatma Gandhi*

Curia Post Vita translates roughly as "Afterlife Court."

I first heard about "a council of elders" in Michael Newton's books and in his interview for my film "Flipside." Michael was a therapist who had thousands of reports about the afterlife before he wrote his first book "Journey of Souls" in 1994. Since his interview I've found other accounts of "divine councils" in the work of psychologist Dr. Helen Wambach ("Reliving Past Lives") to descriptions of "wise beings" and in the near death accounts from Dr. Bruce Greyson (from his book "After").

It sounds like some sci-fi concept based on legal courts; *etheric judges in robes passing sentences in the afterlife?*

However, my use of the word "court" is tongue-in-cheek.

In the over 100 examples I've filmed of people accessing their "councils" they report wise teachers who don't "pass judgment" per se, but act as ombudsmen, like professors conducting a doctoral thesis; asking pointed questions about what a person learned during their lifetime versus what they said they'd planned to learn.

Newton observed people report "two visits" to their council, one prior to incarnation, a kind of "preproduction meeting" where individuals go over what they have in mind or planned to learn, then a "return visit" after the lifetime, where they experience a "past life review" of what they did or did not accomplish.

During the life review people report they experience first-hand all the good or bad they did in their lifetime. This can be disconcerting for some, making the experience feel like a "courtroom" where they're being judged. All those in attendance report seeing them experience the pain, suffering or trauma they inflicted upon others. People report experiencing these events first hand, while the council – sometimes an entire auditorium of participants – watches the person squirm for the mistakes they've made.

In essence, it is a "judgement day" as the person experiencing the life review gets the benefit of seeing how these events were part of a person's overall journey over many lifetimes. It could include events that had a genesis in a previous lifetime, a story point being paid off in this one – or for some to realize events had been "requested" by others asking for help. In these "past life reviews" one could argue that it's akin to experiencing "hell" because the person feels the pain and trauma and suffering they inflicted, but from the perspective of their victims.

But this book isn't about judgments.

I was more interested in exploring and demonstrating "everyone has a council" or that "anyone can visit their council." One doesn't have to have a special ticket, doesn't have to have a near death experience to get in – doing simple guided meditation can allow access to one's council.

It's easier for a person to visit their council with the benefit of a hypnotherapy session; in the multi-hour sessions done by Newton Institute therapists, often include visits to their "council" for advice that can help them on their journey. But people who can meditate, visualize or comment on things in their minds, are capable of visiting their councils as well. Hypnosis is not required, but helps.

It's not my opinion, theory or belief that people can and do visit their councils – in this experiment, the majority of people had never visited their council before, had no awareness they could ask questions or get answers.

When I decided to make a documentary about Michael Newton's work (*FlipsideMyFilm.com*) I interviewed him for his "last interview" at a conference in a Chicago suburb. The topic of the "Divine Council" came up.

A Trip to the Council of Elders

Richard: I've spoken with a few people who've referred to their own recurring dreams of being in a classroom somewhere in the Universe, some working with or without energy. Also, I'd like to know more about "The Elders."

Michael Newton: We get flashbacks from time to time that break through that amnesiac block, folks who've had no LBL experiences, and just ordinary people that don't know about our work. Suddenly they're in a classroom in their dreams and they think "Hmm. That's a strange image; where's that coming from?" Most of us between lives spend time in a spiritual classroom. They are usually described as buildings, a library, or the place where they meet their council looks like a beautiful domed structure and in some cases a temple. Of course, there aren't buildings in the ethereal space between lives, but people free-associate or have flashbacks of buildings; "I'm in a classroom, I have people around me that I know, there's a teacher..."

Essentially we're given instruction by a Specialist Soul in areas we may have a talent or affinity for. They may be areas we'll specialize in after our incarnations are over - when we will be helping others. I often hear about an energy creating class where they're working with raw energy to create certain things. I have the theory a lot of what we see on Earth in terms of plants and animals and geographics has been created by groups of advanced souls.

When we visit the Elders, we talk about our lessons and what we might do differently in the future. We're not standing before God or a Creator or a Source - But people

describe feeling kind of a God like presence at these meetings. It's hard for people to describe it; I need to speak to someone who's not incarnating anymore to give me answers to that sort of thing. Once in a while I got a highly advanced client who was in their last series of incarnations, who'd open the door a little bit, and it's beautiful to listen to.

What kinds of questions would you like to know the answers to from this work?

When I get an advanced client in my chair, I feel sorry for them because I'm a relentless inquisitor. I've asked the question "What does it all mean?" with certain advanced clients. One thing I've learned is that we are only one of many universes. I've been able to hear about nine or ten dimensions, either parallel universes or universes that overlap in timelines, through patients. Once you leave Earth, of course, you're not in linear time anymore, you're in what we call 'now time' - which is past, present and future... that's the best I can do on the question about creation - I wish I could tell you more."

(Flipside: A Tourist's Guide on How to Navigate the Afterlife" Pg. 23)

In the reports I've read of Michael Newton visiting these councils, or in my questions to him, I was not aware of his addressing council members directly to ask them questions. It would be contrary to the therapist's work to ask council members direct question about their own journey. However, I'm not a therapist, and in this book, I ask council members direct questions; "How did they became council members, how long they've been on this person's council, how many councils are they on, if they've ever incarnated on earth or elsewhere before, what's their opinion about this kind of research" etc.

Hypnosis is an excellent tool to access this information, however in this book, these trips to visit councils are from people without hypnosis, not channeling, or any other method – simply asking the same questions. Some subjects know of me, most have never heard of me or this research, most are just accessing what's they're experiencing as it happens in front of them. They learn new information as I do on camera.

None of the direct subjects in the study were aware of my work or methodology (other examples who were familiar I've included later in the book). All had a preliminary conversation where a mutual friend introduced us, said I wanted to do a "Zoom meeting" where we would attempt a guided meditation. She did not mention anything about the afterlife, guides or councils or any of the details of her session, which none were aware of.

I used a simple directive for this guided meditation. It comes from the Beatles song "Lucy in the Sky With Diamonds" and is a simple directive that many have heard before. I'm not asking them to imagine being on a cloud, or in a yoga pose - the concept is simple and effective. I ask people to do just one thing.

Picture yourself in a boat on a river.

When people do, they may remember a boat they've been in during this lifetime – sometimes it's a boat they don't recognize, sometimes they later recognize it as a boat from a previous lifetime. They can describe the boat – if it's wood, etc – and how it is constructed. They can recall if it's a familiar boat or something invented.

They can also describe the river, the body of water that they find themselves floating in – or heading downstream. They can be very specific about such a simple detail, even though they've never done this particular meditation before, since I borrowed it.

After they offer they can "see themselves in a boat" I ask questions about it, about the water involved, and then ask them to "invite" someone to sit across from them in the boat. They may instantly see someone, or they may say "I'm seeing a person in the distance" or sometimes it's merely a "light." If so, I invite the person in the distance to come forward, if it's a light, I'll ask if they can manifest as a person to make it easier to converse – but neither are required. Sometimes it's a loved one, a relative – sometimes it's their guide. I can ask for their guide to sit with them, and sometimes it's a male or female, sometimes a combination of both, sometimes it's a light. The only word \ referent is the word "guide." I assume that their guide knows who they are, so asking for their guide is not something that is foreign to the guide, even if the person has no clue who that might be.

Sometimes the guide is happy to sit this out – because they know that it could be problematic to appear to this person. I always ask if they're familiar with my work – and sometimes they are and sometimes they are not. I ask because if they are, the guide already knows what I'm going to ask next, even if the person I'm talking to does not.

I demonstrated this technique in a podcast with Dr. Drew Pinsky. We both appeared on his wife's podcast, it's in the film "Hacking The Afterlife" where I asked Dr. Drew to invite his guide forward. He said that he saw a light. I asked the guide if we could "visit his council." Dr. Drew said "What's a council?" and I said "I wasn't asking you; I'm asking your guide."

We went in to visit his council live on camera. He saw and met people he's never consciously seen before, and yet they all knew him and imparted new information to him. He got emotional at one point, with one of his council members "blessing him" with an Indian totem. It was new information for him.

He said afterwards that he felt "hypnotized" because he was seeing things he had never consciously seen before, yet as I pointed out, there was no hypnosis involved. Just asking questions.

Everyone has a council.

The number of members changes – sometimes it's composed of "whoever is available." So a person with a council of fifteen might only see five or six of them. Others have less – there's no set amount other than being an average of 3-15 individuals.

In Michael Newton's reports, he found that to be the case – sometimes people report "more people in this room" ("I'm seeing 100") but I've found that we can then ask "Can we speak to the core group responsible for this person's journey?" and the number is often three to fifteen.

So in this book you're going to hear about a number of different councils – some are around five or six, some are around a dozen, some councils meet outside "in the sky" some meet "in a sacred grove" or some meet "in a building." Buildings are different, depends on the person seeing them – some are like log cabins, some are like cathedrals.

People see their core council together – either in a row, a semi-circle or a line. Sometimes a circle. Sometimes around a location. The point is, when they describe a line or semi-circle, I can ask them to "go to the person on your left and let's see if we can address them."

In the book "*Architecture of the Afterlife*" there are a number of councils we visit, including one that "didn't want to speak with us." In one of the podcasts I did with Simon Bown he told me that he had "tried to visit his council" before and they refused to let him in. So during out live broadcast I asked him to return there, and then asked the reason for the lack of entry. They explained it – which basically was "He wasn't ready then." (That transcript is in this book.)

So there's a give and take involved. Not every council member thinks it's a good idea to visit the council for some people. Because they are supposed to "learn about his information" in their own time frame and this form of "skipping ahead" is problematic. That's not often reported, but I'd be remiss if I didn't.

If that is the message one is getting now – at this moment while hearing or reading the book – I suggest returning the book for a refund, giving it back to whomever gave it to you, or otherwise not going any further. What you're about to explore is something that has been unexplored for centuries. And exploring it allows for the possibility of its existing – and ultimately leads to more questions than answers.

Let's begin our journey with an example of someone who visited their council. It's in the film and book FLIPSIDE, and in this case, it's the first past life regression I'd filmed. Paul Aurand, former President of the Newton Institute is conducting a session in front of a class, Michael Newton is a few feet away, suggesting questions on a white board, and a volunteer from the class has just recalled a difficult lifetime where she died in Auschwitz during the Holocaust.

TRIP TO A COUNCIL FROM FLIPSIDE

Paul Aurand asks about the amount of energy she brought to her lifetime;

Paul: Was that adequate? A good choice?

The subject replies: "I thought 39% was enough, but I was wrong, I could have brought more."

You might ask (your guide) if now is the time to visit those wise beings we know as "the council?" As you approach please describe where they will meet and work with you.

It's a formal setting. It's very stately and the floors are marbled. My council is sitting at a table, crescent shaped.

How many are there?

Seven. They seem more transparent than solid and there's an appearance of robes because of the fluidness they have. I see a beautiful royal blue color and light purple.

Is there one central figure?

There's one in the center that will serve in that role. My guide has gone over to stand by the council. I'm standing; I like to stand before them.

And what do you feel standing before them?

Gratitude. I feel honored and such great love coming from them, and of course, my love for them is almost overwhelming.

What are they communicating to you?

They're very supportive but I have some questions I want to ask. I'm addressing the main chairperson, but it's addressed to all.

Does the response come from the chairperson?

He filters the input he gets from everyone and when he speaks, he's speaking for all.

What do you ask?

"How they think I'm doing in this present life?" I also want input about the most recent one.

When you've done that let me know how they respond.

(Laughs) They say "Do you have to ask us the same question every time you come back?" They're tired of me being insecure when I get here; they're asking "What do

you think?" As I stand before them, it seems like all of that becomes so unimportant because this message keeps that everything I do and everything everybody else does is fine, it's all part of the process. Whatever choices I make, they're perfectly fine choices and it's the reaction I have to the choices that creates a problem.

They're saying although some actions are more harmful or destructive, they cause a bigger reaction, and the reaction is important to observe because it's a teaching tool. What's important is once you learn the lesson, let it go and don't keep repeating it, because the more you do that, the more you attract the same in yourself. Just let it go.

Can you ask them about why it was necessary to go through this lifetime in the Holocaust?

The impressions are coming so fast, there's quite a few. One was to experience the importance of family, the love of family and community and to know that sometimes it doesn't go the way people want it to in the physical world. I just wanted to be with them but nothing is permanent.

Another reason was to practice being calm and centered and to conquer my fear. Fear is like a muscle and you can go through something so intense and not be afraid. I was working on that, and all of us collectively agreed to show the world something we needed to learn about hate, about greed, about anger.

Help me understand this.

All participants collectively showed others about love, greed, hate, love, strength, enduring no matter what; surviving the worst on a deeper level.

You mean those in the camps?

Those in the camps but also those that participated in them as well - the perpetrators. It was like there were many polarities being played out and all participants were a part of that demonstration.

So even the ones we would call the perpetrators had a role in this?

(A pause) You know from where I stand, I know this will sound really harsh, but it was much easier to be the victim than the perpetrator.

Don't judge it.

It was harder for the perpetrators because of the pain inflicted on a soul – even though everyone agreed, the pain of knowing you could cause such terrible hurt and suffering was unbearable for many of them. It also taught lessons in courage, learning about standing up for what was right.

That 'being invisible' you spoke of?

There were many of them that were invisible too. They were just going along because of their own fear and learning how much it hurts when we Violate the laws we know to be true.

Are they speaking to you, or are they having you experience this in some way?

They're talking to me but I'm also experiencing it; they're showing me. As they're speaking to me, I see all the events going before me like a movie, and then I feel the feelings. I'm so familiar with what I felt in that body, I'm being given the opportunity to see and feel what the perpetrators felt -- I'm also seeing and feeling what victims were feeling, and if I were to put the two side by side, it sounds terrible, but I'm glad I was on the side of experience that I was on.

Because it was even more difficult to be on the other side?

Yes. Many of them have some corruption that will take healing, will take healing time. Because in order to be a part of this, they Violated something their soul knew was wrong. They Violated something in their own soul. Some were lured by it and fell down into it. Something inside got

carried away; they didn't mean to be that driven to be destructive, but went beyond what had been planned.

There are many lessons; heartlessness, not allowing ourselves to feel what others feel, shutting down and then becoming soulless in a sense. Then they were capable of anything; there was so much fear that if they opened up to what we were experiencing they too would be thrown into the same circumstance. Others were afraid they would be engulfed with the horror and the pain of it all, and many of us on the other side closed our hearts too, the victims. Many lessons about the heart.

What a new perspective in learning. What more did they communicate to you?

That ultimately all souls are... I can't get the word that they're saying. They gave me an image of souls going into the hospital, ultimately the souls rehabilitate... There is no such thing as a throwaway soul. All souls have meaning and all souls have value and all souls have purpose and all souls are perfect. That it's a matter of finding our way back to that perfection after each lifetime on Earth. Specifically they're saying "Everything is as it should be, has purpose, meaning and value as to all the souls that participate."

What do they say to you about your soul's purpose?

They're telling me I'm one of the souls working towards being able to embody this. The part I saw in the classroom is about creating the synergistic energy of love and to acknowledge perfection in all things. Sending that message is very helpful to people as they continue on their path.

Perhaps you have something you'd like to ask them?

"How many lifetimes do I have to do on Earth?" (Laughs) They say "As many as you want; it's up to you." My impression is I'm coming back to continue the work I'm doing.

You mentioned they have deep blue robes. Anything else you notice?

I see a symbol in front of the chairperson. It's virtual reality-like and it's spinning. It's gold in color and there are intertwining different lines, going up. It's almost as if it goes on forever, no end to it. It's a symbol for the interconnectedness of everything. I was able to go inside of it and it's beautiful; inside the center you are a part of everything, are in everything. When you're a part of everything, you are something grand; apart from it – you're nothing.

In a few moments we'll begin our return journey... and you'll be able to take some time to draw this symbol that helps you reconnect... fully awake by the count of ten..."

*****

The above was the first session I had filmed. For me it was startling, as I had no idea how these sessions were conducted, and hearing a person learn new information from their council was a powerful thing to hear. Since this first session, I've filmed over 100, and everyone was able to visit their council.

"Divine Councils" have been reported for eons. From the Wikipedia entry, "The concept of a divine council is in ancient Sumerian, Akkadian, Ancient Egyptian, Babylonian, Canaanite, Israelite, Celtic, Greek, Roman and Nordic texts. Ancient Egyptians describe a "synod of the gods," in Mesopotamia, an "assembly of the gods." In the Torah, there are multiple descriptions of Yahweh presiding over an assembly of "Heavenly Hosts." Examples in the Bible include The Book of Job, The Book of Psalms, John 10:34, The Books of Kings where a prophet has a vision of Yahweh seated among "the whole host of heaven" to his right and left. The Book of Job describes the "Sons of God" assembled, even refers to Lucifer as part of "God's council."

In Chinese theology, deities under the Jade Emperor were the "celestial bureaucracy." Zeus and Hera preside over the divine council in Greek mythology, the council assists Odysseus in Homer's Odyssey. In ancient Rome; Jupiter presides over the Roman pantheon who prescribe punishment. In Celtic myths, the council is a family, in Norse mythology, the gods sitting on "thrones of fate."" (Wikipedia "Divine Council")

If we are to believe councils are mythological, why do they show up in pretty much every hypnotherapy session I've filmed? Are they divine? Or did people who saw them in ancient times transform them into "divine councils" because there was no words to identify them?

I submit it is the latter. That people have been experiencing councils since they began incarnating on the planet. People who had a near death experience have described them during their "life review." They show up in near death research, past life regressions, show up in mediumship cases, hypnotherapy sessions, they show up in examples of meditation.

Having filmed dozens of people using hypnosis to access the flipside, comparing that to thousands of clinical case studies, I became aware that anyone could access these same councils without hypnosis. This book will demonstrate the how. I recommend people use hypnotherapy with a trained, licensed practitioner. I recommend hypnotherapist trained by the Newton Institute as I've filmed many. But there are other methods to gain access to the same information.

There's a challenge inherent in this book for everyone, from scientists to clergy. Conduct one's own experiment. See if one can speak to their guide or council on their own – or ask someone for help with a guided meditation. Everyone can. All those in this book did.

In most of my books, "Flipside: A Tourist's Guide on How to Navigate the Afterlife," "It's a Wonderful Afterlife" book one and two, "Hacking the Afterlife" and "Architecture of the Afterlife" there are visits to councils. In this book I'm going to focus on that aspect of the journey.

Buckle up, it's going to be a bumpy ride.

INTRODUCTION:

"PICTURE YOURSELF IN A BOAT ON A RIVER"

Michelangelo's boat from the Last Judgment

"Picture yourself in a boat on a river
With tangerine trees and marmalade skies
Somebody calls you, you answer quite slowly
A girl with kaleidoscope eyes"

Songwriters John Lennon/Paul McCartney
Lucy in the Sky With Diamonds lyrics © Sony/ATV Music Publishing
LLC

This book examines "Divine Councils" on the flipside. How we all have them. How the vast majority of them are happy to answer questions, are able to help us navigate the planet, and can share insight from their perspective. It's mind bending to consider, but we're speaking with people "not on the planet." Some have never incarnated on the planet.

One could call them "Divine Councils" but then we'd spend most of our time trying to define divinity. Suffice to say they are "etheric" or "energetic" (the work *Akashic* in Sanskrit means "invisible" or "etheric") – but these are people who exist on someone's own private council.

Based on the research, data and footage; everyone has their own council based on all of their previous lifetimes. Everyone has council members who reflect that person's journey. Many council members report they sit on other people's councils. Some represent the same quality on all of their councils, some represent different qualities.

We can ask the council member what their "role" is on the council. It might be a specific quality – like the "Nine Muses of Greek mythology" - each has their own role regarding the individual they keep an eye on. They can be asked "What do you represent on this person's council?"

When asked, they might represent another quality on another council. Some council members sit on "thousands" of councils, others sit on "just a few." Sometimes people encounter a new council member. But the council member can be asked "What role to you represent on their council?" The number of council members is dependent upon the journey of the individual. The number may increase depending how many lifetimes one has had. For example, someone with a large council (over ten) generally means they've been at this for a while. Each "degree" they've earned over the course of a lifetime or many lifetimes, may be represented by the number of council members.

The subjects in this study and book are from all walks of life, different backgrounds. Some are successful business people, some are successful film people, some are younger, older, some have no professional career. There are male and female subjects from all walks of life.

Elon Musk and Jeff Bezos could visit their councils instead of Mars – but none have reported doing so. Paul Allen has spoken to us from the Flipside, and spoke eloquently about his journey (and relationship with Bill Gates) in "Backstage Pass to the Flipside." (And in the documentary on Gaia.com "Talking to Bill Paxton.") Steve Jobs has visited our podcast "HackingTheAfterlife.com" often; Jennifer Shaffer (JenniferShaffer.com) and I interviewed him extensively in our books "Backstage Pass to the Flipside." (Members of his family are also working with Jennifer to speak directly to Steve.) The point I'm trying to make is that an individual's background, education, religion or wealth has little or no meaning in terms of their visits to their council.

Anyone can access their council, and clearly everyone should.

In an interview with the famed channeler Edgar Cayce on the flipside (via Kevin Moore in the book "Hacking the Afterlife") he was asked "why were you so wrong about predicting the future?" Through Kevin, he replied:

> ***Kevin Moore (channeling Edgar): There are strands of possibilities.***
>
> Rich: I assumed the reason you were inaccurate in your predictions was that you were accessing possible future outcomes and I appreciate your reporting that was the case.
>
> *"Not all predictions come true – and not all predictions come to pass."*
>
> However when you were trans-channeling information for helping people with health issues, you were known for accuracy. Were you accessing a previous lifetime as a doctor or someone else?
>
> **Kevin Moore as Edgar Cayce:** *"A group. There is a group."*
>
> Can you bring that group into Kevin's consciousness? How many people are in that group?
>
> *"Eight or more."*
>
> Would all eight individuals weigh in with your prognosis?
>
> *"Absolutely."*
>
> Had those people incarnated on the planet as doctors or healers?
>
> *"No."*

Had they incarnated on other planets or other realms?

"Yes."

Were they bringing their expertise to help you heal people with their expertise?

"You could say that."

Allow me to ask a specific question about how healing occurs; I've heard it called "the healing light of the universe." What is the best method for people to try to access healing or that healing light?

"All the light is contained within each of us. All of everything, all of consciousness is contained within all of us. All one has to do is go towards the light within us. Move towards the light within one's self. The light of the divination of creation, of all-ness, of all-knowingness. Use and bring that light around us. Light is all we are. It's all there is. It's everything."

What would you describe as a good method for us to be able to access that healing light?

"It is the use of meditation. The use of quiet space. The use of calling your divinity towards you. Calling the oneness of who you truly are towards you; your true soul self, your "father in heaven" you may call it – some (call it that), or "the oneness of the universe." Using quiet space… to bring that towards you."

If you could just walk just walk us through the process, if someone who is not feeling well or has an illness, how can they focus this light?

"Just focus the light on part of yourself that needs the healing the most. It may be an emotional healing; it may be a body healing; use the light and focus it on the area of the body that needs the healing the most. Do this even once a day for a minimum of 15 minutes on the area, even using your own hands to focus the light, and you will see a transformation over a period over a number of weeks

towards that area, or less." (Hacking The Afterlife, Homina Publishing, 2016 Pg 97)

After the interview, Kevin Moore said he was not aware that Edgar consulted a "Divine Council" of physicians from other realms who could help him. Edgar Cayce's medical advice including in people who wrote to him, was so accurate that notables such as Thomas Edison, Woodrow Wilson and others flocked to him with their ailments.

(Note: After I'd finished the book "Hacking the Afterlife" I cheekily asked Jennifer Shaffer to ask Edgar for a "book blurb." His reply; "**Tell Richard his book has an appealing thunder for controverting settings that are falsely depicted, for those that need it. The truth we need is, "How we survive our bodies, (arrive) in the afterlife to different situations that make up the past, present, and future outcomes of our spiritual existence." Tell him the book will have people questioning their own disbeliefs and belief paradigms. And that we all, at some point of our spiritual growth, need "upheaval" to make a difference. Rich, you are that translation of the ethers; for now; I'm "The Awakened Prophet." (Jennifer said "he then laughed.")** Jennifer didn't know he was known as "The Sleeping Prophet" so his comment "The Awakened Prophet" is pretty funny.)

An explanation of the guided meditation used for this book:

If helps the guided meditation if someone has had a vivid dream, a memory of something that happened outside their conscious mind. That could be a near death event, an out of body experience or something else that occurred. It could be that they had a dream about their departed loved one, and can remember only a part of the dream.

If someone reports "I don't dream" or "I suffer from *aphantasia*," I ask them if they can remember what they had for breakfast or if they can picture a loved one's face or smell or voice. I'm just demonstrating that memory is fluid when it comes to accessing specific details of another person. I'm not asking them to "remember" as much as I am asking them to "visualize an experience or individual" in real time.

Sometimes people have a fleeting memory – something that happened when they were children. Perhaps they saw a "ghost," saw a relative, or saw "something" they couldn't understand. Recently at a dinner party, a woman said she had a "visit from a demon" in her youth – I asked if she could picture the "demon" and she could. I asked her to freeze the memory, to walk forward and ask this "demon" some simple questions. Before I could ask the questions, she said she "knew this person from a previous lifetime," that he was "teasing her by wearing a face mask" "deliberately scaring her because he could." He showed her the previous lifetime where they were brother and sister, and why he "donned this mask that he knew would frighten her." The emotional fear associated with that event disappeared as she accessed it, all within the space of a few noisy minutes.

Using a specific memory as a key, or gateway, I've had conversations with "ghosts" who often turn out to be someone they knew from a previous lifetime. I've had conversations with "beings" they don't know, have never met, but exist outside our realm. In the book "Architecture of the Afterlife" there are numerous interviews with creatures, beings one didn't know, but by asking simple questions, learn that they have a history with this individual.

By freezing the frame, by creating a hologram of the memory, it allows us to explore it without emotion. A person might be in tears seeing a memory of their loved one, or might associate fear with seeing some being that saw in their youth but by freezing that frame we can move in and out of the frame without any stress or emotion attached.

Then I *suggest* a shift in perspective while they're accessing the memory. (Suggestion because we are accessing a recalled experience.) "I saw my dead grandfather sitting in a chair." "Okay, let's put him back in the chair. What is he wearing?" It goes from past tense to present tense. "I was terrified because I saw an alien in front of me." "Freeze that frame, and let's ask this being a question and have them put the answer in your mind. Are they a tourist? Just visiting? Or is this someone you know or have met before?" It's gone from past tense to present tense. "I saw a gargoyle at the edge of my bed." "Let's freeze the event and ask them a question and allow whatever the answer is to come to mind. Who are you and why are you scaring this person?" The answers are always fascinating. If they were based on subjective reality, the answers would be "all over the place." But because the answers are uniform, they point to a greater awareness of how consciousness functions or incarnation works.

What people report is consistent and reproducible.

In asking the same questions to a group of individuals, we can gather the data from those answers. As Dr. Bruce Greyson notes in his book "After" about his thousands of case studies of near death experiences, "we can gather objective data from subjective experiences." In other words, thousands of people have had a near death event, by asking them the same questions; "what did you see?" or "what did you experience?" we can examine the data objectively. For example, "70% saw a light" "65% experienced meeting a more intelligent being" etc. In all of the cases I've filmed, everyone is able to access previous lifetimes, guides, teachers, classrooms, councils, sometimes libraries. All of these hallmarks are reported in the case studies of Dr. Wambach, Dr. Weiss, Michael Newton – and in the over 100 subjects I've filmed accessing the same information. It doesn't matter if the person is aware of these hallmarks or not, if they have a belief system that includes these hallmarks or not – they all report the same basic hallmarks. And then I can ask them questions about those hallmarks, and ask the hallmarks questions as well.

One might argue "well, those are hallmarks in every movie, book, story about the afterlife." But clearly they are not and are contrary to the zeitgeist of "*afterlife story telling*." What people report is consistent and much more uniform; that we are fully conscious prior to incarnation, that we choose our journey with the help of guides, council members, classmates and friends, that we bring a portion of our conscious energy to a lifetime and the rest "remains home." So if one can devise a method to "bypass the filters" (See Greyson's "After" for a chapter on filters on the brain) via hypnotherapy, mediumship, dreams or meditation, we can access this information and process, get identical results. Consistent reports of new information means it cannot be cryptomnesia, or something we read, saw or heard before in a film, movie or book, or heard as a fairy tale in temple, mosque or church.

Again, the method is basic. Ask people to "picture themselves in a boat on a river." Some hear the Beatles singing the lyric. It's another way to access memory. "What's the boat made of? Where are we?" *"Well, this is a river that I was once in, and I'm in the same boat I was in that day."* "Let's ask a friend or guide to sit across from you. Is that a male, female or a light?" Three options to say *"I don't see anything or anyone"* or *"I am seeing something or someone."* Sometimes it's the outline of a physical image, sometimes a light. I ask the "light" the same questions I'd ask a person. "Can you shift perspective so that this person can see you as a person? It's easier for conversation. Now what do you observe?"

Sometimes the light "manifests" as a person they know. (Sometimes not) I ask "Is this the person that they know, or is this the guide manifesting as someone so we can converse?" The "guides" know the answer. I ask them to "nod" "shrug" or "shake their heads" in response. I then ask the guide or helper the same simple questions. "Is it okay to talk to you? What's a name or letter we can use to address you?" I then ask "Is it okay if we visit this person's council?" I ask "Are you familiar with my work?" If they say "*No,*" they may be reluctant to allow a visit their council because they have no clue why they're being asked to take them to a place they only visit after their lifetime or before the current one.

If they are familiar with my work (I know it's an odd thing to ask, but I do so anyway, as some are and some are not, even if the person is) I'll say "Is it allowed to visit their council?"

It's an odd construct – I'm speaking to someone I know or don't know; they're speaking to someone they may have seen, but rarely have communicated with in this direct fashion. Sometimes they say "*Oh, yes, I've heard of you, you're the guy who asks councils questions*" but the person I asked the question to - does not.

Then I ask them to describe the journey to visit the council, which allows me to hear the quality of what they're experiencing. Some people are in awe of "going into a giant cathedral" some were relaxed to see their council "out in the woods" or some pastoral setting. In this book there's one example of someone who "tried to visit their council" and was rebuffed, "sent away." In that interview, we went back to see if there was a reason for that. "He wasn't ready" was what we were told. But this time, he was.

What comes out of the research is that everyone has a guide. Everyone has a council. Every council member has a guide, every council member has a council. Might be easier to think of this as a giant tree of branches, a giant university with various colleges and classrooms, a giant universe filled with information and memories of all the previous adventures. By accessing our council, with or without hypnosis we can access information and details from all of our lifetimes and many journeys.

What is mind bending is that they can and do answer. They are generally not used to having individuals show up in their sacred council chambers to discuss the journey or process. But I show up with their students, the people they've watched over for all of their lifetimes. And we ask questions about process. What we'll examine:

1. How everyone has a council.
2. How simple it is to access the council.
3. How everyone is connected to their council.
4. How the council members are trying to help us.
5. How they are literally "a phone call away."

The people on the flipside, for the most part, report they're eager to participate in this kind of inquiry. Some of them report it's "important for the fate of humanity." As you'll see – all the people in this book were able to visit councils, recall previous lifetimes, or learn new information about this lifetime. As a dataset, it would be "paranormal" to suggest that one could not access this information since everyone did. Without exception.

We are all here for a reason, all chose this journey for a reason, and you chose to open this book or listen to this research for a specific reason. I hope it helps you fulfill whatever it is you've signed up to do.

Psalm 82:1 "God has taken his place in the divine council in the midst of the gods he holds judgment."

CHAPTER ONE: *A SHIFT IN CONSCIOUSNESS*

A council of Divine hair stylists?

In Isaiah 6, Isaiah enters the presence of the Lord, who is seated on his throne in the temple (6:1). There he meets with the divine council (6:2-3) and is invested with a mission to reveal the deliberations of the council to mankind (6:8-9).

In the following experiment, which inspired this book, nine members of a meditation group were interviewed - eight on zoom, one in person (Kelly). I had met none of them previously, aside from Kelly, and **all** reported they had **experience** with "guided" or group meditation.

I know little about the scope of their group, so I refer to them in this book as "Kelly's group." I know that they've done guided meditation sessions on a variety of topics, but not why they do so.

I'm using only the first names of participants, none of whom I've met outside of Zoom outside of Kelly. I explained to each this was going to be a filmed guided meditation. Interviews ran from 40 to 90 minutes.

KEN, KIKI, DAVID, ELOISE, JULIET, KELLY, MIMI, RONNIE, GIANNI

(Throughout this book I'm using pseudonyms for all of the people interviewed. That's in part to protect their privacy, but also to eliminate bias. They're not trying to impress anyone else with what they see or hear, and I'm not equating anything they do in their life with the reports they get from the flipside.)

Everyone in the experiment was able to do a guided meditation. All were able to access with either a guide or a friend who came to assist. In all the cases, people were able to visit their "councils." Most were not aware that they could visit their councils, most "met" or asked questions and heard answers from members of their council. The councils had between four and twelve (which is consistent with the data and research.)

CASE ONE: KELLY

Kelly and I were having lunch at Hugo's restaurant in West Hollywood, and had no inkling we might try to go anywhere. But based on the fact that I had filmed her four-to-six-hour session with a hypnotherapist years earlier, I guessed she would be able to access some of the memory of what was said, even if it wasn't something she was consciously thinking of. Edited for time and context, my questions are in italics, her replies in bold. (Kelly is not her real name.)

Rich:(recording) Have you done any hypnosis since we last met?

Kelly: No.

And what's your memory of the session?

It was long, like six hours. After years of thinking about it, I don't know whether it *was hypnosis*. It was a combination of the way the questions were posed that allowed me... it felt like a lot of things were in my subconscious that I had wanted to say or thought, but never put into words. And the combination of the hypnosis, and the way that the questions were asked, allowed that to come out.

Did you feel like you were making it all up?

Sometimes.

And in retrospect, now?

I think my eternal quest for, you know, "What is God?" is still not satisfying. I don't think it ever will be.

(Note: As we were driving to the hypnotherapy session years earlier, Kelly revealed to me she really didn't believe she would "go anywhere" because she's a skeptic, atheist, and there was "no place to go," no afterlife, etc. I pointed out the hypnotherapist suggested she write down a couple of questions. In the car, we came up with *"What's the meaning of a shift in consciousness?"* (my suggestion) and *"What or who is God?"* (hers). During her six-hour session she was able to access the same hallmarks as people do in this research, a previous lifetime, a visit with her "soul group" and a trip to her "Akashic library" where she met "a Librarian" who answered her questions.)

Remember, your Librarian said "In terms of the cosmos, a shift in consciousness is no big deal." Which made me laugh, because like on a cosmic level, Saturn running into Venus is a cosmic event. A shift is not so important. He then said, "However, if you want to understand a shift in consciousness, imagine yourself a little tiny crab walking on the ocean floor. And you open your eyes and you say, "Oh, my God, I'm in an ocean!"

Right. I remember that.

But did you have any connection to what you were saying? Visually? As you said it, were you thinking of the tiny crabs in a movie, like "Finding Nemo?"

I remember the answer, but I'd forgotten what the question was.

Because I suggested it in the car on the way there. But you do remember answering it?

Right. (Nods)

> (Kelly: "(A shift in consciousness) is like a massive vast ocean and if a little crab at the bottom decides to open his eyes -- and see that he's in an ocean. That's what a shift in consciousness is. However, the shift is just... it's not as important as people are saying." Scott De Tamble: *Why not?* "We are putting way too much emphasis on things that are not important, like names, giving things a name; in terms of the consciousness of the Earth in the big picture; it's not important." Scott: *Is there something a little more positive about a consciousness shift? Is there a higher purpose? Was it seeded to us by someone in the spirit realm to think about consciousness?* "Yes. That's why it's not important. Any more important than (it is) to think about why a flower seed is planted. It's just evolution." *Excerpt from "It's a Wonderful Afterlife" Homina Publishing 2014. Pg. 326)*

Had you been looking at footage of crabs walking around the ocean?

No.

So if someone suggested this is from your imagination - that wasn't a normal reference?

Yeah.

Your comment about realizing "we're in an ocean" reminds me of how some feel about oxygen. It's got all the properties of water – but we don't see it that way. It behaves identical to the way water behaves. And if we could see it, realize we're in it would we ever pollute it?

I think we're oblivious. We're oblivious to it.

So that's a shift in consciousness. But the other question you asked was "What or who is God? The answer was "God is beyond the capacity of

the human brain to comprehend. It's not physically possible to do so."
That's what I heard.

What did I say?

> *(Scott: She wants to know; "What or who is God?" Kelly:*
> **"Searching for a human concept of God is like looking for somewhere to stop along an infinite wall; it's too vast.** *Talk to us about God as you understand it.* **"Just let go of the intellect and feel it. It's beyond the capacity of the brain to comprehend. However, you can feel it, you can experience God.** *So when you feel God what does that feel like?* **It's not "endless love" the way people describe love; that's just something we can relate to. It's a concept that is much bigger than that. Imagine an energy that connects everyone and everything in the universe. You can call that energy "love." But there is a wisdom to it and that wisdom is what people call God."** *(Ibid)*

Something along the lines of "God's too complex for their brain." But also that "You can experience God by opening your heart to the connectivity of everyone and all things." I thought, "Oh, that's a definition of an epiphany. Suddenly feeling connected to everyone and all things.

I've had many epiphanies. Fact, I was going to share an epiphany with you, before we started. You know, when you, you're in that in between stage when you wake up in the morning? And I have a lot of dreams, and I retain the feeling of them a lot, but this one was f*+king brilliant. I was waking up. And in my dream, I was having a conversation with someone, not in words. But in strictly an emotional language. In other words, I would get a flash of a multiple emotions happening at once to convey it... And they would answer - and then all of a sudden, they got the sense. As if that how the higher universe communicates; with emotion based (concepts) - never words. It's not a language.

So it's like, the emotion you could communicate would be, "I want to go outside and get in my car." Those are the words that describes it, but the emotion would include "the feeling of desire," then "the feeling of outside," and then the emotion of "I want," and then the emotion of how I feel about my car. It (all) happens in a split second.

And by the way, this is kind of what mediums say (about communication with the flipside).

Oh, really?

They translate what they're getting visually or emotionally. Put it into words. And sometimes they get it wrong. You know, like, "did your father die years ago?" And you're like, "No." And they're going "Well, I'm, I'm seeing an image of my father and I'm seeing a person being dead and the number five." They're tying images together.

That's what the conversation felt like when I woke up, and I was having conversations with the universe. And it was just emotions back and forth. And you got all the pictures with the emotions complete. Such a complete understanding of words couldn't go as deep as the feeling I got.

Let's try a meditation. I'm going to ask you some questions and I want you to just say whatever pops into your mind. Do you have any visual reference to that librarian? Do you have one when I ask you that?

No.

When I say "your librarian," what visual comes to mind?

What I remember the most in the past life regression was the old dude Tom. That character stuck with me.

(Note: During her past life memory, she recalled living in a town in Arizona in 1810, a town that exists in Arizona that she's not been to. She recalled details about this town that I was able to look up and verify (in the footnotes of her session in "It's a Wonderful Afterlife." (pg 315) She recalled a "grumpy cranky old man" who was abandoned by his young bride when she asked him to stop for water in the desert, the bride rode away in his buckboard and left him to die. When he crawled over to die under a tree, the hypnotherapist asked "What was that experience about?" and Kelly replied (paraphrasing) "I always wanted to be a cranky old man, and I did it!")

Can you see Tom now?

Easily. Wiry, older. Blue jeans, looks like someone from an old western. Grey hair. I think he looks older than he is, but he's probably around sixty-five.

I want you to picture yourself in a boat on a river. You're in a boat, very calm, but only one person can sit across from you. Let's start with Tommy. I'm gonna ask him to speak to you directly or nod, which is a form of speaking. So, Tommy, is it okay for us ask us a question?

(Kelly nods.)

Is that a nod or "Yes?"

It was an eager nod.

So how are we accessing you? Because this is like a slice of time outside of time?

He's shifting into me, as I'm sitting there watching.

That's unusual. So you're talking to yourself in a way?

Yeah.

So reach over and take a hold of his hands. Are they cold or warm?

Warm.

I want to invite Kelly's guide to chat with us. And is that a male or a female? A light or something else?

A light. White with yellow.

Can I ask you to manifest as a human so that we can have an easier conversation?

A female. In her thirties. Like five foot ten, tall and broad shouldered, athletic and strong. Light brownish hair.

What's a name that we can use to call you?

Annabelle, but that's what I was gonna name my cat so it's on the tip of my tongue.

Reach over and take her hands. Is there any sensation that comes from doing that?

Cool.

Annabelle, I'm going to ask you to warm them up a bit. Can you do that?

Yeah, I feel that.

Color eyes?

They went blue.

Annabelle, is that the name that Kelly knows you as? Or is it something else?

The answer is "someone else."

How long have you been with Kelly?

"I'm always with her. I'm like… her."

Okay, that was a trick question. Annabelle. Are you familiar with my work?

"Yes."

What's your opinion?

(Kelly aside) Nothing came.

How's Kelly doing? Adjustments she needs to make?

I heard "To not be sad." I'm hearing "To stop being alone so much." (Kelly laughs) This is like a therapy session!

Can you show Kelly her life selection process when she chose to be Kelly? Who's there?

I saw a baby. We're outside. Not many people around.

Are you showing Kelly an image of herself as a baby?

"Yeah."

Part of her journey is to be this person born in Missouri and wind up in the Golden State. What's up with that?

"To toughen her up."

Why does she need to be toughened up?

"She's got a job to do. It's related to the place… it is related to the people she's around."

Are you saying that she needs to focus on film? The film industry?

"Yes. Influencing those who make strong influencing." She's saying, "Ask for questions. Ask your question."

Okay, During your previous session, I don't think that we went to visit Kelly's council. Should we do that?

"Yes."

So are we inside or outside?

Outside. Five, five people. Kind of standing in a line-ish.

Go to the first person on the far left. Is that a male or female or a light?

Female. She looks like my guide Annabelle.

May I ask for a name or initial from this first person on the far left?

I got laughter like, when you asked "Can I have a name?" and the answer was laughing. She's "Yellow."

Oh, so let's call her Miss Yellow?

Call her "Y."

Ms. Why. Are you familiar with the work I'm doing?

"Yes."

Is it a good thing or a bad thing?

"Exciting."

What's a word that we can associate with your role on Kelly's council?

"Hope."

Did she earn your role on this council, or do you just represent hope?

"I represent hope."

How many councils do work on? Just this one or others?

I'm getting others but nothing concrete. Hundreds.

And in terms of in terms of our friend Kelly, how do you think she's doing?

Oh, Yellow is like; "Yes, yes!" (Thumbs up.)

So can you put a feeling a sensation in Kelly's body right to remind her of this conversation?

"Yeah. It's that "click." To her awareness, what we're doing… In this next phase in her life in terms of work, life or in terms of romance, all of it, everything. There's a shift that she's resisting though…"

Okay, so how can you guys help her?

"We can let her know that we're here; she's never alone. It was like it dawned on her… like she never thought of that. And we're like, oh, "How can we help?" By being more present."

Are you tethered to Kelly?

"Connected. Yes. Always available."

Thank you, Miss Yellow. Let's go to the person next to you.

It's an androgynous human. More female than male but very androgynous.

What's a letter or name that I can address you with?

She just said "Orange" and she's not being funny. I mean she's… she's like very dry. Yellow was like happy.

So Miss Orange. Is that okay to call you that?

She says, "Oh, it's fine."

But so what do you represent on the council?

"Seriousness."

Define that what does that mean? Clarity?

"No, focus."

Did she earn your position on this council? Because you're representing it for this lifetime?

"Yes. She's very serious."

Can you show her what she's supposed to be doing?

I'm trying to put into words, but I see.... and this amazing. What they're saying is that I keep seeing myself down here in Los Angeles amongst people. And I'm supposed to engage with them. But I don't know why for sure. Like, I'm supposed to actually physically be able to connect with people.

Should Kelly reopen old doors from her career in film?

"And open new doors." I feel like that's what I'm here (for). It's supposed to be like, it looks like a whole bunch of pipes. Like a maze of pipes. I'm supposed to be paying attention (to) inside the pipes between people.

So Miss Orange. Are you familiar with my work?

"No."

But you're aware of everything Kelly does?

"Correct."

However, Miss Yellow is. So why is she more aware than you Miss Orange?

"We don't talk much. That's why - exactly."

Okay, that makes sense. So Miss Orange, let's go to the person next to you; is that a male, female?

"A boy, a teenager. His name is Michael."

Michael, thank you for allowing me to talk to you. What do you represent?

Like.. "The beginning or onset of things."

So you're literally looking forward?

"Looking forward."

And how is Kelly doing?

"She needs to say things. I need to be more with him to have that energy of looking at… "the energy of looking forward. Just the feeling when you get excited about the new thing. Yes."

What's a way for her to be more in touch with you?

Yes. I'm viewing something through this lens. I'm going back and looking at my old job, and I really didn't like this person I was working with. So much so that I left the job. And now it's back to Ms. Yellow. She says, "You know, we've been toughening her up a little bit."

Let's go to the next person on the council. Is that a male, female or light?

A green light. I'm seeing a male. Older again, but not the same age as Tommy.

What do you represent on her council?

"Practicality, pragmatism."

Have you ever incarnated with her on the planet?

"Yes."

You want to show her that?

I immediately saw my dad and my grandfather.

So the same frequency or energy of those two?

"Yeah."

What adjustment does she need to make?

"Instead of the very hard chase to "click over," it's like "to just practice." To "Get out of my head and get on with it." He's taking me back to the (maze of) pipes.

(Note: I think when he says the "chase to click over" he means by trying to "access the flipside.")

So let's go to the last person on the council.

This person is looking somewhat human -- like in a silhouette.

What's a name that we can use?

Something like… Sal. He says, "She's fighting everything."

So what's your role on her Council?

"Overseeing and discerning. It's an emotion that comes through, like giving depth."

What's the difference between wisdom and knowledge?

"Knowledge is something that you know, something that you learn like two plus two equals four. But wisdom is those times when two plus two don't equal four."

Are you familiar with my work?

"Yeah."

What's your opinion?

"That it's good for you. That is good for the people you do it with. But when you're over here, it's not your focus. You're entertaining yourself. Over here, it's not your focus."

What's my focus over there?

"You're old like him." (The council member Sal).

(Note: That's the first time anyone has made that comment to me. Calling out my "higher self" rather than my current "on the planet" self. Outing me as an "old soul.")

Well, in terms of your journey, how many councils do work on?

"Endless. Lots and lots and lots."

But your oversight brings them all together?

"That's what he does."

How does Kelly connect to you? Whenever she needs your advice?

"Both focus and get rid of all the extraneous."

You recommend using meditation?

"Meditation and conscientiously doing contrast. Like zeroing in. When she's feeling scattered, to cut away all the extraneous." He says, "Use pen and paper. Write it down. Make a list."

Does that apply to everybody or just Kelly?

"Everyone; writing is the act of writing a connection to you, a connection to the human brain."

So how do you get information into her?

"Meditation."

A visit to Kelly's Akashic Library

Annabelle, can we go visit this librarian fellow we met before?

She says, "Yep." She says, "But we have to get out of the boat."

Okay, let's get out of the boat and go over to the library. And what does it look like?

Well, we landed in a traditional like, Public Library… turn of the century. Books everywhere like, but then it very quickly turns into like, massive infinite warehouse.

Let me ask if the Librarian is available to chat. I know he's a busy fella.. And you're smiling. Why?

Because he was like, "Oh, you're back." (Kelly aside) I don't know how much of this is in my head.

May I ask for a name or a letter that we can use to address you?

Did ask me this last time?

Last time you said "Call me Five." As in a word that's neither male nor female. So I can refer to you as five?

"Okay, yes. Go."

Five, my question is "Are you the main librarian for our sector?"

He's showing me a mirror. Like have you ever looked in the side of a mirror and seen other dimensions? But they're all inside the mirror. "There aren't separate libraries."

When people focus on their librarian, are they talking to some form of you?

"Yes."

Can you show one of the volumes of Kelly's life to her? What does it look like?

Like a brown leather book. It's big.

What's the cover look like?

No.

So let's open it up. What's inside? Are there words are there images?

There are pages with words, but I can't read them.

So look at the first sentence. Five, tell her what that sentence means.

(It's about) "A time and place. It's a story that has a story." (Kelly aside) But it just feels completely alien to me. But I don't mean "alien.""

It's like a reference book?

"Yes."

But you're not really getting an answer of like, "this is the story of Kelly?"

"Yes."

Five, is this particular sentence for Kelly's benefit?

He says, "You asked me to read it." So he was reading it, but I'm not getting a meaning.

Structurally, does the sentence go from left to right?

Yes.

So if you look at the first symbol on this page, what is it?

(It's) A Golden orb.

And does the orb contain the emotional memories of a previous lifetime? Referring to an event? Something that occurred to Kelly that's related?

The golden orb was the emotion of it, but it's a place holder of that emotion… of a place that I don't understand.

Okay, if I can paraphrase, because we've talked before about these orbs… are they the size of a tennis ball and they retain information?

No, think of an orange, about the size of an orange.

So let's just hold the orb up for her. Take a look at it. And then, Five, if you could open it up for her. See what's inside. What's in there?

Lots of squiggles and lines and colors and geometry that I don't know. Geometry.

This has been repeated before – They are geometric formulas that logically makes sense to somebody who can read them. Correct?

"Yeah."

But they represent lifetimes that Kelly has experienced, is that correct?

"No, in this particular instance, they're about that place."

How many volumes does Kelly have?

"Lots and lots."

Lots of fun?

"Exactly. But the idea of the volume itself is not only of value, but it's also this golden orb, or whatever."

What was the purpose of bringing me and Kelly together today? Did you have a hand in it, Five?

He says he "Didn't have a hand in it. But he knows the purpose."

And did you know that I was going to talk to you today?

"Yes."

So what do you want to tell me about the work or about you?

"Keep going, keep going."

Is it helping people over there to realize they can talk to people here?

"It's like a bridge. And we need a lot of… bridges."

That implies we need them for a reason. Or is this a natural evolution of consciousness?

"It is a natural evolution. But it's got… it's going back to that image of clicking as I was saying earlier. The click (of awareness) You need enough weights on it to trip the click."

To trip the mechanism to shift consciousness?

"So this kind of access is one of many. And there's maybe buildings out there for doing this kind of work or trying to help people make the switch."

Is there any way that we can help others flip the switch?

(Laughs). "Kelly thought the answer would be, "just go out and blast as many people as you can." But that wasn't the answer that came. It's "Focus on the ones who can hear you." Like, "focus on your own people.""

I'm going to ask you a question that probably wouldn't make a lot of sense to Kelly but I'm focused on the process of bypassing filters on the brain. About the process of hearing from folks on the other side. Is it a matter of finding a receiver in the brain?

"The whole body is a receiver."

But my question for you is, is there a specific part of the brain that functions as an antenna?

"No," he said, "An antenna is an antenna."

Let me ask you about the filters. The skull hardens around the age of eight. If he can explain it, so why so why does the hardening of the skull reduce the information or the reception?

"The energy gets denser, humans get denser. It's just that we get denser, harder to get the material through."

Correct me if I'm wrong Five, some people have access to this information because their filters are altered. Hallucinogens or they're like mediums where their filters are off. Is that correct?

This is interesting, he's showing me that it's like history. "Imagine - left to right - is history. And as we're getting closer and closer to our time right now, (where) everything is compacting, getting denser and denser and denser now. That like, throughout history, we're coming to a place where it's really dense. And even people who have been able to see the text of the question you asked, yeah, it's getting denser. It's like it's been compacted." I think he's showing me it's getting harder for people to get the accurate information.

But here we are having a conversation with you. Now, Kelly didn't have to go through six hours of relaxation and hypnosis. We just dialed you up like a cell phone. So why is it easier?

What I'm getting is "It's the people. The people are doing that."

It's funny; we're talking to a guy off the planet in a library somewhere, who's like really super old, who won't give us a frickin' name. It's "five." He says "The people are doing it." What does that mean? Do you mean certain people are doing it?

"Yes."

I heard this the other day from Luana, my pal on the flipside, who said "There actually is no veil. That's just a human construct."

Well, when you were asking me a minute ago, when you said "The veil is getting closer." He was like, "No." He didn't actually see a veil.

I mean, people didn't come up and talk to you all the time before and now they're doing it often?

"They did and they didn't. They weren't consciously aware of doing so, but always have."

So you mean years ago, people accessed you more? Why the lapse?

"This is because we're getting denser, denser, denser, denser, denser, denser."

How do we get denser?

Well, I don't know if I thought of this, or he did - because I like this image. Like when a black hole happens, and they say that black hole contracts long enough it creates another universe? That's what I just saw.

Okay, well, let's talk about that for a second. Energy from our universe goes into a black hole and then becomes another universe somewhere else?

"Correct."

Correct me Five, is this idea of multiverses or parallel universes is incorrect. Kelly and I are having this conversation only here on this planet, and not some other universe. Our conscious energy is here, present, not elsewhere. Is that correct?

"It is." He's saying **"There aren't other universes per se because every single thing happens at the same time."** But again, I don't know if this is coming from me or him.

And I mean, string theory starts with Pythagoras observing how plucking a string makes all the others vibrate. That all matter is vibrating, all matter is music. Is that correct? Is everything music?

"Everything vibrates everything. I turn it into music and turn it into me. Music. Yes."

*****

So it was out of this conversation with Kelly that came the idea for the book. It was her suggestion that I do an experiment with other members of her "group meditation" project. To see if members of her group might have a similar experience. An experiment in consciousness.

I tried to avoid bias by not have the group know anything about me; she only told them that I was asking for an hour of zoom time to talk about guided meditation.

Just a caveat here; once you start reading about councils, considering the possibility of councils, they will start showing up in your path. Dreams, meditations, even every day circumstances. So caveat emptor.

Vanum Populatum - Michelangelo

CHAPTER TWO: "KEN"

My questions are in italics, the answers in bold font. This session was conducted on Zoom with "Ken" in Europe. Ken is a member of Kelly's "meditation group." He doesn't know me or my work, but has done "guided meditation" in the past in a group setting.

Rich: I'm a filmmaker, basically. Some years ago, I started a documentary about filming people under hypnosis, accessing memories. ("Flipside") At the time, I thought, "Okay, this is a great way to prove past life memories to be inaccurate, you know, to show bias." Unfortunately, that's not what happened.

Ken: That was your approach back then?

Sort of. I thought, "What are these experiences about? And is there any way I can film people talking about them?" And then I sort of stumbled upon a hypnotherapist who had been doing decades of focused research in the area. For people to recall the same things was uncanny. I thought a camera is a way to demonstrate what's really going on, without bias.

Yeah, sure.

So I went into the rabbit hole. The research took me to the University of Virginia, and I spent some time with scientists who have been studying reincarnation and near-death events. For over a decade, it's kind of been my focus.

Interesting.

It's how I ran into Kelly. We were talking about it. She was a skeptic; "Oh, come on, really?

That's Kelly!

But she tried a hypnotherapy session. Allowed me to film it.

She did a session?

Yeah, with a Newton Institute hypnotherapist. Those sessions are four to six hours where it's very focused.

I've always wanted to do one of these. Since I first heard about it a years ago, I wanted to do one, because I've met some researchers who have been in the field as well, for quite a while. I've been fascinated by their research. And my whole process has led me to these topics multiple times. Past life memories of children as well. I've always been interested in looking (at) what would come out of me. To be honest, I've had many experiences, but never something (like) I was concretely remembering a past life.

So let me ask you a couple of questions. How long do I have you for?

About an hour, because you say we need an hour or less, but it takes longer than it takes longer. My girlfriend would highly appreciate me not taking two hours.

It just gives me a parameter for how long I can ramble on about my journey before we get started. (Laughs) So you you've had a number of experiences. Have you ever done any meditation?

Yeah, sure.

It's a guided meditation, simply "picture yourself in a boat on a river." I ask you to verbalize whatever it is that comes to mind. I ask to try to not judge whatever comes to mind.

I'm very curious. I can tell you two things that just popped into my mind right now, which might be interesting for your research. I've done something very similar to that once when I was at the "International Conference on Consciousness" in Miami, and there were a few researchers in that field. We did a guided meditation like that, but it wasn't specifically on past lives, but she guided me to choose an animal that I like, and then I had these experiences as that animal. I really did feel it might have been a past life as an animal.

What was the animal?

It was a leopard. I had really interesting experiences through that meditation. But her whole research was about brain frequencies during these meditations. I was hooked up to an EKGs, she recorded the questions and then we kind of compared it afterwards. And that was highly interesting. So she is doing research on the brain states needed for "higher consciousness."

We'll try to do that today.

Okay, so one more thing I wanted to share. It's very timely in my in my life right now because recently - have you heard of *aphantasia*? It's kind of a spectrum of how much you can perceive through your senses without actually perceiving. So when I do the meditation, how much clarity, like the pictures that I see how clear they are, how indistinguishable from real life they are. So I don't really see anything (normally.)

Oh, I have heard that.

I just wanted to say that in the end of the year, I realized through our group with Kelly, I realized I do see stuff. And also like the experiences I told you about, I do see stuff. It's just very uncommon for me.

I appreciate you telling me that. Dr. Greyson's book "AFTER" talks about the filters on the brain, how they block information not conducive to survival. So people may have filters or limiters when others don't. I've used hypnotherapy, mediumship or meditation to bypass those filters. Which we're going to do; so have you ever had a conversation with your guide?

Not a conversation. Wait, I did have a near death experience, which I can't really remember.

I don't want to stop you from telling me about that but covering it would take up hours just talking about that event.

You know how they are. (NDE's)

(Note: I do, have spoken often at the International Association for Near Death Studies IANDS.ORG)

So let me ask you this. What visual do you remember from the near-death experience?

No clear visual. I remember a scene but not the visual part of it. And just remember the part just before I came back to the body.

What do you recall about that?

I was unconscious for a few seconds. I had a lot of friends in the room kind of wanting to wake me up. And I had this wonderful experience at the end - the part that I can remember - I heard them calling my name. And it was like in a movie, where the name was coming kind of from the sky or whatever. I remember not understanding what's going on, and gradually regaining my memory of what situation my body was in.

And then I knew "Oh they are calling me; they want me to wake up." And I remember not wanting to go back, because I had such a wonderful time. But also realizing that I have to (return), I can't just not go back right now. I really didn't want to, but I said, "All right, I need to go back." That is what I remember.

So but so it was audible, you could hear them calling you?

Yeah.

Were you aware of any kind of "looking down at yourself" as you returned?

No. I remember the kind of more of a feeling of (claps hands) coming back in.

Okay, well I'm looking for a key. And this might be the key, the sound. Have you ever had a vivid dream of someone who is not on the planet, like a relative or a friend, grandmother, grandfather? A vivid dream?

No, not that I can think of. I did have a lot of lucid dreams for awhile, I did have an out of body experience within a dream, which I cannot quite remember because it was very quick and fast.

Alright, so I want you to picture yourself in a boat on a river. And while we do this, you can close your eyes or keep them open; it doesn't matter. Can you see that boat? Can you see that river?

Sure.

And just describe it to me a little bit. Is it a big boat, little boat?

It's the wooden boat and it's not big. It's like a rowing boat.

And what river are we in?

Not a river that I know.

Okay, is there a shore on either side?

Not really in the jungle but not in this area of Europe, but more jungle like vegetation.

I want you to slow the boat down so we don't get into any rapids. We're just moving along slowly and floating. Can you feel the sunshine on your face?

No.

What's the sky look like?

Seems a bit cloudy. Yeah. Not very dark, but like gray.

Now I'm going to ask your guide, whoever that is, to come and sit opposite you in this boat. It could be a light could be a male or female. Just put someone in the boat opposite you who is going to play the role of the guide today.

I can't hold on to any form… or any form of it. At first it was… an almost an alien like creature which I couldn't really grasp…

An alien like creature. I don't want you to judge this. I want you to make a holograph out of it. A 3D picture frozen in time. There's no emotion associated with it. Let's go to the one moment where you had a visual of this image. Just describe what you're seeing.

I'd say pretty much. Not classic reptilian-like Alien, but it has like reptilian-like wings. And it has a greenish, greenish-bluish color. And it's quite…. Yeah, I can't really describe it, but like has some horns and stuff.

Just look at the skin, don't look at the face for a minute. Is the skin green or yellow or a combination?

It's blue green. Looks like a petrol like color.

Any emotion associated with this? Take a hold of his hand… is that a he or she or neither?

Probably a "he."

Let's just hold his hand for a second. What's the emotion you feel when you do so? Is there an emotion?

Not sure.

But have you got a hold of his hands?

Yeah.

Just look at your hands with his hands.

They're bigger than mine... like long claws that close.

This might be a startling thing for him as well. But I want you to look up at his face. And I want to ask him to nod, shrug or shake his head. Is it okay if we ask you some questions?

He says "Yes."

Would you put in Ken's mind a name that we can refer to you or have the letter the first letter of a name so that we just have a reference?

He says, "E."

Can I call you Mr. E? Which is like "mystery," if you don't mind. Now, when I say that, does he chuckle or not? What's his reaction to my joke there?

It's a little chuckle.

A little bit of a chuckle is all we need.. Now look at his eyes. Do they close from the side? What color are they?

They are yellow – not completely on the side (of his head) but (are) somewhere diagonal.

Do I have your permission to ask you questions?

He says, "Yes"

Would you consider yourself to be Ken's guide?

He says, "No."

And let me ask you, are you familiar with my work? Are you familiar with me?

He says, "Yes."

Which is an unusual new piece of information for Ken. Have we met before Mr. E?

He said, "Yes."

We have. Well, I want to I want to say that I interviewed another Mr. E, who was a lizard like person in my book "Architecture of the Afterlife" something Ken has not read, and is not aware of consciously. But are you the same Mr. E that I met before that I wrote about?

He says, "Yes."

(Note: This is mind bending information. It has happened before – meeting someone on the flipside who is associated with the person I'm speaking with who tells me that they've met me before. I do recall speaking with a "reptilian" fellow on someone's council, and I do recall using the term "Mr. E" to refer to him – but cannot remember if it was the reptilian fellow.)

Okay, you are? Wow, that's fascinating. What a cool thing. So you know the questions I'm going to ask. Allow me to thank you first.. Oh, let me ask you, Mr. E has Ken ever incarnated in the planet that you're from?

He says, "Yes."

Do you want to put that in his mind's eye? Without any stress or fear just put it in his mind's eye? What does it look like? Are we inside or outside?

Outside.

Look around. What's the environment?

Red Rocks.

Are they sharp or dull?

Yeah, they're sharp. Not completely sharp, not very round.

Both jagged and round. Can you see into the horizon? A big or a small place?

It's a big place. But there's not much going on. There's just this red rock, desert like...

Mr. E? Would you put in Ken's mind what his occupation is on this in this lifetime that you're showing him? What's his occupation?

"Teacher."

Are you a teacher as well? On that on that place?

He says, "Yes."

Is this a place it's in our universe, our solar system or in another realm entirely?

"It's another realm."

Okay, then we won't concern ourselves with identifying the location. I think it's fascinating to hear we've met before. The obvious question would be if I ever incarnated on that planet?

He nods. "Yes."

Well, that's new information. I appreciate that. Let me ask, are we talking about a lifetime Ken has that's concurrent? Is Ken also existing on this other planet while we're speaking? Or was this a previous lifetime?

"It's simultaneous."

Thank you. How much of Ken's conscious energy did he bring to the lifetime of Ken?

"94%."

And how much of his conscious energy is in his incarnation in this other realm?

"13%."

Let's not worry about the math on that one. Is he saying a percentage of the energy that he brought up in lifetime is what he's focused on? Is that correct Mr. E?

(Nods.) "Yes." 87%. (laughs about the math.)

I'll guess you're familiar with Ken's out of body experience when he had a near death event? Why is he not able to access the memory of that? Is there a block in his mind? Were you there when that happened?

"No."

But obviously, this was part of Ken's journey and important for him to be able to access this information. Alright, so if you don't mind, Mr. E, would you take Ken into visit his Council? Are we inside or outside?

"Inside."

Describe what it looks like inside?

It's all made out of stone polished, very high ceilings. Big room.

When I ask "How many individuals are in here," what's the number that comes to mind?

"Four plus us."

And if you look at those four individuals, how are they arrayed? Are they in a semi-circle or line?

Yeah, they are sitting in a line on almost throne like chairs at the end of the room on one side.

Could we go to the first person on the far left? And is that a male, a female or a light?

Female.

Thank you for allowing us to come in and have this conversation with you. May I ask you some questions?

She says, "Yes."

Tell me what does she look like? Just in terms of your visual?

She is short, quite big. And at first, from further distance, I wasn't sure what creature she is. (Closer) A different kind of picture became clearer. Which is that of a grandma. Not a mother like a human grandma, but almost like a cartoonish like grandma. With like gray hair in a bun. Very short. With glasses.

Let me ask you, may I, what's a what's a name or a letter I can refer to as just for purposes of our conversation.

"Isla."

Isla, thank you very much for that Isla. Could you tell Ken what your role on his council is in a word? What do you represent?

"Wisdom."

I appreciate that. Also, that would go with that "Grannie" visual.

"Also ancestors.. ancestral wisdom."

As opposed to innate wisdom?

"As opposed to pure wisdom."

What's the difference?

"Ancestral wisdom is a sub .. A sub, of the pure, pure wisdom and it's more connected to life and experiences whereas pure wisdom cannot be put into any words."

A concept we can't really access. Are you familiar with my work?

"No."

Some council members are and some not. In terms of what Ken is doing with his group, they're trying to access this information to help the planet. Is this an effective method for them to access this information?

(Nods) She's smiling when you mentioned the group.

In terms of that group; what subjects specifically should the group focus on?

"Listen to what the ancient tribes have to say."

How do you think Ken is doing? Any specific advice for Ken?

(Ken gives a "thumbs up.")

Thumbs up? A bit like Roger Ebert's review – but thank you. What is the most effective way for them to get the answers of which they seek?

"Just keep going."

Is there specific advice on how we can reverse climate change?

"Not right now, it will be a side effect of what we are doing, it's going to be -- it's not the real goal, it's a side effect of something else."

In terms of their group and what they're accessing, what about those that are affected by climate change? Is there some specific advice you might give, and how they can help those people?

"They will have to build back from a new place of consciousness; a new starting place. They cannot build back from where they are currently."

So what you're saying is, is that the shift in consciousness becoming more aware how connected we are to everyone and all things, including people not on the planet. That form of consciousness is going to help enable us in what things we should do and focus on?

"Correct. It needs to be the basis from which everything… that will be built from scratch… will have to be based on.. Otherwise, we'll be sitting at a council."

Let me ask, how many councils you sit on?

"Seven."

Could you introduce us to the person to your left? Is that a male, a female or a light?

Male. Very tall and thin. Very, very long neck almost a little bit ant-like, but not really like an ant. It's something I've never seen before. Very, very tall. Not sure they have English words for it.

What's a word comes into mind?

I'm not sure what it means. "Austere."

He answered the question I was about to ask "What do you represent on his council?" Is that correct?

He says "Yes." I don't know what it means.

(Note: I refer to this as "getting the answer before the question is asked." Ken could not know what question I was about to ask, doesn't know why I would ask for a word to describe the council member's role in his life – yet this council member is aware that not only was I about to ask the question, but he provided the answer before I could ask it.)

First I want to thank him for allowing us to speak to him. Is there a name or a letter we can use to refer to you conversationally?

"R."

R like Richard. By "austere" do you mean sort of a focus on Ken's intent? Or to focus intently on something? Show Ken an example of when you helped him be more austere in his life.

It's the quality that I, Ken had experienced as the leopard in that other experience. The quality of elegance and strength and calmness, all kind of combined into (one). Yeah, whatever this is.

The memory he had of accessing the consciousness of the leopard, was that a lifetime before?

"Yes."

It's my awareness that that lifetime choice is not hierarchical, that going from animal to human is not necessarily a step in any direction.

(Nods) "Yes."

It's just a different form of consciousness that correct?

"Yes."

I've also heard that "animals understand the process much deeper, more clearly than we understand as humans." Is that correct?

(Nods.) "Yes."

If you don't mind, can you help Ken to access that leopard again? And let's just ask that leopard, what his main focus in that lifetime, what was the focus of that journey? Why did he choose that lifetime?

"Individuality. Making individual decisions. While being connected on a different level. I can elaborate. So I'm going to speak with Ken in the third person. "So when Ken had that experience as a leopard, there were a few main parts of the experiences. One was the telepathic connection to his "tribe" of leopards. The other was him being alone and enjoying the calmness. But the big one was

that when he has to kill, to survive, it broke his heart. He didn't want to."

Let me ask you Mr. R, is that a common experience? Or was that unique to Ken?

"Unique to Ken."

Ken chose that lifetime as a leopard to learn those lessons and Ken chose this lifetime to learn different lessons? What's the theme of Ken's overall journey through all of his lifetimes? If there is one?

"Ascension."

Thank you Mr. R, I appreciate it. If you don't mind, could you introduce us to the person on your left; is that a male, female or light?

That's a light.

What color? Describe.

Not pure white, a little yellow, but quite, quite white. Quite bright.

Could I ask this light some questions? First, what's a letter or a name that we can use to refer to you for a conversation?

"Ah."

Ah, as in Om Ah Hum?

(Note: In Buddhism, Om Ah Hum means "Body, speech and mind." Ah is represented as a symbol.)

(Nods).

What do you represent on Ken's Council?

"Pure wisdom."

Pure Wisdom. Has Ken had a lifetime where he earned that or is it just that you represent this on all the councils that you sit on?

Can you reformulate the question?

Sometimes council members say the person earned the quality they represent on the council. Did he earn your role in his council?

"Yes. A long time ago."

How long?

"It's been, it's been time."

Are we referring to hundreds of years of years or hundreds of thousands of years?

"It cannot be measured in this kind of ... earth time."

How many councils do you sit on AH?

Not many.

Are you familiar with my work?

"Yes."

I forgot to ask you Mr. R... Are you familiar with my work?

"Yes."

Yes. So Isla was not. But Mr. R and Ah are, which is unusual. If somebody was inventing this, you'd think they would invent a common answer. But in this case, what's your opinion of this work we're doing?

"It's a nice little game."

Is there a value in this kind of endeavor of helping people to access their councils to see their journey from another perspective?

"There is and there isn't."

Are we making it too easy for people to have a journey rather than the difficulty of being in the play itself?

"It depends on the person."

Correct me if I'm wrong; if people are not meant to access this information, then you wouldn't allow them too. Is that correct?

"No."

So people have free will to do whatever they want, including access their council when they feel like it?

"At least, AH is not part of the decision making."

How is Ken doing, AH? What's your opinion of his journey and path?

"He's doing well; he knows that he does, but he needs patience."

Thank you. There's one more member of this council who's here, and we can assume there might be more members that just aren't here. Could you introduce us to the person on your left?

It's difficult to describe. It has features of a… what's the name in English? (gestures)

Describe it in German.

Masshorn… like a lot of… sorry. (Demonstrates a horn in front.)

Like a unicorn?

No, not a unicorn but like the big, big animals that have the big horn here.

Rhinoceros?

Rhinoceros, yes. It has a greenish hue. Has greenish skin. Textured skin (that) also has some spikes.

Similar to our first friend, Mr. E?

"Yes."

Thank you. First of all for appearing here today on this council. Would you give us a name or a or a letter to address you?

"Rupp."

(Note: the word Rupp means "bright" or "fame" in German.)

Mr. Rupp. I understand your name is just a placeholder for us to have a conversation. But so tell me about your appearance. Is your appearance because it's how people look where you're from?

"Yes."

Are you currently incarnated in that place while appearing here?

(Nods) Simultaneously.

Can you tell us where that planet might be? Is it in our realm or another realm?

"He can't tell us. We wouldn't understand. Another realm."

Is your appearance on Ken's council related to making it easier for him to understand? Like a metaphor for a rhinoceros?

(Ken laughs.)

Okay, he's laughing; what's going on Ken?

To me, it's very weird. This kind of appearance. He says, "He did not choose it to help me understand anything, it's just the way he looks."

And for purposes of our conversation, Mr. Rupp, would you show Ken what he looks like to you?

(Laughs) He says, "Very soft and weak."

You see Ken as a light?

(Laughs.) No, it's when he looks at me it's like a wobbly thing. (Makes a gesture) Almost more of a caricature…

Like the movie "Soul?" An outline of a person?

No, no, not like that movie. It's just that he is similar to how I experience him. I focus on his very strong and big appearance… very brutal almost, from this perspective. He focuses on the opposite. He focuses on my soft skin and it like I'm, you know, a "typical human. Very weak."

What do you represent Mr. Rupp on his council?

"Strength."

How many councils are you on?

"Only two."

I would think when people see him on the council, they'd react; "Lock the door! How did he get in here?" Pardon me, just kidding. I think it's fascinating to have this conversation so we can converse with you.

(NOTE: Occasionally I hear something on the track that resembles an EVP. In this case, there is an odd sound in the recording that sounds like breath or laughter.)

Now, Ken, if you can reach over and take a hold of his skin? What does it feel like? Any emotion associated with that?

It's warm and dry. Very dense, let's say. And I do feel a connection. Not sure what emotion it is.

What is it? Is it familial?

Yeah.

Unconditional Love?

Yeah.

"Home?"

Mm-hm. (Nods)

Okay, those three words come up often in this research. A feeling of a connectivity. So correct me if I'm wrong, Mr. Rupp, you are always connected to Ken. If he needs your assistance, or help, he can really just call upon you to charge into the room. Knock things around. You know, if you have a tank as a friend, you might as well invite the tank when a tank is needed, right? So height wise, how big how tall is he? Like the size of a Rhino?

A bit bigger. Let me see. Yes. Six, seven feet.

And you're saying that concurrently you are having a lifetime in this other realm? Is it related to the planet that Mr. E is from?

He says "Yes."

Don't tell me you guys are enemies. That would be weird. Or fight each other?

It's not the same planet, but the same realm.

I understand. And let me just for clarification, how many realms are you aware of Mr. Rupp? Is there a number that you're aware of?

"There's no number he is aware of."

So have you ever shown up in Ken's lifetime in an active way to sort of... get him to change something? And if you have, would you show him that event?

(Nods.) Mm-hmm.

Important for Ken to know that event was something related to you, and your strength. Is there anybody else we need to speak on to the council Mr. E? In terms of a spokesperson, or was AH the spokesperson for this council?

AH was the spokesperson.

Mr. AH, what, what's the primary thing that Ken should take away from this experience?

"That he doesn't need to see us. He feels us already."

Mr. E, I want to thank you for manifesting. So can we get back on that boat? Not all of us, Mr. Rupp won't fit. Is there anything I missed that Ken needs to hear?

"Yes. There is. It is about Mr. E's relationship (to him) and connection to the experiences Ken had as a child."

So you've been hanging out with Ken since he was a kid? Is that correct?

"No, No. I was involved in experiences in his childhood. And at some point, I came back."

Correct me if I'm wrong, Ken has a guide whom we haven't met yet. Would you bring him forward?

It's a light. A male that is approaching (through) the light.

And if you don't mind, you can come forward a little further along the way so that Ken can get a good look at you. Describe what you're seeing.

How to describe like a depiction of like an Ascended Master, like Jesus...

Like a person in a toga or robes or something like that?

Yeah.

What's a name that we can use for you? And if it's Jesus, that's fine. He would know the conversations.

It is.

Now, Jesus, I want you to put in Ken's mind why you've come forward today. Is it because we've met before and we've had conversations before, or do you want to just help Ken in this specific conversation?

It's because he's my guide.

(NOTE: This has come up often in the research, specifically with people who are not Christians, who don't believe in Jesus, or don't believe in any religion at all. Sometimes they say "I'm seeing Jesus, but I don't believe in him!" In terms of the data and research, other avatars do come forward – people have identified any number of them, and Jesus appears to share a frequency of other "healers." I've written a book about the dozens of conversations I've had with people who "see Jesus" including questions about his journey, his reason for showing up at this particular moment in time, currently in the hands of publishing houses.

In terms of this group, it's worth noting that "no guide" appeared to Ken at first, other than a "montage of figures" – which could mean that Ken has many guides, or that his guide didn't want to appear at the start of the conversation. Ultimately it was "Mr. E" who stopped by to help guide us to his council. The questions I ask here are standard in that I ask any guide the same questions when they show up, whether I'm aware of who they might be or not. Ken is not aware that I've had conversations with his guide in the past. But in this construct, I try not to deny what people see, just ask the same questions.)

And Jesus, if you don't mind, we've had quite a few conversations before through other people. When he first started showing up in the research, it wasn't something I was looking for, but at some point, I realized I was avoiding asking him questions. I want you to put in Ken's mind, what you mean by his "guide?" Are you speaking about the frequency that you radiate at, that you're like somebody who is a guide to him? Or are you his guide? As opposed to somebody else?

He says, "I am his guide."

And in terms of his life has Ken been aware of you? Have you ever shown up at some point?

"Yes. Yes. Ken… doesn't… He doesn't like to allow it. But he has sent for me before. He knew that I was guide. But he, he struggles with it."

Okay, I understand. And correct me if I'm wrong. You and I have had a number of conversations before is that correct? Yes. No, or I don't know?

"Yes."

Let me ask you, Jesus. Did Ken know you before when you were on the planet?

He says, "No."

Sometimes that's the case. So Ken knows you from between lives?

"Correct."

So describe how he looks to you now.

"Who?"

Sorry, I meant Ken, how does Jesus appear to you? He's manifesting and using your mind to create an image. So how does he look? What color is his robe?

It's light.

What color are his eyes?

Blue.

Take a good look very carefully. Just get right up there in his face and take a look at them.

Blue with a little green.

Why is it that sometimes you appear with different eye colors? Is it because it depends on the person?

"Yes. Because it's (that) he doesn't have this kind of appearance anymore. So it's just it takes on the form that resonates."

Could you change your outfit into something more conducive to conversation? Because it's always hard to talk to a guy in a toga? Ken, what are you seeing now?

Now he just… he just dissolved his appearance completely. And it's now just the light.

He doesn't want to change his outfit?

(I guess) He doesn't want to.

Jesus if you don't mind, come back into your form with the guy the toga and take a hold of Ken's hands and project to him a feeling or a sensation he can hold on to. Can you do that?

(Nods.) "Yes."

Now what is described the sensation or feeling you're getting now?

(Reacts) Whew. It's like, all of my energy is, is focusing in on my… say crown chakra or whatever, like my top of my SCADA. (*Supervisory Control and Data Acquisition center*) Yeah. Everything's going up and sustaining, focusing here. Almost like pulling me up.

When people talk about opening their heart, are they talking about opening their heart chakra? Are they talking about opening up their energy? Are they talking about opening up compassion?

"They talk about noticing different level of frequencies. Yes, the heart - when they talk about the heart, it's just that the heart is able to tap into a different set of frequencies than the brain. It's always doing that. So when they talk about opening their heart, it's just them, noticing it more. And allowing them to notice it more."

The idea is to open their heart to access compassion? What's a way to do that?

"I've tried to tell Ken how to do it. And he just doesn't comply. Because it's really quite easy. The easiest way is to get out of this whole reference of like "opening chakras," or whatever. Instead, focus on the sensation - focus on the experience they already know from a few moments in their lives, which was when… the moment is when they did receive what the heart is connected to. So bringing

those experiences back into mind and focusing and remembering these experiences, they start to feel their heart more concretely and more often."

In essence, you're saying if they've had small epiphanies in their lifetime, or that kind of experience?

"Everyone has (them), these are things that are not... they don't remember, because they don't see them as special. These are the experiences of... of compassion, of love, of lightness. These feelings, they have, like small moments of experiences everyone has in their lives. They just don't give enough value to them. And they don't understand their connection to what they think an open heart does."

Let me ask you, in terms of what Ken's group is doing, what advice can you give them, the group is general or specifically?

(Laughs.) "I've been smiling, because I told him (Ken) before. And it is just what I just explained, whenever they come together. And whenever they set the intention of doing anything together, they should first tap into that which I just spoke of, they should make a conscious effort of connecting to, of noticing what their hearts are connecting to, and work from that place."

So in essence, a little meditation on connecting to you, or source or connecting to compassion?

"Connecting to unconditional love and the subsets of everyday experience."

In one of my books, someone asked their guide, "What are who is God?" The answer was "God is beyond the capacity of the human brain to comprehend, it's not physically possible to do so. However," he said, "You can experience God by opening your heart to everyone, and all things."

(Ken nods)

Is opening your heart to all things consciousness? An epiphany of what compassion and unconditional love is, is that correct? Am I in the right ballpark there?

"Yes, to the first part, as in "God cannot be comprehended by the human brain." And yes, to "it can be experienced…" What then can be experienced cannot be brought back into the mind, obviously. But when you said, "opening your heart to everyone and everything," the minor "but" is that "you don't (need to) consciously open your heart to anything specifically." It does it by itself. It just opens."

He's talking about the physical act of compassion. So it's not like you have to focus on things to affect them?

"It doesn't have a direction. It goes in all directions."

"It goes in all directions." That's pretty deep Jesus. Dude, you should be a philosopher.

(Chuckles) "I was once."

I heard they didn't appreciate that so much. (Laughs) "Not so much with the Romans." It was a like a weird joke, but the fact that I got a laugh out of you, was pretty funny. Do you appreciate that joke still?

"Oh, sure. Why would I not love (it) when lightness and joy are part of unconditional love? There are levels of humor in everything. The human mind is not made to understand all of those levels in a human lifetime."

I appreciate that we can have a conversation, but I think it's classic to hear you have a sense of humor. Ken, are you aware of any connection to Jesus before today?

Yes. As I said before, it's been difficult for me to deal with. Because at some point in my life, I had the feeling of "hearing Jesus." But I was very… like I didn't tell anyone. I only told my sister. And after she told me that she is aware of (his) Mother Mary. It's been our little secret. But it's been something that has been… this connection has been with me for a while, and I've always tried to find a way of dealing with it, because I come from a Christian household. But I never had a personal connection to another version of Christianity.

Once you start to have a conversation with him, you can ask questions. Is that correct?

"Yes."

Well, that is something we can all do. That idea of shifting your consciousness into another's shoes, and what a wonderful thing be able to do because you get to experience their journey.

"But it's mainly been when Ken was "ready" and I came into his life (revealed his presence) as a Guide. That was when he felt my presence and still needed to find a way how to deal with it."

I've heard people quote Jesus a few times, "We're all just walking each other home." Also that "all religions point to the same garden." Correct?

"Oh, for sure. Mr. E says "He will come back and tell me about this experience as a child when he feels it's the right time."

I hope you'll let me know what Mister E has to say. I'd invite him to come visit me in Santa Monica but I think you'd freak out my family. Thanks to the guides, teachers, classmates, friends. Have you visited your council before Ken?

No. Interesting.

*****

Henri Fantin LaTour. The Guild

"The greater danger for most of us lies not in setting our aim too high and falling short; but in setting our aim too low, and achieving our mark." *Michelangelo*

CHAPTER THREE: KIKI

Kiki has had an unusual life. Married into a family with descendants from a "royal European dynasty" she has seen the gilded side of things in her lifetime. Raised her family. I have no idea how she became part of this meditation group, Kiki is not her real name or nickname, but like all sessions, I try to focus on a person's path or journey and then see how it might match up with others.

Rich: I started making a documentary about a topic that kind of interested me, which led me into people under hypnosis, talking about things that people talk about. What made it unique was that they were consistent. They were talking about things that you wouldn't think people knew or could talk about. And so that led into a discussion with Kelly, who, you know, disagreed. I'm joking.

Kiki: (Laughs) I know her.

I filmed her doing a session. Had to be over five years ago. And she had the same adventure other people did. Afterwards, it was kind of like, "wow, that was weird. Recently, we had lunch and as a follow up, I wanted to know what she remembered or recalled from the session.

She brought it all back as if it was literally next door. She opened that door, walked inside and that sort of spawned this idea of, "Gee, I wonder if other people can access this same information if they know how to meditate." Because of your group, it appears you all know meditation. She didn't go into detail about it but just that you've all had some experience meditating.

Mm-hm.

And so that, for me, that's kind of the key, the idea of being able to visualize and then speak about it, which is kind of what hypnotherapy involves. But in this case, there's no hypnosis involved. I'm just talking to people who have already bypassed the filters. It's like they walk back into the garden.

Yeah.

So let me ask you, and Kiki is that the best name to refer to you?

Yes, Kiki is the best. It's a nickname. But it's a name that at a certain moment, where things happened to really change in my life. Someone started calling me Kiki. And since then, Kiki is like my real name, I would say.

Let's start with a simple meditation, you can close your eyes or not, doesn't matter. A simple meditation The Beatles sang about; "Picture yourself in a boat on a river." Can you imagine yourself in a boat floating on a river somewhere? What's the boat look like?

It's not a small boat. It's not a big boat. It's like middle sized; maybe 20 meters or something like that. Twenty meters would be like the feeling I have. It's wooden. And yeah, it's I think it feels like I'm alone there.

And when you look off the bow or you look off the side. What do you see? Water, land?

Water, fields, trees. Nice, like, spring summer atmosphere around me. It's nice and warm, not too hot. I can feel the breeze that is touching my skin and my face - quite pleasant.

I'm going to ask for either your guide or someone on the flip side, who knows and loves you and hangs out with you and has been around to come and sit opposite you. Is that a male, a female or a light?

Let me see. What is it….? I would say male.

Try not to judge whatever comes to mind. So a male and let me ask him, is it possible for us to have a conversation with you? If you can nod shrug, or shake his head?

He says "Yes."

Describe him as he comes into focus. About how old is he? What does he look like?

He has curls, he is not too old. He is like I would say in his late thirties.

What's he wearing clothing wise?

It's like a white kimono.

His eye color if you can see that?

Blue eyes. Hair color is dark. Black.

Blue eyes. Black hair. If I can ask for a name or a letter. So just for the purpose of this conversation.

It's an "R."

Okay, and if and if he puts a name in your mind, we'll use that, but Mr. R is fine. First allow me to thank you for allowing us to chat with you. And do you self-identify as Kiki's guide?

He says "Kind of."

Does that mean that she has more than one guide or you watch over other people as well?

He says "She's also a guide herself."

Are you familiar with my work?

"No."

I'm asking as it helps me frame the questions.

"Well, no."

Have you ever incarnated on the planet?

"Yes."

Was it with Kiki or would not with her?

"It was with her."

Is Kiki aware of that lifetime?

"I don't think so."

Can we show it to her? Just give her give us an image of or a time and a place? Are we inside or outside?

We are outside.

Take a look at the ground is a grass, dirt? Pavement?

It's like red stone.

Okay, so we're out in the countryside. Let me ask you, is this on this planet? And if it's on our planet, what would be a country associated with it today?

"Syria."

If you could just put a date in her mind.

"1700s"

And if you could show her what you look like in that lifetime?

(Kiki aside) Shall I answer?

Yes. Just so put that image in Kiki's mind so she can tell me what did you look like?

I was, at that time, a man in his fifties.

You're referring to yourself? Mr. R, you were a man in your fifties?

"Yes."

What did Kiki look like in that lifetime?

"She was a girl of around fourteen or fifteen."

What was your relationship to her?

"Um, she was a cousin."

So a relation?

"Yeah."

And if you could put in her mind's eye just the way she looks. What color hair did she have?

Dark brown. Long hair, dark brown. Very bright. Girl who looks very bright and cheerful.

What's her name? Just to be helpful what to be associated with this young girl?

"Sasa."

What was your name in that lifetime? If you don't mind me asking. Just pop that into Kiki's mind?

"Mahomet."

(Note: The name Sasa means "help" or "aide" in Arabic. She either said "Momat" or "Mahomet" Mahomet means "divine teacher" in Arabic.)

If you don't mind, I'd like to take Kiki to visit with her council. Is it possible?

"Yes."

Tell me are we inside or outside?

We are inside now.

What does the floor look like?

Stone. Raised stone – cool gray stone.

Any columns or walls?

They are wooden but open. Like windows between the rooms.

I want to say thank you for allowing us to come in to visit with Kiki's Council. When I asked this question, how many individuals appear nearby?

Five.

And how are they arrayed? Are they in the line? Are they in a circle or a semi-circle?

They are sitting in a circle.

Allow me to thank them for allowing us to come in. I want to say that I won't ask any questions that will disrupt Kiki's path. I appreciate being allowed to come in here and converse with you. If you could pick one, a person on the left to be the first person to talk to? Is that a male, a female or a light?

It's a female.

If you could describe about how old she is, or how she looks?

I think she's in her thirties. She looks very pretty. Black hair, really black hair. Yeah, I think she wears something yellow.

Okay, may I ask you some questions directly?

"Yes."

Please tell us a name or a letter we can use to identify you.

"It's an M."

Thank you Miss Em. Are you familiar with my work?

"Yes."

What's your opinion of it?

"It is desperately needed in this… in these days."

I ask to clarify that some people do know of my work and some people do not. So the idea of why it's important is really the key as to why we're having this conversation. Let me ask, what do you represent on Kiki's council in a word as a quality?

"I protect her."

Protection? And is that have you do serve on other councils?

"Yes, yes, I do."

How many, if I may ask?

"Three."

(Note: The idea that council members serve on other councils is worth examining. Some work on many councils – in the hundreds, thousands – and in some cases just a few. They don't always serve the same purpose on each council – it depends upon the person.)

I appreciate that. Allow me to ask you. These questions that I've asked other council members, do you feel this is an effective method for people that are involved with Kiki's group to access new information?

"Yes, yes, definitely."

And so in terms of their project that they're working on, what is something that you would recommend that they focus on?

"Healing."

How would they how would they affect that? Make that happen?

(By) "Sticking together."

So the group pulling together and accessing each other is a way to help access the information on how to heal people. Is that correct?

"Yes. Not only to heal people, but to heal systems."

That's a better clarification. By "systems" do you mean - because of course the body is a system, we have planetary system, we live in these systems - is that what you are you referring to? All the systems that we exist in?

"Yes."

What is the most effective way to get these answers this these answers? Is it being together and meditating together or is it something else that they should learn by themselves?

"I think… communication."

Because we are speaking to you telepathically, by communication -- what forms come to mind when you say that?

"Communication… also online like spreading knowledge. Yes."

I like to ask is there's something specific, just in terms of changing the climate, changing the planet Earth, healing the planet Earth, that we should focus on more than the others?

"I believe it's more, it's like healing the people's consciousness will heal the planet."

So what would be an effective way to heal people's consciousness? Is it showing people that they can communicate with you on a daily basis?

"No, it is more getting a shift from fear to confidence. Yes, a shift from fear to confidence by knowing that so many people are already working on healing the planet and new concepts. When the masses… when humanity gets access to this knowledge, to this understanding, that there's already a lot going on, they will become confident they will heal, they will lose their fears and they will follow."

Would you please introduce us to the person on your left, which would be Kiki's, right? Is that a male, female or light?

"It's another female. She is young, wild. Not as young as Kiki, but I would say in her twenties, early twenties. She is… pregnant."

And what would be a name or a letter we can use to converse with you?

"Vee as in Victor."

And what do you represent a Kiki's council?

"Victim."

And is this a reference to a lifetime that Kiki has had in the past? Where she's experienced that?

(Kiki aside) I don't think so. No, I think it's (about her) presence.

Based on the research, most council members report they earned their place on a council. And it's sometimes because the person we're talking to, has had a specific experience in a previous lifetime. Would you clarify what that means? Victim?

She's been punished for being herself (in the past)

Do you mean Kiki?

"No, this person."

Oh, I see this. Miss Vee has been victimized. So what you're referring to, is the lesson and knowledge that comes from a person who has been victimized, and realize the reasons for the journey, is that correct?

"Yes, yes, that's correct."

In essence, you're talking about the energy of victimization. The opposite of that energy would be empathy? Like the other side of victimization is empathy?

"Yes."

And so in essence, if Kiki wants to help somebody, you help her with empathy for somebody who's a victim. This is a frequency and a vibration you're familiar with. So she can come to you directly and ask "Help me with this concept. How do I help this person?" Is that Right?

"I didn't really understand the question."

I'm sorry, it was a little bit of a circular question. But the idea is that you represent, you represent the frequency of victimization?

"Yes."

The understanding and knowledge of how a person goes through that. So when Kiki is out in the world and meets someone who is a victim, she can ask you for help in terms of understanding this person's journey, is that correct?

"Yes."

Please, correct me if I'm wrong. From my experience with this research, people choose their lifetimes. And they choose them with their guides, and teachers and council members, all giving advice, classmates all weighing in on the choice. So to choose to play the role of a victim versus playing the role of a perpetrator is an act of courage?

(Nods) "Mm hmm. Yes."

And so, I would just add that in your role on this council, there's a lot that has to do with courage.

"Yes."

Have you ever incarnated on the planet Miss Vee?

"Yes. Many times."

If I may, you're manifesting this visual of being in your twenties for Kiki. Why are you adding this manifestation of being pregnant, with child?

"(Because) As today, women who give birth to children need more protection."

I'm sorry, could you clarify that?

"Women who have children need more protection."

So it's a symbolic, like a metaphor for women who are who are with child who, let's say they live in circumstances that are difficult for them to have birth?

I think "Mothers" is the better word – "Mothers need more protection."

(Note: It's worth noting that "victimization" of women is rampant on the planet. By appearing as a pregnant young woman in need of help is something Kiki is seeing and trying to comprehend. It's a visual metaphor for the universal need for compassion for all mothers.)

How do you think Kiki is doing?

"I think she's doing very well. She's been, she's been through some experiences or more like seeing things that other people don't recognize. And she's doing pretty well. Yes. She's, she brings joy."

That's wonderful. So is there if I may ask, Miss Vee, is there someone who represents joy in her council?

"Yes."

And if we could speak to them, briefly. Is that a male, a female or Light?

That's a light.

And what color is the light?

"Orange."

Can I ask you some questions? Is that more of a male or a female energy associated with that? So I can least use Mr. or Ms.?

"It's balanced. It's male and female."

What does the color orange represent or what do you represent on Kiki's Council?

"It's nurture - being nurtured."

Nurturing?

It is a good... it's a good essence. (And) A good smell.

What's the smell you're sensing?

It's more it's like the smell of a blossoming orange tree or lemon tree. But it is, it is even more it's like... it's like tickling all the senses.

Do you represent nurturing, not only for others, but also of nature?

"Yes. Like existence, like nurturing existence."

Have you ever incarnated on the planet?

"No."

Are you familiar with my work?

"Yes."

Okay and your opinion of it?

"Oh, that's what life is about."

What would your advice be for their group - nurturing the planet, as well as nurturing souls that are suffering from climate change, etc. Is there advice that you have for them for this group?

"Yes, connect with nature, reconnect with nature."

I've heard humans used to be able to communicate with nature, but forgotten how to do it.

"Yes."

What caused the disruption in frequency?

"Technology."

Technology throughout human history? The objects, as opposed to being in nature?

"Yes, yes. But "objects" are something that have been created by humans. And I think it is, because it's useful, it's nothing negative. But the connection with nature is there. There was so much fascination toward human creations, that they lost.... They lost the knowledge, or the connection to their roots. And their roots are nature, they are part of nature. And therefore, they have to, I think they have to rebalance that."

Rebalance. That's fascinating, because it's not like saying we have to stop using technology. Because of course, here we are having this unusual conversation via technology that we couldn't have had a year ago, where you and I and Kiki are connecting on the flipside, through this medium. In terms of speaking directly to nature, could you give people a method that would be simple for them to put themselves in that nurturing position with nature?

"Listening. Just listen."

Do you mean like walking outside and listening or listening to other people communicate?

"No, by going outside - by the sea, by the listen to the sounds and to the words of nature."

Let me ask, is there any more council members that want to talk to us?

Yes, there's one more. A man. He's tall... He seems to be desperate to say something. He's in his fifties or sixties something like that. He's been there for some time. But yes. (He wants to speak.)

What would be a name that we could use to address you, sir?

"T." Something with T.

Mr. T. Please go ahead. What would you like to impart?

He wants to speak to the victim. He says (that) "He never meant to... to do (her) any harm."

Well, tell me what do you represent on Kiki's Council?

"The pleasant male."

The happy male, the pleasant male?

"Yes."

So have you ever incarnated with Kiki?

"No."

Have you ever incarnated on the planet?

"Yes."

And was that a pleasant, happy experience?

"No, it was not a pleasant experience."

I see. And so did you choose those lifetimes to learn lessons about the opposite of that?

"Yes."

Let me ask you this. How many councils do you sit on?

"Just one, this one."

And have you ever had an incarnation with any other members of the council?

"Yes, with Miss Vee."

Are saying that when you participated in that lifetime with incidents that have stayed with you?

"Yes. I was forced to do things that I never would have done if I wouldn't have been forced to do it. Just to save my own life."

(Note: In the book and film "Flipside" a woman who recalled dying in Auschwitz talked about the choice of that lifetime, to "play the role of victim instead of perpetrator." When she got home to her council, they "showed her how it was harder to play one role than the other, as the perpetrators would suffer over a longer period of time." In the film "Hacking The Afterlife" a film executive recalls choosing a lifetime that ended in Dachau. He spoke of choosing that lifetime to "remember the dark" – but that it was "so dark that it scorched his soul.")

Was this a recent lifetime a lifetime in the era that we might be aware of? Or was it a long time ago?

It was like a hundred and fifty years ago.

What you're saying is that even though you chose that lifetime, because of incidents that happened while you were on the planet -- the fear of death, fear of our losing our life, we do things that are above and beyond what we signed up for. Is that correct?

"Yes."

The first person I filmed talked about dying in the Holocaust. And she was talking about how she appreciated from the perspective she has now -- that she chose to play the role of a victim instead of a perpetrator. And as she put it, "because the perpetrators had a harder time recovering from those experiences over their lifetimes." Is this what you're referring to?

Mm-hm. (Nods).

So you had a harder time recovering from those acts?

"Yes."

And here we are speaking about something that happened 150 years ago, but for you, correct me if I'm wrong, it feels more like it happened a minutes or like an hour ago?

"Yes."

This is important to access; we hear it often that "the truth sets everyone free." For a person to come forward and talk about an event that happened 150 years ago, they feel the need to clarify what happened -- even to apologize. It sounds to me like you are apologizing to Miss Vee?

"Yes, I even want to go further and offer her now. My help."

And Miss Vee, can we ask for your opinion about what you're hearing?

"Yes, I can. For the moment, I am not used to getting help. So it would be a new experience. An adventure."

He's referring to a lifetime you had years ago -- But during your life review, Mr. T did you not cover this? Did you guys not work on this? Or talk about it or experience it or go through it?

"No, each one had to move on with his own life and fate. And we've both been through different processes of growth. But it seems that now is the time to address this. Yes."

Mr. T, after this lifetime that you had 150 years ago, where you perpetrated and did these things that were above or beyond what you signed up for – you realized the trauma you created. Did you go through a life review after that, of all the people that you harmed, and hurt?

"Yes."

You never got a chance to sort of, one on one address an individual like Miss Vee and apologize?

"Yes."

So Miss Vee what would be what would be a form of help that he could do for you?

"By being on my side, and um… offering me to have the strength, but helping me to create the strength to – (towards) being independent and still connected.

In this research I've heard people on the other side in the council's say that this form of communication is helping people on the other side to communicate with us.

"Mm-hmm." (Nods)

But this is the first - two people on a council using this form of communication - through someone like Kiki, communicating with each other.

"Yes."

Mr. T., how do you think Kiki is doing?

"I think she's very strong. She's doing very well."

And have you shown up at any point in her life to assist her? Helped her out of a situation?

"Yes, It was like, someone who was… like more in the back. And giving her confidence."

So it is confidence that you impart to her? Is that related to your journey in terms of your strengths? Or, like physical size?

"Yes, yes. Absolutely. Yeah. Yes."

So what's the most effective way for Kiki to tap into you, or anyone in the council - to tap into this council to ask for help in the various disciplines that people give?

"By asking, asking for what she needs, or asking for help in what she needs."

I would like to ask you to take Kiki to her "place of healing." Are we inside or outside?

We are inside. It is like, it's a very central place. It's warm. People are um... yeah, the first word that came up was like a harem, but it's not a harem. It's just a place where it's very, very physical. Sensual.

Physical and sensual. How many other individuals are here in this, for lack of a better word harem?

Oh, many.

And let me ask is this a memory from a previous lifetime?

It feels like it's not. It's not a lifetime. It feels like it's a different... It's almost like a different planet. It's a different field of existence.

Is this a place for her between lives to come and reconnect?

"Yes. Very lively. Very, very lively in a very positive way. Like (experiencing) the joy of life."

This idea, Mr. R, that we live on the planet in a dense world. And we live off the planet in a sort of more mental world, where we can create things and create construct environments. This feels like a constructed environment, but also with the people Kiki's helped over many lifetimes. Is that correct?

"Yes, it is. Yes."

Well, so if you could let now allow her to feel that sensation sort of amplified of this connectivity to these people that are in this place. Are you lying down, standing up or sitting down?

Sitting down and leaning onto others.

I'm thinking of fort near the Taj Mahal, there was a place where the harem would sort of hang out on pillows. How is everyone attired? What is the construct?

It's, it's different. Some of them are nude, some of them are with clothes. But it's, that's not important. It's more like, everybody's just the way he or she feels comfortable. It's more like the energy of being comfortable.

Let's go back to the boat. What else would you like us to explore? Mr. R, what is it you want to impart to her about this journey today?

"She should like… "walk the walk." Like she has done it so far. She should move on to the same energy and the same way."

She's on the right path. She's doing the right thing?

"She's on the right path. Exactly."

Take a look at Mr. R, is he still wearing the same kimono?

Yes.

So where did you get this kimono?

"I bought it at a market. Yes, in the market."

Okay, and what country did you buy it in?

"Morocco."

In the souk?

"Mm hmm."

In Marrakech or Casablanca?

"Marrakech."

Did you haggle for it? Or did you just buy it?

"Haggled for it."

It's been a treat to meet you. And is there anything else you want me to cover? Talk about?

I think it's fine. I think we have touched quite some. Some bases. Yeah, it's great.

All right. There we go, Kiki, here we are an hour later. It's pretty shocking how far we can go in just a short amount of time. Have you ever been to visit your council before consciously?

Not in that way. Or that picture. But yes, I have many times.

And are these the same individuals that you've met before?

Um, no. No, they are very different.

For me that's "new information." Cannot by cryptomnesia. It was fascinating to clarify that... I mean, was this something you'd thought of before?

No, not at all, it really appeared like, it's interesting, because it appeared in the sense that I'm here, or I believe that healing the people will heal the planet. And so this, for me, I've done a lot of healing work in my life. I healed two traumatized families, my own and the family of the father of my children. This was a very important part of my life so far. But I was also surprised, it's something I wouldn't, I couldn't really. I think will take this with me and let it like resonate the next days. Thank you.

*****

Mind bending to say the least. In this session, two council members sharing information that is not only new to the person reporting it, but new to each other. One "never got the chance to apologize" for a previous transgression. It's not cryptomnesia, the subject could not have invented it – she's never seen nor heard of her council. And yet, she learned something completely new about them.

> **"You don't have to be Picasso or Rembrandt to create something. The fun of it, the joy of creating, is way high above anything else to do with the art form."**
>
> *Chick Corea*

CHAPTER FOUR: DAVID

Rich: What did Kelly tell you about what we're doing today? I just mean you, you personally?

David: Well, as far as my understanding you've got a unique gift to channel other people from other sides of the dimensions and part of what we're trying to do as a group is looking at group coherence and…our full selves, just that kind of greater reality that we're part of.

I just want to clarify, I've been filming people accessing this information, filming mediums, or filming people under hypnosis. And in the four-to-six-hour session, they're accessing their guides their teachers or classmates…. And in my case, I learned everybody doesn't need to have that six-hour hypnosis session, to access that same information.

Could I ask that guide to come to visit to help us with access? If I could ask for a name - either a letter or a name to refer to you that we might use.

"Y. a. h."

Nice to meet you. And let me just say thank you for showing up to participate in this grand experiment. And if so, in your mind's eye, how far away is Yah? Far away or close by?

Nearby.

(Note: I didn't ask, but "Yah" is a Hebrew word for "God." It's complicated when someone uses a name that means something in another language, but in England it refers to an "upper class person.")

Is YAH more of a light or a male or a female, just in terms of this presentation or manifestation for our conversation?

Yeah, more of a light.

Is it possible for you to manifest as a person?

Yes.

And if you could describe that person for me,

Just me. (Looks like David).

So like a mirror image of you in a way?

(David nods.) Yeah.

Well, I just don't want it to be problematic in terms of our conversation.

More non-binary.

Are you David's guide, is that accurate?

"Not sure if guide is the best term."

Are you familiar with what we're doing? And why we are having our conversation today?

"Not entirely."

Yah, is it possible to escort David to visit with his council?

"Yes."

And if you could show David the way or where we are. Are we inside or outside?

We're above.

Is there any kind of a structure to this place?

A lot of trees.

Have you ever been here before and your meditations seen it?

Not specifically.

Are there any beings around? If so, how many?

"The Council only comes at a certain time."

(Note: In my experience with speaking to councils, it can be a matter of "inviting them to come forward." What I'm doing is "leading" people to visit their council which is a form of asking them to participate.)

Okay, well, I'm going to invite them to come forward if they don't mind, because that's why we're here to talk to them. And YAH knows what I'm talking about. How many council members can appear and talk to us now?

Six came to mind.

And it's possible that only six are willing to appear for the purposes of our conversation. How are they arrayed? Are they in line? A circle or a semi-circle?

There are plenty of beings - the council came in as a circle.

So there are plenty of beings. But these primary people that are here in terms of the reference word "Council" – you're aware of six, there may be more?

Well, there's seven because I'm there.

First, allow me to thank the Council for allowing us to be here to be in this space to have a conversation with you. May I ask, is it possible to converse with you?

(David nods.) Yes.

Let's go to the person on the far left. Is that a male female or light?

Sort of a greenish color…

May I ask some questions?

(David nods.) Yes.

When you say a light is there a masculine or feminine or neither?

Other worldly hominid. Elf like.

(Note: I've run into "Elf like" entities in these interviews in the past, including what could only be described as a leprechaun. Also faeries, other beings that seem to be mythological, yet they are able to describe their role on a council, as well as discuss the realm they are "from." Like the Elvish group in Lord of the Rings.)

If I could have a name or a letter to refer to you?

"Click."

Spell please?

"Klk."

I'll call you Mr. K if that's all right. If you could manifest or become a little more clear for David. So when you say elf like about how tall is this person? More than two feet in height?

(David nods.) Yes.

Age or physical characteristics, hair or anything like that eyes?

He has elongated features. Greenish gray skin. (Wearing a) Simple tunic. He has slate colored eyes.

Mr. Kay, let me ask if you are familiar with what I'm doing?

(Shakes his head.) "No."

If you could please tell him what is a word that represents your role on his council?

"Discernment."

(Note: He's not aware of why I am asking this question (nor is David) but he is able to answer it.)

Has he earned that over many lifetimes, or is that just the role that you represent?

"It is my role on his council."

How many other councils do you sit on or participate in?

"Many."

Mr. Kay, have you ever incarnated on the planet Earth?

"Only briefly."

So you have, that must have been an unusual experience. Have other people seen you, let's say in their mind's eye, and then that is sort of the source of mythology in terms of elfin characters?

"Yeah, there's many of us there."

(Note: I cannot help but think of the comment my wife made about seeing unique features in people from Wales, and how many of them have "elfin" qualities. I had never considered it before.)

Do you come from a specific realm in the universe where everyone looks like you?

"There are some places where we're the majority."

Although you're not familiar with my research, do you know anybody that I know? Have you run across anybody who might have mentioned me over there?

"Certainly."

Now to the more direct question that I want to ask other members of the council, is this an effective way, talking to councils to learn new information?

"When everyone can speak freely,"

And specifically this project that David is working on with our friend Kelly and others, what is something specific that you can help them with their work?

"It has to seduce or captivate the mind and imagination."

Should they include this kind of conversation with people in a council to help guide them in terms of their work?

"It's all being done by council."

How do you think David is doing?

"This is a time he can shine. It's a new culture now."

In terms of discernment, he's doing what he's supposed to be doing?

"Mostly."

Any advice for David to alter or change?

"He needs to do just more of what needs to be done."

In terms of climate change on our planet, and the thing we're trying to affect, change, do you have any advice for us on that? In terms of what we need to focus on?

"Nobody is paying attention to the margins."

Do you mean the humanity that's being affected by climate change that we're not paying attention to?

"Everyone is so used to a script with (the) familiar players. But that's not what's happening. There's a lot more going on."

What's a way that people can people access this information and stay and be aware of folks on the margins?

"To experience their full selves; they're used to being in a role of audience or a role in the script. And part of what they're doing with the group is trying to experience being different organs in the organism. And until everyone is more aware of what everyone else is doing, then that group experience – that (awareness) otherwise only found in duress, like when a platoon is isolated, and you're dependent moment to moment on the people around you -- that level of bonding is what's the only glue that's ever really gotten humanity through. And I feel like that's where they're at - is lacking the fullness of the human experience."

And is this a way for people to speak to the audience and be onstage at the same time, to realize that we do have a connection with our higher selves or our higher consciousness?

"Yes, being able to change the game, make the game play itself into the next game. And the meta game is "What game shall we play or what game is playing us?" Or "What games are afoot?""

Mr. K, if you can just address the person to your left. Or to the person who's in charge of this council, the council's spokesperson, if you will. Is that somebody we can chat with?

"Grat. He's big. Big; taller than ten feet. Maybe around either or ten feet around. He has orange Skin."

Grat, are you familiar with my work?

"Yes."

What's your opinion of this work?

"We're all in it."

(Note: I have no idea what he means, but can imagine he means that we are all part of it.)

What is your role on David's Council?

"Synapse."

Synapse. Are you the big synapse? The council leader of this group? Did you orchestrate our conversation today?

Today, (and) tomorrow…

What do David and his group need to focus on, in terms of helping people in terms of climate change, or in the margins as Mr. Kay put it so aptly, what is something that they should focus on?

The focus should be "Why is the change changing?" There's this there's this tendency to try to find satisfaction. And that's almost always the problem. Focus on why the change is changing.

So you're identifying the issues that are problematic. What do you represent on David's Council in a word?

"Heft. Psychic… mass."

His ability to traverse those things and bring those elements together? Let me ask you Grat, are you the spokesperson for his council? Or a member?

"There's no one spokesperson."

How many councils do you sit on?

"Many."

How many?

As many as it takes."

Is there anybody else in the council that wants us to converse with them? Or would like to?

Looks like there's one. I'm seeing a blue female.

And if I may ask a name or a letter to refer to you?

I don't know. It seems like um, a portal or something.

Can you reach across and hold her hands for a moment in your mind's eye?

I think she's under water or something.

But can you reach over and touch her or somehow embrace her?

Yeah, I just kind of got closer to her.

What's the feeling when you're closer?

It's like she's a light... she's aquamarine light kind of and bubbling.

Is there a name or a letter we can use to address you?

"Q" comes to mind.

Are you manifesting as you normally appear or have appeared on another planet?

(David nods.) Yes.

(Note: In the reports from the Newton Institute, over 35% of the reports include memories of lifetimes off planet. Some of those include memories of lifetimes on "water planets" where lifetimes take place under water.)

And let me ask if David has ever had a lifetime there?

"Yes. Before. Before (he was) David."

What is that like living underwater Q, is it problematic or fun?

She says, "Everyone's pleasure is shared, where we experience everything together."

Q, is this place in this realm or universe or in another one?

"Another one. I only come here to help out."

Do you sit on many councils?

"No."

What do represent on David's journey on this council?

"Advocacy."

Advocacy, did he earn that?

"It's from previous lifetimes. Yeah. Karma."

I wanted to ask a question to somebody in this sacred grove, if you think that's a good idea. Q, I assume you know what I'm going to ask, is this a good question or a place for me to ask it?

"This is good place to ask it."

I want to ask a question to one of the trees in this grove. What's a way for us to help our planet reverse climate change?

"The future is an inside job… we have to breathe together. The future is an inside job."

(Note: While we use the term "inside job" to mean a crime committed with help from someone – the definition is actually "help from someone living or working on the premises." So in essence anyone on the planet is a participant of an inside job.)

I heard from a tree "plant a trillion trees, because that will reduce carbon and bring the oxygen level up which will cool the planet down." Do you agree with that assessment?

"Yes. It's about how we get along… It's not quantity, it's quality. Everyone appreciating the moment together."

How do you think our friend David is doing?

"Being embraced by the world now."

And Q, if we can go back to you for a second. What's your opinion of David's journey?

"Precious soul out on a limb and has to have another tree to go to next."

You have six people in the council, so you have three more that you need to meet at some point. But we did hear about advocacy. We heard about heft and I'm sorry, Mr. Kay, what was your role?

"Discernment."

Now, I'm going to thank everybody for allowing us to show up here for just brief amount of time, is there anything else we need to talk about?

"It's, um, it's about the evolution of consciousness through collective intelligence. Have you seen the Georgia Guidestones?"

I have not.

(Note: From Smithsonian: "On the stones are ten instructions: *"Maintain humanity under 500,000,000 in perpetual balance with nature. Guide reproduction wisely… etc. Be not a cancer on the earth. Leave room for nature."*)

Well, after a very disturbing first line, some wonderful last lines, "Leave room for nature."

Like the tree telling us to "change your paradigm, change your focus, start to see the world from a different perspective." Easy to say, but you know, obviously hard to do.

Well, they're rooted in it, you know.

Ha, yes, "rooted in it."

It's partially the global situation. The entire sort of breakdown of multiple paradigms at once, which leads to an opportunity for something more emergent to take place. It's participatory environment."

*****

"I saw the angel in the marble and carved until I set him free."

Michelangelo

CHAPTER FIVE: ELOISE

Another zoom session. "Eloise" (not her name) in bold, my questions in italics.

RICH: I'm going to assume you've done have you done meditation before?

ELOISE: Yeah.

I'm going to ask you, in your meditations are you aware of your guide?

Of my guide? No.

Would you like to meet them?

Yeah.

Are you familiar with my work at all?

Not at all.

The idea is of just exploring an unknown place together. Can you visualize and talk about them?

Oh, yeah.

Let's play a game. I want you to picture yourself in a boat on a river. Like the Beatles song.

Yeah.

What does this boat look like? And what does this river look like?

Somehow the boat looks blue. I don't know why a very cobalt blue. the sun is shining, and it's shimmering. If I look at the water. It's shimmering. And it's kind of calm, but you can see tiny waves but not a lot. It's just calm.

Put your hand down on the on those seat. What does it feel like?

Leather. (Pauses) I'm confused because I'm like, "How did I get on this boat?"

What's it made of?

The boat is made from wood.

So when you look over the shimmering water, can you see land on either side?

No. There's a lot of water.

Okay, so you could be at sea in a way as opposed to in a lake? Or a river?

Yeah, it seems like a sea and it's very peaceful.

I'm going to ask you to invite someone to sit across from you. And I would ask for your guide, if they're available.

Someone wearing a lot of white, and I feel like it's, it's, at first it was masculine, but then feminine.

When you say wearing white, you mean like a toga?

Like a robe on... I can see playing with the wind.

Can you identify any features? Does this person have eyes, hair, that sort of thing?

Blonde hair, I can see the hair playing with the wind as well.

Now take a look at the eyes. Are they blue or the green? Are they brown? What are they?

Well, that was just watching an interview on television. And now I'm afraid I'm seeing her.

That's okay, they often use an image in your mind to help you have a communication.

She has very bright blue eyes. Very pure. Everything about her is very pure.

The first question, is it okay if I asked you some questions? And she can nod...

"Yes."

She said yes. So, first question is, are you familiar with me?

"No."

If you don't mind, would you please give us a name or a letter, for this conversation?

Estelle (laughs).

Thank you, Estelle. Are you Eloise's?

(Shrugs) I don't know.

Estelle, give me either a thumbs up or thumbs down, or shake your hand like, I don't know. Are you Eloise's guide?

I'm feeling something like, this side is wanting me to do something like a diagonal.

I understand, it's because Estelle doesn't know me. She will in a few minutes, she'll understand. Take a hold of Estelle hands. And what does that feel like to you when you do so?

Very soft and feminine. And soft. It is, like very precise. I don't know how to explain. It's delicate but fierce… like strong (and) delicate.

Estelle. How is Eloise doing?

There's silence.

Silence is an answer. Is she on the path she designed with you? Or is she struggling?

I saw bright light.

Okay, let's just allow that may be a reply – bright light meaning she's on the right path. I'm going to interpret it that way. But it's Estelle, can you nod?

Eloise nods.

So she's on the right path. It's a little bit like pulling strings at first to try to get an answer, but at the same time, let's go forward. Has there been a time where you've come to help her or give her assistance?

I just keep on hearing. "Yes, yes. All the time. Yes… I'm here."

And do you mean by that? You're always connected to Eloise?

"Yes." I was shown her hugging me from behind, like protecting me at the same time.

Show Eloise what she looks like to you from your side of the boat. How does she look? Younger, older, the same?

I could feel like joy, that joy.

So, let me just clarify. Estelle when you look at Eloise, that's what you see. Joy?

Joy and (that) bright light again.

It's a form of an answer, you know, doesn't have to be in our mundane words or syntax. Would you escort us to visit her Council? Now I know that Eloise doesn't know what that means. But I know you do.

"Yes."

Are we inside or outside?

Inside.

If you could describe it to me, what does the floor look like?

A lot of marble, white marble cold, clean, but serene.

How about how high are the ceilings?

Very high. And again, a lot of light from above.

Okay, columns or any support structures?

Walls, just walls. It's narrow – it's like a path. (I'm seeing) It's like a hallway.

Are there any individuals here?

Just me and Estelle.

Okay, and so I'm going to ask Estelle to invite Eloise's council to come forward. As they approach how many people do you see? And how are they arrayed? Or in a circle? A line?

What I'm seeing is a lot of birds.. Flying like in a beautiful, I don't know... Pattern. (She draws a circle with her hand.) Towards us.

And just if you can, what's a number that comes to mind without judging?

Oh, like it was more like ten but less than thirty.

And so if we could have the sort of primary people in Eloise's Council alight or come down to have a conversation with this. If they could manifest as a person or a light or as a bird, so we can have a conversation? Is that okay?

Mm-hmm. (Nods.)

So I want you to go to the first being in this line. And now as you approach them, first, let me thank them for allowing us to have this conversation. Is it okay to ask you some questions.?

Mm-hm. (Nods.)

Is this a male a female light or what manifests?

(Laughs) It's an eagle. Somehow it's not scary, but I know that it's like, the energy is like I should be honored that it's sitting in front of me. Like a reverence, like a reverential thing.

It a male or female Eagle?

Feels like a male.

So, Mr. Eagle, I appreciate you, alighting and stopping to have a conversation with us. Is it okay, if I ask you some questions, and you can put the answers in Eloise's mind?

He nods.

Are you familiar with my work?

Mm-hmm. (Nods)

You are. And so I just want to point out Estelle is not, but you are. What's your opinion of this work talking to councils?

Like there's one sentence that I keep on hearing is "He knows everything."

You mean the Eagle?

Well, that's a sentence that I hear. "He knows everything."

Is there is there a name or a letter that we can use just for purposes of this conversation to refer to you to differentiate you from the other members of council?

Well, the first name that came was Richard, but then I was like, oh, that's your name!

That's fine. But you know, it's a name that gets around. Richard, is that correct?

(She laughs. Nods)

So Richard, what do you represent on Eloise's Council in a word

There are two words that pop into my mind. One is Alpha. And the other one is something... Omnipresence.

Alpha means "one" or beginning... and omnipresence. Let me ask you, how many councils are you on?

"Twelve."

Do you represent that in other councils, the same concept of alpha and omnipresence?

"Yes."

By omnipresence, do you mean to say that you're always available to Eloise at any time?

"Yes. I'm here always."

Let me ask, you are appearing today as an animal. Let's say that we understand the visual may be a metaphor. Have you ever incarnated on the planet Earth?

I didn't know why. But I saw a Lion.

Okay, well, that's an answer. Richard, you have incarnated on the planet Earth as a lion?

Mm-hmm. "Yes."

You chose that journey? And did you learn all the lessons you wanted to learn in that lifetime?

Somehow, it's a "No."

Has Eloise ever incarnated with you at the same time?

"Yes."

Would you show her a lifetime that you have known Eloise on the planet earth or anywhere?

Hmm. I saw like a lot of rocks.

Richard, are these is this location on the planet Earth? Or on another planet?

This planet, earth.

If we were going to draw a quadrant but it'd be north, south, east or west on the planet,

Southern Africa.

And if I was going to pick a country that it is now where these rocks are, what comes to mind?

(laughs) Mozambique.

The whole idea is trying to get information from somebody we've never met before. It's new information. And in that lifetime, would you show Eloise what she looked like in that lifetime? A male a female?

Hmm. Again a female and a lot of hair.

What century was this? It's just put it in her mind a date?

A long time ago.

So pre-BCE, as they say?

Yeah, it's like, very far away from now, very far away from the civilization of now. And a very simple primitive life.

I'm going to ask you a couple of questions. That may not make sense to Eloise, but they will to me, why did she choose that lifetime? What did she go there to learn?

"The basics of life of how to be with how to learn the role of human versus animals versus nature."

Richard, what was your role in that lifetime?

"Guidance."

Were you with her also as a human? And if you could just show her what you look like then?

Hmm. It feels as if it's still the animal. The lion.

Just to clarify. So what you're saying is that you have incarnated as an animal? Is that what you're telling us?

"Yes."

I just want to clarify some things. Only because people will ask this idea of a hierarchy of going from animal than up the scale to human That's incorrect. Is that right?

"Mm-hmm" (nods). "Yes."

I imagine people who are connected to your council - and you're with them, you're teaching them a lesson at some level. Is that correct?

"Yeah."

And so how is Eloise doing?

"Good."

Little bit different than Estelle. What do you want to show her in terms of our conversation here?

"Strength."

She's got it but forgets she has it?

"Yeah."

I'm going to ask you a couple of specific questions. Is what we're doing an effective method for the group that Eloise is involved with? To get answers from the flipside?

"Yes. "

And is there anything specific you can give us in terms of their group? And what they need to focus on?

"Listening to each other."

Do you mean like listening with empathy, or listening with insight, listening without ego?

"Being there together and truly listening, seeing each other and recognizing each other."

Let me ask if we're in a group accessing information or talking, is it a stronger form of communication? Because we're all in a group? Or is one-on-one the stronger way?

"One on one."

That seems to be the best way in terms of these interviews. If I do it in a group setting, it's very difficult, but one on one, it seems to be more clear.

Mm-hmm.

If there was one thing for us to focus on a terms of our climate, in changing climate, or the effects of climate, what would be like a paramount thing to focus on?

(Nods.) "Temperature."

Bringing the temperature of the planet down by planting more trees because there's more oxygen?

(They're) Showing me water.

If there's more oxygen in the atmosphere, that will occur, is that correct?

Hmm. (Nods.)

I think it's bears repeating the more plant more trees and plants that we plant, the more oxygen we have and the more carbon and disappears. And the cooler the planet gets.

I'm hearing "Listen to… deep listening to everything" will solve a lot.

Do you mean listening to animals as well?

Hmm, "Yes. Yes."

What's a method for someone to access someone like you? What's the what would be a one, two, three?

"Be an Eagle."

Do you mean like step consciously put yourself into an Eagle?

I feels like, I feel like I'm talking from the lion's perspective. I can constantly feel his presence, his warm presence, his hair as if he's talking right now.

Richard, how have you done that with her? Have you opened up that door?

I am opening – (and) she is opening the door.

I've heard about where people can, in a deep meditation shift their consciousness into another creature or another being. Is that what you're talking about? Something like that?

(Note: The Six Yogas of Naropa refer to an ancient Indian technique of shifting one's consciousness into the body of an animal.)

(Nods.) Hmm. Just be.

Be the creature you're thinking of?

Exactly.

How many of this council are here, Richard?

Four.

If you could introduce us to the person to your left. And to Elisa's right. Who's the next person on the council?

Again, it's like this very colorful bird. A beautiful, colorful bird. It's a Toucan. Male.

Are you familiar with my work?

"Yes."

What's your opinion of it?

He's laughing, I don't know why.

I love that response. I asked a question you don't know the answer to, but he does and he's laughing. Why?

I don't know.

What would be a letter or name to refer to as Mr. Toucan?

Mr. Toucan is ok.

What do you represent on her Council?

Joy.

More comedic joy or just more joy?

Like, "This life is joy. It's not a comedic joy. It's like the sense of being, of knowing, the joy of being joy, of lightness, of laughing at and with life and everyone."

How many other councils do you sit on?

Two.

So, in terms of Eloise, how's she doing?

He's laughing.

(Note: Just an observation, I'm asking a member of the council questions, and the response is laughter. Not something that someone would create or invent – because it's new information to them as well.)

Are there any adjustments she needs to make?

"Lightness."

Lighten up? Let me ask you that question again. Is this an effective method to communicate with you?

"Yes."

And so how would an average person speak to their guide? What would be the most logical way to do so?

"Be still on and tune in."

If Eloise wants to talk to you tomorrow, let's say, would she visualize a Toucan?

(Nods). "She knows that I'm here. She knows that I'm sitting on the shoulder, she just has to touch her shoulder and she knows that I'm here."

If I may, why are you guys projecting this frequency of flying beings? Of birds? If there is a reason?

"Perspective."

Tell me what do you mean?

He shows that flying... the flying is a way of getting perspective of seeing everything, of also knowing that you don't have to stay in one place. And that the traveling can give you new insights, can give you a broader view of all this happening.

I've heard before that you're able to travel at the speed of thought.

(Nods.) "Yes."

So, in essence, when people see an angel, or when they think they're seeing an angel or some creature with wings, that's not that different than seeing someone like you, is it?

Shakes her head. "No."

So in terms of this journey, that Eloise is on, what some advice to her on how to stay in touch with you? Let me expand that into the group that she belongs to. What is something that they can work on specifically?

(You mean) What the group can work on?

Yes -- some focus that you would recommend the group to focus on, that they haven't already?

To be together, like, really be together as (their conference) in Barcelona, like the being together will help a lot will give a lot of more information and focus.

Is it possible for the group to do like a meditation together?

"Yes."

And then ask for your participation?

"Yes."

Let me ask you, have you ever incarnated on the planet Earth?

"Yes. As a human. A man with a mustache. He looks a bit like Einstein."

Well, let's ask Mr. Toucan. Was this guy a scientist?

"He was a very intelligent man and inventor… like an older white man."

What was the first name of this fellow?

"Again, a "Richard." I think they're telling me like the names don't matter."

Nikola Tesla was quite taken with pigeons. And he seemed like he had some real communication between pigeons to animals. Was he accessing the same thing we're doing?

"Yes, of course, of course."

I love that he says it that way. Thank you, Mr. Toucan. Is there anything else?

"He was laughing because the moment you've learned so much, you've seen so much and understand so much about the world; that makes you laugh at everything that's happening. It makes you laugh about what we're all trying to do here. Like how much we're trying struggle."

Like a comedy life on Earth? I've said it before we're doing this kind of work it allows us to sit in the audience of the theater while we're watching ourselves, perform on stage.

"Exactly."

And that upsets some people. They get upset to hear that. Like "Oh, my God, all this suffering is really just part of a play that I designed?"

"Yes."

But from your perspective, you find it amusing?

"It frees you up the moment you realize that you shouldn't take it that seriously. The playfulness, the joy that arises."

If you can just introduce us to the person on your left, which is on at least his right. Would that be?

A White Swan. Female.

Are you familiar with my work?

"Yes."

What's your opinion?

She shows me something like softness like, she shows me the care. That's it. It the care that goes into the work that you do. The care and the love.

May I ask you how you think Eloise is doing?

"Wonderful."

So we seem to be getting higher praise as we go along.

(Laughs)

What is something that we can tell Eloise's group that would be a benefit to them and their research and their focus?

"Beauty - imagine how beautiful things can be how beautiful life is and protect the beauty."

What do you represent Eloise's Council a word or concept or quality?

"Beauty slash serenity. The purity, the silence... like the absence of pollution, the essence of things."

How many councils do you work on?

"Eight."

On each council, is that kind of the same quality that you bring? Beauty and serenity?

"Yes."

Have you ever incarnated on our planet?

No answer.

That is a form of an answer. Have you ever incarnated on another planet?

"Yes."

May I ask you some questions about that planet?

"Yes."

Is it in our universe or in another realm?

"Another realm."

And has Eloise ever incarnated with you on that planet in another realm?

"Yes."

Without any stress, or judgment, let's take a look at what that lifetime was like. If you could show that to her. Are we inside or outside?

"Outside."

Describe what you're experiencing.

I can feel a lot of wind. Soft wind.

Buildings, rocks, water, trees?

Water, like water, of course. But flowers, there's a lot of beautiful flowers and other insects. I see a butterfly, like a lot of butterflies and trees, a lot of beautiful trees like old wise trees. It's very peaceful and magical to be there.

Miss Swan, if you could show her what being you were incarnated as, in that place?

She is a swan. And I am her baby. I can see myself being protected by her wing.

So this other place has earth like qualities because it has trees and water etc. Are there any humanoid beings on this planet?

"No." She says "It's to show what the absence of human beings does to the flourishing…"

Well, let me just ask Miss Swan, so is this place that you can incarnate, a place of serenity? Would somebody choose this lifetime after like a lifetime of difficulty somewhere else?

Somehow, (I'm hearing) "It is for someone who has earned it."

Okay, so it's like, your victory lap?

"Not particularly. It's when someone's like, well, maybe when someone's been through a lot of evolution, evolution, evolution, evolution, and then like, they can go further, and then they'll end up there to see like to experience the rest that they need."

In terms of Earth years, how many years would a life exists there, let's say of a swan?

(Feels like) "Eternity."

For a long, long, long time? Is Eloise currently incarnated in that other realm while being here? Concurrently? Some four part of her conscious energy is there?

"Yes." She says – "One foot in… and it's her strength."

What percentage of Eloise's conscious energy is in this lifetime as a swan?

Twenty… twenty eight percent.

And how much percentage in Eloise, here?

The other (amount).

I've heard that the number fluctuates – yet we always have a part of our conscious energy back home. Is that correct?

"Yes." I have another message coming at me - is it okay if I share?

Yeah, please.

"The whole purpose of this (report) is not to show that that the human should be absent from planet Earth, but it is to show the balance. Like if we human beings know how to balance our

presence on Earth and know how to not be superior to other life, then we will have mastered it."

Where did that message come from? Was that from anyone in particular, or the whole group?

The whole group, everyone bringing in his energy.

"Balance is the key." How do we as humans, find that balance?

"Listen."

Listening?

"It's like if you listen to the water, if you listen to the animals, if you listen to the state of the planet… of nature, then you'll know what's going on. And then you'll know what to do."

You mentioned that earlier about shifting one's consciousness into that. Because everything has the right to exist, because it chose to be here?

"Exactly."

Thank you Ms. Swan. And if I may now turn to your left. Is there one last person who's available to speak with us?

(Laughs.) It's a squirrel!

Is it a flying squirrel?

Yeah.

It's Rocky the flying squirrel!? Sorry, I couldn't resist. We have a theme going here. Is that a male or a female?

It's a male.

What can we call him?

He likes "Mr. Squirrel."

Okay, Mr. Squirrel. Nice to meet you. May I ask you some of the same questions?

"Yes."

Are you familiar with my work?

"Yes."

Your opinion?

The word that popped up in my mind was "Gathering." He says, "You're doing a good job gathering."

Like gathering nuggets. Squirrel humor. And how do we how do you think Eloise is doing?

"Good."

In terms of her group that she's working with? Do you concur with what everyone said here about listening and focusing? Is there anything you'd like to add to that?

"Yes." He shows me warmth, the warmth of being together. Of dropping our shields, of truly showing up as ourselves.

Have you ever incarnated in this world?

"Yes."

And what was that like?

(Laughs.) "Tough life."

When was it? Was it within us the previous century, or?

"Yes, quite recently."

Oh, then I can see why that would be really difficult. How many councils do you work to work on?

(Laughs) "Forty."

And what's the quality that you represent in terms of Eloise's Council?

It's "gathering." Like he "Has the ability to manage and to distribute food and his planning skills; like he's a very peaceful. And he speaks up when he has to speak up. Meanwhile, he focuses on his planning, on knowing when to share."

He's gathering nuggets of information?

"Yes."

Is the value for Eloise in terms of that gathering of people for her?

"Nurturing."

Has that been part of her journey?

"Yes."

Is there anything that this council should focus on specifically?

"Trees. The well-being of trees."

Would you do me a favor Mr. Squirrel? I'm sure you're familiar with and are friends with a tree?

"Yes." He says, **"It's the reason why he's not on earth anymore."**

What happened?

"It's that the trees are suffering. He was someone's heart but he was murdered. Because a tree was murdered."

Are you saying you were a tree on earth?

No. He was (living) in a tree.

You were in a tree when this incident happened?

"Yes."

What happened?

"Humans were chopping the tree."

What country?

(Aside) I don't know if squirrels exist there, but I keep seeing the Amazon.

(Note: Flying squirrels live in southeast Asia, and the red squirrel lives in the Amazon.)

While incarnated as a squirrel, are you able to communicate with the trees?

"Oh yeah. Every squirrel knows how to."

What kind of what things did you communicate about?

"We communicate about everything -- about danger, about warmth, about the current state of like - it's almost as if, as if they hold hands. So they support each other, and knowing when to go where -- they tell each other everything."

So in terms of your relationship with a tree, let's just say one specific tree, what is what is your opinion of humans?

"Yeah, if only there were less than more. Because they don't really see us."

Can we bring forward a tree that Eloise can communicate with?

"Yes. It's already here."

Eloise, put your arms around the tree. What's the bark feel like?

It's a very old big tree... like a yew tree.

What are the sensations that are coming to you?

"Warmth, love and wisdom."

In terms of warmth, is it a familiarity?

"Yes."

Some words that come to mind, what would they be?

"Safety."

Unconditional love, perhaps?

"Yes. Protection."

And now, Mr. Tree, if you don't mind, I know this is unusual. I want you to put in Eloise's mind, the most predominant way that we can help climate change.

"Spend more time in nature."

And how, how would that benefit?

"Because then you'll understand how important it is how important the effect is on human beings. And then you'll learn that you can't live without- - so then you'll protect it. And fight for it. And even help it to exist."

Did you used to be able to communicate with humans?

"Yes. Always."

And what happened when humans stopped being able to communicate with you?

"The word that keeps popping in our mind is "damage." They start damaging when they stop talking. They disconnected from us. And then somehow they feel it's okay to, to treat us as something that they can use; consume. But when we're more than consumption, then things they need they human beings placed themselves superior to us. But what the moment they start connecting with us, they realize that we're really equals, like we need each other."

Killing the thing that gives us oxygen seems to be a crime against humanity?

"Exactly."

So the answer is to listen more. And at the same time, spend more time in nature. Because then you become more aware of nature. Is that correct?

"Yes."

I want to turn to back to her guide Estelle for a minute. What is your opinion of what we just did?

She loved seeing it happen. She could guide us to these to this other dimension and help us meet these animals who are really beings just like us.

So is this a place that Eloise can go on a regular basis?

"Yes."

And would you be her escort?

"She doesn't need me. But if she needs me to be there, I'll be there."

Estelle, take Eloise to her place of healing. And are we inside or outside?

Well, both. It's in England.

Does Eloise spend a lot of time in nature with animals?

"Yes."

Let's take her to her place of healing. Describe the environment. Where are we?

Next to my house. A very old big tree with a wooden bench.

And are you sitting there, standing, lying down?

Looking at it.

A nice place to go. Is there anything Estelle you want to show us or show Eloise?

"Nothing more. Just enjoyment."

Is there anyone no longer on the planet that Estelle you think Eloise should talk to communicate with?

It just is something that popped up in my mind was the work that I'm doing here. It somehow put it in perspective – like who I should invest my energy in to and letting go… or like whom I should invest my energy in and whom I should be letting go.

I want to thank you all for allowing us to do this kind of conversation with you.

You've got a very, very beautiful energy, Rich. I really like the joy that you bring. I will remember you saying, "like Mr. Toucan."

*****

CHAPTER SIX: JULIET

Juliet's comments are in bold, my questions in italics. Juliet is not her real name.

Rich: You said you'd seen a podcast and had a glance at my bio online but have no idea what I'm going to ask you. I just asked, "What's your familiarity with meditation?"

Juliet: I am familiar with meditation.

There's also people who do meditation where they can imagine that they can see people and converse with them. Is there anything like that in your path?

(Shakes her head.) No. There is one thing. I get a very clear picture of when my father passed away, of what he was doing at the very moment and how he was feeling.

Have you ever had a conversation with him since he's crossed over?

No.

What's his name, if you don't mind me asking?

Ben.

When I say, "Let's pretend we're on a boat, in a river," what do you see when I say that? What kind of boat is it?

It's um.. it's a boat with a motor, it's very old. It's made of wood. And it goes slowly on the river.

When you say River, is that a river that you know, or is this something new?

I might know it; it's a broad river. I once did a cruise on the Nile. And it could be something like that, but I'm not sure if it's the Nile.

Let's turn the motor off. I don't want you to go too far or too fast down this river.

It's not a fast motor. It doesn't have a sail, so it has to move somehow.

I appreciate that. When you look off to the shore, what is it?

It's palm trees. And it has, it has this golden glow, because the sun is really shining from a certain angle. It has a very golden glow and with palm trees and some vegetation. In the distance less vegetation, but close to the shore, a lot of vegetation.

I'm going to ask if your guide could come and sit across from you. I don't know if you're familiar with your guide. But let's ask your guide to come and be in your mind's eye. Is it a male, female or a light?

It's a male and it has light.

If you could just kind of give me a description; can you see facial features or color eyes or hair?

I can only see the silhouette; I cannot see the face or .. he is sitting across from me, around me. But I cannot see his face.

First, let me thank you for coming forward to converse with us. If you could put the answers in Juliet's mind. First of all, is it okay to ask you some questions? You can nod shake your head or shrug?

"Yes."

Are you familiar with my work?

(Nods.) "Yes."

If you could put in Juliet's mind a name or a letter so that we can refer to you.

I have a guide. His name is Gabriel. I'm not sure if he's here.

Well, let's ask this figure that sitting across from you. Are you Gabriel?

(She shrugs.)

So not Gabriel, that's fine. But you're somebody who has shown up to assist us and you're familiar with the conversation because you're familiar with me. First, I want to ask you, how is Juliet doing?

"Fine."

Since you're a friend of hers, I'll assume that... a have you ever had a lifetime with Juliet before?

"Yes."

And if you could put that in her mind's eye just to give her a glimpse. I won't ask her any questions that are going to alter her path. But if you could just show her - are we inside or outside?

We're inside… but I don't know where it is.

Inside is it a structure a building? What does the floor look like?

Oh, I thought it was something else. No, we are outside.

And so what does the ground look like? Is it grass, dirt?

We are sitting on the boat and the floor is wooden planks and were sitting across from each other. We're leaning on something, I don't know exactly what it is, but it's brown.

And if you could put in her mind what Juliet looks like to you? Same or different?

"Yes, she looks the same."

If Juliet can take hold of your hands, or the idea of your hand, what does that feel like? Are they rough? Are they soft? are they hard? Are they cold? Are they warm?

They're normal, they're not cold. They are a little bit more fleshy than I would have expected them to be.

Is there any sensation or emotion associated with holding these hands?

I like it.

Is there a familiarity?

No.

Could you bring Gabriel forward so that we can show Juliet some other things? Or are you going to be our guide today? It's fine. Either way.

Gabriel is here.

Thank you Gabriel. Appreciate you coming by to help us have this conversation. How do you think Juliet is doing?

"She's doing good. Although she's had a lot of struggle."

Are you familiar with the kind of questions I asked or my work?

(Shrugs) "I don't know."

So one guide is familiar with what I'm doing. Gabriel can we bring Juliet to her Council? Are we inside or outside?

We are still outside; we're still sitting on the boat.

Gabriel I want I want to bring Juliet to visit and meet with her council. Can we do that?

(Nods.) "Yes."

How are we traveling?

Flying.

And if you could characterize that - are we find fast? Slowly?

We are flying…. Slowly.

When we arrive? What is it in your mind's eye? Are we outside? Are we inside a place?

We have stopped at the stairs of a temple.

And how many stairs do you see?

A few.

Describe what you're seeing - what's the floor look like?

It's made of stone. It's made of tiles. I'm looking for the word in English.

Smooth or rough?

Yeah, it's "polished." Polished tiles. It's very nice. Warm.

Is there a color associated with them?

They're beige.

Are there any other structures inside this room?

The columns in there are big. Very big.

Gabriel, would you show her how many people are in her council? Just a number that comes to mind?

Five.

How are they arrayed? Are they in a line? Are they in a circle, or a semi-circle?

There's a long table, and they're sitting behind the table, all of them in the line.

If we could go to the first person on the far left; is this a male, female, a light or something else?

It's a male. He's middle aged, but I cannot see his face.

Okay, and how is he dressed?

Black, in black. It's not a toga and it's not a suit… I cannot really identify what he's wearing.

What's a letter or a name that we can use for you on this council?

(The letter) "L."

Mr. L. What role do you have on Juliet's Council?

It's "the Past."

So history and the past? Or her past?

"Juliet's past."

And in terms of what Juliet is working with her group, is this an effective method for them for people in her group to learn new information from people on the other side?

"Yes."

And is there something specific that they the group her group should focus on in terms of this research?

"A circle."

What do you mean by that?

"It's the idea of really sitting in a circle and belonging to a circle."

I see. We've heard this from other council members, that idea of listening with empathy, and really hearing what other people have to say, and connecting to what their ideas are. Is that correct?

(Nods.) "Yes."

In terms of a specific question that I might have, which is about climate change or affecting climate change? Is there anything that you can give us in terms of advice?

"They should focus on the circle - of being circular."

Could you manifest as a face for Juliet so she can see your features? And it doesn't have to be something she's familiar with. But is it somebody she knows? Or has met before in her dreams?

(She shakes her head.)

Not someone she knows. Can you manifest as a person?

(She nods.) He says, "I can."

So tell us what he looks like. What color hair? Eyes?

A male. It's blonde. He doesn't have so much hair. I would say he's about sixty. He's got blue eyes. And he's got he's got white skin that is not tan.

And Mr. L, how many councils do you sit on?

He says, "Fifty-Five."

And so, in each council do you represent the same kind of idea of the past?

"Yes."

Is that related to Akashic libraries?

"Yes."

Would you show Juliet what her library looks like? Describe what he's showing you.

It's a huge, huge, a very old library. And it has many, many stairs and has many, many letters.

And correct me if I'm wrong, I'm aware that the word itself Akashic means invisible or are etheric. But do people access the library prior to incarnation? Look up things they might want to learn?

"Yes."

Is there a way that people can access their library outside of what we're doing? I guess my question is, "Is it easy for people to access a library in terms of meditation and asking for help?"

(Shakes her head, no.)

Are you familiar with a librarian, for lack of a better term of this particular library of Juliet's?

(Nods.) Yes.

And in May I ask you Is that is that librarian responsible for all libraries? Or just Juliet's?

Just Juliet's.

(Note: If he had said, all of them, I'd have suggested interviewing the Librarian.)

Mr. L. Have you ever incarnated on the planet Earth?

"Yes."

And have you ever had a lifetime with Juliet?

(She shakes head no.)

Please introduce Juliet to the person to your left and her right. Is that a male, a female, a light or something else?

It's a female. She's very light. She's got a white dress. It's a beautiful dress. It's an old dress and it (the dress) doesn't have any arms. She's blonde, she's about forty. She's got a beautiful smile. And she's big, big blue eyes.

What would be a name or a letter that we can use to associate you with our conversation?

"Grace."

That's amazing. Grace. Sorry, couldn't resist. What do you represent on Juliet's Council?

"Love."

Love related to grace as well?

(Nods.) "Yes."

How many councils do you work on? A lot, a few?

"Over 100."

Do you represent that same quality on the other councils of grace, of love?

"Yes."

How do you think Juliet's doing?

"She's full of love. It's a good thing."

Do you have any advice for her or direction for her?

"Keep up the love."

I always ask, are you familiar with my work?

"Yes. It's a good connection."

The reason I ask is to demonstrate some people on councils do and some do not.

I can feel her reaching… from somewhere through her… and touching me and also touching others.

Can Juliet take hold of her hands and describe them.

They are soft, but that's not the point where we are really touching. We're having a heart connection. There's white light coming from her heart to my heart. It's a beautiful emotion.

Is there a familiarity?

(Nods.) "Yes."

Miss Grace, what's the best method for Juliet to access you when she needs you?

"By practicing love."

Do you mean by opening the one's heart?

"Yes."

I'm just trying to clarify what that literally means. How do we open our hearts?

"Juliet has this practice that she's giving unconditional love to people on the street that don't know her. And then we touch."

If you could introduce us to the person on your left. And Juliet's right. Is that a male female or light?

It's a male. He's wearing a brown suit, but he has a head that is between a fox and a dog.

Is it okay if I ask a few questions, sir?

(Nods.)

Are you familiar with my work?

(Nods.)

How about if I call you Mr. Fox?

(Nods.)

Mr. Fox, why are you manifesting this visual for Juliet? What's the purpose or meaning behind it? Is it that you've had lifetimes as a fox or a wolf?

"It's a sign of hope for Juliet."

Is that what you represent on her Council? You're skipping ahead with an answer..

(Nods) "Yes."

So you represent hope. And so please, if you could sort of connect those two, how hope and this idea of an animal or a fox are connected as a metaphor?

"Whenever she sees the picture of a fox she feels at home and not alone. So she's guided and supported."

May I ask you, have you ever incarnated on the planet Mr. Fox?

"Yes."

And have you in Juliet ever shared the same timeframe on the planet?

"No."

When you were incarnated on the planet, were you a human or an animal?

"I was an animal but I was also human." (Both at different times)

In that incarnation as an animal, what was the predominant feeling or lesson that you were trying to learn during that journey? In other words, why did you choose that lifetime?

"I wanted to... I wanted to learn to be very fast and I wanted to have um.. I wanted to have babies."

My question is, in terms of getting everyone to agree, including your children, including your parents and siblings, and whoever else was in that Fox family. Did you guys work that out in advance?

"It was very easy. We were in tune. We didn't have to work it out. It was it was obvious."

Was that within the past few centuries here on Earth, or was that a long time ago?

It seems (like) it was a long time ago.

And what advice would you give Juliet for her group, on what they should focus on in terms of these, what they're trying to accomplish with their group?

"They should stick with the group meditation and, and stick with the topic. And they should you should work out to specifics via meditation."

And in terms of meditation, this idea of asking questions, does that bear fruit?

"Yes."

Because in some forms of meditation, people access whatever comes to mind, which is a one way, but this is a little bit of a different format, where we seek you out to ask questions directly?

(She nods.)

Okay, you're nodding. Thank you Mr. Fox. Could meet the person to your left, and Juliet's right. Is that a male female? Light, or something else?

It's black and it's like, a little black wind. I don't see somebody sitting there, but it's black, and I don't see any form.

May we ask you some questions, and you can telepathically put that into Juliet's mind?

"No."

All right. And if I may, I let allow me to ask, is there a spokesperson for this group?

I'm not sure who is there... I'm also debating with Gabriel, I'm not sure who it is who wants to speak. (a beat) It's Mr. Fox.

Mr. Fox, what's the reason for the person on Juliet's council who doesn't want to speak? This person has been with her for all of her lifetimes. Will conversing with them upset her path or journey?

(Shrugs.)

Sometimes council members don't want to participate because they feel like it would alter this person's path. Is that correct, Mr. Fox?

(Raises eyebrows, shrugs.)

Let me turn to Gabriel for a minute. Gabriel, if you don't mind, could you come forward? Is there anybody else on this council that Juliet needs to speak with?

(Nods.) "Yes."

So if that person could come forward, please. Is it a male, female or a light or something else?

I'm not sure yet. It has to manifest... I'm waiting... it's a woman. She's around 50. She's got a very tiny nose. Brown hair. Brown eyes.

How do you think Juliet's doing?

"I think she's got a lot on her plate but somehow she's keeping up."

And what do you represent on her Council?

"I'm the fun and the joy."

How many councils do you work with?

"Very many."

On each council, do you represent fun and joy?

"No."

If you don't mind, what would be a name or a letter we can use to associate you with our conversation today?

"Joy. It's Joy."

I've heard this and have observed that people retain their sense of humor on the flipside. And in terms of joy and fun; what would you characterize as fun or joy on the flip side where you are?

"Joy is a feeling for something, something good. And joy is in something fun."

Are you familiar with my work?

"No."

Let me let me ask you this Joy, the Black Wind person that we weren't able to communicate with. I'm going to assume that they are not familiar with my work. And is that correct?

"I guess so."

I just wanted to characterize the reason that they do not want to communicate with us is because they don't see the value. Would that be a correct?

"No."

Why do you think that is - they didn't want to communicate with Juliet?

"It's not the time."

Thank you. So you have five people on your council. And I think Joy, you're the fifth one correct?

(Nods.)

In terms of what we're doing here, do you recommend it something that everyone should do? Or does it require something like Juliet's group with focused meditation?

"We do it, but it's very powerful, what they're doing and it's a very interesting discovery. So it's the first step before they can show other people. The work they're doing, they're learning how to do this. And once they know it better, or they figured it out much better, they can learn, teach it to other people."

Was there an event in Juliet's life when you helped her?

Nods. "Yes."

The idea of showing it to her is to remind people the council members are always available.

Nods slightly.

Let me ask you, is there anything else that she needs to hear from the Council today?

"Move."

What do you mean by that?

It has something to do with piling people up … piling something up very fast. Okay, so a little bit to do with time, pressure. It's (referring to a) "time to do something."

Oh, "move." You mean like get to work?

Mm-hm. (Nods.)

"Get to work." It's a great admonition. Gabriel, could you show Juliet "place of healing" where she normally comes back to between lifetimes. Are we inside or outside?

We are outside. Juliet's garden where were a lot of things are growing and this is the place to heal and to and healing... Gabriel, he's embracing me. And he's doing that right now.

So Gabriel, you know what I'm going to ask next? Is this a good question to ask?

Nods. "Yes."

So I'd like to ask your dad Ben to come forward into this garden into this place into this place of healing, where we can connect to people who are no longer on the planet. How are you doing?

"Good."

Who was there to greet you when you crossed over?

A bartender.

A bartender, that Ben knew? Right? Somebody you knew in this lifetime? Or just a guy behind the bar?

(Nods.)

So that must have been a little startling or surprising to see?

(Shakes her head no.) "It was a good thing."

So what was that experience like for you? So can you tell Juliet who this bartender is? Is this like somebody that's on your council or a guide, or a teacher?

"It's not a pub, it's a little bit something like a bar. In in no specific light. It's no specific room. And the tools are made of the color silver. And it's a beautiful bar. It's not very big. And there's only one person and the bartender."

He's not an avatar; just a bartender?

"It's only the bartender. It's really nice sitting at the bar chatting with somebody. But nothing specific."

I appreciate that. Ben, how do you think your daughter's doing?

(Laughs) He's worried.

Are you helping her? Have you shown up to visit with her and she's not aware of it or you could show it to her?

"No."

So who are you hanging out with Ben, on the flip side? Are you attending any classes?

(Shrugs.)

Many people talk about classrooms. Could you show your one of your classes or your favorite class to Juliet? Where are we inside or outside?

"**Inside. There's about thirty students.**

And how are they arrayed? Rows of chairs or auditorium style?

It's a library and sitting on the desks of the library. And some people are also standing on the stairs.

And, uh, please allow me to apologize for interrupting this class. Could I ask the teacher a question?

He says, "Yes."

Could describe how this teacher looks?

It's a male standing in the library. Holding a book, looks very conservative, safe, serious fellow.

What is this class? If you could put this into Juliet's mind?

Some kind of men's class, it has something to do with building something.

Like architecture? Or objects?

It's more like building machines.

(Note: I've been to visit many classrooms since I began this research. Each one seems to be involved with moving energy, or the creation of energy.)

I understand. Is it a specific object that you're working with?

It's airplanes.

Professor, if you could hold up an example of the kind of airplanes or objects that you guys create are or manifest, that you're working on? What does it look like?

He's holding a little plane that's a double decker (biplane). Very old; it's very old.

Are you literally talking about the physicality of building an airplane? Or a metaphor?

"It has something to do with learning. And being a man."

Let me ask you, sir. Have you ever incarnated on the planet Earth?

She shakes her head, "No."

Are you familiar with my work?

"No."

So you're teaching the idea there's a relation between the airplane and masculinity or between flight and thought, intent and manipulation of space and time. And that's all related to masculinity?

He gives a slight nod, then a shrug.

So how do you get into this class?

"Through the door."

Very funny. So let me ask. What's this class about? Try to give us a little more descriptive concept so we can understand it. It's about constructing objects that are able to fly?

"Yes."

And it's also about your intent and how to create objects?

"Yes."

I've heard that in the creation of an object it requires time, pressure, and intent. In terms of, of putting intent into an object you're going to create, what does that entail? Is it something to do with your heart or belief or is it something to do with your mind and creation?

"It's both. It's a heart to mind (equation) and in the heart. Okay, yeah. It's (also) just thought."

Ben what's the best method for her to access you when she has a question? Some people say bring out a photograph because the photograph has captured time, space and frequency. Is that valuable?

She nods. He says, "Yes."

Do you have any questions for Ben?

I would really like to know how it is on the other side. I get the feeling it's very good, but I don't know why.

Interesting to hear that we might find ourselves in a pub. There was an episode of the Sopranos where one of his crew had a near death experience and they asked "Were you in Heaven?" He said, "No, I was in hell. I was the only Italian at an Irish bar. And it was St. Patrick's day all the time." **(Laughs.)**

Let's thank Gabriel, for allowing us let's thank the first person we met that was in a boat, who stepped aside, so Gabriel could lead us. And thanks for all the answers

Well, thank you very much. It was really very nice because I really get the feeling in guided meditations of being here, and he brought me there, but now I know it and can go back. You opened the door for me and opened things for me.

*****

CHAPTER SEVEN: MIMI

Again, this is a zoom conversation with someone I've never met before. Her name is not Mimi, that was my grandmother's nickname, and I'm using it in this example.

Rich: First, how are you Mimi?

Mimi: Very well.

Are you familiar with my work at all?

No.

Better that you're not.

Yes.

It's kind of what I've been doing the past years, helping people to access other information, higher consciousness stuff. And can I assume that you've meditated before, done meditation? That sort of thing?

Oh, yes.

And in terms of your meditations, are you familiar with your guide?

Um, I'm aware of many.

And have you ever had a visual of your guide like a person?

Like, oh, yeah. Many, many times.

Okay, so that's kind of what I use as an entry point, to this kind of guided meditation. How long do we have together? About how much time do you have?

As much time as is just necessary.

I appreciate that. We'll see probably like an hour or something like that. We'll see where we go, we'll see we get anywhere. Can you "picture yourself in a boat on a river?" You can close your eyes or not, it's up to you.

Yes. Oh, Clearly.

And tell me what the boat looks like. Is it big or small? What is it?

It's wooden carved from one piece, one solid piece of wood.

By the way, does this boat is this boat familiar to you? I mean, have you constructed this boat before? Or is this a memory of a boat that you knew?

Not in this lifetime. I've not encountered this boat, but it's familiar to me. The architecture is familiar to me.

So if I could ask one of your guides to sit. Is that person a light, male or female? Whatever comes to mind, try not to judge what you see.

I'm seeing a person with seems to be a male with dark skin. Very strong, muscular. Strong features. Tall dark hair. Really light eyes. Silvery.

He can nod, shrug or shake his head to my questions or answer them. Can I ask you some questions?

He says, "Yes."

Is there a name or letter to address you?

"Ishmael."

As in "They call me Ishmael?" Nice to meet you Ishmael. Are you familiar with me or my work?

"Yes."

That's interesting. Because our friend here Mimi is not. What's your opinion?

"Very important."

Would you show Mimi what she looks like in this boat to you?

I see a woman who has dark skin, very long, dark hair. Very strong. A mother.

Is this someone you incarnated with before? Or are you just showing her a previous lifetime?

"Yes."

May I ask are you indigenous person from a particular country? And if so, tell us place on earth.

I just got, I guess a picture. I will share with you what I am trying to decipher.

Please.

So when you ask indigenous there was a "Yes." That form, that body is indigenous. But they themselves aren't of form. (There's) the time and location where we knew each other. Regionally identifiable but they're not of form.

In terms of region was it in North America, South America, Africa? If it was on earth, what was the region?

South America.

I just want to ask, is there a country associated that we would know with this time period?

No.

So is pre civilization as we know it Brazil, etc, Venezuela all those names those terms? Is that correct?

No answer. But I look around at the environment, I would say "yes" to that.

Like Amazonia?

I think what he's trying to say is "Don't focus on that. Because that's not important information."

(Note: As if to say "by calling this place a country it limits our ability to speak about it. It reduces it to a time frame and a historical record. What we need to address is information over many lifetimes.")

I appreciate that. I was going to ask, could you and escort Mimi to visit her council? Even if she's not aware of what that means, you are. And if you could tell us, Mimi, are we inside or outside?

I am in complete darkness. Complete dark and void. I do not see Ishmael. I see these columns of Light. And if I look closer, they're beings.

And if a number comes to mind of how many beings are in front of you?

(counts with her hand) Twelve.

I kind of liked watching you count as well.

(Laughs.)

I want to thank everybody for allowing us in here. So how are they arrayed, these beings?

It's circular.

Let's pick one, go over and stand in front of them. Is that a male, a female or a light?

I feel a lot -- a lot of emotion. Like my body feels trepidation and it's shaking. I guess the only word I could say is reverence. It's special really.

Let's go to the first person that you can address and ask them if it's possible to ask them some questions.

Yeah, well, I see symbols.

Can you describe them?

I'm seeing geometric patterns that are sort of an interlocking layers that seem to be emanating from them.

Are you familiar with these shapes? But is that something you've seen before Mimi?

Yes. I have seen different layers of different fields. This is a little bit different. I can't really describe them. I mean, I can't translate it into words.

I'm going to ask them some questions about that. Let's go to number one, whoever wants to self-identify that way. And do you see a male or a female or light associated with geometric symbols?

It's a light, but there are features that I could identify as, maybe a being. I could personify it in some way.

Is it okay if I ask this light some questions?

I'm just seeing more symbols and the color of the light is changing to bluish. Sapphire. So there's communication. They're communicating.

Can I ask you to manifest a little bit more in terms of features only for the purpose of this conversation, so that we have someone to identify if you could give us a name to identify you?

I see a line with two strike marks.

(Note: A horizontal line with two parallel lines at an angle. What comes to mind is a variation of the "not equal" sign in math.)

What do you represent on Mimi's Council? And maybe that'll give us an idea of what that symbol means.

"Future."

Her future? Let me ask you, is that symbol that you showed her associated with that?

It's not coming as words, but it seems it's a form of "architecting" my access to the future, like a core piece of something that exists now, that is essential for the future.

Let me ask you some simple questions and put the answers in Mimi's mind. How do you think Mimi is doing?

It's just a feeling… the color changed to this warm like glow. There's a tenderness. A soft light.

So let's call a warm glowing tenderness as a "yes." Doing okay or well. Is that correct?

(She nods.)

So this is a way we can communicate. It's like somebody's talking to somebody in sign language. Now we know what that feeling represents "doing well." Are you familiar with my work?

Yeah, there's all these colors. There are all these colors shifting.

So a more emphatic yes? Is that what all the colors shifting means?

There's energy moving up. So the question you just asked, there's a feeling that came over me -- of inviting more of whatever they're

acknowledging. So it feels very affirming. And when asked about their energy, there is color shooting up this column. There's like a magenta. There's a propulsion to it.

So if I can characterize that as something along the lines of, "I'm aware of your work and it is, that it is helping people to connect with their councils?"

I'm just noticing; it feels like a "yes." Affirming. But there was also a piece of wanting to say "not helping to" but "already assisting," that is, you're working together.

When they see symbols or geometric shapes, are they seeing like these symbols as metaphors that you're emanating? Or are they symbolic of a specific being?

I heard "Code." That's the word. "Codes. Code transmission."

Thank you. That was a much better answer than my question.

I'm just seeing now that I'm seeing these symbols. And they're indiscernible... I can't translate it. Because it's what's embedded within it. I can't stop the transmission of the symbol and put a meaning on it, or translate it. I just receive it; they just said "You can see it." They just said that you can see it as well.

If you could introduce us to the person on your left, moving to the right down the line? Is that a male or a female?

Very strong female energy. And I'm glad you said to their left and my right. If you're going the other way and there was like "Nope. Nuh uh." To the right, is a strong white column of light. Almost a tight cylinder. Very precise.

What's a name or a letter we can use to it identify you for the purpose of our conversation?

"Truth."

She's skipping down and answering my question about what she represents on your council. Do you mean truth in terms of the "truth will set you free?" Or do you mean truth in terms of Mimi's experiences?

I see a symbol. There's a circle. And it has a point in the center.

So our word "truth" doesn't really express what that means?

"No."

Let me ask you "Truth" Do you sit on many councils?

All I'm getting is "There's only one."

Just one okay, that's fine. Do you mean or is this you in all councils or one council or the or do you mean just this one? This one particular Council Mimi's?

There's one council. But there are other representations of The Council, which is still the one council.

(Note: This is an interesting philosophical point. All councils are "council" – saying that "all councils are one council." Not literally, but figuratively.)

Have you ever incarnated on our planet?

"No."

How's Mimi doing?

(I'm seeing) There's like this electric storm.

Well, I love the way these guys communicate.

So this pertains to incarnation. This was a continuation of what you had just asked. And it just quickly went around; when you asked if any of them incarnated? It was "No." And then this electric storm occurred, showing me that I am, that we are how they incarnate. We are the representatives of the manifestation of who they are.

Of the Council?

So the answer to your question, I wasn't sure if that electric storm was to show that counterpoint. Because it looks like I am… them. I am this being, so there really isn't a separation.

Very interesting. It's a little bit like seeing yourself on stage and in the audience at the same time. If I can ask you Ms. Truth. Are you familiar with my work? Because sometimes members and councils are not? Some are?

"Yes." There's a thumbs up. (Observes) Well, it's a solid focused column within the column... that's very... (uses her hands to show a direct line going up and down). That one was a very solid (reply), not a propulsion, but it's like this sort of anchored light. And uh... there's much to do, there's a propulsion and that energy. Like, innervating, like the statement to me is it's like putting energy into the system. And the other one, I feel like I'm looking at the energy that's being held within the system of your narrative.

Is there a spokesperson in this group?

There's someone over here... (points) actually all the way around to the opposite of where the original was.

So like number 11 or 12? Somewhere in there?

Eight.

Are you seeing a male or female a light or a symbol?

I'm seeing red. This is focused – the core of it, it's white. But then it sort of emanates out as red. An orb. I'm just seeing a lot of layers and layers and layers and layers of images.

Is this a more of a male or female or neither energy that you're sensing from this red person?

Feels more male.

And if I could ask for a name or a letter to reference you?

It's a symbol, like a long rod that tapers at the end. And there's a horizontal bar that crosses the top. Not at the very top, but just down a little bit.

Okay, let's just say something like a T, but different than a T.

Like a T but the bottom seems to taper and curves a bit.

We'll call him Mr. T for now, just because it's a reference. First how is Mimi doing? What's your opinion of Mimi's journey?

I see a symbol which almost turns into what looks like a sword on to my back. And there's a feeling of power yeah, that's, that's like...

Warrior-like?

Yeah, a really solid quality to us. Very, I can feel the gravity like now I can feel gravity. Like it just, locks me in.

What quality do you represent on Mimi's Council?

I'm going to try to translate it because the word is "faith."

Faith, a great word.

"There are many other words, trust. It has these other qualities."

It's almost poetry as it's also metaphor. So faith and trust in her own abilities? Faith in herself or faith in others?

"It's the same."

How many councils do you sit on, work with?

"I see there's one. There's only... one. (Observes, corrects herself) All right, there are others. I'm seeing there's one principle one, but then I'm seeing the infinite ripples of these others. It's like the multitude of the reflections of all the other representations."

I'm going to ask some questions related to the group that Mimi's working with - is this an effective method to learn new information, talking to councils?

"Could you re-restate that question?"

I'm saying is talking to council members an effective method to help?

"Yes."

In terms of their project, what specific focus should they be focusing on? Should they be talking about process? Or should they be focused on results?

Wow. That was... I'm seeing a core and all the ripples of that in the core... I'm seeing the process is the result, the result creates the process. It's actually not linear. (Circular) That these are the same

thing. But how do I identify where I am in relation to that? Oh, that was the answer. "For each of us to identify, because we are the process, we are the results."

What is the most effective way for this group to get the answers they seek? Is it related to what you just said that this the process is the result as well?

I'm seeing mirrors reflecting back… I'm just seeing how they are around me. Mirrors, mirrors reflecting.

So what does that metaphor represent? Are you saying the answers are within the mirror to look at one's self?

Yes, it's very clear. They're right here. Mirror, Mirror, Mirror. There's nothing beyond these mirrors. It's all reflecting back.

Is there anything we can do on the planet to help, reverse climate change or find new alternative methods of energy by accessing you guys to help guide us?

Okay, so the same; the mirrors are still here. Everything that you said, climate change and reversing and these things, it is the reflection of ourselves. We are what is being reflected. The things you just said are within us.

So the answers we seek are within us -- that realizing that we're connected to all people and all things, and the planet and how consciousness works by focusing on that we will find these answers something like that?

It's instantaneous. The reflection that we're seeing with the reflection that we create, we're creating that reflection, we're creating these… and I'm seeing images of disasters, and pain, and all these things.

If we focus on the images of healing, and focus on connecting to each other, that's a way of changing the paradigm, changing the experience within the mirror. Something like that?

Yes, that we are accurate reflections. I'm seeing this now in the mirror showing me "me," but in, in the different facets of my life, I'm seeing the people in the moments. This kind of looks a life review.

What's occurring is a reflection of my state of being, and you asked about contacting them. And so we are an accurate reflection of them. If we've seen these introductions, instantaneously, we are an accurate reflection of them. If somehow these layers have this other distortion.... (Even then) when accessing them, we become accurate reflections. And then what we see and perceive accurately reflects that.

Once we are aligned, then the external experience will accurately reflect what it is that we truly embody.

"How can we prove to people, skeptics, that this is an effective method?" My point is by showing that we can visit a council is evidence that councils exist. Is that correct?

There are a few parts of that question. I think the question was first, how do you prove it? So what I was seeing was, myself, evolving or expanding. And then with that, it seems, there was skepticism, and there was this distortion in the field. And it just went (falling away). Then I was seeing all these other pieces distorted, it seemed like tightly bound, like puckers in this really beautiful web, little puckers of skepticism. By focusing on my evolvement, these pieces just "poof" (disappear) – I'm not able focus on them at all, because they don't really exist. If I bring them in, I create them. "There's nothing to prove when I am the proof."

It's almost like tuning in a stereo and, and dismissing all the frequencies that are not needed. Once we strengthen those spider web links, we focus on the outcome instead of the puckers of doubt?

"In terms of climate change, by focusing on the puckers, we make them exist."

In terms of reports of "evil" - are those also distortions that we create?

"Yes."

Is there anybody else in this council that wants to come forth and have a conversation with us?

"Everyone one is illuminating." (Lighting up)

Oh, like raising your hand. Who comes forth?

They're showing me that when one is communicating, that they're all… communicating, they're one.

Allow me to turn back to your guide Ishmael. Could you take Mimi to her place of healing? Even if she's not aware of what that means you are. And if you could just put in our mind, are we inside or outside?

I'm still in the boat. And he's rowing. I'm sitting in the boat and I can feel the grain of the wood.

Did you create this boat?

"We did."

Ishmael, put a sensation somewhere in Mimi so that she can feel this place. And if you could describe that emotion or that sensation, what's the emotion associated with this boat?

"There are many emotions. The only word that came was hope."

Hope. Lovely. Some people describe a feeling of unconditional love.

Oh yeah, there's that.. And yes, it's interesting when my feet are in the woods, I see things like this long enduring space. There's so much love and so much protection, so much support. It's tremendous. But it's a glimmer of hope, the joy of this.

You've had a visual of this canoe in the past this dugout canoe something you crafted with your friend before?

No.

Ishmael. What else do we need to look at? Is there anything else we need to talk to? Where does where would Mimi like to go?

I just looked down on my own (body) .. I'm covered in scars… the sense that I get from him is, he's here to protect me.

Ishmael Are you showing her this traumatic memory in order for her to realize that she's okay?

There's something about "It's what I volunteered for. It's not traumatic. It's essential awareness, awareness, awareness."

And when you say volunteered for, are you referring to choosing a lifetime that had conflict or a lifetime that had essential learning involved?

"Agreement."

Ishmael, can you show her the life planning session before that lifetime where you were all together, and she was talking about the agreement? Were you there?

Everyone was there.

And now when you look around do you see people that you know, in this lifetime?

It's endless... the images are endless.

Ishmael let her see a few people that are, or have been in her life, she might know them now in this lifetime, that have been instrumental in her journey.

I'm seeing the face of my mom come forward and then instantly I see her shift to that of a man. And now she's child. Just like all these different iterations or something of this, this representation,

Is Mimi's mom on the planet still?

No.

Does she want to have a chat?

She'd love to.

Just sit across from our friend Mimi here and if she could hold your hands for a second, and just take a look at you now. What's your mom's name?

Alice.

Alice is it all right if ask you some questions you can nod shrug or shake your head?

She says, "Yes."

Let me I'm going to ask you a couple of questions that Mimi doesn't know the answer to if you don't mind. Who greeted you when you crossed over?

"A light.

Was it somebody related to Alice? Or was it her guide or a council member?

Yeah, she's like "maybe a guide." One of the council.

Let's ask Alice if was in a happy experience by crossing over. Did you realize your journey?

"Yes."

Who are you hanging out with on the flip side?

(gestures to herself) Me.

Let me ask you, Alice, how do you communicate with your daughter?

She does through animals. There's a lot of animals here and horses and goats and chickens and wildlife. I live in the middle of a national forest.

Alice, can you show her how you do that? How do you access the frequency of these animals so that she thinks of you or remembers that you're close by? What's the process?

She's showing me a dream- she showed me a hummingbird and how it redirects movement -- just showed me it's like lucid dreaming.

So just to clarify, Alice, what you're doing when you get a hummingbird to get into Mimi's face, asking the consciousness of the hummingbird to perform a task for you is that correct?

Correct.

When she meditates, can you show up and tap her on the shoulder and continue this conversation?

Mm-hmm.

And what are the lottery numbers for this Friday's lottery?

(Laughs) Now she's laughing hysterically.

Can I just say, that is the one joke that I tell that I always get a laugh from somebody on the flipside. And what I really appreciated about it was that Mimi didn't laugh but saw that her mother was.

She's laughing... hysterically.

Because the last thing I need is a lottery winner. I mean, come on.

That's what she just said, "Why would she do something so horrible to you?"

Thank you. Alice, you did two things at once, which is you told the joke. They retain a sense of humor and besides the connections of family and home and unconditional love, there is humor. So that's a wonderful thing to observe.

Yeah. She's laughing so hard it's making me laugh. She loves that.

Oh, well, I'm sure there's many more comedy things that's going on for Alice. She's having adventures.

"Correct."

Alice, are you taking any classes on the flipside?

"Yes."

Would you show one? Would you show it to Mimi? Because I've piqued your interest. What is the class?

"It's like an amalgam of physics and fine arts, physics and Fine Arts."

If Alice you could show the teacher in this class, is it a male a female or a light?

A light. Yellow light. Flat yellow, iridescent yellow. Moving yellow. Vibrating yellow.

Alice, could you introduce me to the teacher for a second here?

(Nods).

Are you familiar with my work? Are you familiar with me?

(Mimi laughs.) Um. I just saw that, that this is the subject that you are teaching this world. "Yes."

I loved your reaction. Mimi's reaction was like, what, a class? That is what I'm doing. And so you're familiar with it? Have I ever interrupted your class before? And I apologize for doing so.

She says "All the time!" But says "There's no such thing as an interruption."

Let me ask you, physics and art? In terms of your teaching are you showing students how the creation of ideas, the creation of books and music and painting is also related to mathematics and physics?

All the same. Not different all. Not even dissimilar. I'm seeing these insane brushstrokes being then distilled down into the mathematical formula of every single arc and movement in the color. And they are the same thing.

But in terms of painting, but let me ask you, this professor, in terms of intent-- of connecting your heart, opening your compassion and heart and empathy to your work... How do you inject that into the mathematical equation?

She said, like this, (waves her hands like a painter) this stroke of this seeming color that created a form, and then I'm seeing the mathematics behind that but then there was - it moved into like a wave form of sound. There's also a sound associated; you can play the song of each of these movements of everything… of everything that seems visual is actually a sound as well. And then when you just ask that there was the sound, or like the energetic pulsing of, of like one heart. And, and that also has a very specific sound and a song that-- that registers. And that that creates form in the same way.

I had an interview where I met a teacher who taught how to create objects. Her class was creating pink crystal. There was a formula on the chalkboard the teacher explained the symbols, the way you described symbols earlier of each person on your council. One symbol represented time, the other one intent, and another symbol represents pressure over time. So intense pressure over time, with intent creates a crystal.

(Nods) Correct.

There was also a ringing tone to it. Sound is frequency, color has frequency. Music has frequency, my voice has frequency, if you want to go into quantum mechanics, everything is vibrating in the universe. So it all has frequency.

She just said… "Even our thoughts, our thoughts, our feelings."

Our thoughts, and feelings?

"Everything has frequency. She just showed me climate change and weather patterns and bees. And the thought forms that create the ripple that coming into form are actually knowable."

I've read that some birds can anticipate weather patterns six months in advance, so they change their mating habits. So it's the idea of they're in touch with the frequency of what's happening so that they know in advance these things will occur. Is that something what you're describing that being in touch with how the frequencies work is a way for us to understand how to change it?

Correct. Because there's some facet of this that seems like our mental field or capacity. The capacity to identify the art form… (on cue her son interrupts her).

Right on cue! So what a fun adventure, like going to Disneyland and getting an E ticket.

Yeah. Yeah that was wonderful.

*****

At some point, I felt like we were speaking in such metaphors that it was difficult to get a concrete message from the experience. That's why I asked for her mother to come forward – because when someone is able to access a loved one no longer on the planet, everything becomes more concrete, more solid. And she too was able to walk us into a classroom on the flipside one about art and physics. A wonderful metaphor for how we navigate the planet, the frequencies involved, but also the frequencies that include that love that never dies.

CHAPTER EIGHT: RONNIE

Another zoom session, this time with Ronnie who is in bold font, and my questions are in italics. Ronnie is Dutch and lives in Holland (not his real name.)

Rich: So, and I've been talking to your group for the past week, almost like every day.

Ronnie: That's great.

I think you're number 9.

Such a great group of people.

Hey, yeah, very cool. And, you know, all around the planet.

Yeah.

So you're the only you're the only second person who was even vaguely aware of stuff that I've been doing. You've had some experience in in meditation? Tell me?

Yes. Well, because of this group I've been, I've been the one leading meditation. And so it's, it's kind of been a powerful tool for the group to embody. And I've taken that into exploring meditation more deeply.

I start with a Beatles lyric. Picture yourself in a boat on a river. What kind of boat are we in?

Wooden boat. Canoe.

And please describe how long it is?

I guess it would be an average size. I would say maybe nine feet.

And is there room for more than one person?

Three or four.

If you could just sort of look at the river or the waterway that we're on. What's that look like?

A good size river. The water is kind of like muddy river water.

But how wide is the river?

I would say like 40 feet wide or 50 feet.

What's the shore like?

There is nature all around. No palm trees, it's sort of like a Midwest setting.

How fast or slow is this boat going?

It's going at a consistent pace. Not fast or slow. So I can appreciate the nature around you.

This is a wonderful place to start. Because it's calm and it's easy to access and I'm going to ask Ronnie's guide to sit down in the boat opposite him. And when I say that, what comes to mind? A male, a female, a light? Could be somebody you've already met before? I don't know, but it's up to you.

It was more of a feeling.

Is that a male or a female or a light?

Uncertain.

Okay, let's ask them to sit across from you - your guide. And I'm going to assume that they know what I'm doing because they wouldn't come unless they were approved of whatever it is we're going to do or where we're going to go.

It's a man. It's my friend, Robert.

Take hold of his hands. How does it feel in terms of his hands? Are they warm, cold, rough or soft?

Rough. Warm. We are about the same age were young, but he looks just like healthier. He is wearing like muscle shirt.

I just want to ask Robert a question. He cannot shrug or shake his head. Is it okay to ask you some questions?

He says "Yes."

Robert, are you familiar with my work?

"No."

Are you his primary guide?

"No."

But you've come forward because you're going to help us with this conversation today. Is that correct?

"Because he asked."

I appreciate that. So, Robert, would you help guide Ronnie into visit with his council?

"Yes."

Are we inside or outside?

Inside.

And so describe it? What does it look like?

Like… what's it called… a lodge. Wood floor. It's like a cabin in the woods.

Is it alright for us to talk to Ronnie's council, and when I say that how many individuals come to mind?

"Four."

And how are they arrayed? Standing, sitting, in a line, in a semi-circle or circle?

Sitting around.

I want to thank you for allowing us to come in here and have this conversation. And if possible, Robert, would you escort us up to the first person to your left? And is that a male, female or light?

"Female."

Describe about how old or what does she look like?

"She looks young, but she's… I've known her as an older woman."

So you recognize her. And what name can we use or letter can we use to address her?

We'll call her Gela – her name is Raquel.

Gela, thank you for allowing us to have this conversation. And may I ask you some questions directly?

"Yes."

Are you familiar with my work?

"No."

Gela, what do you represent on Ronnie's journey?

"History. Everything that's come before."

How many councils do you sit on?

"Many."

Over 100? Less than 100?

"Enough."

And on each council do you represent the same concept or different concepts?

"Different."

Have you incarnated with Ronnie?

"Yes."

Has he known you from a previous lifetime?

"No."

So this is the first your first go round with him. How's he doing?

"Good."

What's your opinion about Ronnie's group that he's working with?

"It's inspiring. To see my generations after me do so great."

What they should focus on, is this an effective method -- coming to the council to ask questions?

"It could be better. More open, more transparent. To talk about this research openly as a group."

Is there anything that we can do just in terms of climate change to reverse it?

"It's hard -- there's so much to be done."

How many lifetimes have you had on the planet?

"Three."

Gela, would you do me a favor and introduce us to the person to your left and Ronnie's right? Is that a male a female or light?

It's a male.

And if you could describe him please.

Well-dressed individual. In his 30s.

Is this someone that Ronnie recognizes or is this somebody he doesn't know?

He knows him. Not well.

And what's a name or a letter we can use to address him?

Edward.

Thank you for allowing us to chat with you. May I ask you some questions?

"Yeah. You can call him Lalo."

Okay, very good. Lalo. If you don't mind, are you familiar with my work?

"Not really."

So far, that's three out of five who are not aware. But first, what what's your opinion of how Ronnie is doing?

"Good."

Is there anything he needs to work on?

"He knows what he's been working on lately."

And is that that he's on the right path?

"Yeah, to continue to do it."

Is there any way that you can show him that he can connect to you in this way? Some sensation perhaps in his body?

(Ronnie startled) Holy shit, the smell of tobacco. (Gets emotional)

I'm sorry to bring something up that causes that emotion but I also want to say it's new information.

"Yeah. I'm sorry." (wipes away tears.)

What kind of tobacco did he use? Was it cigarettes? Cigars?

A pipe.

Please, Lalo, If you don't mind, show him your pipe? Are you still using a pipe?

"No."

How did you create that sense so that he could access it? What's the process?

He says, "I'm here." (aside) I don't know.

Well, I mean, let me ask you, the memory of smoke is very specific. Did you tap into those engrams and synapses that are in Ronnie? Did you generate it in some other fashion?

"I did. I tapped in."

How are you generating that energy so that they can access you?

"Because that's what he wanted."

I assume you've been on the planet recently. Is that correct?

"I have."

I want you to put it in Ronnie's mind who greeted you on the other side when you crossed over?

"My father."

And was that a happy reunion? Or was that disconcerting?

"It was complicated."

And some point it wasn't complicated, correct? Like you realized where you were?

"Yes."

In terms of the relationship; at what point did you realize that you were the architect of that relationship?

"I didn't realize it."

Can put in Ronnie's mind, your life planning session when you chose to be Lalo - before you incarnated? And you were accessing some of the people that were going to participate in your lifetime, including your own father, right?

Mm-hmm. (Nods)

And try to describe where we are. Are we inside or outside?

"We're at the door. A door. Outside."

Tell me about the door.

"It's a glass door. It's a barbershop."

And is that barbershop associated with some part of your life in this lifetime?

"Yes."

Let's just follow this construct for a second. We're outside looking in?

"Correct."

Populate that barbershop with some of the people that were key in your lifetime.

"Yes. My brothers."

Have you had other lifetimes with these folks?

"I believe so."

So, when we leave the planet, where do we go? I mean, I've heard people say it often, that we return home?

"Back to the family."

I've heard it often described as a feeling of non-judgement, of being with family, of unconditional love. Are those correct terms for the experience?

"Yes."

Lalo if you could put your hands into Ronnie's hands while he's standing in front of you, and generate that feeling of family. So he can experience what you experienced when you went home?

(Leans forward, nods slightly.)

And what do you represent on this council and a word?

"Guidance."

Would you please introduce us to the person to your left and Ronnie's right. Is that a male a female or light?

"Male. Older man, mustache. Black hair. In his 40's."

And if I may ask for a name or a letter to address you with?

"Hector."

Hector, I'm going to ask you what I've asked the other ones. Are you familiar with my work?

"No."

No. What's your opinion of what we're doing?

"It's fascinating."

Hector, what do you represent on his council?

"Love. To help him find love and peace, Love for himself and for others."

Now, let me ask you, how many councilors do you sit on or work with?

"Not many, a few."

Do you represent that same quality on their councils or something different?

"Not all of them, but most of them."

That concept of love? When you say to help him find love, or help him love himself? Are you referring to an unconditional kind of love? Or something more specific?

"Understanding of love, the understanding – to know what that means to bring peace to him."

I've heard it described by someone, that love is the idea of opening your heart to everyone and all things. Is that an accurate description of what love is?

"Yes."

Have you ever had a lifetime on the planet Earth, Hector?

"Yes. A long time ago."

And if you don't mind, could show him that lifetime, are we inside or outside?

"We're inside. An educational building."

Where on the planet?

"Near Texas."

And what if you don't mind just put a year in his mind.

"1700s."

Texas in the 1700s. Is this a school for indigenous people or a school for people who are from Europe?

"School from where we're from."

Okay, so it's a school for European based people?

"No."

Indigenous people?

"Yes."

And what kind of topics were you teaching there?

"Science."

Let me ask you, Hector, are you still teaching a class like that on the flipside?

"Yes."

I want to introduce Ronnie to what you're saying. Would you take us to that classroom that you are currently a professor or teaching and allow us to see if we're inside or outside? What does the classroom look like?

"There's walls with no ceiling."

Just look around. How many people are in the class?

"About 10 people."

And if I was going to ask you for a name on the curriculum, or above the syllabus, what would be a name that we would call this class? What form of science?

"The connection of the stars in the mind."

Is this an astrophysics class? Or something more specific?

"The connection of the spirit."

If I asked you for how long you've been teaching this class, I would assume that the answers are like a long, long time?

Mm-hmm. (Nods) Yes.

Do you occasionally incarnate in between classroom exercises?

"Sometimes."

I've met a teacher who described 25 years of a lifetime on Earth felt like a five-to-10-minute break from her class, because she stepped out of the class to incarnate on the planet. Does that sound accurate?

"Yes."

I would like to ask you about this connection to the stars, spirituality and astrophysics. Are you talking about, like the healing light of the universe? Are you talking about moving energy? What's the focus of this class?

"As far as things are; (how) we're all connected."

Scientists talk about something called dark energy or dark matter? I'm guessing that it's has to do with consciousness. Are you referring to consciousness is how it all we're all connected?

"Yes."

And if you could put in Ronnie's mind, what's the medium of consciousness? Is it like water, energy, light?

"Its energy."

And this interconnectedness?

"It's hard to explain, we don't have enough time."

But am I on the right path here talking about how we're all connected like the ocean?

"You're close."

I've read Rumi say that we are all not just drops in the ocean, but the ocean in every drop. Like that?

"Yeah. On Track. Yeah."

Hector, you've known Ronnie for quite some time, I would assume. Have you been watching over all of us lifetimes?

"Yes."

Would you show him one that is important. Are we inside or outside?

"Outside. We're on an island. Bali. 1800's.

Was he a male, a female or what was his role?

"A male. He owned land."

And what was the primary reason for this lifetime? What did he learn?

"Farmed. He learned about business. He was a good businessman."

Was he married? Did he have kids?

"Yes."

Any of these people that he was with in his current lifetime?

"No."

But he but he knows them all correct?

"Some of them."

(Note: That may mean "knows them via his higher self.")

When he does a meditation can he access you directly?

"Yes."

If he's having a dream where he's talking to a guy with a moustache, it's likely going to be you, correct?

"It will."

I can see that there's much more to learn from you about this class and how consciousness works, that's up to Ronnie to check out. Is he a member of the class by the way?

"No."

Who would we consider to be the spokesperson for the council?

"Raquel."

Now that you've heard what we're doing, answer, you're asking these questions, what's your opinion of it?

"It's interesting. And it's been a long time since I've had a conversation like this."

Do you recommend that people do this more often? Correct me if I'm wrong, but it's like you're tethered to him. And he you're always accessible, correct?

"Right."

And so all he's got to do is, what would be the most valuable thing?

"**Just to know that he's… we're here for him.**"

Are there any specific messages you might have for members of the group or for his friend Kelly?

"**It's your decision to make an impact. And so if you want to do it, you have to do it now.**"

That they should publish something they should create something or, or just continue to do this kind of work?

"**That it's a decision. And if the decision is to work together, something great can happen. And if not, the chance for impact may go by.**"

What else would you like to say Raquel?

"**Thank you. He has to go.**"

Lalo, you gave him a visceral memory. Have you ever put pipe smoke in his nostrils?

"**No. Never.**"

So in a way him doing that would be a way of letting him know that you're always available, isn't it?

"**Yeah.**"

And could do it any time? Correct?

"**Correct. I've done it to others.**"

And who in Ronnie's life is most connected to you guys that he needs to sort of have a conversation with?

"**His Mother.**"

Thanks everybody for the journey and the trip. And Robert, let's park the boat. Very good. And that's it.

*****

CHAPTER NINE: GIANNI

Another member of the group that I'm meeting on Zoom. None of the group members have met or discussed the conversations we've had up to date. I'm asking in italics; replies are in bold. Gianni is a pseudonym.

Rich: You were saying you've come without much knowledge about me or what we're going to do.

Gianni: Exactly. Outside of this being a group coherence or group synchronicity experience.

Well, that is kind of what we're doing. So just to clarify, you've had experience with meditation or guided meditation?

Yes. I've done a past life regression hypnosis and between lives hypnosis here in Maryland.

So you've already opened the garden gate. In your sessions, were you able to meet a guide or someone like a guide?

I so the first one was just a past life regression hypnosis (session) and I did call up my higher self. I got the name of my higher self and it was a very interesting entity as well. It was a long time ago; we also had an earthquake literally at that the moment that I came out of the session. Earthquakes are not very common in Maryland at all.

I don't know how you pulled that one off. Pretty cool.

And then you know, learning about Shiva and these three aspects and so forth.

Why don't we do this? Because you've meditated before and that's not an issue. Let's do this Beatles meditation. "Picture yourself in a boat on a river." So tell me what does the boat look like?

It's a long canoe.

Is that a single person canoe or like wider?

Single person canoe. It's more of like an indigenous dugout, canoe.

Put your hand on the side of the boat. What does that feel like? What kind of wood is that?

Kind of polished. Mahogany. Walnut maybe.

Did you make this canoe?

I don't think so.

If you if you were able to look at yourself, what do you look like sitting in the boat? Do you look like you do today?

The same. Shaggier haircut.

I want to ask your guide to come and sit across from you in the boat. And when I say that, your guide knows what I'm talking about. But just allow whatever image comes to mind. Is it a male, a female? A light or neither?

It's a light.. a silver shining light.

First, let me thank your guide for coming at this request. And if your guide could manifest as an individual or something easier to converse with, would that be a male or a female?

It's connected to this cosmic sloth named Cebu.

All right. So you're getting an image of Cebu?

Yeah.

Have you met Cebu before?

I have through ceremonies.

Let's just allow this construct to be our construct, but I also I appreciate the name because that allows me to ask direct questions. First, Cebu, are you familiar with this work I'm doing?

"Yeah, of course."

And what's your opinion of it?

"It's always fascinating to just uncover more layers and kind of go back through the veils of it and remove the veils."

How is Gianni doing?

"He's doing pretty good actually. He's continued to find his path and find these symbols and signs and synchronicities that are that are meant for him."

Did he plan this journey or have random things sort of influenced his journey?

"It's always a bit of both. It's (that) the destination is always known but the side trips are always up to him."

Can we take Gianni to visit his Council?

"Oh, he's got several councils. In fact, which depends on which one we want to visit."

(Note: Based on the research we only have one council for our current journey. Council members have their own councils, but I try to zero in on the council we need to speak with.)

I'd like to converse with his council primarily responsible for his journey and with members we can access. When I say that, Cebu knows what I'm talking about, so, yeah, are we inside or outside?

We're in space right now.

Okay, so outside, in what feels like outer space. Is there any structural aspect to it?

Well, there's a there's a table, which is a circular table with the symbol in the middle of a star seed.

What's a star seed?

It looks like a four-pointed diamond with a curved ... tail.

Is this symbolic of this council or of Gianni's journey?

I think it's one and the same actually.

How many individuals are here at this table?

Well, there's twelve by twelve. So each council is a council of twelve in a circle (with twelve other councils.)

I'm going to ask Cebu to direct us to the council that wants to talk to us today. Are they in a line? A semi-circle? Or a circle? You said a circular table?

Yeah. It's a full circle.

Take a look at the person to the far left, whoever that is. And is that a male? A female or light?

This is a bird tribe member.

If you could describe that person?

He is a winged bird, like a six foot (tall) winged bird. And it's almost a mix between a parrot and a blue bird.

First, I want to thank the Council for allowing us to come in to talk with you. Can I address you with some questions? This person for the blue bird tribe?

He says, "Yeah, yeah, let's go for it."

Is there a name or a letter that we can use to identify you?

"Blue Ray."

Blu-ray? So can I call you Ray? Or blue?

(Laughs.) "Either one, blu-ray, that's fine."

And what do you represent on Gianni's council?

"A Phoenix quality."

So if I can paraphrase rising from the ashes rebirth?

"Yes."

How many councils do you sit on Blu ray? Just one or many?

"It's kind of difficult to explain. It's a multi-dimensional council. So you're pulled in -- each aspect of yourself is pulled in multiple places."

Many, but it depends upon the individual that needs this knowledge?

"Or the task at hand."

Have you been with Gianni for all of his lifetimes?

"Can't say actually."

Do you represent this quality of rebirth for other people are mostly for Gianni?

"Anyone that calls on me can access the same quality. He's connected to this phoenix energy in some way."

Let me ask you about Gianni's group that he's working with. What's something that they should focus on?

"I think that when you need to ask another council member for that answer."

Are you familiar with my work?

"No, I haven't seen it."

The reason I ask is some council members are, some are not. So how is Gianni doing?

"He's doing incredible here. There's 12 bird tribe members and he's been able to meet many of them."

Blu-Ray, would you introduce us to the person to your left? Who's the next person in our group here?

On the same Bird Council. It is an owl.

What do you represent?

"Wisdom."

And what would be a name to refer to you?

He's goes by "Mr. Who."

Very funny. What's the difference between wisdom and knowledge?

"Wisdom is the true knowing... it doesn't require any book learning, it's almost a re-remembrance."

Versus knowledge being something you learn through experience?

"It could be through experience through reading or through story, but wisdom is true embodiment."

What's your opinion of this group that Gianni's involved with? What can they focus on to get the results they're looking for?

"I don't think that they've actually figured out the result they're looking for."

Can give them some guidance?

"I think this process of connecting to spiritual councils, galactic councils... it is a very powerful process, and especially (in terms of) group coherence or visualization."

What's your recommendation in terms of doing this kind of research?

"I think it'd be a fascinating experiment to see if it could be done together."

I'm going to assume that you can show him your true essence, outside of the metaphor of an owl of knowledge and wisdom. What would it be? A light?

"Yes. it would be a just a rainbow color... a rainbow mesh – it's almost like shifting sands - like each time you look at it, it's a different rainbow like color."

I'm curious as to how you present yourself to, let's say, other members of the council, or your own council. Do you have those people that advise you, do you have your own Council?

"I've never been asked that. But yes, we do. In fact, because it's kind of a constant, ongoing, almost a fractal."

Yeah. And if you don't mind, would you show Gianni a visual of your own council? What they look like.

"In fact, (it's) quite similar… a circle. And then you have all the colors of the rainbow radiating out of that circle."

If you could just talk about that for a second, you have access to your council and I assume other members of this council have access to their councils. So this idea of wisdom is magnified?

"Yeah, it's just a fractal within a fractal within a fractal. It's like the Russian nesting doll, each unit holds the entire consciousness of that other unit."

Mr. Who, thank you. If you could introduce us to the person to your left.

We're actually going to move to a different Council.

Whoever we need to speak with. Who do we need to talk to?

Well, we can go in a couple different directions. We have a few people that have passed on, that are part of this council now…

Let's go to the first person who wants to speak to us. Is that a male, a female or a light?

That's a female. Her name is Barbara.

And is this someone that Gianni knows?

"Yes."

Was that a happy encounter?

"It's always a happy encounter."

And just in terms of that journey, were you aware of what was happening? Or was any of it surprising?

"It's a beautiful reunion I had anticipated for a long time."

Are you familiar with my work?

I am. My full name is Barbara Marx Hubbard.

Nice to meet you, Barbara.

"During my time on Earth, I was responsible for helping create the 12 categories of co-creation."

Do you know our friend Kelly (who organizes the group meditations)?

"I don't know her."

So what's your opinion of this work, Barbara?

For decades, I've been expanding on this idea of there are twelve categories of just what's needed for the world to come together. And so Gianni and I have come together around that he's also been given that same vision, and that's why this work seems so important with his group, because it's one of the sacred categories.

(Note: Barbara Marx Hubbard who was a pioneer in spiritual research, who formulated the concept of "12 councils." As noted, in the 100's of sessions I've filmed, there has never been more than one council in a person's mind's eye. But the idea that "councils are related" is reported, each council member has a guide and each has their own "council.")

Barbara, why did you settle upon the number 12? Certainly, not all councils are twelve. I've run into many councils that are five and six. Some are more, fifteen or twenty, but some are less. Why the number twelve?

"Twelve is a quite a mystical number if you go down that path."

So Barbara, who does he need to speak to on his council?

"I do have one more message for him for his group that he's working with. And it's to find the twelfth member, or to allow the 12th member to be a spirit. To hold a place for their higher purpose. Because they have 11 members."

Eleven's a good number.

"What the numbers are, definitely activators, that numbers are powerful. And some numbers are just meant for that individual. Some are universal numbers."

So the main comment is that he needs to find the 12th member?

"Yeah. The member is for the group. And what how will that how will that help the group manifest or get their goals that they seek. I recommend a conglomerate of one representative from each of their councils."

Tell us a way to access their guides. What's the best method?

"Each person is going to have their own shorthand or shortcut to it. And if they've already called on them, it's really an invitation. It's an asking. And it can be as simple as drawing a symbol that represents that council, it could be as simple as asking or requesting for that council. Gianni has learned that he asked for GPS which has guidance protection and source connection. And that brings it forth."

Okay. And so is there anybody else in the council that Gianni needs to access or meet with?

Cebu sits on this council and oversees the council in some way. So I can bring him forth again.

All right, Cebu have you ever incarnated off the planet?

(Note: There's a zoom glitch – recording stops. Off camera the question is asked whether Gianni has incarnated as well on another planet, and the answer was "Yes, in the Sirius B constellation." He speaks about how he looks to others on the planet, describes a blue tone or hue to his skin.)

Rich: Is this blue skin or the blue hue of his skin the source of the mythological characters that are in Hindu mythology? Those have blue skin are from this same planet?

Gianni: "Yes."

Have you met or know the Hindu fellow known as Krishna?

No, but the consciousness of Krishna, or the awareness of Krishna. Certainly, because this is a part of the process.

(Note: In the research I have interviewed people who self-identify as Hindu deities, including Ma Durga, Vishnu and Krishna. So asking them to "stop by for a chat" isn't outside the realm of possibility in this kind of conversation.)

So if you want, do you want to ask him to stop by and now? What's his opinion of what we're doing?

"Let's bring forth Shiva."

Okay. When you say that, what's the visual that comes to you?

The visual is the individual with the with the three stripes on his forehead, the trident in his hand and the blue skin. And he is simply sitting there in a meditative pose.

And we are talking about Krishna, Vishnu or Shiva?

Shiva.

Can I ask you some questions?

"Yes, if you make a quick."

Why, have you got a date?

(Smiles) "Lot of things to do here."

Are you familiar with me?

"No."

Are you familiar with my lifetime in India as a devotee? Me, Richard, are you familiar with my lifetime in India?

No matter what the energy around that (question) -- there's, there's a strong energy connection.

(Note: In the book "Flipside" I recount my second "past life regression" with the Newton trained hypnotherapist Scott De Tamble (whom Kelly did her session within Claremont.) During that session, I had the memory of being a Brahmin priest in Kerala, could see the makeup that I put on my forehead each day, my home, wife, and the temple that I oversaw, as well as the "piece of Mt. Kailash" that was in the "holy of holies" inside the temple.)

I just was curious if he was, because I went around sporting those same things. (Wavy lines made up of white Ayurvedic makeup). So Vishnu, how do you think our friend Gianni is doing?

"He's doing as well as he can. He's leaning into separating what is his own mythology (versus) what's his own creation. And what's his greater work here?"

And let me ask you, if you have any specific advice for our friend. I'm sorry my computer is doing kind of weird thing. I always assume when there's a glitch, there's possibly a spiritual reason for it.

Going back to that earthquake, as well… as all (is) connected.

(Note: The hard drive on the portable disk had filled up and was kicking us out of the zoom conversation after each minute. Rather than continue in that fashion, I wrapped things up.)

I want to thank everybody in the council, all of you. Is there anything else you need to show Gianni?

"The only thing to show him is that he hasn't met all 144 members of his council yet. And he continues drawing and bringing them forth and they each show up in the right time."

All right, well, and this is an effective method for doing so. Thanks again everyone! **End of Session.**

As noted – not everyone has 12 council members, and not every council member has 12 members in their council. However, it is interesting to note that someone can "access the members of the council's council" if they ask, and can ask mind bending questions about how the process works. It's in these "beyond the average question" sessions that we can hear specific information about the architecture of the afterlife.

*****

So that ends the experiment portion of this book. Nine individuals, none of whom had met their council in the past, the only thing they had in common is that they could do guided meditation. In terms of a dataset; 100% saw members of a council, all were able to communicate with members of their "council." All had a guide or trusted associate lead them into a place they'd never visited before. All learned "new information" during the session, so it could not be categorized as cryptomnesia.

As noted with the session of Kelly, while she did a hypnotherapy session first, she had not visited her council. Details of the hypnotherapy session done earlier had gone out of her conscious mind – she felt as if she "could have made them up." However that doesn't account for her repeating the same hallmarks, or conversing with a librarian in a library, seeing books there. Other people have reported identical experiences, although the library itself appears reflexive – that is, some see monitors and microfiche, some see stacks of books, some see scrolls or tennis balls of light. In this instance one of her "orange globes" was opened up and she could see "geometric shapes and squiggly lines" inside.

Others have reported the same – and further that the geometric shapes "retain information from previous lifetimes." In essence, what we are doing in these sessions is accessing a person's Akashic memory – outside of time, and learning new information about their path and journey that they chose.

It's not my opinion, theory or belief that everyone has a guide, everyone has a council, or that everyone has chosen their path and journey – it's what the overall data, research and footage show – and is reinforced by this new information.

I'll leave it to the scientists, philosophers, religious folks to parse it, box it, make sense out of it. However it does lead us into the next part of the book. Speaking directly to scientists about consciousness, but at the same time doing the exact same experiment with them. One is a neuroscientist, research fellow at Harvard Medical School at Mass General in Boston, the other a neuroscientist trained at a prestigious university in his country (but preferred to remain anonymous.)

Let's see how they fare with the same parameters.

> *"I've always believed in a higher power. You can call it God, you can call it Jesus, Krishna, Buddha, Allah, I don't care. I really believe we are all a part of God."*
>
> **Olivia Hussey**

CHAPTER TEN: THE NEUROSCIENTISTS

AKILA WEERASEKERA, PHD

Here are two other sessions done around the same time, one with a Neuroscientist who reached out to me through Quora, where I moderate a forum "Hacking the Afterlife." Akila was one of the 20 prize winners for the recent Bigelow price for "Proving the Afterlife Exists."

BIO: *"In March 2019, Akila received his PhD in Biomedical Sciences from the University of Leuven (KUL) in Belgium. His PhD research centered on the non-invasive assessment of the onset, progression and therapy monitoring of amyotrophic lateral sclerosis (ALS) using magnetic resonance spectroscopy and imaging... Akila was involved in a number of external research projects related to brain tumors (mice), addiction, aging, neurodegenerative diseases. As a research fellow at Dr. Marco Loggia and Dr. Eva Ratai's Labs, he's focused on chronic pain related. He's a cricket player, writes articles for a Sri Lankan newspaper on Buddhism, science, international politics and Eastern philosophy." Currently a Postdoctoral Fellow at Harvard Medical School-Massachusetts General Hospital in Boston.*

My questions are in italics, Akila's replies in bold.

RICH: Did you get a chance to watch my film "Hacking the Afterlife?"

AKILA: I watched it last night.

(Note: A general discussion ensued of how memory works, and Akila's research into the "putamen caudate system" in the brain. A discussion of the work of Dr. Viola Pettit-Neal and her reference to the "antenna" of the brain. Akila is working with brain scans (MRI) to further research how the brain filters information or receives it.)

Rich: My point is, that I think you should do brain scans of mediums. (For their ability to "connect to the flipside" to see where the locus of the filters might be that prevent others from the same information.)

Okay, let's try a guided meditation. The most simple meditation I know is the Beatles song; "Picture yourself in a boat on a river." I suggest to people that they invite someone you know to sit with you. Do you have grandparents not on the planet, someone you might like to talk to?

My maternal grandmother. She and I were pretty close.

Her name?

Seelavathi.

Picture her sitting across from you in a boat. See if you can see her. How old does she look?

Older, in her seventies.

Did she pass in her seventies?

Eighties. I wasn't there when she passed.

What's she wearing?

She always wore a white sari.

What color is her hair?

Grey.

I'm going to ask her to nod, shrug or shake her head. Is it okay to ask you questions?

"Yes." (Nods.)

My suggestion is to reach over and take her hands in your mind's eye. Are they soft, hard, warm cold?

Warm.

How do you think your grandson is doing?

Hmm. "Great." (Akila laughs.)

Do you approve of what we're doing this conversation?

"Yes."

Put in his mind who was it that influenced him to reach out to me that you know. Was it you?

Seems like someone else.

Can I ask that someone else to come forward?

"Yes."

Let's invite that person forward – male female or a light?

Don't see anything.

Let's ask Seelavathi – was it his guide that suggesting this conversation?

She says, "Yes."

Is his guide a male, female, or light?

Male.

Does he want to speak to us, or not?

She's not saying anything.

Seelavathi, what is important for Akila to learn today? Something he needs to hear or focus on?

Something like "don't give up."

Nice. There may come a time along the line – you mean don't give up in the research? Or in general?

Research.

Seelavathi would you introduce him to his guide – doesn't matter what he presents himself as, for the purpose of a conversation.

She's not saying anything.

Look around. Can Akila's guide come by and chat for a second?

I don't see anything.

I'm asking him to help you – but that would mean that he doesn't want to chat with us or doesn't know why we want to chat with him. Seelavathi, what's something besides "Don't give up?" Have you shown up to visit him?

(Akila aside) She's smiling.

Put it in his minds' eye where and when that happened.

(Closes his eyes) – it's like, I don't see clearly... a white and black cross. Like a grid.

A white and black grid? Let's ask her – are you saying you're in the research, is there a symbol or place associated with this grid, a location?

A location I think.

Some place in Sri Lanka, or someplace in Boston? What's a good place to chat with you?

I think it's a temple.

Did Seelavathi go to temple?

Always.

What kind of temple was it?

A Buddhist temple in Sri Lanka.

Is the crosshatch grid like a place or a shrine room?

In a shrine room.

In the holy of holies – sometimes there's a cross hatch grid?

And in this temple, above this is the cross hatch.

Like a mosaic?

Yeah.

Seelavathi, are you saying it's easier to chat inside a Buddhist temple?

She says, "Yes."

Is there a place in Boston where you live?

No.

Of course any Buddhist temple would suffice wouldn't it? Doesn't have to be Sri Lankan Buddhism, he could go into a Buddhist temple Boston?

"Yes."

(Note: I'm asking leading questions because I can. I do have a memory of being a Brahmin priest in Kerala, I do have a memory of being inside the holy of holies, and while I'm asking these questions, I'm seeing the same thing I'm speaking of. A black and white mosaic tile or screen. It's why I ask the questions in the order I've asked. He is capable of saying "No, that's not it" – and people often do. But in this case, it was a bulls eye.)

I have a Tibetan friend in Cambridge, I know there's a large community there. So Seelavathi, I want to know the lottery numbers... for Friday.

(Laughter.)

What is it you want to show our friend here in terms of his journey? Is this something important for him to focus on?

The word "Success" came to my head. But (the answer came) in English.

Well telepathically – she doesn't have to speak in Sri Lankan or Malayalam... what do they say instead of namaste?

"Ayubowan."

I've been to Kerala – ayubowan?

Means "have a long life."

I'm saying that to you Seelavathi. Namaste, ayubowan.

She's smiling.

Do you want to show Akila his council?

Her face has no emotion.

I understand – but I need a nod, shrug or shake of the head. Can you escort him into visit his council?

(Shrugs) Maybe.

So let's do that. I'm going to ask your guide, who remains anonymous – since she says he's around, or feels he's around and it's a guy – can we walk Akila into his council? Are we inside or outside?

Inside.

What's the floor look like?

Checkered.

(Note: I realize now that she may have been projecting an answer about "going to the council" before I asked the question.)

Marble or wood?

Marble.

Look up at the ceiling. How high are they? Tall?

Yes.

How big is the room – big? Medium size?

Medium, it's darker .. I can see like a middle.

So in your mind's eye – first I want to thank your guide for bringing us here, if we could lighten up the room a little bit, how many people are here?

Four.

How are they arrayed? Are they in a line or a semi-circle?

Sitting. In a kind of semi-circle.

First person to your left – on that semi-circle. Is it ok to talk to you?

"Yes."

First I want to thank you for allowing us in to talk to his council – first person on the left, is that a male or female?

(Reacts.) Doesn't look human.

Don't judge it. What do you mean by that, "looks alien?"

Yeah.

Without judgment, could I get a name or letter to refer to you?

(makes a face) It's kind of like an insect kind of look.

Don't judge it. What's a letter or name?

"L."

I'm going to call you Mr. L is that ok?

"Yes."

Of course you're speaking telepathically to our friend, so he can hear you – thanks. What do you represent on Akila's council? What's a word?

"Knowledge."

May I ask, has Akila ever incarnated on the place you're from? Mr. L?

"Yes."

None of this will bother him because we're talking like scientists about data - If you don't mind, can you show him the place, is it a place in our galaxy, solar system, universe or in another universe?

"It's like a dimension. Another realm."

Is the place where these people exist, does everyone look like you?

"Yes."

Without any stress, or disconcerting thought, could you show Akila what he looked like in that place? A bit like you?

"Yes."

What is the purpose of this design is it related to your environment? The physical makeup of who you were.

Hmm. Doesn't say … anything… about it..

Can you fly to move in that environment?

"Not fly, but yeah."

What color is the skin?

"Green."

Take a look at his eyes. Does he have eyes? If so, what color are they?

Black. Pitch black.

The emotion is knowledge so if you were to reach over and grab hold of Mr. L, what's the sensation of doing that?

Power. Strong power.

You represent knowledge – would you consider yourself a leader of his council?

"One of the four."

Are there more council members that aren't here now?

There seems to be more.

Do you sit on other councils besides Akila's?

"Yes."

Thousands, hundreds, dozens?

I get the feeling hundreds.

Let me ask you this, Mr. L. Are you familiar with my work?

He says "yes."

What's your opinion of it?

"Going the right way."

I've yet to hear "going the wrong way," but I appreciate that. Can you introduce us to the person on your left? A male or female?

A female.

Can I ask you a few questions? Describe her.

An older lady. Silver greyish hair.

If there's a name or letter I can use to address you?

The letter A.. A something.

What word or quality do you represent on Akila's council?

"Compassion."

Compassion and knowledge – two excellent things to know. Did he earn this quality of compassion from a lifetime?

"Yes."

Can you show that lifetime where he learned compassion? Just a glimpse?

Seems like taking care of people.

Like a large group?

"Yes."

Was he a doctor or like a warrior?

Like a doctor.

Was it on the planet earth?

(Chuckles) Something *like* planet earth.

(Note: Not a question I often ask – but to clarify, I start with "what planet was this lifetime on?" Sometimes it's not on earth.)

Something like earth but not exactly. I understand. Taking care of beings that had ailments?

"Yes."

That's fascinating, because compassion isn't always assigned to doctors and he's probably carrying it through to this lifetime, is that correct?

"Yes."

Are you familiar with my work?

She smiles.

(Laughs) I ask because some on the same council some are not. Do you approve of what we're doing?

She smiles, "Yes."

How is Akila doing?

"Wonderful."

How about the person to your left? Can you introduce us to him or her?

It's an older man with long hair. And a beard.

May I ask for a name or a letter?

"W." As in wisdom.

Mr. W, thank you for allowing us to speak with you. How do you think Akila is doing?

"Going the right way."

Thank you sir. Let me ask, how many councils do you sit on?

He says "Many. Thousands."

I'm sorry Miss A – how many do you sit on?

"Hundreds."

I mean, it's not a contest, I'm just asking to give reference, in case I run into you in another session. Mr. W. what do you represent on his council?

"Wisdom."

So, how is wisdom different than knowledge?

He's saying, "Knowledge is something acquired, wisdom is something you sort of bring to a life, each lifetime."

Are you familiar with my work?

"Yes."

Let me ask, am I accurate when I talk about Buddhism as a peerless philosophy about the nature of reality but not so correct when it comes to the afterlife?

"Somewhat."

The reason I ask is because, in terms of the afterlife, am I correct in saying that people do choose their lifetimes and choose the journey they're going to be on?

"Not always."

That's a clarification – In other words, some people just allow their guides to choose exactly the path and say "Here's what you're doing" and they trust their guides to know what they're doing.

"Yes." And seems like… it's also (that) incarnation – that you meet with this guide, not somewhere, but like, not like "home" as you say, but it's also an incarnation that you have the ability to choose, but not everyone.

"But not everyone does choose." I just want to clarify; it is correct that people can turn down or defer a choice if they don't feel up to it?

It depends on them. Depends upon things like karma, depends on the energy.

(Note: "Karma" in Sanskrit means "energy" or "action.")

I've heard this before; someone says "I don't think I can do that again, because I suffered immeasurably" and the guide might say, "Okay, you will have to do it eventually, like a lesson, like a class and eventually the class has to be fulfilled."

"Yes."

It's a small distinction but people on the planet feel they have no control over it and what you are saying sir, is that people do have some control over it?

"Yes."

Anything you want to tell Akila?

"Just to continue."

This person to your left?

Doesn't look human.

Is this a male or female presence?

Feeling of male.

May we speak to you?

"Yes."

What's a name or letter we can go by to address you?

"G."

Like golf? Or god?

He's got golden armor on, but he's not human.

Is there an animal or creature one would associate with this person?

I can't see the face clearly, just the body. It's black and gold like shiny armor – the head is clear.

What do you represent on his council?

"Power."

You mean in terms of controlling events?

"No, like attitude."

Mr. G, how is Akila doing?

"He needs to be more confident."

To get more power? Can you put a sensation in his body to remind him to access you?

I actually see fire. Not flaming fire. Some type of a ..

Warmth?

Yeah.

Let me ask you Mr. G, are you familiar with my work?

"Yes."

Not everyone is. How many councils do you sit on? –

Seems like many.

Thousands?

"Yeah."

Do you get asked questions like this a lot?

"Not many times."

Do you think it's something humans should figure out how to do?

"Yes."

Put it in Akila's mind how he can do that – help others to do it – but also this is something that will take time for him to take this knowledge and put it into his work. Is that right?

"Yes."

Is there anything he needs to be wary or careful of? My feeling is truth sets everyone free.

"There may be obstacles."

Can you give him a forewarning, put that feeling of flame – so he's talking to someone, "maybe I shouldn't share this." Is that correct?

"Yes."

Am I correct in saying that truth sets everyone free and that people should share everything?

Yes. He's saying "We met for that reason."

So who put us together?

Seems like the council.

Are you the leader of this council?

"Second in charge."

Who's the leader?

"W."

I appreciate that – Mr. W, you're in charge of this council are there missing council members?

"Yes."

How many more?

"Two."

I've never asked this before, what are the others doing? Working with someone else at the moment?

He doesn't say.

Does that mean it's not important for us to know?

Yeah, or maybe we're not supposed to know.

Out of all your council members, four are willing to chat with us – two are not to be known yet, is that correct?

"Yes."

Mr. G, since his guide brought us here – could you show him his guide now?

Yes. Male. Middle aged. Blackish hair. Brown eyes.

A name or letter, to identify him?

(The letter) "U."

And may I ask how do you think Akila is doing?

Seems like he's saying "going the way it's supposed to."

Was that okay to talk to his council?

"Yes."

I'm going to guess that you're not aware of the work I've been doing.

He's not saying.

My point is to understand why you were reluctant to speak with us initially. Just wanted to point out it was an interesting conversation. Each council member – the words power, knowledge, wisdom, compassion – these are all the highest things that people can achieve in a lifetime. Am I correct about that Mr. U?

"Yes."

So the people advising him are really wise – and the people I've met over the years, not everyone has that experience. By the way, is there a term or word for your planet Mr. L, what would it be?

He's saying "it's not like a planet, more like a dimension."

Do you have a word for it?

It's more of a sound.

Thank you – is there anything else U?? can you take him to a place of healing, where he normally returns after lifetimes. Could be inside, outside. Can you take him there?

"Yes."

Where are we?

Outside – by a lake, trees…

I'm going to ask you to hug a tree. Can you do that?

Yes.

Is there an energy or consciousness associated with this tree?

Yes.

Male or female?

Male.

Associate a name or letter with this tree?

Like R.

Have you ever incarnated on the planet earth as a tree?

He says, "No."

You're here representing tree – your consciousness is representing tree, is that correct?

"Yes."

How can we on the planet earth help affect climate change – what's a way for us to change the climate?

"Go back to old days."

Meaning?

Like, "Live like one with nature, not separated."

In Akila's work with the brain, his work with consciousness, how is that related to the construct that he's seeing right now. Seeing a mental construct of a place that he's created over many lifetimes?

"Yes."

Is he creating the characters or do they exist under themselves?

"Everything is part of a creation."

However members of his council are their own creation, correct.

"Yes."

But they're participating in his mental construct – whether it's a male with armor, or a female – to focus on the caudate and putamen complex. Is that the key to how the brain receives information from outside it's conscious awareness or is able to communicate?

"It's part of it."

What does he need to focus on?

"(That) There are other structures involved with this."

(Note: In our email exchange prior to this conversation, Akila mentioned the pioneering work of a scientist Dr. Viola Pettit-Neal. There is little literature about her online, but what I could find included her doing "channeled" sessions in the 1950's and 1960's where she would access a "higher being" who could answer questions about the physiology of the brain. She popped into my head, and since he's researched her work, I thought it wouldn't be hard to access her on the flipside.)

Because we can – let's ask Dr. Viola Pettit-Neal to stop by or her associate – either one.

Viola.

Nice to meet you Dr. Viola. How does she look to you?

Old.

Viola, what do you think of Akila's work?

"He's going the right way."

Is this new information for Akila to hear?

"Yes."

I'm trying to differentiate between that and wishful thinking. What's he missing in terms of his research, or you think he should focus on?

"To repeat what we found." (Her research)

You're saying he needs to recreate with the latest equipment that your information is accurate?

"Yes. To validate what we found."

In this model that you've demonstrated, you called it an antenna. Is it a form of an antenna for the receiver of consciousness?

"Yes."

If Akila is able to prove this antenna is able to pick up information, that would be a way of proving consciousness exists outside the brain?

"Yes."

Okay, let's get a high five from Viola. What's the best place for Akila to sit down and access you?

"There's no specific place."

I mean in his house, his bedroom, backyard – where's a good place to chat with you?

"In the bedroom."

This would be a place for him to access you?

"Yes."

Let's bring everyone together, Seelavathi, Mr. U, we appreciate you giving us this guided tour, everyone on the council – what a wonderful way to enjoy a Sunday afternoon. Any last words?

"No."

*****

Rich So that's it – you've recorded this, and when you look back at it..

Akila: You were saying these things and I was getting these pictures in my head. Did I create that?

I think the answer is yes, everything in your head is created.

Is this something I want to hear?

The key is new information – transcribe this word for word – focus on the details "I'm seeing a person that looks like this" Allow me to say if you were creating members of your council, you likely wouldn't have started off with an insect alien.

That was weird.

If I had a nickel for every time I've heard that!

*****

CHAPTER ELEVEN: DR. CARLO THE NEUORSCIENTIST

Dr. Carlo (a pseudonym) is a neuroscientist who has been published in both science journals and writes books about consciousness studies. This is our second filmed interview, the first where I attempt to visit a council with him.

My questions are in *italics*, Dr. Carlo's replies are in bold.

Rich: I got an email from a neuroscientist, asking questions about the research. We did one of my guided meditations to see if we could go anywhere.

Dr. Carlo: Okay.

This scientist reached out because of my responses on my forum Hacking the Afterlife on Quora – he shared some research he had done via Viola Pettit-Neal's research. Have you heard of her?

No.

Dr. Viola Petitt-Neal was a scientist in the 50s, who worked with another scientist (Shafica Karagulla "Through the Curtain"). Viola was doing the same kind of channeling work Jane Roberts was doing with "Seth" but as a case study. Viola was focused on the mechanism of communication or access. "How are we able to communicate to spirit?"

During her sessions, she was accessing a teacher on the other side – this idea of talking with teachers shows up in my work, as I've run across many accounts of classrooms. I've had mind bending conversations with teachers via mediums or people without hypnosis involved.

Right.

I don't know what you've been doing for ten years – by the way, he was one of the winners of the Bigelow prize.

Oh yeah?

Yes, one of twenty. But I wanted to hear your thoughts about the caudate putamen system in the brain?

Yes, I know it.

He has been studying MRI brain scans of "highly motivated individuals" to see if highly motivated people have a different kind of brain. He showed me his lecture of the caudate putamen system (CPS) - I've done some research into Richard Davidson's work and the amygdala, I'm sure you know about that.

Yes. Oh yes I do.

For lack of a better term, to me that structure functions like an antenna – inside the brain.

Yes.

After our conversation, I wondered, what is it that allows people to communicate, bypass these "filters" – are the filters located within the antenna? He was showing me that in the slides the Caudate Putamen System was clearer or more pronounced in the subjects. Smoother as opposed to less defined.

In the MRI scans?

Yeah. Let's say there was a difference between this and the average people so I thought of you – not to focus on highly motivated rich people – but to use the same focus you did on nuns to access that information, I'm suggesting focusing on mediums, because they already are bypassing the filters; but the study doesn't have to be only mediums..

It's primary … the Caudate Putamen System is involved in the reward phenomenon…

*As a term we might use, I came up with **"intenna"** instead of antenna – it's a process, or system, let's say for lack of a clever term… an "intenna" to access information from outside the brain.*

You could contact Andrew Newberg because he has lots of scans. He's In Philadelphia.. and he's been investigating what's going on in the brain, spiritual experiences…

Is he with a university?

Was with University of Pennsylvania, now with Jefferson.

Are you friends with him?

No, but he knows me.

So I can put you in my introduction...?

Yes. Sure. There's a Brazilian team in Sao Paolo who have investigated mediums, they have the anatomical scans...

That's great. I know some amazing mediums who work with the FBI, NYPD. Jennifer Shaffer and I have been doing this for years... so I have a lot of data. About a year ago we took it online as a podcast. When we start our program – the question is "Who wants to talk to us?"

Wow.

Sometimes it's someone I've invited - I ask the same questions; "What was it like to cross over? Was it instantaneous, was there difficulty?" Each is different – each has a process. Some believe they would fall into a dream. One former atheist described it elaborately. I asked "When did you realize it wasn't a dream?" (Harry Dean Stanton) He described a road trip from 1967 and they had a flat tire – that's when he realized "wait a second. We didn't have a flat tire." And his friends said, "We know." He said they gave him a "soft landing."

Oh. Interesting.

I'm suggesting that you are not aware of these other journeys, but you can be.

Sometimes. (I am).

If someone does meditation, hypnotherapy, LSD, one can bypass those filters.

I've done all these things, including rebirth and breathwork.

You've done a guided mediation?

Yeah.

It's great you answered my question before I could ask it. I was going to ask if you had MRI scan files – instead of doing it myself, someone else has done it.

Yes.

Maybe they're on to it – answered this question.

I don't think they have asked this question.

Speaking of planning journeys, shall we try one? Do you want to see how far we can go?

Okay, fine. Should I close my eyes?

It's up to you. I know you a little bit I want to go to that day when you had an epiphany.

I was eight years old.

Have you been back to that day?

Yes, I've talked about it in documentaries and books last few years.

I talk about it too – is there a more dramatic day in your life you'd access?

Oh, several – (laughs) – I was raised in a tough environment… but it wasn't fun.

Hold on that's part of the theater, I'm talking about the backstage stuff a vivid memory, seeing someone not on the planet.

There's one thing when I was about five or six I was having a recurrent dream and during the dream it was my mother in the basement of our old house, but she was transforming into another mother, but the other mother was demonic. Not my mother, who was extremely nice, kind and gentle.

What's your mom's name?

Celine. Three years ago she passed away, made her transition.

I'm sorry. Okay, that's all I need. I'm glad you told me about that event because that allows me to access something else. I want you to pretend she's across from you now. Picture her as a guided meditation – picture her sitting across – how old is she?

She was about thirty-eight years old. Around forty years old.

I want you to see her present tense. How does she look now while you are imagining her?

Thirty.

Color of her hair?

Black.

Wearing makeup?

No, she's wearing black glasses.

Her dress. Clothing?

It's more like a tee shirt something nice with pants.

This tee shirt – color?

It's a pale kind of .. (computer freezes)

I think we overloaded your system. You're back. You can hear me. We're outside of time it's not a problem.

In my case I've always experienced problems with electronics in my lab.

It think it's because the frequency is being amped up – so Celine, don't freeze the computer screen. So the tee shirt is pale.. what color?

A light green.

Her eyes?

Her eyes are brown.

In your mind's eye, pretend you can reach across and hold her hand. How's the feel?

Warm. Soft.

Celine is it ok if I ask questions directly?

"Yes." She nodded.

Thank you - I appreciate this. I know you know that I know your son – first question; "How do you think Dr. Carlo's doing?"

(Laughs.) She says, "I'm too serious and I'm working too much!"

What's fun – I'll ask – did Dr. Carlo make that up or was it yours?

Hers.

In terms of your journey, I want to ask about this dream morphing was that accurate or imaginary?

Imaginary.

I don't want to judge it but let's talk about morphing was he accessing the fact he's known you over many lifetimes?

She says "That I've known her for several lifetimes, but this creation was a mental creation because I was an anxious child."

Thank you – in terms of previous lifetimes can you show him one, what country are we in?

France. Eighteenth century. In the countryside.

Were you his mom, sister?

A married couple.

Would you show him what you look like in that lifetime? Describe her.

I see a woman who is about thirty to thirty-five years old, petite, not very tall, five foot two inches perhaps, she's wearing the costume of the time, it's hard to describe – it dates a few centuries ago.

Celine, show him what he looked like in that lifetime. What did your husband look like?

Tall skinny guy, older because he has grey hair.. I'm a farmer.

Out in the countryside, what was the name of the town?

It was part of a region of France; Burgundy.

Was that a happy life?

Yes. A tough life, but a happy life.

If you don't mind Celine, I want you to go to the planning session where Carlo is choosing his parents or you're choosing him – can you show him that?

I see a room and sort of screen, and images on the screen of my future parents.

Wow what a cool image.

I'm with people surrounding me, but light beings of sort – to the side.

Look around this room – or have whoever is doing the projector – scroll forward to your previous wife – why did she choose you?

We've been together over many lifetimes – over lifetimes. And sometimes what I get is that we were friends, enemies, lovers, all the various possibilities.

That's interesting. Celine, would you introduce Dr. Carlo to his guide – might be a man, woman or light.

A light, but a masculine type.

If you don't mind, could you manifest as a person so we can have a conversation? Whoever you want to pick as an avatar is fine.

Someone in my family on my father's side – great grandfather...

If you could give us a first name?

Gerard.

If I may – are you actually manifesting as his great grandfather or were you actually him?

Apparently he was my great, great grandfather.

Thank you for coming. How do you think Dr. Carlo is doing?

"Just fine."

Let me ask you a silly question – are you familiar with my work?

"Yes indeed."

What's your opinion of it?

"Thumbs up."

Reason I ask is because not everyone is, not everyone gives a thumbs up – top the next question, is it possible to visit Carlo's council?

"Yes."

Describe where we are.

Inside some huge building structure.

Describe it – wood, marble, glass?

More like – marble.

How tall are the ceilings?

Like very, very high ceilings – a different type of structure. More like a cathedral.

How many people are in this room with you?

Five.

And how are they arrayed – line, circle, semi?

I'm in between and there are two on each side and one behind me.

First allow me to thank your guide Gerard for bringing us here – is it all right if I ask some questions about Carlo's journey.

It's possible.

Start with the first person on the left. Male, female?

A light being and seems to have both masculine and feminine characteristics.

Androgynous. Can you give us a name or letter to address you buy?

"X."

How old does this person appear to you?

It's a light being – so …

Indeterminate?

Not possible to determine.

What word would you use to work to represent your role on Carlo's council? The quality over all of his lifetimes?

"Truth."

Is the lifetime he's leading now, is it about revealing truth, setting people free?

"Yes, in terms of the science of the mind, brain and consciousness and later on in the more general level," he says.

How do you feel he's doing?

"He's doing what he needs to do."

Are you familiar with my work?

He says that all of the entities standing there are aware of it.

What's the value for people what I'm doing?

Very important. Very important for the future. For humanity.

I just want to ask - this epiphany he had when he was; did you orchestrate that, or who did that so he could see how things fit together?

(It was) "All of us."

May I ask in terms of the structure of the council – is the number, more or less?

There are others, but I can count five of them at the moment.

Correct me if I'm wrong – Carlo shouldn't see all the council members because he'll meet them later on?

Correct.

The person next to you X, is that a male or female?

Female.

What does she look like?

(Chuckles.) She has blue skin. Pale blue skin.

How old is she?

She appears young, twenty to twenty-five years old – but I have the feeling she's quite old.

What's a name or letter we can use to identify?

"Lyra."

I'm sorry?

"In human language it would be Lyra."

Thank you Lyra. What word or concept do you represent on Carlo's council?

"Expanding reality."

That's interesting. Let me ask, the nature of your blue skin – is that a choice to manifest that way or does it relate to a lifetime you've had somewhere, where people had that color skin?

What I'm hearing is that "she's from another planet, another system."

Has Carlo every incarnated on that planet with you?

She says, "Yes, Pleiadeans."

Is that a star system?

"Yes. It's a star system."

In terms of the planet he's incarnated on – is there a name for it, that specific planet?

There's a name for the sun – but we have a name for it on planet Earth. Alcyone or something like that.

Would show Carlo what he looked like when he had a lifetime on that planet?

Yeah. (A pause) I was – I see, I was a male about seven feet tall, blonde hair, blue eyes, pale blue skin – look very human some differences with us humans.

Lyra is this a place he's had many lifetimes?

She says, "Yes."

So why did he choose a different place, this journey as Carlo on earth.

"Because it was needed."

Expanding reality? How is he doing with that?

She smiles.

I know you're familiar with my work – anything I need to adjust?

She says, "Just keep going the way you do."

What a delight to meet you. Carlo you're looking at her – put your hand into hers and tell me what that feels like.

A lot of soft – at the same time from her emanates a lot of strength, but wisdom at the same time. She was she is someone working aboard a ship a huge ship and they've been apparently fighting in our galaxy against dark forces.

Why did you show that to him? Has he been doing that fighting or just you?

No, she provided the information – Why? Because I've been doing pretty much the same thing aboard their ships before.

Let me ask you about this term "dark forces." Are you referring to other beings in our universe or in another realm?

"In this physical universe, this galaxy."

Of course everyone is an alien, we all choose to incarnate, even those who incarnate as dark forces could be friends of ours.

"Yes."

Do they consider you a dark force?

(Dr. Carlo chuckles.) "Yes, yes, they do."

I find that amusing for you to call them that, they're your old pals – that's a topic for another conversation to find out who they are, shift our consciousness to them – help me with this, but I'm going to assume the person behind Carl is the lead council member.

Yes.

Does this person want to chat with us as well?

No. He prefers not to.

I assumed that's why he's behind you – let me ask this question, the reason you don't want to identify yourself because it's not the moment to do that?

He says, "Exactly."

You're not hiding anything?

"Yes."

It's just not the time – but tell us, lead council member, what do you represent in Carlo's life?

"Wisdom."

Thank you – and if I may should we speak to anyone else on the council?

He's sending me back to my own guide.. Gerard.

Gerard, thank you to your council – is there anything else Carlo needs to see or hear today – a place of healing where he goes between lifetimes to recover?

He says that I "need to meditate more, to take the time to do that."

Put that into his mind – oh, I wanted to ask Lyra, when you touched her hand, you had that feeling that sensation? What was that like?

She says, "Yes. It's a transmission of energy."

I want to point out that's a wonderful way to start a meditation to remember that feeling of that transmission so you can access what they had to say to you. Lyra are you always connected to Carlo?

"We are."

Is there anything else he needs to see?

"Not at this time, no."

Let's thank everyone for this adventure... Thanks to everyone for showing up.

"You're welcome," she said.

****

Rich: (Conversation continues) So, that's it. I've spoken to dozens of council members – each one comes from somewhere else – and report that they sit on multiple councils. You mentioned at least five...

Dr. Carlo: I couldn't see all of them.

I thought it was fascinating your council member said "We are all aware."

Do you sometimes meet people from other planets?

Almost every time... the Boston neuroscientist – in his life he'd had some odd UFO events – and I found that when people have a lot of UFO studies, it's their subconscious being aware.

I did.

She even gave you a location – Pleiades. But I try to focus on the experience that's unique to you. So the Boston guy saw a life-size insect-being on his council. Our conversation was disconcerting for him.

I can imagine.

And I was saying "I've seen reptilians before, nothing to worry about – show him your skin. Is that skin or is it armor? Have you ever incarnated on earth?" This fellow said, "I wouldn't stoop so low."

(Carlo chuckles.)

Lyra said she was "fighting dark forces" – that would be a human construct. Plus they may see her *as a dark force. It's that thing of separation; we're not separate, we have the illusion we are... Also – those two concepts "truth and expanding reality" – with Akila one council member said he represented knowledge, the other wisdom.*

They said "Knowledge is something you learn; wisdom is something you're born with."

I studied psychology before neuroscience, so I have heard that before.

But when you focus on new information that's not in your memory – like Lyra, a blue person and you're holding her hand – if I was going to construct that, it's very difficult to have someone say "I've never heard of you" or "We are all familiar with your work" How could you know that answer?

I could now.

You answer it succinctly – "we're all familiar with your work Richard; it's important" – on some weird world, it could be Carlo being polite.

No, I'm not like that.

When one says they know me, and the other says he doesn't – it's mind bending. I've had some say "because of you we're getting a lot of people coming up here and asking us questions" What can I say? Thank you!

*****

Gerard von Honthorse – The Concert

CHAPTER TWELVE: *OTHER COUNCIL DISCUSSIONS*

ANDREW

Andrew is a financial analyst from England. He reached out to me to do a session over Zoom. His comments in bold, my questions in italics. Andrew is not his real name.

Rich: Have you done any hypnotherapy before?

Andrew: I did two hypnotherapy sessions with a Newton Institute trained hypnotherapist.

Was that successful? The first one was more successful than the second correct?

The first one gave me tons of food for thought. And all sorts of things came up, I wouldn't have expected. But you know, I don't know what my expectations are. Whenever I read some of your books. It feels to me like people are having these like perfectly lucid, Technicolor, high definition experiences.

That's my fault. Because, of course, people do meander and don't really feel like they do anything. I edit their experiences. A six hour session edited is only 20 pages in a book.

I had lots of things happen. And actually, it was amazing how much recall there was afterwards. I still came away from it, feeling like, "Did I just make all of this up?"

I started doing this kind of thing we're going to try today, just asking questions without any hypnosis or drugs... unless you've taken them.

I've never smoked a cigarette, the only drug I've ever taken is Ayahuasca. That's it.

Oh, dude. You're way ahead of me.

It was kind of funny. In a way. You asked about my first spiritual experience, and when I look back, you know, this whole thing I've said about the shiver-chills, I think I've had that since childhood. And when I had my Ayahuasca experience that actually referenced a meditation experience I had, which made me wonder, what was

my first experience? It's sort of feels like, "I think this is new, but it really isn't." I had one experience where we had an issue with family breakup. I had a whole bunch of books to sort through and when I looked at the books I've bought over the last three decades, I realize I've rebought the same titles again, again, again. So there's some things on NDEs and other stuff and I think, "You thought you have a new interest, but actually, you've had the same one every decade."

What a funny way to see the theme of your life. I think it's fascinating you can access stuff that happened before. Memory appears to be almost sacrosanct. There's no delete key in the mind, so everything that happens to you is recorded, not by your brain, it seems that your brain works like as a URL or a reference link to where the information is stored off site in another database. The Akashic library, let's call it that.

I am the exact opposite. To the point that I wondered whether I had some trauma, because I can only remember things for a year or two. I listen to other people talk about, you know, all these memories from their childhood. For example, I have children and the memory of their birth has faded. It's faded in a sense that the picture fades, but I can kind of remember the feeling. And that's true with almost all my long term memories. I have no real memories of childhood; I just have some memories of emotions mostly. And without any kind of pictures or clarity, or what have you. To the point where, you know, people say "What do you mean, you can't remember anything for your childhood? Something really bad happened?" I don't think it did.

I know what you're saying. But memory doesn't have a delete key. So everything is recorded, including this birth of your children. But the fact that you can access it now, that's the second thing. We can do that via hypnotherapy or meditation. Which is what we're gonna do - a guided meditation. And the reason I'm confident that we're going to do something, mainly because I've been doing it for so long.

I guess if I were to look at my three different types of experiences, I think the first spiritual experience I had, happened in a meditation quite similar to the LBL Newton hypnotherapy session - it was all a little bit gray. Lots of stuff came up. But at the end, I was thinking, "Yes, is that me or not?"

Then if I want to contrast the Ayahuasca experience, it was, "boom!" That was as real as real can be. But then, this energy chills thing. It's not visual at all. It's feeling and it's so strong, I've convinced myself it's external. I spent a long time trying to say, "Am I just doing it to myself? If I'm asking questions, am I just asking myself questions. What is this?" I still don't know that. But that's a very real kind of feeling.

Let me ask you this. How long does it last for?

The actual sensation, it's like in the center on body, then spreads out. And if it's not particularly strong, it will go a little bit up towards my head, then a little bit down towards the floor. When it's really strong, its gets all the way to the limbs.

Where does it begin?

Right in the center. (Points to his chest) I don't know if the heart but it's somewhere in the middle of the chest, it almost feels like it's from a point. And even though it feels like it's coming from something outside me. But it starts at a point right in the middle of my chest sort of thing, and then expands out.

Okay, let's explore this. A friend can bring on the Kundalini experience at well, even though he's not a trained yogi or anything. He says that experience is like an overwhelming feeling of intensity, "ten times a full body orgasm" as he puts it. I point out that he's a coach, takes cold showers, walks miles a day, stretches for hours – almost the same way a yogi might practice Kundalini yoga. But how intense is your experience?

How intense does it gets? It's like a pulse. If I do pulse after pulse after pulse, the reality is I don't really know how strong can get because after about three or four waves of this, it just feels too much. And I stop it. And so maybe I'm a coward, I should just keep going, but it just feels like "Whoa, this is a bit too much."

Here's what I want to do, I want to ask you to go somewhere with me, we're gonna play a game, so I just want you to picture yourself in a boat on a river somewhere,

Should I close my eyes at this point?

That's up to you, whatever is easier. Picture yourself in this boat on a river and tell me what does the boat look like?

Sort of like a kayak type thing. Okay, like a, like a big one. You could fit four to six people in it.

Look at the material it's made out of what's it made of?

It's made out of wood. Wooden sort of, cross beams or seat type plank right across the middle.

And does this seem like something that was made? Hundreds of years ago or years ago or longer?

I would say a few years ago; not very modern but not ancient.

Take a look at the water that you're on.

It's quite clear, but it's, it's moving or we are moving without anyone rowing. So it appears to be flowing.

How wide is this river? Is it a river or lake or sea?

It's a river… And I would say, maybe three or four boat widths (across.)

What can you see on the banks?

Mainly trees. They're not very tall. I would say sort of, quite Leafy. Not like plants, but somewhere between a plant and a tree if you like.

Does this scenario or scene look familiar? Or is this new information?

Well, it, it almost feels like a sort of a mash up of, like, sort of somewhere in Europe and being in like a mangrove type place. So neither one nor the other.

I'm going to ask someone to come forward to sit in this boat with you. I want to ask your guide. Even if you're not familiar who that is. I'm going to ask for a primary guide, let's just say call it that way. He or she knows what I'm talking about. And so ask them to sit across from you in the boat is that a male or a female or light?

I would say it's a male. It's very indistinct. But unlike when I did the exercise myself earlier, it feels like, I don't mean this in a negative way, but quite a dark coloring.

As if it's obscured from view. And so I first I want to thank him for allowing us to have this conversation. And just can you describe what he's wearing?

I suppose it's sort of blurred; it doesn't look like formal dress. But it's dark colors, like black or navy blue.

Robes or trousers or shirt?

Trousers and some kind of top.

Can you see a hair color?

That's kind of weird, because when you said that, sort of the visual is a little bit dark. But at the same time, the thought of light came to mind. Almost like a conflict. I would say lighter, blonder hair.

Okay, the word light comes to mind because I'm not going to ask him if he can turn the light up a little bit. In other words, lighten up this image so that you can see him a bit more clearly. Is that possible?

That was sort of weird when you asked. He became more see-through but the body shape is still there. How to describe this? It's as if the body is made of like, different colors twisted together. Not a single color.

That is what light is, multiple colors all blended together to become white. So if I may ask him some questions. Can you give us a name or a letter from which to refer to you? Whatever comes to mind.

The letter L came to mind.

Thank you, Mr. L. I'm just going to call you that for the purposes of this conversation. And let me ask you, are you familiar with my work? He can nod shrug or shake his head?

"No." But also, it felt like he's patting my hand into his hand.

So let's ask him to nod, shrug or shake his head no. Does that part of the hand mean "Yes?"

He said "Yes."

The reason I ask, to give an example of our way of communication. Are you his primary guide, L?

I've totally lost the image of the boat now. It feels like I'm kind of shooting upwards.

Funny, he's anticipated my next question. My next question was, "Can we take Andrew to visit with his council?" Is that where we're going? He's in a hurry.

(Note: I'm fond of reporting "Ask questions and when you get a response before you can ask the question you'll know you've made a connection." I asked "Are you his primary guide?" He responded by showing him "shooting upward." The next question was going to be; "Can you take us to visit his council?")

We're going somewhere, like into space.

Okay. As you get to the location that he wants to take you to, are we inside or outside?

Well, like it feels like we've sat on some rocks, but the rocks are kind of in space, rather than... (on the ground.)

That's fine. So we're outside and there are rocks. And so I think, is it a comfortable place to sit?

Yes. Okay. It's kind of weird. I mean, sort of like being in orbit.

Not so weird for me. So we're outside, we're on some rocks. Try not to judge what you're seeing. Just let it come forth. And so Mr. L, if you could put into Andrew's mind, the number of people that are on his council, how many would that be?

Eight.

Is it possible for us to address some of these council members? If you look around, you may see them.. How are they arrayed? Are they in a circle, semi-circle or aligned standing or sitting?

I'm on a rock and there's some other rocks in front of me. And they are sort of, in a little bit of an arc. It's not a semicircle, less than a semicircle. But it's not a straight line, either. Like ten o'clock to two o'clock. Something like that.

I appreciate that. First of all, may I address the council and say, Thank you for allowing us to visit and have this conversation. I will try not to ask any questions that will be disruptive. Mr. L if you could help Andrew, access the first person on his left in this line of people? Is that a male a female or a light?

The image I'm getting is a male, almost like a very small male. Like a little.. wizardy goblin type.

Try not to judge it. When you say wizardly goblin do you mean like his long ears or hair? More Yoda or more like a leprechaun?

No, no, kind of small body. Long beard and a big, big, long, pointy hat.

Oh, like a Merlin hat?

But on a very small figure, or someone's like a dwarf wearing a hat

That's fine, thank you. May I ask you some questions directly, and you can put the answer in and just mind. Is it possible?

He says, "Give it a try."

Thank you, and what's a letter or a name that we might use just to address you in terms of this conversation?

"Jay."

Mr. Jay. I'm honored to meet you. And it's a treat for me to be here to have a conversation with you. And to ask you some questions about Andrew's path and journey. First question, how do you feel Andrew is doing?

(Andrew aside) He's kind of chuckling.

Okay. Chuckling is an answer. If you can tell us what is your role on Andrews Council in a word?

The word "mirth."

Okay, mirth, comedy, laughter, enjoying life, the joy in life. All those things are related. How many councils do you sit on Mr. Jay?

The number twenty-seven came to mind.

Thank you.

It's not as if he's talking to me… that just somehow the answer came to mind.

They do communicate telepathically, the same way we do in dreams. I appreciate that. That sounds like a logical number. And let me ask you, do you represent mirth on all of those councils?

I can't tell whether he's teasing or not. He kind of held his glasses out… he has ring glasses – (Harry Potter glasses) and he kind of held his ring glasses out a little bit… and said "it's mirth and wisdom." But again, with a little chuckle, so I'm not quite sure that he's saying "Yes" or by saying "It's mirth and wisdom" as if he's teasing a little bit. He's a very playful character.

Could be a combination of all three, as mirth and wisdom are related to each other, and by holding out his glasses and making that observation, "mirth and wisdom" are arguably the same things. Because they both aim at the truth. You're telling the truth to people in a funny way, but in a light way. But let me ask you, Mr. J. Dr. J, are you familiar with my work?

He nodded.

What's your opinion of it?

He kind of put his head back… and I can't really see what he's saying or doing.

Well, he can give me a thumbs up or a thumbs down. Or a wave of his hand, like "so-so."

That, okay, so now he's just being… playful. He… he sort of put his right thumb up his left arm down and then sort of kept switching.

That's hilarious. "Yes, no, yes and no." It's good for some not good for others. But it's I'm assuming it's good for Andrew?

In response, now he's got two thumbs up. Yes, his whole thing seems to be playfulness. You know, "We shouldn't take ourselves too seriously."

Let me ask you, Jay, do you normally look like this? Have you ever incarnated on Earth before?

I'm getting "Yes."

When you were on Earth, did you look a little bit like the way you do now?

I'm getting an image of almost like an Adonis type figure, like a real chiseled, good-looking man.

Interesting. Have you ever incarnated with our friend Andrew here? The same time?

"No."

But that Adonis looking fellow, was that on Earth? Or somewhere else?

"That was on earth."

And how many years ago was that? Was that I mean, just for us for reference was that we like centuries ago or recently?

I'm getting images like a few years ago. Yes, sort of a picture of Romans but sort of like wearing...

A toga?

No, but like a legionnaire who is topless wearing the Roman skirt that the soldiers would wear.

(Note: A "Spartan skirt" was the name for the cingulum straps that hung from the waist of a soldier or gladiator.)

Well, let's ask Mr. J. Are you giving him an image of that time period? Was that when you were alive? On the planet Earth?

"Yes."

Where was that by the way? Was that in Rome, or was that just in the Roman Empire?

I don't think it was Rome. I'm getting a picture of like an arid area, but quite a remote area.

Could have been Egypt or any part of the Empire which included the Sahara and Sinai, from Morocco to Babylon in the East.

He's showing me a landscape that reminds me of Sedona; Red rocks. Quite arid and dry, and a little bit of an orangey red tinge to the soil.

Was that in Syria, or one of those areas? Sumeria? North Africa?

When you said the first thing you said he sort of, Yes, he looked quite proud. And he stood up tall and then sort of stared into the distance.

I like his sense of humor. Like "Ta-daa, you got it. That's it." Like tapping your nose. Right on the money. I appreciate that. Now, let me ask you about mirth, the idea of mirth? How is that related to Andrew's journey? Is that something he needs to be more focused on?

What I'm getting is that, that he is very proud man. And he, Yes, in a way he's chosen now to have this form, this playful form. And that that's important for me not to take myself too seriously, too.

Well, thank you, Mr. Jay. And the idea is, of course, and correct me if I'm wrong, people on our council, or people on Andrews Council are always tethered to him or connected to him. So he just needs to sort of ask for help, in terms of connections, is that correct?

Okay, he's doing a little dance for some reason.

I'll take that as a yes. Like, ding! Yes, correct. I'm going to give you my happy dance for that one. But it's also playful, which is, of course, why he represents mirth. Yes. That of course, is the answer!

It's kind of like he's teasing. Like, as soon as you said he's always there, he turned his back on me. But in a way that wasn't really true. Kind of just teasing.

Funny. So Mr. Jay, I really appreciate talking to you. Would you mind introducing this to the person to your left and Andrew's right. Who would that be? Is that a male a female or a light?

Female.

Describe.

Okay, it's a complete contrast. This is almost like a sort of Princess type figure. Very regal. And so there's this this kind of comical figure right next to her.

She is serious?

Yes, not stern, but sort of...

Austere?

Very serene.

How old does she look?

Before you asked that question, I would have said thirties. But as soon as you said that, it was like she showed that she's incredibly old and sort of like, she embodies different ages. So she suddenly still looked beautiful, but much, much older, like in her eighties, nineties. Now back to her thirties again.

Thank you for allowing us to talk to you. And if I may, or may I ask you for a name or a letter to address you?

"Lily" comes to mind. It's kind of weird for me, that name doesn't fit to the picture.

Thank you Miss Lily, how do you think Andrew is doing?

She's just smiling with quite a radiant smile. Like I mean, literally radiant as if there's some light coming off her face.

I'll take it from that you think he's doing a good job or he's on the right path?

Yes, I think so.

So let me ask you in terms of Andrew's experience, sometimes he gets these shivers. Is that you guys on the council giving him that message? Or Is that him creating that? Who's creating those shivers for him?

When you asked that, all of them together, turned and kind of looked towards a light. That's a fair distance away.

All right, that gives us somebody to talk to in a minute, but before we get to that light, let me ask you, Lily, have you how many councils do you work on? Are you part of?

She says "Just six."

I appreciate that. Oh, what's a word that you can that you represent in Andrews journey?

"Calm."

So that serenity that you exude? Do you also represent that another councils?

I have this image as if she is more transmitting that to other councils, as opposed to being on other councils. She's helping other councils rather than participating. I've got this image of her radiating this calmness to other council members in different groups. Not necessarily being a member of those councils.

Have you ever incarnated on the planet on the planet Earth?

I'm getting this image of somewhere else – far. far up - feels like "up."

Has Andrew ever had a lifetime on that place that you're referring to?

No.

Lily, do you want to show us that place that you've incarnated on before, just to give Andrew a taste of what it's like to be off planet and somewhere else? Is it another realm? Or is it in our universe?

It didn't feel like another planet felt more like a kind of a higher place. Like a realm, more than a planet.

Lily, do other people in that realm, do they project an image of themselves the way you've done today, sort of like multiple ages and times?

The image I'm getting is that they, they tend to project -- it is more light than she has in this form. But a lot of them don't even bother with that.

Does everyone kind of look like you back home, or do they project the form they prefer?

She's kind of showing me that sort of thing. It's like they look a bit humanized a bit. It doesn't really matter. But the essence is a sort of calmness and light and serenity. Yes, they all have that. But it feels like she's gone to a bit more effort to look humanoid.

Are you familiar with my work?

She says, "Yes."

What's your opinion?

The image that comes to mind is that she's showing light coming down, sort of from her to Earth and then sort of splitting into different places. I think that means it's a positive message. But it's basically spreading a little bit of light all over the planet.

Just to clarify, are you saying this kind of work of speaking to councils? Like they can tap into the process?

The image I get is like this sort of light calmness, sort of going down and soothing the planet, a little bit of soothing people. So it doesn't feel like she's commenting specifically on the question of what you do. But she's sort of saying, that type of work that can spread that calming light is all good. And it's almost what you do is a form of that, as opposed to the only form of that.

If I compare and contrast the two we've met, the first person we talked to was sort of reflecting human existence and Lily feels like, she's coming from a way higher level. Almost a more abstract level.

And how did Andrew earn your role on his council?

The feeling I'm getting from her is that it's not about earning it. It's about needing it. And to see this image of her just bathing me in this calming light. Like I needed this help, as opposed to earning it.

So my question is, can you feel that light that she's bathing you in?

Yes. I can feel something. It's more than a visual. But it's not like if I touched the table, but I can feel it touching me.

So Lily, please amplify or make that a stronger feeling in Andrew so that when he feels this, he knows that this is you reaching out to remind him to connect to serenity.

When you asked for that, I got my shiver-chill feeling.

the question I would have for you, Lily, when everybody looked past the council towards the light, is that a person that we need to communicate with?

There's two separate feelings here. When she showed that light, I could feel the energy around me like surrounding me. Then when you said "Can you sort of amplify it?" I felt that coming from within. It feels to me that whatever this feeling is, is coming from that light. And it doesn't feel like a council member or person.

So let's go forward to that light.... Is that a portal? Or is that a like is it like something generating a light?

I'm going right up to it; I don't know what it's portal or not. It's so it's not like a sun because it's not hot. But it's a bit like a sun. It's a bit like a, like a ball of energy. But it's not fire.

But you can feel that energy. Is there any emotion associated with it as you're closer to it?

It's a little bit scary, like not scary, as in evil or malevolent. Powerfully scary.

This is why I want you to make it a hologram. Because you can have no emotions associated with a with a hologram.

Oh, I didn't do that. What do you mean by hologram?

Take a photograph of it in your mind's eye, what you're seeing. And then freeze it, like a like a hologram and make it three dimensional.

When you said make the hologram, take a snapshot, it felt like it sort of froze. It was like stopping time if you like so it's not moving. Yes, that's my hand onto it.

Stopping time is what I mean by a hologram. So what is the sensation when you put your hand on it? Or in it?

Well, it's not solid I mean, I haven't got further than a few centimeters, because I guess I'm still a little bit nervous. But if I put my hand into it, it's like, Yes, it's kind of like putting your hands into a cloud. But as you get close to it, it really isn't.

I want Mr. L, your guide to stand right next to you. And I want him if you don't have he doesn't mind, tell us "What is this that he's accessing?"

"Not a portal, it feels much more like it's like a well, you can draw on."

Like the source of a well, and, you know, if we were going to go down this philosophical path, we'd ask questions about who created this well, and where did it come from, etc. Based on the research I'll assume this well is created by all of us that there's no separation between us and the well. But it is something that we call upon or need to use, is that correct Mr. L?

So as soon as you said, "it's created by all of us" I did get the impression now that the world itself or the sphere has an identity.

Male, female or neither?

Male.

May I ask some questions and you this entity can put the answers in Andrews mind is? that possible? Do you get a feeling yes or no?

It's kind of weird. It's as if, like it's sort of hovering a little bit above us - in front and above us. I don't know what that means.

Okay, well, I just want to I want to get permission to ask you questions, this entity that is associated with this energy.

I'm going to guess yes, because it's not moving away.

So there's an entity associated with it. Are there other entities like yourself? More than one, let's say so, you know, many - that that people have created a specific energy source?

"Yes."

So it's more than one?

"There are more like this, him."

Some who've had a near death experience, or experience something like this during meditation or a hypnotherapy session, associate this with God or the word God, because they don't really have another word for the experience. But what you're saying is, there's more than one. Is that correct?

It feels more like an angel than the god.

Can I ask you to manifest as a male, from this male energy, manifest as a being so that we can have a conversation with you? Can you do that?

It's like, almost like a superhero – not a superhero because it's made or light, but it's got that sort of superhero pose. It's floating in space but has one knee up and one down, like a superhero pose to me. Not showing off, I don't know. It's just hovering.

Is there a name or a letter we can use to associate with you just for purposes of this conversation?

Okay, this sounds nuts. But the word that came to mind was the word Orion.

I appreciate it. And the word Orion is that a word you're using for us to reference you or to other people refer to you as Orion?

I just get this image of like, a series of elements sort of spinning very, very, very fast around his head. If you can imagine like, not planets, but like objects orbiting his head, but so quickly that it forms like a disk. Like Saturn's rings or something.

Ask to slow those down slow because we're outside of time here. Are they geometric shapes like fractals or they are they do they look literally like planets?

I'm not sure if he just put that thought in my mind as soon as you said that. It did look more like the pyramids or some kind of geometric shapes as you said that.

(Note: In the first week of filming people with hypnosis for the film Flipside, one of the subjects reported seeing "geometric shapes" whizzing around. In subsequent reports, I'd ask them to "slow them down" and people have reported that these geometric shapes are like the Akashic library, as the shapes carry "all the memories" from previous lifetimes.)

Let's just pick the pyramid because that was the one that you saw. Just stop it and allow him to examine it. Like if he was going to open up the top of this pyramid and look inside, what would he see?

So he's doing what you said - before you even asked that question. He kind of plucked one out of the ring. But it's not a pyramid. It's a more complex.

I appreciate it. He anticipated the question before I even asked it. And show him the contents. What do you see? Like mathematical constructs, geometric shapes? What's it composed of?

Okay, so it's a little bit weird. It's like if this geometric shape, and he then kind of broke it in half, but then it could fold onto itself. And then you kind of repeated that until you basically just had a point and then nothing left.

Sort of what a fractal is, recurring geometric shapes. A mathematical construct, but it's repeated. Orion, is the content of the shapes related to personal history? Like the Akashic records - are these shapes that are related to your journey through all realms and lifetimes - or related to Andrews journey?

The thought or the image I'm getting is... along the lines of when it was all spinning together into one mass, that's a combination of all of these different ones. But each of the individual ones is the right one for an individual person.

Almost like a library that's spinning around?

I don't get the sense of a general library. I get the sense of like, what you were saying before, in a way this is like the unique signature or signal for each person.

I appreciate the clarification. Let me ask you this around why are you showing this to Andrew? Is this so we can have a conversation about this? Or is it just that the way you look and we happened to notice it?

It's feels like when I feel what I feel, there's a unique any key or unique signal for everyone to connect to this. And that's kind of what I'm feeling.

Orion, do you represent a person on Andrew's Council, are you like the spokesperson for this council? And that's why everyone sort of deferred to you and looked over towards you?

No, feels much more like he's a resource closer to different councils.

Like Lily, you too are a resource for other councils Is that correct?

Yes, but it feels like Lily does sit on some councils. And he really doesn't.

In terms of your role, if you could give us a word or a concept or quality that we could use to describe what it is you represent for all these councils, what would it be?

The word "contact" came to mind.

Do you mean like connection?

(Note: It just occurred to me he could have also meant "like the movie "Contact.")

Yes.

Or communication? Do you that facilitate communication or contact?

Yes, I think so.

That's fascinating. And so when in terms of when you went to see Orion, and you said he was like, a light that was set apart?

I don't get the feeling that he hangs out with any council. He's kind of there. And the councils are there. And the councils were pointing to him. And he's helping to facilitate contact.

I appreciate that Orion. Do you have your own guides and council members in your journey?

There, I get an image of a connection up. Further up.

Orion has his own compatriots, his own advisors his own, is that correct?

I really get the feeling the last bit is correct. He has his own council, but that he is a resource. He's a part of the fabric.

Somebody who sort of oversees this kind of process?

Oversees is the wrong word - feels like he is he is providing a role. He is facilitating connection, but it's it feels like a very personal thing, like you'd have to get the council to interact with him, as opposed to the council interacting with him. if you get what I'm saying. Almost like an infrastructure provider than he is a council member. And... he has his own council.

I like to point out that there's a myriad there's millions of different roles that people could play. And he's playing one. Orion, have you ever incarnated on the planet Earth?

No.

Have you ever incarnated anywhere?

Well, this is kind of weird. Okay, the sense I'm getting is that... he ...it almost feels like he is made up of things that have incarnated but in the form that he is now, he's never incarnated the if that makes any sense.

He's saying it's like he represents a number of individuals. In terms of contact, are you talking about all of humanity or referring to other beings throughout all universes?

No. It feels like human souls have kind of joined together to form something. And that something isn't just, you know, a collection of a number of human souls, but it's a new thing. So in that sense, he's never - individually incarnated. But the things that came together to make him have. He's given me the image of six individuals.. as if six souls have kind of come together and merged to create him.

So he's aware of their incarnations, he's composed of all six. Something like that?

Yes, but it would be wrong to only think of him as a collection of six souls. Because when they came together, they formed something new.

I appreciate this Orion, manifesting as somebody so that Andrew could see you. And let's return to his council now. And is there a spokesperson in the council that might want to communicate with us?

There's somebody sort of, in the middle towards the right. Not all the way over the right, but just a little bit right of center.

Male, female or light?

Light.

Describe this color or light?

It's green. I would have said male, but doesn't really feel like male. So maybe it's just somewhere in the middle.

A word or a name that we might associate with you?

G came to mind.

Okay Mister or Miss Gee. What do you represent on Andrew's council?

The word "love" just came through.

Are you familiar with my work?

"Yes."

And what's your opinion of it?

The phrase that came to mind is "don't go too fast."

Do you mean in terms of me or do you mean in terms of Andrew or both?

The feeling I'm getting is that it's very valuable for people who are ready to receive it. But I was like a feeling that.. like, don't force it on people be there for people who want to hear it. But they have to ask.

The ones who need to hear it will find it and ask questions about it, or reach out to their guides or councils. Those that should hear about it, will.

A little bit more specific to me. It's something along the lines of it's like showing me that fear serves a purpose. That sometimes I'm impatient. And Yes, that sometimes fear is just bringing me to the right point to do something.

Fear compels you to practice, to learn how to do something. Do you overcome the fear by practice, and by learning?

He's saying that sometimes I'm too impatient. And it's as if fear is their way of just getting me to slow down a little bit.

Mr. G. How many councils do you appear on?

I just had an image of his arm stretching out and sort of, you know, kind of going over a lot of councils. As far as, my eye can see if you like.

A lot. Thousands?

I would have said more. Hundreds of thousands but not millions.

Could give us a definition of what love means?

The thing that came to my head was "respecting other's freedom."

Is that different from unconditional love? Or is that the same?

I'm getting a sense it's the same. But he's trying to tell me that, that I need practical instruction. If you say "love unconditionally," and you don't have a definition of love, what does it mean to do that? Whereas if he tells me to respect others freedom, then I kind of know what to do.

Love is hard to define, if someone has never felt love before, very hard for them to sort of open their hearts to everyone and all things.

I'm getting the sense it's almost a melancholy freedom, he's showing me that there is a kind of burden of love that, if you respect other's freedom, then Yes, you're sort of opening yourself up to suffering… others can hurt themselves. The loving thing in some situations is to realize you can't fix it, you simply have to allow it. Allow it and I guess suffer along.

We've heard that "One can experience God by opening their heart to everyone and all things."

The image and feeling I'm getting is that, "If it's good enough for God, it's good enough for you." So in a way, the biggest gift is to give them their freedom.

Because of course, one person suffering may be a method of helping another person to experience the opposite. Can't experience joy unless we've known suffering, can't experience love unless we've known the opposite.

I got a really strong sense that he was agreeing with everything he was saying then, except the end bit where the thing you were saying that something along lines of suffering is another frequency of joy …

But that idea Mr. Green represents love in a way in a way that's very profound. It's love without conditions or judgment, including what's going on the planet. Is that correct?

Yes. The feeling I'm getting as he was saying, "what other kind of love is there?"

Andrew had an experience with Ayahuasca; what was going on? Was he creating an imaginary world? Or was he visiting the real world?

Neither - the sense I'm getting is that he was seeing a real world... Well, there is no real world and imagining there's the world; the same.

The mental construct of it?

Yes, sort of it like we gave him a different filter, or he saw through a different filter. So it's all the same thing.

Could just show him the genesis of a shiver that he might have?

So the sense I'm getting is that I am the gatekeeper to that.

If you could just talk about that a little bit what the heck does that mean?

Means the signal if you like.... the connection is always there. Yes, so it'll be like me turning the radio on.

And so when you're turning the radio on, is it a way of saying pay attention to this?

I have a feeling of there's not just one... I have like this image of a child talking to a parent. Sometimes you need to share. There's not one reason why you make that connection.

Andrew's self, his Earth self is in the sandbox in the playground, and the child is in the playground turning to Andrew the higher self and asking, "What the hell does that mean? Why did that event occur?"

I get much more the image of Andrew connecting to other things.

When you say you're the gatekeeper is that you, Mr. Green, or is that Andrew?

Andrew.

I've heard consistently that we bring a portion of our conscious energy to a lifetime, how much did Andrew bring to this lifetime? Just a number pop it into his head?

The number forty percent.

Can I ask you what the other percentage is up to at the moment? Is he incarnated in somebody else? Or is he attending classes?

I got an image of the rest being diffused, like spread (out). The image I got was - was a cloud and it was on the edges of that cloud.

I want to ask Mr. L to escort Andrew into one of the classrooms he's attending. Tell me are we inside or outside?

Feels like a sports class, which is weird because I'm definitely not athletic.

Try not to judge it. Alright, so a sports class. And how many are we? Are we in a room or outside?

We're outside. It's like a weird sport, I don't know how to describe it. A cross between a bobsled and boating on a river. It's almost like Yes, like some strange bobsled. It's like a very narrow river. Only centimeters across. And then with banked edges, like a bobsled track. Then riding on some kind of bobsled, a cross between a luge and like a little boat.

How many members are in this class?

Twenty-five.

What's the purpose of this class?

Like the purpose of this event is to learn to live with fear.

We talked about fear earlier. I'm going to ask Mr. L to introduce us to the teacher of this class, whoever that is, is that a male or female or light?

It's a female. But similar statue stature to the first council member. Short.

Is it possible for me to ask you a couple of questions? I promised that to interrupt your class too long.

"Yes."

Could you give us a name to address you?

"**Rona.**"

Correct me if I'm wrong. This is a class you teach in how to deal with fear. Is that correct?

"**Yes.**"

In terms of your students, so they can do they all construct sort of events that would include fear within the event? Or is it everybody working on the same luge, the same kind of River Run?

"**No, there are unique elements. There's like a starting point that the whole class builds. And then people have their own individual fear element on top of that.**"

In terms of the class, is twenty-five the number currently participating?

I'm getting the sense the maximum class size is twenty-five. Currently there are fourteen participants.

Rona, have you ever incarnated on the planet Earth?

"**Yes.**"

Are you actually physically on the planet now and teaching?

No, she's just teaching.

How many lifetimes roughly? Had you gone through before earning this accreditation?

Two numbers come to mind. Thirty-seven, the other is nine hundred.

Thirty-seven lifetimes on Earth and nine hundred lifetimes overall?

I think so.

Can she give me a thumbs up or thumbs down?

It's a thumbs up.

I understand because we have a lot more lifetimes than we're aware of. And so I appreciate you being so succinct and precise. In terms of Andrew's journey, what does he need to focus on in terms of letting go of his fear?

The image I'm getting is of rolling with the environment as opposed to fighting. The specific image in relation to this course is that people think they have to do a whole bunch of steering, but you can actually master the course by simply letting yourself roll down the whole course.

A bit like Luke, in Star Wars trust his instincts and trusts himself?

That conjures up an image of still too active. I think what this is simply saying is it's like, changing your attitude, it's sort of "enjoy the ride."

How often does Andrew participate in this class?

I'm getting a sense that every so often "he needs reminding." So it's a course he has to keep on taking, but it's not an everyday thing. It's when he forgets.

Are you familiar with me? Or my work?

Another thumbs up.

In my work, I've run into other teachers and had conversations with other teachers. Do you feel like this is a valuable tool for people to understand that they can communicate with these teachers?

I'm getting like a mixed message that for some people, it like helps them roll, they can relax. And then for some people, it's a distraction. And for some it could become an obsession. So it depends on the person. They could be too busy focusing on the flip side to actually enjoy the experience on the planet.

What's a way that I can include some kind of instruction or direction in that way to remind people what would be something to remind them the reason they signed up for their planet or signed up for their lifetime or their bobsled? Is there anything I could say?

I'm getting a sense to remind them how silly they're going to feel when they kind of get to the flipside and they've learned nothing, done nothing. A little bit like a child who's like, you know, you kind of at the end of the summer holidays, you go back to school and you report on what you did during the summer holidays. And you don't want to be the kid that just did homework all summer holidays.

You don't want to be the kid who just reports they did homework over the summer. That's annoying. Thank you Rona. What does Rona symbolize or represent?

This is really weird because but the image Rolling Stone came to my mind.

Rolling down the river or a rolling stone. Rona. Is there anything that Andrew can do in life that will help him consciously overcome fear?

I'm getting a sense of -- that fear is telling you, you're not listening or you're not ready, so that when you feel fear, you should be asking. "What's the lesson I'm missing? What are they trying to tell me?"

And if we can now escort our friend back to the boat, put him back in the boat on the river. And sort of let him feel sort of the energetic healing light of the universe that he's so eloquently tapped into, while he's sitting on this boat.?

It's really funny. I'm on the boat, but I'm kind of sitting backwards. And this boat is moving at quite some speed. So I'm feeling very uncomfortable with this. Then I'm getting the feeling the word "Trust" came up.

Andrew let's stop the boat. Freeze the boat outside of time. The boat's not moving. You can freeze that frame at any time – look in any direction you want, you can turn around to see where the boat was going.

Okay. That works.

Let's give thanks to everybody that showed up today. Thanks!

*****

Council of Nicea

CHAPTER THIRTEEN: REVEREND WILL

I did a guided meditation with Reverend William's wife. I had never met him prior to this session, but he was aware of my research through his wife. (William is not his real name.)

Rich: So have you ever done any hypnotherapy?

William: No, but let me give you a thumbnail sketch of my journey. I've made my living as a psychotherapist in my adult life. I'm also an Episcopal Priest, and do parish ministry. And now I am doing virtual programs that I do recordings. I work one on one and in groups with people on Zoom, as well. I live on the East Coast. My wife found you through Jennifer Shaffer, the medium you do the podcast with. So my life has been extraordinary. I've done some really neat things, exciting things. I'm turning seventy-four this year, and I'm working as hard as I've ever worked and enjoying it tremendously.

Wow. That's great.

My wife is a true fan of yours. And she's done some work with Jennifer Shaffer. She really thinks that this would be fantastic for me to delve into this. And I do too.

When I first started doing this research skeptics would argue bias, hypnotherapists trying to affect a cure. Difficult to prove an experience isn't cryptomnesia. But eventually, it doesn't matter if the end result is someone is healed.

Right.

Nice to know we have college in Boston in common.

Yes, I was at the Episcopal Theological school on Brattle Street in Cambridge. Graduated from the Boston University School of Social Work in 1975.

I got my BA in Humanities from Boston University in 1978, probably hanging out at same pubs in Kenmore Square.

The other thing I will say, is that in my own journey, I have moved, not completely, obviously, but moved more and more out of my identifications. My, you know, wanting to present myself, as I have moved more into my own authenticity, I have found that more stuff arrives that's not in me, but it's through me.

So what was your first conscious thought that you'll be doing the kind of work you're doing?

When I was probably about four or five, they asked me what I wanted to do. And I said, I want to be a garbage man. "Why do you want to be a garbage man?" Well, I get to ride on the runner of the truck. And I only have to work one day a week, which I thought was brilliant.

If I may, nice metaphor for what you're doing now. Dragging out people's trash, compacting it, and making it disappear.

And I get to work on Sundays. I was told that when I was seven or eight, my mother asked me what I wanted to do. And I said to her, "I want to feel every feeling that any other human being has ever felt."

Do you remember saying it?

I remember feeling it more than I remember saying it.

Have you had any experiences like a near death event, or something where your consciousness was altered, and you saw people, or even a vivid dream?

I have dreams in which my deceased parents will show up a sense of them. My sister who passed away. I remember a couple years ago I went to bed saying, "I want to know who my guardian angel is." I woke up and said aloud "Xander." My wife said, "Pardon me?" I was aware he wrote it in red for me and the X was much bigger than the other letters; Xander.

About a month ago, we were visiting my son, daughter-in-law and granddaughter. I woke up and I said to my wife; "I the worry." She goes, "what?" I said "I the worry. Help me remember that because I'll forget it." She said, "What are you worried about?" I said, No, no, not worry, but *whiri*." Later I looked it up and whiri a braiding technique used by an ancient Polynesian people who ended up in New Zealand and it's how they braided things together to make them stronger.

Well, it turns out that that's exactly what I do in my work. I take different themes that that don't belong together. And I put them together so they cast a new and different light on themselves from the other. I do a lot of work in terms of larger groups. I divide people into triads and give them time to talk about things. So that's another weaving. I had never heard of "whiri" before.

(Note: "Whiri" in Māori is a verb "to braid.")

That's great. By the way, what's your sister's name?

My sister's name is Lindy. My parents Bill and Jean.

That gives me that gives me some parameters and some places for us to visit. Do you ever use meditation in your work?

Oh, God. Yes. All the time.

Let me ask you to picture yourself in a boat on a river. You can close your eyes or not, that's fine. It's up to you. Try to imagine what this boat looks like and what the river looks like. And tell me tell me about the boat.

It's an old steamship. It's going down a river that's quite wide, maybe kind of like the Mississippi or that stature.

Is it a paddle wheel boat?

Yes, it's a paddle wheel boat.

Does this boat seem familiar to you? Or does it seem like new information?

Vaguely familiar.

Where are you on the deck? Are you on near the paddle wheel? Are you at the front?

I'm on the top deck.

And what river are we on?

The Mississippi comes to mind. I don't really see anything on the side. It's all kind of marsh after the river, the banks are kind of marshy. I don't see any houses.

What state are we in?

Mississippi.

If you could just look at your shoes, what color do you have any kind of shoes? Do you have brown shoes? And are you wearing a suit or leisurely clothes?

I'm wearing a dark pants, a lighter shirt, maybe even a white shirt and kind of a leather vest.

Okay, and what's and as we look at this fella, about how old does he look?

He looks about late thirties.

Does he look like a worker? Or does he look like a traveler, a tourist?

Not a worker, perhaps a traveler. Have a neat trimmed brown beard, kind of parted, kind of wavy hair.

Name?

George... Phillips.

(Note: There are a few George Phillips born in Mississippi in the 1800's.)

Let's get him to nod, shrug or shake his head. George, is that your name?

"Yes. I'm his guide."

Are you familiar with my work?

"Yes. You are doing an important service."

George, you're probably aware that this conversation was going to happen today. Is that correct?

"I've been waiting."

I want you to escort William to visit his council, it could be inside or outside.

It's inside. The floor is – there is a circular configuration. And there's a kind of a raised platform that goes all the way around in a circle. It's not wood or marble. It could be stone.

Are there any structural beams or pillars or anything holding this place up?

No, there are just walls around the circle.

I want to thank William's council for allowing us to come and visit with them. How many individuals are here?

Twenty-four.

If I could address William's immediate council. How many people present themselves?

Five.

How are they arrayed? Are they in a line, a circle?

They're in the circle of twenty-four people. They'll just speak from the circle. They're sitting.

Let's go to the first person on your far left. Is that a male, a female or a light?

A male.

First, I want to thank you for allowing us to come and be here. Could you give us a name or a letter so that we can identify you for purposes of discussion?

It's the letter Bee. He's older. He has a trimmed beard that sort of goes down. I don't know how to describe it. He has a receding hairline with dark hair combed back. Brown eyes.

Mr. B, if I could ask you what is your role? Or what's a word that would identify your role on William's council?

"Wisdom."

What's the difference between knowledge and wisdom?

"Wisdom includes being includes the wholeness of being more than just knowledge, which resides in the head."

In terms of your role at William's council, how many other councils do you work on?

"Three."

Do you represent wisdom on all three?

"I represent different facets of wisdom."

Have you ever incarnated on the planet?

"Yes."

So, Mr. B, how's Bill doing?

"He is doing very, very well. He's on the trajectory that he's been called and created to be on."

Could you show Bill some incident in his life where you were involved with helping him?

"I have worked with Bill to help him be transparent in his work. I have specifically worked with him around different occasions, different moments in time when he has been especially transparent, and it's been my work to show him the effect of that on other people."

Are you familiar with my work?

"Yes, I am. My opinion is that this is *the work*. This is the work that helps people to ground in something bigger than their individual lives."

Very interesting to hear it put that way. And it Mr. B, could you introduce us to the person to your left?

"Yes, a woman. She is older, gray hair. Glasses. Her name is… Nora.

Nora. So are you familiar with her? Have you met before?

I don't recognize the image before me.

How do you think William is doing?

"I think William is doing very, very well."

And what do you represent on his council?

"I represent - and not me alone - but I help to represent the feminine aura."

And if you could help us with what that means.

"It's the development of the part of William that knows how to how to yield, how to surrender, how to open, how to be receptive, how to love more deeply, how to nurture."

Is it related to compassion?

"Compassion is part of it. Absolutely."

Have you ever had a lifetime on the planet with William?

"Yes."

Could you put that in his mind? Where are we? Let's just go to a place on the planet when this occurred.

Late 1700's. It looks like England.

Nora, if you could show William what he looked like in that lifetime. Was he a male or a female?

"He was a male. I see him as a young boy. I was an older female. I was his neighbor. And we had a beautiful friendship, he would sometimes wander to my house and have tea, and we would talk."

And is that related to his journey in terms of compassion and listening?

"Absolutely."

So in essence, he's been a listener for quite a few lifetimes?

"Yes."

If you don't mind, could you introduce us to the person to your left. Is that a male, female or light?

A female. Her name is Betsy. And she's five years old.

And what do you represent in William's journey?

"I represent the striving of all people, the attempt on their part, to just make it through life. And my job is to get William's attention. So he sees me. And as he sees me, his capacity for compassion and loving grows."

How many councils do you work with?

"This is my only one."

And have you had a lifetime with Bill before?

"Yes, I have. I was a, a young girl who had great difficulty walking. William lived in the town where I lived. And although we never spoke directly, I knew he saw me. And feeling seen in that way, meant everything to me. It was a previous lifetime, but it wasn't all that long ago."

Let me ask you, Betsy, are you familiar with my work talking to councils?

"No, I'm not."

Why did you choose a lifetime with a physical difficulty? What did you need to learn from that experience?

"I needed to learn how to receive compassion."

In terms of becoming a member of William's council, it's my understanding that people sometimes will join a council based on some event that happened in a previous lifetime, almost like Bill earned your presence. Is that accurate?

"Yes."

His compassion for you, allowed you to become part of his journey?

"Yes."

What's a message you might give to people about seeing people who have physical difficulties?

"Most people simply do not recognize the power of seeing. We look at people and think of their use to us, or how we appear to them. And when one person can truly be so present in in the capacity to truly see another that seeing is healing. It wasn't like I was cured of my difficulty walking, but I was healed on the inside."

That's beautifully put, powerful to hear. Do you mean empathy or putting your stem cells to use?

"It includes some of all of that. But, it's truly letting go of all of our stuff, the stuff that usually runs around in our minds, letting go of that in order to really open to the reality of the other."

Is there any advice that you might want to give to William about his current path?

He's doing precisely what we are guiding him to do.

If you could describe Betsy, what color hair does she have?

Curly brown hair and laughing eyes. She's got a little kind of twinkle in her eye.

Shirley Temple-esque?

Yes.

Betsy, could you introduce us to the person to your left and to William's right?

Yes. This is Albert. Albert is quite tall. And he has white, totally white hair. And a full white beard.

Albert, are you familiar with my work?

"Of course I am."

Well, Betsy, isn't. Fun to see members have mixed awareness. What do you represent a William's council?

"I represent the position of sage."

Tell me about that. How does that work for Bill?

"For me, it has been the accumulation of many lifetimes and I find myself at this point representing sage, the position, the post of sage and it's my job simply to oversee everything."

Do others consider you the spokesperson for this council?

"I'm not the spokesperson, but everybody recognizes my many lifetimes in my post of sage."

And have you had any lifetimes with Bill?

"Yes, I have."

Is there one that you might show him?

Ancient Greece. We're in the countryside outside of Athens but not in the city itself.

And is there anybody in William's awareness, like a name that exists at the same time period.

"Epicurus."

(Note: That would be 341-270 BC. "Epicurus was an ancient Greek philosopher and sage who founded Epicureanism, a highly influential school of philosophy. He was born on the Greek island of Samos to Athenian parents." Epicurus was a prolific writer, writing over 300 books yet only three of his letters survive.)

It's just to give us a time frame and time period. And if you could show Bill what he looked like in that lifetime.

"I knew him in that lifetime as a young maiden."

So where you a follower of Epicurus the philosopher? The term has carried into our time period meaning an afficionado of certain things. Is that accurate?

"Yes, it is."

Was it part of your philosophy to curate your enjoyment of things? Or was it more deep?

"It's deeper than that. I understood life through a reflection of death. That to live well, one needed to learn how to die well."

I'm curious about when you crossed over in that lifetime? You had religious and philosophical beliefs about the afterlife. What was your experience? Was it surprise? Or was it exactly what you thought it would be?

"Oh, it was, it was a surprise on the other side. But everything that led to my death was well planned out."

You're presenting to William as an older person. But in terms of time, I've heard it exists relatively different so that 2500 years ago feels more like last month. Is that accurate assessment of time?

"It's like there are different pockets of time. And the idea that it's one straight linear line is, is very, very superficial. There are pockets, almost like eddies. One can go from one eddy to another eddy, without going through the whole river. So that, yes, you can jump around."

And what about when someone's conscious self runs into someone from an ancient era like yourself. You may be incarnated, and your incarnation may be having a dream accessing your wisdom. How does that work?

"There is an ongoing conversation. It's not just between distinct and separate individuals. It's almost like there's one conversation. And we can tune into it in many different places, in in many different times, and in many different ways."

So when you say you represent sage, do you mean as something related to history?

"It's related to completion. I oversee completion. And my, my perspective, helps to bring things to a certain completion."

If I may, you're like the author who helps people to finish the third act of the play that they signed up for?

"Yes. But it's not necessarily a conclusion or an ending, a completion. I help people find the fullness in where they are and in what they're doing. And that that could be the final act. But that isn't necessarily the ending."

Like a playwright sort of helping people see what the themes have been throughout all the plays, they've performed it. Could introduce us to the person to your left and Bill's right. Is that a male or female or light?

It is a male. His name is Jonathan.

Are you familiar with my work?

"Yes, I am. It is so important, and this work aids, Albert's job of completion, to see the fullness of things, and the and the in the rightness of things."

What do you represent on William's council?

"I represent "love.""

How would you define love?

"Love is certainly much more than a human feeling, or sentiment, it is an acknowledgement of the true validity. And a justification of the other to be able to embrace the other in their fullness and their authenticity, without needing to have this person be what I need them to be, or to fulfill any of my needs."

People have talked about the experience of unconditional love when they get back home, as they call it. And if you could just sort of let us know what your opinion is about that idea of unconditional love.

"It's where we come from. And it's where we're going. And the job of each developing evolving human life is to begin to taste that and to enact that more and more."

Have you ever incarnated on the planet?

"Yes. I have many times many times and also with William."

If you could put one of those lifetimes into William's mind.

"The late fifth century in Italy, outside of Rome. William and I were true, dear friends."

What was the purpose of that lifetime?

"To look beyond striving to look beyond accomplishment. To look beyond success."

And was it a difficult lifetime?

"The times were uncertain. There was a shifting and some thought a collapse of civilization. And Bill himself what was indeed very successful, very prominent. But in our friendship, I helped him learn and he helped me learn that there's more to life than success."

Jonathan, how many councils are you on?

"I am on ten."

Do you represent love on all those different councils?

"I do."

I've heard this term "Love, love." The idea of loving what love is, what love could be. And I've also heard that love is the key to everything in the universe. What's your opinion about that?

"Both are profoundly true. In order to get there, it's not just that we have to climb some sort of ladder to achieve the possibility of love. What we need to do is much more surrender some of the things that get in the way. Because although many don't know it, we are made for love. That's what we're created for. And as things and other ideas build up in our mind, that gets covered over. So the path to love is not one of achievement. It's one of surrender."

I've also heard this concept that in order to experience God, one can open their heart to everyone and all things. Is that accurate?

"Of course, it's accurate, because God is the summation, and the spirit within absolutely everything. You don't have to go anywhere to find God, you just have to tune in. And wherever you are, and, and on whomever your gaze falls, that is the divine."

In that construct, God is in everything, and in everyone. And everywhere. Is that related to consciousness or to, let's say, dark energy for lack of a term energy that's, you know, that make the sort of the medium that is the universe?

"It is what life is."

It's hard for people to wrap their minds around because of the separation, we constantly go through boxing things up. Is this something that you helped build with in his work?

"I have taught him this, and others have taught him this."

Let's go back to that moment when Bill was eight years old, and saying something along these lines, was that you tapping him on the shoulder? Or was that his own creation?

"That was the fullness of the council. We were we were all participating, leaning in towards him in that moment, trying to set him on up a path a trajectory, where he could fulfill his deepest longings and highest calling."

Just in terms of storytelling, and how things work out, I'd guess that other councils try to help people with that sort of thing, but they miss it, or they don't hear it, or the trajectory goes in a different way. Is that correct?

"Yes, and the individual may only be ready to take in some of the teachings and not all the teachings. Where we have we have many

lifetimes and we're learning over all these lifetimes. Some are younger than others. And they haven't had the same number of lifetimes to learn. And some have experienced lifetimes that are very, very difficult and it's hard to learn things. Although often times great learning comes from hardship. But all councils are working towards this kind of purpose. And in doing what they can."

George, I wonder if we can maybe converse with some other friends that Bill is aware of; is that possible?

"Sure."

First, I'd like to talk to Xander. If that's possible, is there a Xander in his journey?

There is a Xander. Xander has darker skin, is tall and thin.

Have you had a lifetime with Bill?

"Yes, I have. We are on a slave plantation. It's in Mississippi."

How does Bill look in this memory?

"Bill is a small black child."

And are you related to Bill, Xander?

"No, I'm the plantation owner."

And what was the purpose of Bill's lifetime on this slave plantation?

"To understand what it feels like not to be free, not to be free in one way, but to learn to be free in other ways."

And let me ask you Xander, was your role? Was it a negative role in his lifetime? Or was it a positive one?

"We went through what all slave owners and slaves go through. But Bill taught me something, something that I had to keep secret my whole life."

What was that secret?

"I saw the freedom in his eyes. And I learned from him how to be free, even though I was the slave owner."

So if you could put it in Bill's mind why, what that was about when you appeared to him in a dream, were you just stopping by to say hello?

"I function as a kind of agent for his council. I'm a bit of a go-between, between the council and Bill."

When Bill is in the midst of doing something or on a journey or trying to figure something out, and he needs help from one of the council member, you work as a go between?

"I do."

Are you like one of his guides or a primary guide?

"I am a primary guide."

So George is a friend and somebody who helped us to access the council today?

"Yes."

Xander. Were you the one who put the word Whiri into his mind?

"Oh, yes. Oh yes."

What were you talking about?

"I was just showing him in a delightful fun way of reflecting to him what he was doing, but using something that he was completely unfamiliar with."

So that he would remember it so that when he woke up, he'd have this completely new word?

"That he would be reminded to look beneath the surface."

And to clarify, the "whiri" is like rope?

"It's like braiding. It's stronger in the braid than it could be with a single strand, or even a double strand, or with three strands if they weren't braided."

And in terms of those braids, if you could just focus on that for a second, are they a representative of something symbolic? What are they?

Yes. We tend to look at things in an individual lives kind of way. And the way we do that in this modern life of ours in that we take what we think is an individual thing and hold it up to the light in order to see and understand what it is. But when you can put two things in relation to each other, they seem to bring forth something beyond what either one of them could be on their own. And they reflect a different kind of reality to each other. And when you can do that with three, you get a whole new reality that emerges and a whole new understanding of those three different things than you could if you saw them separately. It could be anything. It's not that there are specifically three that need to be combined. It is it is the combination process itself the braiding process itself, that is so important."

Thank you Xander. What does Bill need to see or visit?

"I'd like to show him how he has touched and is touching other people."

So what would be a visualization of that?

"It's a sunset. It all is evident in a sunset. The beauty, the serenity, the completeness of a sunset is a manifestation reflects Bill's work in this life."

Is Bill a fan of sunsets?

"Yes and sunrises and moonrises and the whole thing."

Could you take him to his place of healing?

"It's a forest. It is a lot of trees. It's a lush, moist, deep, luxuriant forest."

Can you go up to one of the trees and put your arms around it?

"I can feel the vibrational connectedness of everything that is there, through that one tree."

Is there any kind of sentience with this tree?

"Oh, of course."

And is that a male or female?

"It's somehow a combination."

If I may ask this tree a question. What's a way that we humans can be in touch with you?

"Be rooted, be rooted in the earth. Put your hands up to heaven and know that you are the intermediary between heaven and earth."

What do you recommend humans do to alter the deleterious effects of climate change?

"Share. Stop accumulating, stop striving, care about those around you. It's so incredibly simple."

Was there a time in human history where we could communicate with trees and we've lost it?

"Of course."

What precipitated that change?

"The change was necessary. We had to let go of that feminine connectedness and embeddedness in nature, to grow our intellect. What we need to do now is not abandon our intellect but recover that sense of the nature, connect that with this fantastic intellect that we have created so that there can be a linkage, a connection between the differentiated parts."

What is a way for humans to connect with that idea conceptually?

"Jonathan would tell you it's love. And the way you get to love is not by climbing but by surrendering. So meditation helps let go of things, to surrender some things and that can be very useful but the answer to your question is love."

Before we go Xander, let's bring his sister Lindy forward. Can we do that?

"Yes. She's been she's been waiting."

Lindy, tell us a little bit about your journey. Who was there to greet you when you crossed over?

"All of the ancestors and our mother and our father. It was incredibly happy."

What have you been doing? Where have you been hanging out? Who do you spend time with?

"I can't describe it to you because we wouldn't be able to understand it."

Have you been keeping an eye on Bill?

"Oh, I always keep my eye on him."

Is there any kind of incident or something that you can put in his mind that he's not quite aware of where you stopped by to say hello?

"Well, (my brother) Bill helped me to die. And I asked him to help me because I didn't have a clue. And in my life, I was pretty tight and in my own constructed box. But I knew I wouldn't be able to die from within that position. So I asked Bill to help. And he did. My months, my weeks of dying were the happiest weeks of my life. I felt free and unencumbered in a way that I never imagined that I could."

What was it like for you to see your parents Bill and Jean again on the flipside?

"All the misunderstandings just melted away. All the disappointments and misgivings; all of that was gone. And I saw in them their deep love for me and my love for them."

And Lindy if I can ask you just to access this experience when you chose Bill and Jean as your parents, or agreed to participate. What visual comes to mind?

"I suppose it's a little bit like planning a hike, you can kind of look at a map and kind of imagine how it's going to be. But when you really start traveling, it's all brand new and full of all kinds of surprises."

So even though you might have the map, suddenly you come across a bear or you come across something you didn't expect to be there? Did you accomplish what you set out to do?

"I did. And more. I did and more. My journey was about first creating a box. And then learning how to be deconstruct the box. But at the learning was a steep, steep learning curve in the last weeks of my life."

In terms of planning were you aware on the map that there was going to be this steep cliff before you got to the end?

"No, no. When you're living your life, you basically don't have access to the plan. You're just living your life. There is a plan when things get started. But once life goes into motion, you're not aware of the plan."

Are you aware of Bill's plan? Or is that something you're not really allowed to talk about?

"Oh I know Bill's plans. Quite obvious; always was."

Is there anything you want to show Bill? Something you can pop into his mind?

"Yes."

I mention it because it's new information. Not something Bill expected to hear today. Xander, let me ask you about the design of your logo that appeared in William's vision. Why did you specifically choose red letters?

"Red is the color of blood. But red is the color of joy as well. I wanted to make it distinctive, so he couldn't simply find the writing in the fonts on his computer."

Xander, have you incarnated again since your journey with Bill?

"No, I haven't."

Are you kind of waiting for Bill to come back so you guys can work out another scenario?

"That remains to be seen."

So Xander if you don't mind, could I have the lottery numbers for this Friday's lotto?

He's laughing. He laughed.
*****

Another council of Nicea

CHAPTER FOURTEEN: MIRELLA

Mirella reached out to me after doing a session with the medium Jennifer Shaffer. (JenniferShaffer.com) (Mirella is not her real name.)

MIRELLA: My family is from Lebanon, originally from Turkey but family is originally from Armenia. I am currently living in a midwestern city.

RICH: Have you ever chatted with your council?

No. I feel people around me, especially as I'm trying to fall asleep. I'll feel a presence swaying. At one point, I was so tired, I was like, "just stop."

I've heard that. I think you just tell them, "You're allowed to come here. But you're not allowed to wake me up!"

I always say "Meet me for coffee." I'll go downstairs and they never show up.

Oh, that's funny. So who are these folks? Friends?

I don't know.

But when I asked that question, what comes to mind?

Like either my soul cluster or like my ancestor.

Have you done meditation before?

Yes.

So this is a very simple meditation. Picture yourself in a boat on a river. You can close your eyes or keep them open, it doesn't matter. Whatever feels most comfortable for you. What's the boat look like?

Painted white. Bent wood. Formed wood with like a cross bracing.

What's the water look like?

A still lake. There are trees on the shore. It's pretty dark out but it's a comfortable place.

I'm going to ask your guide to come forward and sit across from you on the boat. When I say that what comes to mind a male, female or a light?

Hard to tell; it's a form. I'm seeing a triangle at the top.

I'm going to ask your guide to manifest as a male or a female or light for purpose of our conversation.

Okay. I'm seeing a light, slightly feminine features, about seven feet tall. It's hard to keep it from fading into a mass of light.

What color is the light?

Golden.

I'm going to assume your guide knows what I'm doing or approves of what we're doing. So I'm going to ask if it's okay to have a conversation. She can nod, shake her head or shrug.

The light got bigger.

I'm going to take that as an okay. Reach over and take hold of her hand or hands. Describe what that feels like. Are her hands cold, warm, soft, or hard?

Cold.

I'm going to ask her to warm up her hands please. See if she responds - can you do that for her?

(She nods.) They're warmer.

Okay, thank you. It's a way of showing she can respond to what we ask. So what's a name or a letter we might use to address you? What's the first name or letter that pops in your mind?

M.

"The Divine Miss M," thank you for allowing us to have this conversation. Have you ever incarnated?

"Yes."

Have you ever incarnated with our friend?

"No."

Are you familiar with my work?

"Yes."

Can you take us to visit her council? Are we inside or outside?

Inside. The floor is marble, dark marble. It's almost like they're in deep space…

When I ask how many people are there, what comes to mind?

Eight. In a semi-circle. They're sitting down.

Let's go to the first person to the far left. Is this a male a female or a light?

The image is fleeting.

A male or female presence?

"Female. Almost ageless."

267

Is there a name or a letter we can use to address you?

"Kay."

Miss Kay, what do you represent or her council?

"Healing."

Have you ever incarnated on the planet?

I'm not getting a yes or no.

(Note: When I don't get an answer to a direct question, I move to questions that are simple, or are opinion.)

How's our friend doing?

"She's getting there."

How many conversations have you had with her?

"I talk to her all the time."

What form of healing do you represent?

"Spiritual."

In terms of her healing abilities, what do you want to tell her to do?

"Trust."

Miss Kay, would you introduce us to the person to your left?

A male. Between fifty and eighty. No hair.

What do you represent on her council?

"Humor."

How many councils do you work with?

"Hundreds."

And in terms of Mirella, how she doing?

"Great."

So that's a little different than "getting there." What's a name or a letter we can use to address you?

"Han."

Have you ever incarnated on the planet, Han?

"Many, many times."

Have you ever incarnated with our friend?

"No."

Please put one of your lifetimes you had that was particularly fruitful, or humorous or funny.

I'm seeing Asia. Rural, mountainous with lots of trees. About 500 A.D.

What did you accomplish in that lifetime that made you think of it? What was the journey?

"Calmness and also humor."

Almost like you can endure a lot if you've laughed at it?

"Yes."

I've heard that laughter is a fast way to change a person's disposition.

"Right."

Correct me if I'm wrong, Han. You're always connected to her?

"Yes."

Could introduce this to the person to your left?

(Aside) Every time I switch people I keep getting a flash of like a Nefertiti like persona.

Well let's examine that for a moment. Is this somebody on her council? Or is this somebody that is trying to get her attention?

Something they want us to look at.

Who here on this council of eight represents like the lead council person or the spokesperson? And if they could come if she could go over to see them? Is that a male or a female?

A light. Yellow at the top. And a white point at the bottom. Like a feathering of light that comes with a point.

Where is this person on your council, in the middle or the end?

Towards the right. The image is turning into feathers actually.

What feathers are associated with this visual? A bird?

An eagle.

Try not to judge it. Would be a name or a letter that we can use for reference you?

"Jay."

And what do you represent under council?

"Wisdom."

Could give us a definition of wisdom versus knowledge?

"Wisdom isn't something learned; it exists and unto itself. Knowledge is something you gain."

(Note: It's a question I've asked often in this book and the answers is always the same.)

How many councils do you sit on?

"A lot. More than one hundred."

My question is "What's up with this memory. Was that related to a lifetime you'd like her to examine? Something to do with Egypt?"

(Note: An image of Nefertiti; instead of examining if it's specific, I ask about the era the image represents.)

"Yes."

Who's going to help us talk about this? So let's just take a minute to examine this lifetime. Show her what she looked like in that lifetime. Tall or short?

She is thin and tall. Covered hair, she's wearing it short and it is covered. She has black hair and is wearing red lipstick. She's about thirty-four.

Is she wearing any jewelry?

A ring.

Let's take a look at that ring. Is there any drawing on it? Or carving?

It's a big light. Like amethyst. And there's like a gold notch that's pulled together. Her middle finger.

So where are we on the planet?

Africa. I was African.

What's the name of the country today that we would associate with this time period?

Sudan.

Let's look at the color of your skin. Is it golden, brown, or black?

It's black.

So if you can just reach over and take a hold of her hands, tell me what is the feeling or emotion?

"Trust."

What year is this?

I'm getting fourteen... or one hundred and forty-one.

Before or after the common era, before or after Christ was on the planet?

"Before. 141 B.C.E."

So is there a city associated with this?

"Khartoum."

(Note: Khartoum is the capital of The Sudan.)

Are we in a royal family of some sort?

Yes. The ruler.

A princess or royal family member?

A Queen.

How did she achieve that? Through her bloodline?

"Through sabotage. Somebody took over for her, got her out of the way."

Let's go to the last day of that lifetime. What's happening? How was she killed?

(Aside.) I'm just going to trust this. "It was someone else in the family that had somebody that was her servant poison her."

So poisoning from a servant?

"Yes. It was because she wasn't going to keep doing things the old-fashioned way. It's almost like she was too strong."

Why did you choose this lifetime? What was the lesson the primary lesson you're supposed to learn?

"Resilience."

How does this resilient lifetime relate to our friend's current lifetime now? Why are you showing it to her?

"She needs to see the strength she once had."

Can you transfer some of that strength to her?

"Yes."

What was her name?

"Rania."

I think Rania means Queen in some languages.

(Note: Rania means Queen in Sanskrit, Arabic "glittering" in Hebrew, "One who sings" or "Song of God" and in Greek; "Heavenly.")

I think she was supposed to be the Queen.

Well, let's do this – imagine that Rania is standing opposite you. And have her transfer some of that royal energy into you, that strength. Can you feel that?

"Yes."

So let's just talk a little bit about this kind of feeling of because Rania, you lived over two thousand years ago. What does it feel like for you? Talking to us now?

"Feels slow."

I've heard this before that twenty-five years on earth feels like five to ten minutes over there. So in essence, you lived two thousand some years ago. So that would feel like to you, like last week. Does it feel that way to you?

"Correct." She keeps making me feel her nausea for some reason.

Well, that's the memory of the poison?

"Yes."

Alright, so Rania let's do a meditation. We know the poison doesn't exist, that body no longer exists. Your body suffered through it. But then you went home. Correct?

I'm feeling angry, like this happened because they wanted her to feel like she was wrong.

But your meditation today is to let go of that anger. It doesn't serve you. You don't need to hold on to it. You can set it aside you can always tap into it if you need it. For purposes of our conversation. Just let all that go.

Yes. I'm sensing like, here's that pain and then with the transfer that you asked for, I'm watching it subside.

Are you familiar with my work?

Now I am.

Let's ask what's up with the person that appeared in her bed? Who is that?

Her grandpa.

Thank you, Ranie. We're going to shift over to grandpa for a minute. What's his name?

Hieronymus.

What a great name. How old does he look in this visual?

Sixty.

How's our friend Mirella doing?

"Very well."

Put your hands in her hands. And how do his hands feel?

Strong.

So why did you stop by? To let her know that you've always got her back?

"Yes."

Let me ask him, who was there to greet you when you crossed over?

"My brother."

And was that a happy reunion?

"Yes, happy."

Allow me to ask this question that Mirella isn't aware of. Are you taking any classes?

"Always."

I want you to put in Mirella's mind your favorite class. And just show her. Are we inside or outside?

"Inside."

How many people are in this room?

"Seven."

Look around the room. Can you see the teacher?

"I see the teacher because I am the teacher."

What is the class subject? What will we call it in the syllabus?

"Love and Knowing."

So the subtitle for this class might be "love and knowing the energy of connectivity" something like that?

"Yes. The energy of connectivity. Sure, call it that."

Okay. But the reason I ask it is because the class is about how people connect. Is that correct?

"Correct."

So, when you say the class is about love, what do you mean?

"It's like learning to feel okay. Learning to heal. Healing others."

Empathy, compassion, stepping into somebody else's shoes? So stepping into somebody else's shoes would demonstrate connectivity. I rarely meet a teacher who's a relative. Do you teach other classes?

"Just this one."

Is there anybody in the room that she recognizes that might be one of one of your students?

One of his daughters, actually.

That's an unusual thing to visualize. Is she on the planet or off?

She is not on the planet.

One of your daughters. So this would make her Mirella's aunt. Let's talk to her for a second. What do you want to tell her about her journey from your perspective now?

"Trust yourself, live your truth. It's not always gonna make sense because it's new (information)."

Who did you meet when you crossed over?

"My father."

So please, if we could ask for Mirella's dad to stop by. And let's put him in the boat. How old is he?

In his forties. Linen shirt, beige pants. He's wearing three necklaces. Red, blue and gold.

Is this clothing that you know or have seen him wear before?

No.

So this is new information. Could you tell us his name?

Hagop. It's Armenian.

Hello Hagop. Tell us, what's the significance of those necklaces? What do they represent?

"Friendship."

Did you earn them in your lifetime?

"Yes."

How's your daughter doing Hagop?

"Amazing."

Who was there to greet you when you crossed over?

"Drago. My father."

At what point did you realize that what you had been told about an afterlife was different?

"Right away. It's like a recollection."

So what do you think about your dad hanging out in Mirella's house, waking her up at night?

(Mirella aside) He says he's there sometimes, too.

How do you physically manifest jewelry or things that she can see?

He was a jeweler. So it's not hard for him to create.

So what are the necklaces made out of?

They are stones, then like… wrapped in gold.

How is it that you can create things? What's the process?

It's almost like he doesn't want to, but I don't know how to describe it. Like "I try it. I'm always there. But I try not to take up space." But he doesn't want to disturb me.

Can you take her to her place of healing? Are we inside or outside?

Inside a place that seems religious, like a small part of a cathedral. Like they showed me the shape of a dome. "She's been there many, many, many times."

Are there any objects in there?

Water. It kind of just flows. I don't know where it comes from.

Walk into it. How far up your legs does it go?

To my waist. I can't tell if it's like cold or hot because it's like more pure energy.

This would be the place to reconnect with the higher self. Where would Mirella normally go after that?

"You go back to work."

To work, meaning she go and hangs out with her classmates and teachers?

"Wherever the work is."

Yes, well, the work that you do is healing. It's a healing kind of work that you've been doing for many years and continue to do and now you're tapping into. Is there anything that she needs to focus on?

"Trust what you're hearing, trust what you're given. You're learning to do it more and more."

*****

"There are things known and there are things unknown, and in between are the doors of perception."

Aldous Huxley

CHAPTER FIFTEEN: LILIAN

Lilian is a friend from Argentina. We were having a general discussion about some dreams she had of her boyfriend, who passed away. I suggest we see if we can do a meditation about those dreams.

Rich: We are in Manhattan Beach at an outdoor cafe. So we're going to play a game. And there are no right or wrong answers. There's only whatever comes to mind. Now, have you done any meditation?

Lilian: No.

You mentioned having a dream about your boyfriend Mark who passed away. And you were walking on a bridge where you got separated. Is he walking next to or in front of you?

He's standing near me.

I want you to walk over and stand in front of him.

Okay, I'm opposite him. The moment (in the dream) when he let my hands free.

Freeze that frame. Just roll the frame back a second. Before your hands let go. Sort of move over and look at him. And now describe how tall is he? Is he taller than you?

Is a bit taller than me. And he's got a little beard the color of his hair. His eyes are green.

What does it feel like to hold his hand? What emotion comes to mind?

Security. Love.

Unconditional Love?

Yes. A feeling of home. (She cries)

What clothing is he wearing?

I see him in a T shirt, jeans.

I'm going to ask Mark some questions. Do you mind answering them for me?

"Go ahead."

Who was there to greet you when you cross over?

"My mother."

Was that a happy reunion or were you shocked?

"Happy but expected."

Was I correct in the assessment you knew it wasn't meant to be that plan you had with Lilian?

"I see now it wasn't."

So your mom was the first person to greet you?

"Yes."

Have you seen other friends and family?

"Yes."

Was your journey planned in advance? Did it work out the way it was supposed to?

"You don't need to plan ahead when the pieces came together."

Okay, so what's up with you leaving early? What was that about?

"I needed to leave Lilian free."

Have you guys had a lifetime before?

"No."

So you you're not aware of any lifetime that you and she have had together.

I'm seeing a little baby. A beautiful baby.

Mark, is this a visual of her from when you knew her before?

"Yes."

When did you plan to meet up?

What comes to my mind is when I was born that year.

So you knew her before she came to the planet?

Correct.

Put in Lillian's mind where the two of you lived together before.

Like an island surrounded by water. I'm getting Australia.

Mark, I want you to show her what you look like in that lifetime.

Taller, blonder and wider.

And were you a wealthy person or worker type person.

Someone working with nature.

Mark, I heard you worked with snakes. Is this part of that journey, working with animals in another country?

"Yes."

What year was this?

"Nineteen sixty-three."

How many lifetimes have you guys had together?

Eight.

Did you put us together today Mark?

"Yes."

And what does she need to know about your journey here?

That I regret not having spent more time with her. It was intense because it was the best part of my life.

In essence, you showed up during the second act of her life, as opposed to the first half of this play. And this was the best time for you to be together with her. Correct?

"Yes."

Okay.. And so now, have you tried to reach out to her before?

"She was in too much pain, and complaining too much about me leaving her."

But now?

"Now it's better because she can hear me."

What's the best method for her to access you like meditation or being in a quiet place?

"In church."

Mark is what you are saying is that you will always with her on some level?

"Yes. I will never leave her. I will provide for her."

Well that's new information. When you say provide, speaking financially, also emotionally as well?

"Yes."

So what does she need to focus on in her life that's going to help her? What does she need to focus on?

"To be happy without me."

Can you show her that place of healing place, where she goes in between lives to be healed; is it inside or outside?

It's in the clouds.

Describe the feeling you're having while here?

Peacefulness, silence. Happiness, gratitude.

Let me ask you, is visiting Lillian's council an important thing for her to do or should we save that for another time?

"That's important."

So would you walk her in to her council?

"Yes."

Are we inside or outside?

Inside. There are marble floors.

How many people can you see in here?

Twenty.

I'm looking for a core group of individuals that we can speak with on Lillian's council

Five. Some are lined up in front.

Go to the first person on the far left of this line of five. Is that a male or a female?

A woman with long hair. She's fifteen or sixteen.

Thank you for allowing us to ask you some questions. Are you familiar with my work?

She says, "Yes, everyone here is."

And is that because of Lillian's awareness?

"In part. But also not in part."

What's the other part? People talking around the water cooler?

"They know about it."

May I ask for a name or a letter to address you?

She says, "Her name is *Jean*." (French pronunciation)

Jean, nice to meet you. What word represents your role on her council?

"Familiarity."

Do you mean in terms of recognizing frequency or recognizing people?

"Frequencies is a good term."

How many other councils are you involved in?

"Twelve."

Do you function in that same role on those other councils?

"Depending on the person and how much the person needs to heal."

Let me ask you, how do you think Lillian's doing?

"It's hard for us."

And do we see light at the end of the tunnel for her?

"Yes."

Would you introduce us to the person to your left? Is that a male or a female?

A male. He looks about thirty-five.

May I ask you some questions? What's a name or a letter we can use to reference you?

"Jay."

And how do you think our friend is doing Mr. Jay?

"It's been hard. People will help her. They're clearing obstacles."

You're familiar with the research, what's your opinion of it?

"You are helping people with your books."

Let's go to the person on your left.

She is a black woman in her 20's.

What's a name we can address you with?

"Miriam."

Thank you. Miriam, what do you represent on Lilian's council?

"Balance."

How many councils do you sit on?

"A few."

Have you ever incarnated on the planet?

"Once."

Would you show that to Lilian?

"In Italy... as a white person."

Thank you... Was it with Lillian?

"No."

And how is Lillian doing balance wise?

"She's going to get through this. She is going to get her balance back."

What's a way for her to do that?

"Through her friends. And I will help her with this. I will support her."

Miriam. Interesting name. Are you related to the famous Miriam of biblical fame?

"In a way."

Are you related to Miriam of Magdala or that Miriam who had a child in a manger. Are you aware of them?

"I wasn't aware of them until I came."

You weren't aware of them until you came to Earth and incarnated? Have you run into Jesus since then?

"Yes. Between lives."

Do you mind if we ask him to make an entrance? Please describe what you're seeing.

(Note: If I have the opportunity to ask Jesus questions, I always try to ask the same ones.)

(Pause) I'm seeing he's here. He has shoulder length hair. His eyes are deep brown.

Look carefully. Is there any other color in his eyes?

"Yes. Light." (Pauses) His smile is the most reassuring thing in the world.

Would you take hold of Lillian's hand? And now describe what you're feeling? Does it have that same kind of familiarity that you had with Mark?

It is the same.

A feeling of being home? Or of unconditional love?

Yes. Both.

This is a question for Jesus, but Lillian won't know what I'm asking. What do you think of this book that I wrote that Lillian doesn't know about?

"It's a book that will help a lot of people. Some of the things you say are not... it's mainly more for interpretation. But on the whole, it's a book that will help a lot of people."

It does help people to address you, and not only as an avatar and somebody who can heal people, but also as a person who still exists that they can contact. Are you aware that I tell people that you still exist, that you that you can communicate with them? Is that annoying to you?

"No, it's not annoying. And telling people is like "you're spreading the gospel."

(Note: Gospel means "good news." In that sense, I suppose it is.)

The Gospel according to Martini? Okay.

He's smiling. He says, "It's a good thing."

Because I do tell a lot of people just talk to you directly. "Ask Jesus."

"That is the best thing people should know. That we can communicate."

I've quoted you as saying the Bible is metaphor. Is that an accurate quote?

"It is metaphor. But at the same time, the reality is so big, that it's not easy, even for the church, to explain it as it is."

Now, well, let me ask you, is there anyone in the church that's aware that you exist this way and can converse with you in this way?

"Many, many do.. but they don't admit it or confess it, because then the hardest or the most conservative part of the church would be against it."

Does Pope Francis talk to you? Do you have conversations with him?

"He was the chosen one."

But we know how he got chosen. At the same time, he seems like a very interesting fellow. It seems like heart as in the right place, but do you converse with them? Are friends with him?

"I am a great friend of his. I lead him. He started the change that is needed for the church."

Okay. Well, you and I have had conversations about this before. The story of your life is incomplete. But I've asked you many times and you've said, "The truth sets everyone free."

"That is true. I know this will provoke a great crack inside the church. Many people will feel disappointed."

Okay, but truth sets people free even for the disappointed. What do you want to tell our friend Lilian? The idea that she can see you and talk to you at any time is it must be a revelation for her.

"She always knew."

We talk about opening your heart to other people. Certainly, we're talking about a metaphor of compassion. But is the heart center, something to do with consciousness? It's a science question.

"Yes, certainly."

So consciousness is connected to the heart as well as the brain. Is that correct? Or is it more heart than brain?

"Yes. But it's also a metaphor. Because the heart is an organ and what we put in the heart is what is really important."

What do you mean by that? We've heard from a guide that "God is beyond the capacity of the human brain to comprehend. However, if you open your heart to everyone in all things, you can experience God."

"Anyone can experience God if they open their hearts."

But that would imply that God is not a person, but more a medium, like opening yourself to the ocean, or consciousness.

"Well don't forget. I'm God as well."

Very funny. In that construct yes, we all are. Jesus, I want to talk to you about the Trinity for a minute. So what is the Trinity? Father, Son? And what?

"The Holy Ghost."

Let's just talk about the clarification of the Holy Trinity.

"Nobody could clarify (that) for the human brain."

Originally written as Pneuma in Aramaic and Greek, then Spiros or spirare in Latin which means "to breathe." So originally it was Father, Son, and Holy Breath. Breath or pneuma seems to be a metaphor for consciousness. So we're really talking about Father, Son and Consciousness. Is that correct?

"Perfectly right."

That's fun to hear.

"This era, we should call this period "When we feel you know which way to go, it makes you feel more conscious about where you are."

Thank you sir. And is there anybody else in the council that needs to talk to us?

It's like a little kid.

A little kid. All right. Let's invite him to come forward. And who are you sir? Have a boy or girl.

It's a girl. Maisie.

Nice to meet you Maisie. How old is she?

Five.

Maisie are you part of Lilian's council?

She has wings.

You represent somebody on Lillian's council, is that correct?

Yes.

What is your role in a word on Lilian's Council?

"Keeping the flame of innocence alive. I'm in charge of not letting it die."

Maisie, have you ever incarnated on the planet?

"No."

So can we call you an angel? Is that the word we should use to refer to you?

"It's close. Almost correct."

I'm clarifying. Have you ever incarnated anywhere else? That's my question.

"No, but maybe I will incarnate."

So it's a possibility for you. Why would you do that?

"To Learn. To learn and grow."

Let me ask you about your wings. A physical manifestation of a metaphor? Or a real thing?

"**Light.**"

Let me ask you, Maisie, is this a construct that you created to represent speed or speed of light or speed of thought?

"**It's something I created, it's a construct.**"

Is it a metaphor that represents the fact that you can, correct me if I'm wrong, you can move between realms?

"**That's right.**"

And how do you do that?

"**I go because I want to go.**"

When you go do you shift your energy or your frequency? Or do you actually go to a location and like, going through a portal or something?

"**I shift my energy.**"

About how many realms do you have access to?

"**Five.**"

(Note: An interesting conversation. I'm asking an "angel" to describe the process of movement between realms. She says she has access to five, that she could incarnate if she wanted to, that the wings are metaphor for light.)

You can traverse five different realms? How many more realms are there?

"**A few more.**"

What is your occupation in each of these realms? Are you healing? Are you helping?

"**Supervising. Who needs help? Who needs to grow or learn?**"

Let's focus on this realm because I understand this one better. If you're going to help somebody, how would you do it? Would you orchestrate events around them to change or would you work with their frequency directly?

"Depends. For most I work with the frequency of the body, if this takes too long or doesn't work, as I expected, I can help by physically making things happen."

So what you're saying is, that sometimes you try to intervene with somebody, and they don't respond. And why is that? Is it because of their humaneness?

"They don't vibrate at that frequency. They don't want, they don't vibrate at the frequency, that they need me to address."

When you show up to help them, they're not aware of you, they can't see you. Because they don't believe they can?

"When they don't perceive it, they don't perceive it."

Do you slow down your frequency to theirs?

"Yes. I have to."

And just as an example, how much do you slow down? By half, by a third? More?

"About a third, roughly."

So correct me if I'm wrong. Someone is in need; you want to help or you're called to help. You lower your frequency to show up. Are you communicating with their higher consciousness, their soul or higher consciousness? Are you communicating with the person inside the body?

"Their higher consciousness."

I really appreciate you answering these questions. And I know Lili is not really aware of what I'm asking in terms of frequency. So you're talking to the higher self, even then they may not be able to figure out what you're telling them.

"Many are blinded from outside things."

When you stop to help somebody, are you trying to generate some form of love or unconditional love?

"Yes. That is the key, that's a key foundation, without it it's impossible."

So love is the key to consciousness, it's the key to life. That's amazing. And so someone who resists learning, is it because over their many lifetimes they've learned like the wrong lessons?

"They didn't learn the lessons, that is why they cannot understand."

Let's say that someone's not listening, they need the unconditional love, but can't focus on it. So how would you manipulate the people around them in a subtle way? Or show signs?

"I get their attention focused. Perhaps on a television show or I will show them something that will ring a bell and then try to catch their attention. Maybe through a program or maybe through somebody they meet. Maybe through a problem, too. Because then we have to figure out how to get out of it."

Do you show up to people after they cross over and remind them? "Okay, it's me."

"We meet before, sometimes."

Are you familiar with my friend Luana?

"Yes."

Thank you, Maisie, I really appreciate it. Is there anything else you want to impart to our friend here?

"Keep the serious in a sense, but not too serious."

Have fun? I like that. So Maisie is about five years old and blonde or brunette?

Blonde and curly hair, and blue eyes.

Have I ever met you before Maisie?

"No."

So Lilian have you seen Maisie before?

"No. But she's a type of an angel. But when you look at her, like the prototype of an angel, prototype of an angel, almost like a cherub."

Who is your guide, Mark? Is that a male, a female or a light?

It's a male. His name is Neil.

Neil, first, thank you for helping us do this. What's your opinion of what we just have done?

"It's amazing for people on that side."

Do you have any advice for Lilian?

"She's doing better. It's hard, but she's doing better. And I take care of her."

Neil, you're always tethered to her, like a rope to a kite?

"Yes. That's a good image."

*****

Not Maisie, but close. Rossino Uffizi

CHAPTER SIXTEEN: MIKE THE DIRECTOR

Mike is an old friend of mine, a successful film director, and I've known him for around forty years. His films have made over 250 million dollars, and he's done over 50 projects. We've never discussed my research into the flipside, and while having coffee together for the first time in ten years, I told him a little about it. Instead of talking about it, I asked if he wanted to take an adventure.

He said "fine." For the purposes of this interview, the pseudonym I'm going to use is "Mike."

Rich: So, okay, we're here with Mike. I'm gonna ask him to picture himself in a boat on a river. You can close your eyes or not; doesn't matter. But I want you to just say whatever comes to mind.

"Mike": I'll close my eyes. (He does) I'm seeing a long river in the jungle, I'm in a small boat. There are steam operated small motors moving the boat.

Does that imply a time period?

No. But the boat is made out of wood.

Looking on both sides of the river do you see jungle or palm trees?

Dense stuff, less palm trees, more dense tropical foliage going up.

I'm going to ask for Mike's guide to come and sit in this boat. When I say your guide, what comes to mind? A male, a female or a light?

Female.

Okay and first let me ask her if it's okay to ask her some questions. And she can nod. shrug or shake her head "No."

Who are you asking?

Her. She can put the answers in your mind's eye. See if she will nod, shrug or shake her head "no." Is it okay to ask you questions directly?

"She nods."

Describe what she looks like. How old is she? Just allow that to come to your mind.

She has… brown hair. Dark eyes.

What's she wearing?

A simple dress. A red dress.

Can she give us a letter or a name we can use for this conversation?

"Dee."

Miss Dee. So allow Mike to take hold of your hands and tell me what that feels like.

Cold.

Miss Dee, could you warm them up for him? So you can feel them warming up?

Possibly.

This is just to show how you two can communicate. You asked her to warm them up and she's done so. But to proceed I need you to nod. Is it okay, if I ask questions?

She nodded. Said, "Yes."

First Miss Dee How's Mike doing?

"Good. Really good."

If you have you been with him for just this lifetime or other ones?

I think just this one.

Sometimes guides change or tag each other out like team wrestling. Miss Dee, I'm going to ask you a simple question. Are you familiar with my work?

"No." Not familiar.

I ask because it helps me with what questions I can ask. I'm going to ask you to take our friend here to visit his council. He may not know what that is, but you do. And so are we inside or outside?

Outside.

Describe what you're seeing. Are we above the ground or on the ground?

We're still on the water. We're still in the boat.

I'm going to ask Miss Dee to take him to visit with his council members. So put that in his mind's eye. Are we inside or outside?

We're inside.

Take a look at the floor. What does it look like?

It's a wooden floor.

Color?

Medium dark.

Any structural columns or something holding this place up?

No, very simple.

And how high are the ceilings?

Fourteen feet.

Take a look at how many people are gathered in this room?

There are five people.

Miss Dee, I appreciate you taking us here. I'm not going to ask any questions that will disrupt Mike's path if I can. So how are they arrayed? Are they in a line? Are they the circle, semi-circle sitting or standing?

Standing in a semicircle.

Go to the first person on your left of the line; is that a male or female or a light?

A young girl.

Tell me about her hair and eye color.

She has blonde hair. Blue eyes..

What's a name or a letter we could use to identify you?

The letter "Oh."

Miss Oh. First, thank you for allowing us to talk to you. Are you familiar with my work?

"**Yes.**"

Mike's guide is not yet she is. What's your opinion of it?

"**It's good.**"

Okay, is it important or something people should focus on?

"**They should (focus on it).**"

Now what do you represent on Mike's council in a word?

"**Reassurance.**"

Related to "It's okay or go ahead?"

"**Yes.**"

And did he earn that from you, specifically in a lifetime? Or is this something you've represented for all of his life?

"**For all (of them.)**"

If you could clarify that a little bit. What do you mean by "reassurance." Everything's gonna be okay?

"**Yes.**"

Important to know everything's gonna be okay. No matter what?

"**Correct.**"

How's Mike doing?

"**Doing good.**"

You have any opinion or thoughts about his recent marriage?

(It's a) "Very happy thing."

Took them long enough. Just kidding. Thank you so much, Miss Dee. Have you ever incarnated on the planet?

"**Yes.**"

Incarnated with Mike?

"No."

(Note: In a longer session, I might ask Dee to describe her lifetime and what she learned during it, but in this case, I move on to other members of his council.)

Miss Dee. Can introduce us to the person on your left and Mike's right. Is that a male, female or a light?

Yes, it's a male.

And about how old does he look?

He's older.

And may I ask you some questions, sir?

He says "Sure."

Tell me a name or a letter that we can use to identify.

"Ah."

Mr. Ah. What do you represent on Mike's council?

"Oversight."

Oversight is different than reassurance.

"Yes."

So you've been keeping an eye on him and all of his journeys for all this lifetimes, correct?

"Yes (I have.)"

And how many other councils do sit on?

"Many."

The same for you, Miss Dee. You sit on many councils?

"A few."

Okay, so less than, but Mr. Ah. How do you think Mike is doing?

"I think he is getting through, okay."

Is there anything you should be focused on in terms of his career or life or journey? If you just want to give him some advice?

"No. He should keep doing what he's doing."

Are you familiar with my work, speaking to councils?

"Yes."

What's your opinion of it?

"I'm skeptical, but I think it's good."

Well, let me ask you in terms of your skepticism, do you mean whether it's actually accurate or do you feel like it might not necessarily be valuable because people are cheating?

"I think it's generally accurate."

Okay. And the idea is that by having a conversation - because it's Mike who sees you, he knows what you look like, right? By the way, Mike do you recognize this guy in any way? Or is this a new face for you?

No, I recognize him now.

Someone in your lifetime?

Similar to my father.

Oh. Well, let's ask him that question. Mr. Ah. Are you his father?

He says "Yes."

(Note: Because I want to nail down that this really is his father, and not someone who looks like him, I ask him to show Mike his "life planning session" as only he would be aware of that.)

This is a weird question, but if you could show Mike his life planning session, where he chose you as his father, if you could just show him the visual of that, and so he can see who was there? Who else was there?

Me and his mother.

Let me ask you who was there to greet you when you crossed over?

His mother and his daughter.

Was that a happy reunion?

"Yes."

So are you hanging out with them now?

"Sometimes, yes."

And let me ask, can you show Mike kind of what activities you are participating in now?

"Thinking. Walking and thinking."

Please clarify this. When you say thinking and walking, it's constructing environments with your mind?

"Correct. Because you're no longer in the denser world. And over on that side, everything is mind."

(Note: Mike hasn't read any of my books or is aware of my documentaries where people talk about constructing reality on the flipside, how the act of walking or viewing things is a mental construct. This is in line with the research.)

And so what kinds of things do you construct? Or think about?

"I think about complexity."

Complexity. By the way, are you taking any classes over there?

"Yes. I'm teaching."

If you don't mind, if you would put in Mike's mind what the topic of your classes is? And even if he doesn't understand it, you can just tell him what the title or the course headline for your class.

"It's about thinking past (beyond) what appears to be the case."

Thinking past what appears to be the case?" How many students in your class?

"One hundred."

Let's say you're in class, and showing students how to think in deeper ways? What would be some kind of a lesson?

"It's about not simply accepting everything exactly as it appears to be."

So looking at things from multiple facets, and do you teach them how to put themselves in the shoes of others?

"Yes, and how to how to do this without judgment."

Is that something that Mike can bring into his work as a film director? Or does he do that anyway?

"He can always do it more."

So when he's creating a character or creating a scenario, he can try to live it or create it as a construct?"

"Experience (it) as another person would experience (it)."

Have you ever shown up to Mike in his sleep?

"He's not aware of that."

Could you show him a dream or some occurrence where that happened, you were there observing, and you can show him where he was?

"Yes." (Nods. Mike smiles.)

Was that a moment of joy?

"Yes."

When Mike wants to contact you, what's the best method for him to reach out and have this kind of present tense conversation with you?

"Meditate."

But also by looking at photographs, correct?

"Yes."

And I want you to show him something. So a photograph is a hologram of time because it captures time and space and frequency. So when he sees a photograph of a loved one to just address them in present tense?

"Yeah."

When you have a party, or get together, speak of them in present tense, because they are there. Is that correct?

"Yes."

Let's talk to a person on your left. Is that a male, female or light?

It's a male. In his 40's. He has dark hair.

Is this somebody that Mike knows from his lifetime?

"Yes."

What can I call him?

"Jay."

Mr. Jay, have you had a previous lifetime with Mike?

"Yes."

Before the one that he knows you from?

"Correct, yes."

Would you put that in his mind's eye? And where are we inside or outside? Describe the location?

We're in western state in the mountains.

What does Mr. Jay look like to like?

Kind of like a mountain man.

Look back at yourself, or what do you look like?

Young, innocent, fresh faced, young kid.

Okay, and are you guys mining?

No, we're exploring.

Put a date in Mikes mind without any judgment to what's the first thing that comes to mind?

1872. It's in Colorado.

Was there anything that happened to you to guys that you might want to explore or look at?

No. We're free, mostly (concerned about) the dangers of the wild outdoors.

Why did Mike choose that lifetime? What was the lesson in that lifetime?

"The lesson was to appreciate the world that we were in at that time."

A visceral experience of life or what goes on. What do you represent on his council?

"Appreciation."

Well, I appreciate it, Mr. Jay. We've got a couple more people to meet. If you could introduce Mike and the person to your left and his right. Okay, is it a male or female?

A female. In her thirties. She has brown hair.

A name or letter to identify you?

"Bee."

What do you represent on Mike's council Miss Bee?

"I represent his sense of humor."

Have you been with him for all of his lifetimes or just recently?

"Just a couple."

How many other councils do you work?

"Ten to fifteen."

Okay let me ask you. Are you familiar with my work?

"Yes."

Can you put some comedic thing that occurred that you were responsible for putting in this path?

(Laughs, remembering) "I made him fall." Oh my gosh, it's hilarious.

So you're the banana peel? Letter Bee for banana? Were you the one responsible for us meeting today?

"Yes."

Appreciate that. Miss B, I want you to introduce us to somebody else on the council that he needs to talk to.

"Okay, this will be the leader of the council."

(Note: Here it is again, someone answering a question before I could ask it.)

Anticipated the question. That's usually what I asked for it next. So and is that a male, female or light?

"A light. It's mostly white, a little bit of yellow in it, but mostly a warm, white light."

May I ask you some questions?

"Yes."

What's a letter or a name that we can use to associate with you?

"Eye."

What quality do you represent on his council?

"Vision."

What do you mean by that? Vision of awareness of surroundings? Or into the future?

"All of it."

And how many councils do you work on?

"Hundreds."

Are you familiar with my work?

"Yes."

And do you have an opinion about it?

"Yes. I think it's good."

Correct me if I'm wrong but it helps people to be aware that these council members are always connected to them?

"Correct."

So in times of need, or even in creative crisis, they can turn to a miss comedy Miss B and say, I need a punch line. Or to you, Mister "Eye." In terms of in terms of Mike's journey, what is it you'd like to tell him that he should focus on?

"To keep his eyes open."

And is there anything in terms of this research that people should focus on?

"Opening doors. And they should keep their eyes open."

(Note: "The Doors of Perception" by Aldous Huxley goes into details about the many doors of perception we keep closed, but need to open.)

Have you ever incarnated on the planet?

"A long, long time ago."

And let me just ask you for my own understanding. Why is it you're appearing and not manifesting as a person?

"Because I was a person a very, very long time ago."

And is this your preferred way of appearing?

"Correct."

I've not asked this question before, is there anyone on this council who is also on the council of someone in Mike's life?

"Yes."

Do any of you guys have any messages for (that person)? She may not be aware of this kind of work.

"We talk to her all the time."

Is she aware of it?

"Oh, Yes."

I want to turn back to your guide for a second. The person that we met at the beginning, whose name escapes me at the moment, what was his name?

"Dee."

Mr. Dee. So what's your opinion of what we're doing here? Now that you've seen it?

"I think it should be helpful for Mike, the idea he can access this group at any time."

Anybody else do that he needs to see in this council?

"No. He's good."

Okay. Before we depart, would you take him to his place of healing? Is he inside or outside?

"He's inside. It's like a hallway connecting a number of rooms. At the moment he's just walking."

Is there any kind of light or visual associated with these rooms?

They are lights coming from (each of) the rooms.

Do they hit his body?

Yes.

And is it a linear kind of experience, as he's walking down the hallway, he's reconnecting with different facets of his life?

Something like that.

Let's go to the end of this hall, when the process is finished? And what's the emotion or feeling that he gets from us kind of standing there sitting there?

Relief, release.

Back to his natural state, a release of all the trappings of incarnation?

Yes, a release of all the trappings.

Almost like an actor getting off stage and dropping props and costumes.

Right.

Show him a visual of himself standing there, from your point of view of the, what does he look like?

He's smiling. He's younger. Like eighteen.

So let me clarify Dee. This visual that he's manifesting, this is the preferred frequency he radiates for lack of a better term?

"Correct."

When we run into people in our dreams that are younger, we're actually accessing the frequency that they like to radiate. Is that correct?

"It is. Sure."

Dee, can put a sensation in his body now, so that he is aware of it? And then it's like your bat signal when you're when you want to get his attention? Or, you know, he doesn't have to tell me what it is, but it will be somewhere in his body, that you can generate some kind of a feeling. Can you do that?

"Yes." (Mike smiles enigmatically.)

Alright. So let's go back to our boat in the river. And let's just be aware as Mr. Dee points out, anytime he closes his eyes he can access him. Is that correct?

"Yes."

Okay, let's dock our boat. (Mike opens his eyes, blinks. Raises an eyebrow.) So that's it. What do you think of that?

Cool.

*****

Moses and the Council of Seventy – Jacob de Wit

"In dramatic writing, the very essence is character change. The character at the end is not the same as he was at the beginning. He's changed psychologically – maybe even physically."

Robert Towne

CHAPTER SEVENTEEN: *RANDOM COUNCIL VISITS*

MAO FROM CHINA

This is a friend of mine from China. For purposes of this interview all the names have been changed and represent pseudonyms. (His name is not Mao).

Rich: So to recap, we've already spoken to your grandmother Yuan, who was sitting on the boat in the river with you. I asked her if it was possible to bring you to visit your council, and she said it was okay and has brought you into this room. You described a room with marble floors and high ceilings.

We are at the first person on the left of these five members. What's a name we can refer to you?

Mao: It's Lao.

Mr. Lao; are you familiar with my work?

"No."

What do you represent on Mao's Council?

"I represent dreams."

(Note: Lao means "consoling and rewarding" in ancient Chinese.)

You mean dreaming of things?

"Nostalgia."

Interesting. Nostalgia refers to the memories of good and bad things happening.

"Correct."

How many councils do you work on? Many? Do you represent that same thing?

"Yes."

How do you think our friend is doing?

"Not too bad."

I just want to point out this is a council member, somebody who represents watches over you? Correct?

"Yes, I do."

And you are watching over him now?

"I am. We are."

So, can you put a sensation somewhere in his body to let him know that you're always connected?

"Yes, I can." (Mao reacts).

Okay. Very good. And that's like a bat signal. So whenever you feel that sensation, you'll know they're trying to let you know like everything's okay. And have you ever incarnated on the planet Mr. Lao?

"Oh, Yes."

Let me turn to Yuan for a second. Have you ever had an important event with our friend you want to show him?

Yes. Outside. We are in the backyard of her place.

You're in her backyard. And what's happening?

She is showing me the day she was taking me around and then she handed me plant with a flower in it. It was in a pot. And she was teaching me how to put water in it and then grow the flower.

Why did you want to show this to him?

She show him "How things work."

Lao, if you don't mind, would you please introduce us to the person to your left? Is that a male a female or light?

A female. She's sixty-seven.

May I ask you some questions directly? What's a name or a letter we can use to refer to you?

The letter "R."

And how does she look? Is she Caucasian? Is she Asian?

She's Asian.

And so Miss R, how do you think our friend is doing?

"He needs focus. To be more focused, needed more focus, to be more determined. Needs to do better time management, more detail focused and needs a lot of work to improve him."

Are you familiar with my work talking to councils?

"No."

So my question to you is, you feel like he should be more detail oriented, what is your role on his council?

"The role is to supervise and to kind of push him to be a better person."

So helping him focus?

"Right."

And so, have you ever had a lifetime on the planet Earth? Miss R?

"No, no, no, no."

Okay. Where do you normally incarnate or have you incarnated somewhere off planet?

"It's always the same point in another universe."

Let me ask you, has he ever had an experience incarnated in this other universe?

"Yes."

Is he aware of that?

"Yes."

And is he doing the same thing on this planet?

"Not so much. He talks too much. He doesn't take in the advice from a lot of other people."

I'd like to speak to the spokesperson of this council, wherever that is, if it's possible.

"Yes. Okay."

Is that a male, a female or a light?

It's like a white light. Like Yuan.

Is it vibrating? Is it moving? Or is it flat?

Energetic.

And you can see various colors within the light?

Some shadows as well. Some gray.

May I ask you some questions, and you can just put the answer into his mind.

"Yes, sure."

And what's a what's a name or a letter we can use to refer to?

"Hope."

I think you're skipping ahead. So do you represent hope?

"Yes."

Are you on many councils?

"Yes."

And are you familiar with my work?

"Yes."

The reason I ask is because that's different than the other two council members. It's new information. If you were gonna make it up, everybody would either be aware or not aware. So Hope is aware of it but the others are not. What's your opinion of what I'm doing?

"It's a good thing, for people to come down and then help them to look back. And then also it helps them to look back and think forward as well as to have hope.

****

CHAPTER EIGHTEEN: CATHY

Cathy reached out to me after a session she had with the medium Jennifer Shaffer. Jennifer appears on our podcast, "Hacking the Afterlife." Every now and then Jennifer says one of her clients has insisted on this form of examination via guided meditation.

Rich: I'm going to ask your guide Michele to do me a favor, you probably already know what it is. Would you mind walking us into visit with her council?

"Yes." I felt like he already knew what you were going to ask.

I always find it unusual because you know you've made a connection when you hear an answer before you can ask a question. Describe the path. What does that look like you're on your way into your council? Are you inside or outside? Or is the is it a structure? What is it?

I'm inside. Although when you said "the path," it flipped through a couple things and ended on a green pasture. But now I'm inside.

And as you're walking in, what does it look inside?

Think of a dome. Very high ceiling. Warm golden light.

And take a look around how many people are in here.

Eight comes to mind.

Michele, you've been here with her before. Is it okay for us to come in here and ask questions?

"Yes."

In your mind's eye, how are how are these eight people arrayed? Are they left to right? Are they in a circle?

At a table.

Have you ever done a session where you ran into your council before?

No. (Cathy aside) Can I digress a second? I did go for a weekend at the Omega center that Dr/ Brian Weiss gave. He did a regression in a big group setting, but not me personally.

That's great. Look at all the time we've saved. All right let's start with the person on the far left. Is it a male or a female?

Male. Brown hair. Medium length. Sturdy looking. No beard. Blue eyes. Thirties.

May I ask you questions?

He says, "Yes."

And could you give us a name that we could use so that we could converse? Or a letter of a name?

The letter A. But then the name Adam came to mind.

Is Adam the right moniker for you?

"Okay."

How do you think our friend Cathy is doing?

What comes to mind is "Good." But it comes with a feeling a little bit of for me of anxiety of... I guess, being judged, or if it's good enough.

Okay, but that's coming from you, not him. So that's why I'm asking him. How is she doing? Is she on the right path?

"Yes."

Are you familiar with me asking council members questions?

"Absolutely. I'm hearing *"I've talked to you before."*

So we've actually had a conversation before is that correct?

"Yes."

Would you put it in Cathy's mind? Did we meet during one of these conversations? Was it a male or female who introduced us?

Male.

What do you represent on her Council?

"Integrity."

And how is she doing with that?

"Doing good but sometimes she sacrifices a bit so as to not upset someone else or... she will do what they would like; it's done out of compassion."

Let's ask him can you put a sensation in Cathy's body right now head to toe somewhere, almost like a bat signal so when one of these issues comes up, and you'll know it because you'll feel that sensation. Can you do that?

I feel a lightheadedness.

What do you want to say about integrity?

"Try as hard as you can to hold on to your own integrity in the face of things that are happening now."

Thank you. So it's almost like adversity can be a lesson in integrity?

"Yes. It'll serve you well, (integrity) it's so easy to let it go." And what that translates to me is, it's not that I've let go of my integrity, (because) it's always been very important to me. But it gets challenged when people do things that they shouldn't."

But the challenge is there?

"Yes. And today, it's even harder to hold on to. And applies everywhere." What came to mind is that "If you hold on to a sense of integrity, it can help with the anger."

Adam, would you do us a favor and introduce us to the person to your left? Is that a male or a female?

Female. She morphed... started out as a younger blonde, long haired woman then morphed into a beautiful older woman.

And if we can ask you your name?

Elana.

Elana, if I may, is it okay to ask you some questions about Cathy's journey?

"Of course."

How do you think our friend is doing?

"Good."

Are you aware of my work?

"Yes."

And if I may ask, from where?

"I heard from others."

I ask because some are and some are not, which is an unusual construct when talking about what we're talking about. What do you represent and Cathy's journey?

"Creativity… and kindness." (Cathy aside) I don't know why both of those.

How many lifetimes have you been watching over her?

"Many."

How many councils do you sit on?

"Fourteen."

Adam, I forgot to ask you. How about you?

"Eight."

Back to Elana. So you both represent forms of creativity and kindness along with integrity. Is that correct?

"Yes."

And creativity in terms of the journey of all her lifetimes, or mostly this one?

Mostly, this one.

In terms of "kindness" is that just in the nature of who you are? You're a kind person or are you talking about Cathy's journey?

"No, I represent a kind female."

Let me ask, you morphed a second ago. Why did you show her these two different individuals?

"It's her two images of women."

Like a metaphor or universal image?

"Yes. But Cathy's image of women was based on sort of an ideal. But her sense of women is much more grounded in a depth of feeling which has to do with kindness and more of a feminine spirit."

Have you ever incarnated on the planet?

"Yes."

And what's your opinion of how people are treating the planet these days?

"Um, unkind. Opposite of what I represent. It's not good."

You think we can do something about that?

"You've said it before; plant a trillion trees. You somehow have to elevate the energy of kindness and it will translate to the planet to doing more of the right thing."

Let's take a look at Elana, what is she wearing clothing wise?

It's kind of like a white robe. Elana has a gold necklace.

Elana, let me ask you about that gold necklace. Is that something you earned or something Cathy earned?

"That is something she earned."

And please put in her mind's eye how she earned it.

"Through strength. It's a symbol of strength, feminine strength." Some might say it was like a collar, but it's a little bigger.

Has Cathy ever seen this object in her lifetime?

No.

But you're showing it to her now. It's new information.

(Cathy aside) Not any particular thing that I've seen.

Let me ask who on the council needs to speak to us? Anybody raising their hand?

Yes, but I can't see an image of who they are.

How far down the council?

Middle. Three quarters.

Let me ask you what image comes to mind. Is this a male or female?

Male. Looks like maybe a twenty-year old boy. Hair is Brown, eyes are green.

And how is he dressed?

In a white robe.

What's a name or letter we can use?

"Gee."

Hello Mr. G. Is it okay if I asked you some questions?

"Yes."

How is Cathy doing on her path and journey?

"Good."

And what quality do you represent on her Council?

Oh, this is interesting, I'm getting "A sense of ambitiousness, youthful playfulness, wholeness."

Do you represent that quality for all of her lifetimes or this one in particular?

"All of them."

And did she earn your position on her council or did you choose her?

"I chose her because she all too often forgets me."

If you could just talk about that a little bit. Are you familiar with what I'm doing?

"Yes."

I mean, people can find this research offensive, outrageous, crazy. But I always like to point out it's also fun. We're on a Disneyland ride here, and we appreciate you participating in it.

"I appreciate your sensation."

Thank you, Mr. G. You're no relation to Ali G. Are you?

(Aside) He says "Yes," but I don't know who that is.

That's funny – he gets my joke, but you do not. Sascha Baron Cohen is "Ali G." It's been off the air for a long time. So you find what Ali G is doing is pretty impish?

He says, "Yes."

Very good. But you don't know who Ali G is Cathy?

318

I don't I feel like I do. I may have heard the name.

That's why I wanted to clarify. So. Mr. G, if you could say something to the actor who plays Ali G, what would it be? What's the value of what he's doing?

He is "lightening, lightening, lightening."

I understand. Lightening our load. Enlightening. Does Cathy know the other person whose council you are on?

"Oh, yes." (Cathy aside) I'm not getting who it is.

You're not going to show her? That's fine. So could you show her something in her life that was silly, wacky, that she wasn't aware that you were responsible for?

There was a memory of a couple of moments of just total laughing, laughing out of control. Finding something hysterical.

Out of control laughter. It can change a person's health and disposition.

I can't really place when that happened.

He associated it in your mind with something that was physical, that most people have had the experience, hopefully in their life where they're laughing uncontrollably.

What's coming to me is that he's also on (my friend's) council.

Mr. G. Can we ask were you responsible for these two getting together in some way?

I hear "A bit."

Mr. G put it in her mind the moment they met the moment they recognized each other.

Well, (she and her mate) met in eighth grade outside of a Junior high school, and had a bit of a connection. But the real meeting was in Junior High cafeteria. I had a friend that we would eat lunch together and in front of these new boys who were so cool, she and I used to spit bananas between our teeth during lunch, and we got in big trouble because we were supposed to impress these boys, but we didn't care. What I'm hearing from Mr. G is that he orchestrated that silly moment I had. After that encounter somewhere in me, I knew (this was her mate).

But we what was the feeling? Knew what?

That I wanted him to be interested in me. And it was something bigger than to wish that he would like me. And interestingly, we ended up dating for just a couple of weeks. And then he went out with another friend of mine. We ended up best friends for years. And we didn't get together until much later.

That's the moment I was looking for, outside of time. Let's shift our focus back to your council again. Let's ask the spokesperson for your council if they want to have any words for you.

Well, I see a male. And he looks like Rip Torn.

Where is he sitting?

The middle.

Sir, may I ask you some questions? How do you feel Cathy's doing?

He feels more judgmental. That's why I'm seeing that character from that movie.

(Note: She's referring to Rip Torn in Albert Brook's movie "Defending Your Life." The film comes up often in the research, Michael Newton mentioned it in the interview we did on camera. I've asked Albert about it, if he was aware of how close he was to what people report about the "council" in the afterlife, he was not.)

He has a big sense of lightness about him but (also) a little bit of a severity. In response to how I'm doing, he says "Very good. She has to listen to what she needs to do more. Less judging of the path or past."

May I ask you for a name or a letter that we can use to address you?

Mr. L.

How many councils do you sit on?

"A lot."

What do you represent on Cathy's journey?

"Holding her to task." I don't know why I'm saying this, but it's "Expectations."

Mr. L. what's your opinion of this work? Are you aware of it?

"Very much. It's necessary."

Please, elucidate why.

(Cathy aside) I'm going to repeat what I heard. "For the survival of human beings."

And when you say that, do you mean for the natural evolution of human beings, or specifically humans have gotten to a wall, and in order to get over the wall, they're gonna have to adjust?

"Concern for human life on Earth, reaching a point of difficulty. And yes; it is needed (this open channel to the councils) to open up channels to go forward. To evolve, and in some ways to hold to a task. We need to be held to a task; it isn't quite the direction we might be going with some of these snags."

Mr. L, is there something you would like us to impart to somebody listening in or reading this to get in front of humanity?

He says, "Don't judge this and if it is the right direction, to have consciousness keep evolving and to communicate, (it means) you're going in the right direction."

Mr. L, what should Cathy focus on?

What comes to me is "I need to be less invested in the outcome."

Less invested in the outcome, but learning to love unconditionally?

"Yes." He's put in my mind a dream or vision of shadowy figures I thought might represent spirit guides. And I woke up with the words "Just be kind."

Which one of you guys suggested that – anyone want to raise the hand?

It was Mr. L.

"Just be kind." "Let go of the outcome." So let's first let's thank everybody in the room. Oh before I forget, let's ask Bernie, your dad, how he thinks you're doing. Put him in the boat.

He says "She's doing just fine!"

****

CHAPTER NINETEEN: SIMON THE PODCASTER

Simon is a hypnotherapist and a member of International Practitioners of Holistic Medicine in the United Kingdom. Simon has a podcast called "The Past Lives Podcast" I've appeared twice on.

In the podcast (#53) we did some years back, Simon asked me a question about councils. He said "I did a life between lives hypnotherapy session. And when I got to the council of elders, I was there with my spirit guide. And the guy at the front of the Council of Elders basically stood up and said, "What the hell do you think you're doing here? Well, we don't want you to come and talk to us."

I said, "I wish I had been there. We'd go back and ask them what that was about." Two years later, I made my attempt to sneak Simon in to visit his council. It was a fascinating trip, and can be heard in its edited form on Simon's podcast (#119). This is my edit of that conversation. As we began to record:

SIMON: I was saying before we started recording that I did a between live session and went to the council of elders. I got to the council of elders, and it was like a Greek amphitheater. And there were people there in togas, they looked quite old. And the guy at the front who seemed to be in charge, he just kind of looked at me anger, and pointed away. And his whole demeanor was kind of like, "How dare you present yourself to us? What do you think you're doing coming here?" And I kind of found it funny at the time. I still look back on it as something amusing. It wasn't upsetting.

Did you just walk away?

Yes. Walked away.

Did your guide go along with you for that?

Yeah.

Describe your guide to me.

Well, that's that was interesting as well, because when I first met my guide, it was when I got to the soul group, and my guide came over. And he was kind of a joker and smiling at me and making jokes. And he looked like a person. And then he quickly changed into someone else and then someone else again, and then quickly, into different forms, even Chewbacca. He was laughing and I got the idea that what he was doing was saying, like, "I've lived all these lives. I've been all these people. Don't look at me now and think I'm just this this person. Right?"

Did you get a name for him?

No.

Can we talk to him now?

I suppose so.

So you have a visual of this guy, let's pick the Joker, because that's the word that jumps out at us, right? So visually, just describe what you're seeing. How far away is he?

Six feet away.

How tall?

About six feet tall.

I want to ask him a question. Is it okay if I ask you a direct question, sir?

Yes. I don't know if I'm just imagining all this, but he's kind of like tapping his watch. He's like, "I've been waiting for this for ages."

Great. What's a name that we can use to call you?

I hear Abbie.

Nice to meet you, Abbie. My pleasure. I'm in Santa Monica. You're somewhere off planet. And here we are having a conversation. So describe how he's dressed.

The Joker from Batman.

Okay, which Joker because there were quite a few. Okay, because, you know, there's the cartoon version. There's that Heath Ledger version.

It's more like Joaquin Phoenix. It looks funny. Very skinny and colorful. He's kind of going like this. (Makes "finger pointing" gesture.)

Very good. Firing on all cylinders. I'm gonna ask you to do something because I think it'll help Simon to address you. Can you shift into another persona that's maybe more familiar or comfortable for Simon than Joaquin Phoenix?

I'm kind of seeing a female now. Twenty-five years old, white hair. Not blonde but white hair. Blue eyes. A white dress.

Abbie, can I ask you a question? Is this how you sort of see yourself normally? Then you present to your friends?

She says "No."

So why did you choose this particular avatar for Simon?

Just because he's, it's easy.

It's easy. Okay, thank you. Well, that makes sense. So blue eyes, is the hair long or short?

Long hair, down to her elbows.

Have I ever met you before, Abbie?

"No."

Have you ever heard of me or the work I've been doing?

She says, "Yes."

And what's your opinion of it?

"It's hilarious. You're a troublemaker." (Simon aside) I'm just telling you exactly the words that are just coming straight into my mind. I'm not thinking about it.

Simon had an experience of going to visit his council and being turned away, can you tell us why that happened?

"It wasn't the right time."

Is it the right time now?

"We can try. We can have a go." She's kind of dancing around. She's being very playful.

Abbie, would you take us on a trip to his council??

She said "Yeah, let's go!"

Describe what the visual looks like.

There is this kind of a huge golden ball that's floating towards us and then doors opening up. We're getting inside it, inside the ball that takes us to where the council is.

Okay, but let's hold it there. Describe the floor of the council.

Just kind of white light.

And is there a ceiling?

Just two or three feet above our heads.

How many individuals do you see there in the council?

Eighteen to twenty.

How are they arrayed?

It's like a Greek amphitheater. They're all in togas. It seems like this is exactly how it was before. And the guy that prevented me from coming in last time is on his way over.

Don't focus on that guy. Just leave him alone.

Right.

(Note: I'm trying to avoid getting bounced again, so I thought perhaps to avoid the fellow altogether. However that doesn't work.)

We're gonna go up to the first council member on the left, and ask this person if it's all right to ask some pertinent, respectful questions?

Yeah, so standing in our way, this is the guy that told me to leave as last time.

Let's freeze this now like a hologram. How does he look in your mind's eye? Is he tall, short, thin?

I'd say he's five foot ten, about seventy years old. Gray hair, bearded, balding. He's wearing a toga and it's got a purple stripe on it. I'd say one stripe. Yeah, all of the council members have got a toga with a colors on them. And the colors symbolize something, but I'm not sure what it is.

Is it okay, if we ask you some questions?

He says, "Yeah, it is." When I first got here, he was quite grumpy. It seemed like he was saying…

Yeah, let's not focus on that. Sir, please give us a name that we can use to address you?

"Joe."

Let me ask Mr. Joe, are you aware of this work that I've been doing?

"Yes."

How did you become aware of it?

I'm getting from him, "We all know you."

Okay, makes my job easier. Joe, have you ever incarnated on the planet Earth?

"Yes."

Have you ever incarnated with our friend Simon?

"Yes."

What's a word that represents your role on Simon's Council?

"Father."

And let me ask you, how is Simon doing?

"He's doing better than he has done in previous lives."

Joe, can I ask you, what does the purple stripe represent?

He says, "He's a junior member of council."

Is there anything you want to pass along to people?

"Don't take life so seriously. You get lots and lots of lives. And this kind of goes without saying, the people that you meet in your life, anybody you see anywhere; they are souls. And sometimes we can judge people by the way they look or some little interaction, but realize that there's a lot more to people than you might just see; don't dismiss people."

If only we could see that we're all connected. Is that correct Joe?

"Yeah."

And would you show Simon how you're connected to him?

(Simon aside) It's (about) lots of lives together. He was on the earth a lot more than I was before I started. That's what I'm getting. He's progressed. He's a lot further along the path. When he got to a position where there was my council of elders, he wanted to be a part of it. And they allowed him in. That's why he's a junior member.

How many of Simon's lifetimes have you participated in?

"Lots and lots."

Joe, can you do us a favor because we'll come back to you. Could you introduce us to the person to your immediate left? Is that a male or a female or light?

A female. She's, let's fifty-five, short blonde hair, six foot tall, quite slim. She's got a gold stripe on her toga.

May I ask you some questions?

"Yes."

Are you familiar with this work that I'm doing?

"Not so much."

So not all are. If you could give us a name that we can use to call you?

"A."

Miss A, what does the gold stripe represent? Is it part of his spiritual evolvement or does it represent your journey?

She said, "I'm in charge."

Miss A, why did you let Joe chase him out of here?

I'm not really getting anything from her about that. Regards to Joe, I'd say he's got a kind of very human personality and demeanor. But she seems a lot more serious.

Is that your demeanor or it's just because you've been around a long time?

"I've been around a long time."

Have you ever incarnated on earth?

"No."

Have you incarnated anywhere that Simon has been with you? Have you incarnated off the Earth?

"Yes."

I understand that answer, Simon may not. (Over 35% of the reports from the Newton Institute include memories of lifetimes off planet.) Miss A, would it be okay, for Simon to visit that place?

She says "Yes." I'm also getting "You have no idea about what is out there in terms of dimensions, or universes or other lives. You have no idea."

Well it is a question I often ask and I appreciate the ability to do so now. If you don't mind, put in Simon's mind where this planet that you've incarnated on before, is it in our universe or in another realm?

"Both."

How long ago was that?

"Eons ago."

In terms of putting him on that planet, are you inside or outside?

Outside. It's in water. It's like water (based). They closest thing I could say to explain is that they are dolphins or whales or something, but it's different to that.

Dolphins are considered advanced intelligence animals, we have yet to understand how they communicate. So let's just allow that when do you see a dolphin that could be to represent a being on this water planet? Is this correct Miss A? Am I on the right path here?

"Yes."

So on this planet, was it a complete water planet? Or were there spaces that were not water?

"There are spaces that are not water."

Would Simon or you participate in being on those spaces outside of water?

"Always under water."

Some have observed that oxygen on our planet has the same function as water, but we don't experience it that way. It's H_2O, very close to O_2, but functions like water. Is it like that?

She says "It's not the same for that planet."

Is there any kind of social organization? Family members? If you could describe it.

It seems like "You're born, but there are no families. But there's a collective; everybody looks after everyone else." What I'm getting is, "It's much more advanced spiritually than Earth. And that they're well aware of a lot more things than we are."

Is Simon aware of anyone in his lifetime now that he's shared a lifetime with on that planet in the past?

"No."

(Note: In a previous podcast, Simon referred to an event where he saw a UFO, of being abducted and how he "gave a sample of his DNA.")

Are Simon's experiences with UFOs related to people who might have had lifetimes on that planet in the past?

What I'm hearing from her is "On that planet, that's where souls go to rest."

Okay, vaguely meaning that there might be somebody back there who incarnated in another planet somewhere and eventually connected to you in the way that you're connected. Is that correct?

"It's a very slight link, because it was such a long time ago and such a long distance away. And when she says distance, she doesn't mean physical as we would measure in this universe. It's spiritual in relation to other dimensions and universes."

Did this existence happen prior to the big bang of our universe that we're in now?

He says, "The "Big Bang" has nothing to do with it. This is both another place, another dimension."

(Note: As if saying that the "creation of this universe" is not related to this other dimension or realm.)

So is Simon ever going to go back there?

"If he wants to."

I mean, to visit or hang out. Do you ever go back there to hang out?

"Yes."

What quality do you represent on Simon's Council?

She says "She's in charge of the whole council."

When we show up to a council, do you all assemble, show up to have this conversation?

"We're always here. No matter where we are, we all can always come together. But when we come together, that's just a small part of us, because we can be off doing other things at the same time."

I've heard this before, that our council members are always tethered to us. Is that an apt description?

"Yes; they're always looking over."

What's a physical way for Simon to connect with you?

"Meditation and music."

Would it be a music that he likes or that you like?

"It's him playing music."

Should he think about the image of your face that he's seeing now?

That's not needed. She's kind of saying you're getting the wrong idea of who she is. And what she does.

People ask me all the time, what's a good way to connect to them? You just gave him two obvious ways. In terms of meditation, should he visualize you? Or are you automatically connected?

"The connection is there all the time; it's just opening up the barrier, the veil, and you have to get into the right frame of mind, you have to change your focus."

Is there anyone else on the council we should speak with? Who would like to speak to Simon?

I'm seeing them all putting their hands up kind of like their kids in a classroom.

Miss A is that all right?

Miss A has left.

Okay, a busy person. Let's go to the person next to her. Who wants to visit with us first?

Female. About thirty something.

Okay, describe her. What does she look like?

She has dark hair. Dark skinned as well. And she's got a blue stripe on her toga. And she says something about logic; she represents logic.

And what does the blue stripe represent?

She's laughing. She says "Middle management."

That's funny. And what's a name we can use to address you, ma'am?

"Arie."

Can I ask you some questions? Is that okay?

"Yeah."

How's Simon doing?

"He's doing fine. He's an old soul."

Have you been with him through all of his lifetimes? Or are you a recent person like Joe?

"Some of them never live lives and yet look over people's lives…" She says, "I do the same for her."

Say that again?

She said "She says she's lived lots of lives with me and she's watched over lots of other lives."

Do you want to put a lifetime in his mind and we can briefly take a look at?

This is the one from (when) I did my life between life session. A young woman in Germany who was burnt as a witch.

I'm sorry to hear that. Are you familiar with this work I'm doing?

"Yes." She says "I've been watching Simon."

You're aware of it by watching Simon, is that correct?

"Yes."

(Note: I'm clarifying. By repeating questions it allows them to change or alter their answers if we didn't hear it correctly the first time.)

Is this this something people need to hear, this exploration of councils?

"Yes. (It is) Important."

Why?

"People have to realize that they're not alone. And they're at some times when you're having a human life, you can get very depressed, very lonely, and you feel that you've been let down. And that you have no backup, or there's no one there for you. But you have got to realize that your soul guides are (always) there and your councils are there. You've got to find a way to get in touch with them, and they can help you out. And they're always trying to help you out."

Thank you. Arie, what's a logical way for people to access their councils?

"Opening your mind and doing meditation."

How many councils do you sit on?

"Thousands."

And how about Joe? How many does he sit on?

"Three."

What would you like to impart to people that are tuning in to this podcast?

"They're incredulous."

But what would be something that you can impart to people?

"Simon's not sure if he's imagining all this, and none of its real. And that's one of the problems they have as well. They try to communicate with people and they try and produce these signs.

And most of the time, people on earth see the signs, but they don't recognize them for what they are, or they just ignore them. And so for these council members, they say "It gets frustrating. They're trying to communicate, and the humans don't pick up on it."

(Note: The signal disappears. Takes a few minutes to get it back.)

(Simon aside) Hang on a second, I lost you there. Okay, that's a bit better.

Let's ask her. Was that you guys interrupting our signal or was that just an anomaly on the planet?

"It's not them." She's laughing.

I'm glad we can make you laugh. Alright, so Arie. What are the lottery numbers for this Friday's lottery?

Now she's counting her fingers.

How many did she have? Just kidding. I think I need a bonus number.

She says "It doesn't work that way."

I always ask and almost always get a laugh. We were asking you about imparting wisdom to the planet.

"I'm saying keep busy. Just be aware that you're not alone. And there's always backup for you."

Can you introduce us to the person to your left?

"Yes. This is Fred." He's wearing a toga with a black stripe on it. He's smoking a cigarette. He's looking kind of grizzled, almost like a Clint Eastwood scowl on his face. He's about sixty-five.

Fred, can we ask you some questions? How do you think Simon's doing?

"He's doing fine. That's no surprise."

What brand of cigarette are you smoking?

"It's Marlboro. The real one," he says. "There's no filter in them."

So have you had a lifetime on the planet with Simon?

"Yes, briefly."

And where did you pick up Marlboros? Was that from a previous lifetime?

"California in the early sixties."

Where did you live in California in the sixties? If you don't mind me asking.

"San Diego."

(Note: Simon grew up in the U.K. San Diego is not a city he knows.)

What were you doing in San Diego?

"Business."

Was it a happy life?

He says "There was a lot of trouble." And that he "got mixed up with the wrong people."

And let me ask you, what quality do you represent on Simon's Council?

"Pain." And he's saying, "Hey, I got the black stripe." He seems a bit moody.

Fred, you represent pain and you're wearing a black stripe? Does that represent pain?

"Yeah."

And what kind of pain? Physical, emotional?

"Emotional."

I don't think I've ever met anybody who represented pain or something that we would consider "negative." But how did you get this gig? Did you choose to be on this council and did Miss A invite you in?

"They asked me. I could go to a lot of councils. But I don't stay very long."

How many councils do you work on?

"It's thousands."

That's interesting. Talk to us about pain, what is it?

"There's all sorts of pain, emotional pain, sometimes we don't even know that it's creeping up on us. Sometimes it's very sudden." He says "He's had lots of lives or he's experienced all these things. So he knows what he's talking about."

And how do you function with the other members of the council? Are you helping people with their pain? Or are you inflicting pain?

"*Processing* pain. Members of the Council are grateful that I'm here. But they don't want to spend much time with me."

Fred is this your choice to teach this process which you've experienced from many lifetimes and on many different councils? There must be a positive outcome from this, otherwise you wouldn't do it.

He's saying, "Pain is sometimes the quickest way to learn a lesson that will really teach you something." He says "These eight, (he's kind of using his thumb, like he's pointing over his shoulder at the other council members) saying, "You know what, these other council members, they're a bunch of pussies."

(Note: That's a first.)

Fred, I appreciate meeting you. So what did you learn in that lifetime of pain in San Diego?

"It was trust. And being you thought you could trust somebody and they double crossed you, and you put your whole life on the line, and they knew it - but still, they didn't care about you at all. They just took you for what they wanted."

Once you crossed over, correct me if I'm wrong, you had a life review.

"Yeah."

How many people are in your council?

"Twelve."

How do they think you're doing?

He says "There's this tremendous sense of unconditional love amongst the spirit world. And they felt really sad for him." But at the same time, he's kind of saying, you know, "My council is not a bunch of pussies. These are mafia guys."

Oh, interesting. Well, Fred, would you like us to go and talk to your council?

He says, "No, you don't want to do that."

Why?

He says "That's a bunch of tough guys. They don't want to talk to you."

I just want to clarify something, Fred. You're not talking about negative energy or negative aspects of being on the planet. It's not that we don't want to talk to them because they're "evil" but intense and focused, is that correct?

"Yeah. But they can give you some of the best things you would ever need. But it's painful to go through."

And are you familiar with what I'm doing? Fred, have you ever heard about me?

"Yeah."

You think it's a good thing or a bad thing?

"Okay. Since you're one of the nice guys."

Well, kind of you to say. But the journey, the performance, is something they signed up for. Is that correct?

"Yeah."

So you were in the life planning stage when Simon signed up for his lifetime?

"No."

And so at what point did you enter into this process?

He says, "You can't equate time on Earth time."

But I mean, recently?

"Yes."

And are you assisting Simon in processing pain?

He says "No," and "It's like this." He says it again, "This council is a bunch of pussies. They don't know anything about pain. They needed to consult me on certain ideas." And now he's using a lighter to light his cigarette.

Focus on that for a moment. What kind of lighter? Zippo?

He says, "Yes."

Anything printed on it?

"There's a picture of a tank."

(Note: From Zippo's website: "From 1943 to 1945, every Zippo made was shipped directly to post exchanges and Navy ships around the world. Millions of Zippos were carried into battle by American troops across the globe." Standard issue for U.S. servicemen in Vietnam. Many have their units or mottos emblazoned on them. "Death From Above." Simon is not aware of this.)

Is this related to your lifetime in San Diego?

"He's saying yes, he says, "It was his trip through Vietnam.""

Did you pass away in Vietnam?

"Just served there."

What was your name in that lifetime in San Diego?

"Allen."

Fred Allen?

I'm getting nothing now.

(Note: There were a number of Fred Allens who served in Vietnam from the San Diego area.)

It's almost like he's taking your questions and he's answering "He doesn't really care."

I understand. He's a tough guy. Fred is still playing a role. Showing him the images of what playing this role would be. Because he looks like Clint Eastwood smoking a cigarette, he's got a tough guy lighter. It's all part of that performance. But could you show Simon what you look like to the other council members?

It's a ball of light. And now he's laughing. He says, "Okay, fair enough. You got me."

What color is the light?

It's white with gold flecks that keep appearing and disappearing above or below or throughout. It's almost amorphous but at the same time undulating…

But the flecks of gold are moving in and out?

Yeah. One of the flecks of gold represents Fred's age and wisdom. He's saying "The older you get, the less gold you got."

So like a nurse or a doctor who shows up to save the life of a patient?

He's saying "It's more like saving the work of the council."

You're like a master technician, who they call upon to come in and save the day?

Now he's now he's kind of saying "No, no, don't put me on the spool. Don't make some grand guy. I'm just another one of the workers."

(Note: I'm not familiar with the term "put me on the spool" but fishermen are. "Wind me up" or "blow smoke" are other terms like it.)

We're among council members who are really good at what they do and they've been doing it for a long time. Anything you want to tell Simon about his journey and path that he needs to hear?

He's saying "You've got nothing to worry about. I'm not here because you have some pain coming at some point in the rest of your life."

Okay, were you called to help in a general way or a specific way?

"Remember that time doesn't exist (per se). So I could be helping out at any point."

Just a general notion that you're here to help Simon in terms of any kinds of pain?

"Yeah. He's kind of saying, "I've never seen this guy (before)." He's saying "It's like he's a consultant; they need him for like ten minutes to get his advice. And he comes in, does his bit and he's away again."

So give us an example.

He says, "Okay, somebody's dying. You have an incarnate, so they know somebody very close to them who's dying. This (one) counselor doesn't quite know how to handle the whole emotional side of it, so I tell them how this person's going to feel, how they're going to process it, what help they'll need. What signs they need, whether or not the person has died. How they're going to make contact in a very obvious way."

Like dying in a hospital?

"Yeah, (like) trauma in a hospital. He says "He's talking about the life of somebody who is a family member of the person who's

dying; he's not dealing with the dying person, but (with) the family member who is going to feel the pain of the loss."

Do you help give them signs to let the person know the person still exists, so they will no longer be traumatized?

"No. There may be people who grieve forever, never really get over it." And that's where he comes in. He says, "It's about the pain. It's not about relieving the pain. Pain is a lesson that has to be learned. We all have to learn it at some point in some life."

I've heard of guides helping people with grief, encouraging them to move grief to nostalgia. Grief being painful memories, and nostalgia being a combination of sad and happy memories.

He says, "Sometimes that's not the plan. Sometimes the grief is part of the lesson and that people might live years and then die and never get over the grief."

But is it okay to help people to overcome their grief because their loved ones still exist?

He's saying, "There's nothing wrong with that. But that's not his job. That's not what he deals with."

Fred, I'm saying, while you're showing people how to deal with grief, you can also show them because we have free will. We don't all have to experience endless grief, do we?

He says, "No." He adds, "Well, who do you think you are, giving me a job? Are you the boss?"

Thanks Fred. I'm just saying it's an option you can choose to add to your work helping people.

He's laughing and says, "Now I know why you've got a reputation as a troublemaker."

Oh my gosh, that's funny. Thank you Fred. Let's go to the person next if you don't mind. Male or Female.

She's a female. Sixty. She's wearing a toga with a blue stripe and gold stripe on it. And she's an Indian lady. And she's got this. You know, the red dot on the forehead?

A Bindi?

With lots of gold jewelry.

May I ask your name or a letter??

"The letter S."

May I ask if you've ever incarnated on the planet? And this is why you're dressed like this?

She says, "Yes."

Are you aware of what I'm doing or my work?

"No."

Where have you incarnated on the planet?

She says, "Yes, in India, She said it was her favorite life. In Kashmir.

And what would you like to tell us about Kashmir?

"Very hot. Lots of great food. She had a very loving husband her whole life. That's why it's one of her favorite lives."

Have you ever incarnated with Simon?

"No."

What do you represent in Simon's Council?

"Life."

And what's the blue and the gold stripes represent?

She says, "She's an observer."

What did you think of the conversation we just had? Was that normal for Fred or was that I was annoying him?

She says, "Oh, that's just Fred. We all know that's not really him. It's just a cloak he likes to wear."

Let's focus on your lifetime, were you Hindu, is that correct?

"Yes."

So what was it like for you when you departed that lifetime, and became aware of the between lives realm?

"It was no surprise, no surprise."

And in terms of religion and the concept of reincarnation. Reincarnation doesn't work the way it does in the books.

"Yes." She's using an analogy I've heard before. She says "Time is like a river. And then you're on the riverbank, you're outside of time, and you can walk up and down the riverbank and dip your toe in any part of the time stream your life." She says "You can reincarnate. You could die today, and then reincarnate in another era."

I've heard we wouldn't learn anything if we went back in time, plus we'd have to get everyone else to agree to have the same adventure.

She says, "You always learn, you plan to have a life where you learn a particular lesson, and you go to that timeframe where you would best learn."

How do you think Simon's doing?

"He's doing fine." She says "She's just there to observe the council and they don't have to do a lot. Sometimes the council is working hard, twenty-four hours a day. But Simon doesn't need that support."

Okay, how many councils do you observe?

"Thousands."

And do you participate in any?

"I observe, most of them who participate are the most senior ones." She wants to talk about this time thing.

Okay, go ahead, please.

She says, "You have no idea about the dimensions of the universe or how it all works. And this thing with time, and being able to step into any point of time; that's how it works."

I understand we can go back to visit any point of time on the timeline, but we are not living that life by observing it. Is that correct?

She says "No." She's standing now and has hundreds of people behind her. She says "These are all my lives from all different points in history. And that some of them existed at the same time. So I was incarnated twice in the same time period."

I've talked to people who are concurrently alive on another planet in another dimension while here on this planet. I understand you've had all these lifetimes, some were concurrent, but you've never gone back and lived the same lifetime again. Is that correct?

"Yes." She added that "She never needed to."

But the answer is "Yes, Richard, I never have lived the same lifetime again." So that is correct?

"Yes."

I just want to be clear, because I understand you've had many, many lifetimes. But we don't live them over again, do we?

"No. But we can incarnate at the same time period as one of our other lives. So we're living two lives at the same time."

Yes, I've heard that. Two lifetimes at the same time, as we bring a portion of our conscious energy to each one. Would you like to describe two lifetimes that you've lived at the same time?

She says, "No."

So let's examine a life where you were living concurrently?

She's showing me she's showing me she's accepting a cigarette from Fred. She's ripping the paper off the cigarette and putting all the tobacco into this really ornate pipe, and she's lighting it up and smoking a pipe. She's showing me a man in a very sharp suit, kind of like Sinatra, somebody like a successful white businessman. But then on the other side, she's showing me a black woman on her knees scrubbing a kitchen floor. She had both of these lives at the same time.

Were they both in America? Or are they both in different parts of the planet?

I'm getting he was Florida sort of area. And she was in the south but not in Florida.

Should we ask questions to either person?

She says "No, there's no point."

Has our friend Simon ever done that?

"Yes."

When?

I'm getting nothing from her. She's kind of holding the pipe and pointing it at you and kind of say, "Hey, you know, you'll get it (eventually)."

By the way, do you have any opinion about what's going on in India today?

She says, "Oh, dear. Oh dear, there's too much. Too much separation in the people. There are too many people with too much money, and then many, many people with no money; too much poverty." She said, "We don't need this from a soul level, that you can learn so much from living a life of poverty. But there's too much of it on Earth. There everything is out of balance.

So what do you recommend that we do?

She said, "There's not a lot we can do. We just have to let it run its course."

That's a perfect answer for someone who is "just an observer."

"That's my job," she says.

But we could use some advice on how to save the planet, stop pollution, change the climate, how to turn fresh water from saltwater, in an inexpensive way, how to stop global warming. These are all things that you have a unique perspective of, Miss S. How can we save our planet?

She says "A lot of what is there is needed on the soul level for people to learn lessons. If there wasn't suffering, then there'd be no chance of anybody learning the lessons. But she says there's a lot of young souls that have not lived many lives. And they don't have perspective."

Well, can we give them some perspective, by speaking about this, by talking to you directly?

She says, "They've got to live their lives and learn their lessons. And this takes, from the Earth point of view, hundreds of years. She's mentioning a person but it's political. Let's not say the name on the podcast.

Is there anybody else in the council that needs to speak to us?

"No."

Is there anything you guys want to tell me or Simon?

"You're doing good work getting the message out there."

Abbie, can you take him to his place of healing. Are you aware of what that is Simon?

"Not really."

But Abbie is?

"Yeah."

So Abbie, walk him there. Is it I inside or outside?

"Inside. She's given me a headphones. So we both got headphones and are listening to music. It's disco. I can't say a particular song. Maybe it sounds like Disco Inferno or something like that. She is dancing. It's light inside, but a huge drop off in the middle. There's a tub of energy."

Describe the tub.

Gold around the edge. It's full of shimmering blue water that seems to be alive. And it's lit up almost like it's luminous water.

Very good. Why don't you climb in there?

She says "Make sure I get my headphones back. I don't want them ruined."

Okay, don't go all the way and just go up to your neck. Just slide in there. What's it feel like?

It's first like, the water is the same temperature as my body. So when I slip into it, and I do go right under it's, it's like my body dissolves. I can't feel it anymore because it's all the same temperature or the same feeling.

Okay, and why is this a place of healing?

Its energy. She says it's kind of like it regenerates. But the soul is immortal. And it doesn't lose energy. But at the same time, this adds energy.

Abbie, correct me if I'm saying anything wrong, but the two of you create this kind of environment together, or was it just you?

It was Simon. It was assignment. She says we're here right now just show you what it is. It's not like Simon needs to load a healing (program.)

When he does that he has this experience of what what's the feeling. What quality of this experience comes to mind?

She's saying "it's kind of like drugs." Suggesting it's like heroin or LSD or cocaine or something. (Simon aside) I've never taken those drugs. Never had the opportunity.

So any, anybody you want us to meet or talk to?

"No." They're saying "Hey, you know what? We're busy."

Before we go, should we discuss this alien abduction experience that our buddy Simon had in his youth? Was that a memory or dream? Is that something he needs to examine or explore?

She said, that's all done now. No need to worry about. It's all in the past.

(Note: It's been a long session. Every reason for me to wrap this up. But something stops me from doing so.)

But let me ask Simon when you remember this event? Were there other people around?

Yes. There was a few. I haven't talked about this on the podcast. So none of the listeners would know about it about how I saw my alien abduction experience. While I was going through a past life regression. It just happened to come up during the session.

Well, but I just want to focus on this little moment here within the moment. Are you lying down? Are you standing up?

Well, are you talking about specifically when there are other humans there? Yeah, yeah, I didn't really interact with them. Right at the end, I found myself in this small white room with bench seats with clothes all over the floor and everybody was getting dressed, but nobody was talking to anybody.

Can you see any of them?

I can see them now.

Okay, let's just pick one person. I want you to turn it a hologram like a freeze frame. So there's no emotion associated with this conversation. Try to go closer and take a look at them. How tall are they?

About our feet tall. Color skin is dark grey. The eyes are large almond shaped eyes, a typical kind of gray alien. There's a mouth. Just a small slip for a mouth.

So I'm going to ask him a question. Is it okay?

Yeah, he's turned around now and he's looking at me.

Is he male or female?

Neither.

Can I have a letter or a name to address you?

"Q."

Thank you, Mr. Q. Are you familiar with what I'm doing?

"No, not at all."

Can I ask you some direct questions?

"Yes."

When you are seen by people, are you just flying by? A tourist?

"No."

Are you here to see Simon specifically?

"We see lots of people specifically. He wouldn't be here if we didn't want him to be here."

Have you met Simon before, Q?

"Yes. I have met him in his physical (form). He agreed to this before he was born on the condition that it would be something that would not interfere." (Simon aside) What I'm getting from is very emotionless. It's kind of robotic.

Q, can you show us your planet?

He says he's from "the factory."

Is that factory exists in our universe?

"Yes." It's like he's suggesting he's not a natural being, but that he was genetically engineered to do his job.

If you can, point us to where your planet exists, or where is the factory?

"You can't see it from the earth. It's beyond."

It's beyond our knowledge. Is that correct?

"Yes."

Okay, and how many times have you been to Earth in your lifetime Q?

He's saying, "I live here."

I want you to focus on where you originated. Before you first came to Earth. Are you physically examining Simon (when here) or are you a theoretically or energetically examining Simon?

Both. I'm physically here. It's like he's saying "It's outside of time. It's outside of space."

Q, let me ask, have you taken Simon's DNA back to your factory and manufactured somebody else?

"No," he's saying, "You are underestimating operations on Earth."

What's the operation?

He is kind of saying… "The human race will need to be replaced." Not because "the aliens" are removing them. And not because the human race will die out. It's kind of an evolution. It's an upgrade. Like an artificial evolution upgrade."

Upgrade! Okay, let's call it that. Because replace is a whole different concept in our lore. "It's a cookbook!"

(Note: Sorry, couldn't resist. Referencing the "To Serve Man" – an iconic Twilight Zone episode.)

Perhaps "upgrade?" Because "replace" can mean something's defunct or should be fixed. Upgrade allows for an update to allow consciousness to change. So are you talking about an upgrade in consciousness, Q?

"Yes."

So our physical brains do not let enough through?

"Yes."

And that's related to the filters on the brain. Is that correct?

"Yes."

And people who bypass those filters, doing what we're doing - which is what we're doing, we're bypassing those filters. Or if we had a near death experience, or if we have deep hypnosis or LSD or an out of body experience, a near death event, etc - we can bypass the filters so that we can access you. So are you trying to help humans to bypass their filters?

"Yes."

By this upgrade, okay. So ultimately will be able to converse with you?

"Yes, mentally."

Telepathically. And when will this occur? Or is that important?

He's kind of getting confused. It's like he's kind of, hesitating, as if he's thinking, "Hang on a second. I shouldn't be talking to this guy."

It's alright, Q. I've talked to others saying the same relative things. You're part of a group from the factory that's helping upgrade human consciousness so "we can communicate with beings." We've all incarnated, all of us choose to be a being; is that correct? So far?

Sort of, he's saying that the human race… Kind of like saying "It's part of a community. And it's not all about the human race, because you humans look to human centric (thoughts). You look at yourselves the whole time. You look at the Earth the whole time, you don't realize that there's so much more out there that you are a part of, and it's all connected. And that's one of the problems with humans. But that is also what makes the earth such a great place to learn lessons."

Have you ever incarnated on Earth?

"No."

Would you like to?

"No."

If I may, you just said it was a great place to incarnate and then said "Nah, not interested."

(Note: I ask complex questions for a number of reasons – including seeing if there's a pat answer or if we can learn new information.)

He says "He's busy. He said that the body that he has (now) lasts about four hundred years. And then he just goes back to the factory and gets another one when the time comes."

Can we go visit your family?

He says, "He doesn't have a family like what humans would call a family." He said "You might say that he has a soul group or a council of elders. If you call that a family."

If you could describe what that planet is like where the factory is located?

(Simon aside) What I'm seeing is a desert, a very scrubby desert with lots of rocks on it. He's saying, "Simon wouldn't want to walk around on here even last very long." What I'm seeing is like, the whole solar system is full of technology. And okay, this isn't the people that make him, this isn't where they're from, this is just one of their factories.

Q, take us to the place where the people who make you were made? Is that allowed?

He's kind of saying, "You wouldn't understand it. It's in other dimensions or another universe. These different beings, you'd see them as higher beings or even godlike, but they don't want to be viewed like that. They're just the same as you. They would never want to interact with you because they don't… because you would respond like that."

In the course of this research I've met quite a few people from other dimensions, higher dimensions, let's say, and we've had this discussion, I'm more interested in your journey. As you've said, in four hundred years, you'll go back, and now you'll go back to your council and your soul group, correct?

"This is possible, but he would just go and take on another body and carry on the work," he says.

So you're not aware of going back to your council and talking to them?

He's saying, "No, I've done that. I don't need to do that yet. I've got other things to do."

Do you have any friends from your soul group, currently on our planet that are from the factory?

"They're all from the factory."

Why do you call it that?

He says, "The bodies are genetically engineered" and he's kind of showing me loads of these, almost like huge glass bottles with the new bodies in them. "They're like fetuses and they grow inside this bottle. And when they're adult size, they come out and then their souls, jump in them and they're incarnated."

(Note: It's a mind-bending description, and I try to just continue asking questions.)

Why this particular design? If you're visiting Earth, why not design them to look more human?

"We don't need to." I think that this is kind of him saying "We've got everything sorted. We're done."

So let me ask you the size of your eyes… are the related to the light that's on the planet when you were walking around out there?

He's saying "The eyes are a conduit to conduit to a soul. They facilitate telepathy with the humans."

Ah, very interesting. So the eyes are more like an antenna and a receiver?

"Yes." He's saying "The nose and the mouth and the ears are unnecessary, but they'd be (there) to make the humans accept them more easily or something."

So you don't eat or other stuff?

"No. More like a robot but physical. Robot is a pejorative term, but more like a mechanical creature, let's say, a created creature."

Do you have emotions of love and loss and rejection or any of that?

He is saying, "With the human body, you have emotions. And they trigger chemicals to be released into the bloodstream, perhaps dopamine or adrenaline, and they make you feel emotions really intensely. But none of that happens with him."

(Note: It reminds me of the comedy show "Resident Alien.")

So have you ever experienced unconditional love in your lifetime, Q?

"Not in lifetime, but in death time."

Correct me if I'm wrong. But it sounds like your journey is that of a selfless being, helping others, and you agreed to show up as this entity to help others knowing that it was going to be devoid of human emotions?

He says, "You are saying that you are too human by saying I have never been human. And you shouldn't impose human life on me. It's human centric."

(Note: As a human, I can't think of another way to be.)

I'm sorry – let me clarify. I'm pointing out that if you and I can share this conversation about unconditional love, which you have experienced in the afterlife after your journey. You have friends who have, is that correct?

He says "He hasn't." But he says "He could do it." He said, "He has no desire to be a human on Earth right now."

I know you don't want to interfere with our evolution as a culture, but what should we think about when we run into someone like you?

He's saying, "We're not here on any kind of…" (Simon aside) He's saying the word "evil," but that's not quite right. He's saying "It's sort of as if he's saying that humans would see them as evil (if they met him)." He says, "There is just too much tribalism among humans. That's why they don't show themselves very much." But he's kind of saying, "If anybody ever does see them, it's because they want to be seen. They don't make mistakes like that."

Correct me if I'm wrong, part of your mission from the factory is to help humans to drop this illusion that there are other beings, animals, trees, other beings that are different than them; that we're all incarnating for a reason, we're all choosing to be alive or to be whoever we are. And once we come to that unusual understanding, we allow ourselves to meet people like yourself, Q?

"It's something you mentioned (before), which is that it's important for Simon to reconnect with (aliens). He made the agreement to donate some of his DNA before he even came to the planet. And even though he agreed to do it under the (agreement) it wouldn't disturb him or make him freak out. It doesn't seem to matter, because humans are not aware of the fact that they existed prior to incarnation. Not aware of any of that. So but the fact that he is able to access that, to say, "Sure, come and get a DNA sample."

Are you guys trying to figure out a way to conceive humans in the factory?

We're moving to the next stage now.

Is the evolution of the human race to learn how to remove the filters?

He is saying "The next stage isn't a few years away. This takes hundreds of thousands of years."

Simon and I met through this research, talking to people on the other side. Does this accelerate change, allowing people to hear about it in their lifetime?

"No."

So Simon and I are just twiddling our thumbs because it's going to happen anyway?

He's saying "It's all part of the message. The realization that there is more to life, more to the universe, that the near-death experiences, (the process) of reincarnation, they're all different messages."

Q, are you on Simon's Council? He mentioned about twenty people in the back.

"No, I don't do that. Not ever."

Well, maybe once you learn a few things you could become counselor. I'm teasing you.

(Simon aside) He doesn't seem very amused.

Okay, so what's a good joke in the world of Q? What would be amusing to you? You must have humor.

I got the word "religion."

That's pretty witty, and dark at the same time. Are you making a joke how religion is ridiculous and hilarious?

"Yes."

That's really dry wit.

He says, "There's definitely something to religion. But you humans have got it all wrong." He's saying "You don't understand the bigger picture. They took religion and dumbed it down to the human level."

Would spirituality be a more accurate term than religion? I've heard "God is beyond the capacity of the human brain to comprehend, but we can experience God if we open our hearts." Is that accurate?

He's saying "God isn't separate from people. We are all a part of God. And you shouldn't view God as being separate. from us. When the soul enters the human body, it's being put in a box, the lid shut, all the sides are shut. There's no windows. Don't forget that God isn't separate from you, you are God. And you were all a part of it. We're all connected. And that unconditional love is all a part of all of us.

Where are you now Q? Physically on or off planet?

"Underwater. On this planet. Under the sea."

What would be the nearest port or country to where you are under the sea?

He's saying "He's between New York and Paris."

Are you moving around the planet in a ship? Shifting dimensions?

He says, "We have it both ways. If we want to be seen, we'll get seen. And we don't have a factory where we build them. We can just click our fingers and they appear and then we go wherever we like."

May I ask you about the UFO that was seen off the fantail of the US Navy ship that they recorded?

He says, "It was staged. We knew what would happen. It's like, we don't have trouble viewing time. We can go forward; we can go backward. And we knew how this would come out. We knew how the pilots would be able to film it, and how it would be released and people would see it. And that's what we wanted. So it did dance in front of the cameras."

Very good. So how do we access you Q? Do we have to meet up physically?

"No. We don't have to meet physically. I've sent dreams before," he said. "It's all part of the process of making you aware that there's more to life than just this… and what you experience in flesh and blood."

So when did you first visit Simon? How old was he, Q?

"Six months."

And you got all the DNA out of him that you need?

"We finished with that a long time ago."

And the DNA that Simon has provided? Is it just stored somewhere?

"It goes back to the factory."

And do you use wormholes to get there?

He says "It is interdimensional travel you wouldn't understand. He's saying that he can have a body there and a body here. And he'll leave this body and join that one. In a split second."

So you're holding onto this specimen? And it goes into a special tube?

"Yeah, we'd make more humans (with it). I don't need to be there. When the specimen gets there someone else can work with it. He says there's billions of him. Not (Simon) but billions of these bodies that are in (existence.) He's also saying that they there are many Earth like planets where humans live. And the beings are like us physically. They live on other planets living other lives, and some of them are aware of Earth.

So the DNA goes back to the factory. And then it's used to create what?

"Not a human. It's like on Earth, you normally get a man and a woman to produce a baby, but you don't get an exact replica of one of them." He says, "It depends on the filters. He says it's a kind of a fine art to tune the filters. And they always don't always get it right."

But I mean, do they return to some other planet? Are they sent off as babies?

"Yes, sometimes they go to the same kind of place. There are lots of planets that interact with this kind of being, completely openly, (where) there's no such thing as "UFOs." They're well aware of aliens."

Simon's DNA becomes mini-Simon. Does that energetically go into the womb of some woman on another planet?

"Depends where they're supposed to go. Some planets don't have a family structure like we have on Earth, where there's a mother and a father and children. And so the women are quite happy to receive an egg. They might go to a planet like Earth, abduct a woman and put an egg in them without them knowing or wanting. He's saying that these women would have agreed to this before they were born."

You're describing the earth as a source to create beings around the universe. Or is it just one of many factories?

One of many factories. He kind of says, "You humans didn't just evolve on Earth." It's like he's saying, "this isn't the origin of the human species."

It's fascinating Q, because you seem kind of human.

He says, "He was created. When they when they designed him, they took away most of the emotion. The soul was still there in the background."

Why not more like humans?

He says, "Then he wouldn't be an efficient tool. If you had a hammer that had emotions, it wouldn't be so easy to use it. To hammer in nails."

So you've got a lifetime of four hundred years and how far along are you?

"One hundred years left." He says, "I'm like this for a reason. All this has been considered." He says "This is all part of the process. This is influencing you a lot more than him." He added, "When he says "you" he doesn't mean Richard. But humans."

I appreciate the ability to ask questions. I know it's unusual for you, but obviously we could do it more often.

And it's as if he wants to. He'd like to.

Okay, have you ever had the need to converse with Simon like this before?

"No."

So why did you allow it today?

It was just there. He says, "He's interacted with thousands of humans. There's nothing special about Simon."

I understand. But none of those humans have asked you questions?

None.

Not that we're patting ourselves on the back, but this is the first time in your three-hundred-year existence that you've been asked these threshold questions?

"Yes."

Okay, so we've altered your path, my friend.

He says, "Maybe a little bit. That's it." (Simon aside) We went way beyond time. (Simon aside) I was just letting the voice come through, letting the words come through and just telling you exactly what I heard... I wasn't trying to analyze it, just tell you exactly what was coming into my head.

*****

CHAPTER TWENTY: SKIP AND JANE

STORY TELLERS

My friend "Skip" (not his real name) is a story teller. "Jane" (not her real name) is a prolific award-winning story teller who has worked with a number of other award winning story telling folks.

I just want to recap.

In my dinner conversation with Skip, we started speaking to his guide "Lavinia." She said she has been his guide for many lifetimes. She reminded him of a lifetime where he worked as a blacksmith in Virginia in 1865. He didn't seem like a totally carefree guy as my friend is now. In this memory, he said that he "died in his sleep." He recalled that his name was Smith, and his first name was Evan.

(Note: A number of Evan Smiths in the Ancestry records from Virginia or nearby who lived in the 1860's. I always check.)

I've asked his guide if we could visit with my friend Skip's council. At the moment I reach into my pocket, put my cellphone on our dining table in the restaurant, and begin to record.

At this moment in time, he was able to see "three council members" sitting among six chairs.

Rich: May I say, thank you so much for allowing us to converse with you I think it's going to be helpful for our friend on some level, I don't know what, but we're starting with the person on the far left. Is that a male, female or light?

SKIP: A female.

And a name we can call her?

It's "Michelle." She's about twenty-seven. She has black hair, dark hair, and light skin. She has a dress on and is wearing like a black shawl.

Okay, so does she look familiar to you in any way?

She looks like my mom.

Michelle, are you familiar with my work?

She says, "Yes."

What's your opinion of it?

"It's accurate."

(Note: We've been friends for a while; Skip's vaguely aware of what I've been up to in this field, as the topic wasn't something we focused on. He seemed chagrined that his council member was aware of my work as he was not.)

The reason I ask is because sometimes they are not aware, and some on the same council are. Michelle, is it accurate to describe you as a council member on Skip's Council?

"That would be correct. Yes."

And so what quality do you represent on this council? In a word?

"Patience."

Would you like to show him the lifetime where he learned that lesson? Patience? Or should we move on to talk about other things?

"It was a lifetime where he lost his family towards the end of his life. It was in the 1900's."

Towards the end of his life in what century?

"The nineteen hundreds."

He lost his family? Was that in the life as a blacksmith in Virginia? How did he lose his family?

"His wife killed herself."

I'm sorry to hear that. But if I may, our friend here has carried those stories forward into this lifetime. He's a great storyteller. Is that true? Michelle, would you characterize it that way?

(Nods) "Yes."

And what how do you think our friend is doing?

She says, "Just fine."

So he is on the path that he's supposed to be on. Thank you. Michelle, would you introduce us to the person on your left? Is that a male a female?

"Male. He has like cotton pants and no shirt. He's black. Eighteen years old. His name is "Bill."

Thank you for talking to us Bill. Are you familiar with my work?

"No."

(Note: As above, two members of the same council, one is aware, and one is not.)

Bill, how is our buddy Skip doing?

He says, "Excellent."

And Bill, what do you represent on this council?

"Perseverance."

First "Patience" and now "perseverance," two very key things. Just in terms of his journey now, his stories revolved around perseverance?

(Note: Skip looks surprised at what he's hearing.)

"The story is about him."

I'm sorry? Oh. You're saying this is Bill, as in the actual Bill our friend has told a story about?

"Yes."

(Note: This detail seems startling to my friend, as well as to me. "Bill" lived a century ago, was falsely accused of harassing a white women and was tortured and hanged in his home state. My friend Skip has told the story of what happened to him; it was horrific – a young black man in love with a young white girl; he was falsely accused of rape by her family. The family and neighbors hunted him down, had him stripped, flogged and whipped in public. There are public photos of his naked broken and hanged body. Despite torture to make him "confess" Bill's story never altered. He died a courageous man who refused to lie about what happened.)

I just to clarify, because this is, of course, this is always a little bit disconcerting, when somebody you know, shows up on your council. So have you always been a member of Skip's Council? Or are you a council member who is embodying what Bill looks like to remind him of this frequency or energy?

He says "I've always been a member."

So you were a member of his council, even in a previous lifetime?

He says "Yes."

So let me ask, why did you choose such a difficult lifetime for yourself and your own path? If you can access why, or what lessons you wanted to learn or teach?

He says, "It was about love."

A very profound lesson in love that, that a person can go through anything, if they love somebody. How do you think our friend Skip is doing with his lifetime?

"He's doing excellent."

And, and so are you inspiring him in some way with these stories he's telling?

"Yes."

And can you give me some lottery numbers?

He's laughing.

It's always tough to get a laugh from someone over there. Thank you sir, is it true that our mutual friend can always access you?

"Yes."

Can you put a sensation in his body that he can feel? So he knows that you're here nearby and trying to advise you?

(Skip nods.) I've got it.

Bill, can you introduce us to the person that's to your left, is that a male or a female?

Female.

Thank you for allowing us to talk to you. And what's a name that I can use to refer to you?

"Terry."

How does Terry look to you? What's the visual?

She has on glasses. She has curly hair.

And about how old?

Forty-six.

Terry, are you familiar with this work I'm doing?

"No."

Two out of three. But you've seen what we're doing, what's your opinion of asking council members questions?

"Seems harmless."

How do you think our friend is doing?

"Exactly what he's supposed to be doing."

Can you say that again?

"Exactly what he's supposed to be doing."

I asked you to repeat it because sometimes it's hard to comprehend that we could feel like we're not getting anywhere, spinning our wheels, because we always feel we should be doing more or better. But he's doing exactly what he's supposed to be doing?

"Yes."

What quality do represent on Skip's council?

"Confidence."

Have you been giving him confidence through all his lifetimes?

"**Yes, all of them.**"

Terry, let me ask a question on behalf of our friend. We can't ask about the future because it hasn't happened yet. What would you like to show him?

"**That something big is coming around the corner.**"

Terry, I just want to be able to put this in context. So we heard patience. We've heard perseverance, and we've heard confidence. Now, what about these other three chairs? Are these guys busy?

"**They're around later.**"

What do those folks represent without getting into too many details?

"**Focus, calm, and planning.**"

Focus, calm and planning... like engineering? Are these qualities that you often think about in your work as a story teller?

Yes, I do.

So now we know why. Terry, can you put a sensation that's different than the one Bill created for him? The reason I asked Bill is because I know he's really influential. But Terry is different, someone Skip doesn't know – can you put a sensation in his body so that he knows you're always connected and tethered to him?

"**Okay.**"

Is there anything else you want to show Skip? And Lavinia, of course, you're here as well. Is there anything you want to show him? Like, sometimes people like to go and see the library? Sometimes people want to go and see a place of healing. Or a life planning session?

I'm seeing a big crowd. The crowd is listening to this.

How many people are in this crowd? Just roughly?

"Thousands. Maybe ten thousand."

Are these people that our friend has known throughout his lifetimes?

(Nods) Yes.

And so they've come to gather to hear him as an artist, is that correct? And so when you look out over the crowd, just describe the place we're in is in an auditorium,

Literally, it's an outdoor area. The rows go up.

Look at the people. This is a weird question I've never asked before. Could somebody in the front row stand up and answer a question for us?

Okay.

Who are you guys?

"We're friends." It's a guy. He's standing up.

What's his name?

He says his name is "Peter."

Peter, what do these people, this crowd here represent for our friend?

"People seeking people seeking the truth."

And Peter, what would that be in your case? Is it watching something that our friend creates something that speaks to the truth?

They want to listen to something I have to say and "how to bring more justice... bring more justice to the world."

Lavinia did you orchestrate this audience or who, who came up with this idea?

It was Terry. She's smiling.

Well, that's a beautiful thing. And thank you Peter in the front row for standing up. We appreciate it. Peter are you alive now? Or is this your higher consciousness speaking?

He says "He's alive now."

What's your second name?

"Thompson."

So Peter Thompson, if I ran into you, at some point in my life, you wouldn't have access to this memory?

"Right."

Well, allow me to thank everybody that's part of your crew, your council members. I've heard this before, and it's worth repeating. They're always connected to us no matter where we are in the plan. So even when things look really dim, you just ask for help. You've opened the door, just open up the door and ask for help. Thanks everyone!

*****

JANE

The following was recorded in a noisy kitchen at a party. I'm speaking with Jane (not her real name) and she asked me about what kind of work I'm doing. Something prompted me to just "give it a shot" to see where we might go. We met some decades earlier at an "industry event" in another country, but I don't think she's aware of it.

In this noisy enclave, she was able to picture herself in a boat on a river.

The boat seemed "more like a raft." Her husband (who had passed) showed up to sit across from her on the boat. She was amused because he was only wearing boxer shorts – and it was a pair she had never seen before. (New information). She was able to hold his hands and they seemed warm. He was able to "nod" to let us know that he was happy to have a conversation. He seemed younger, before his passing.

Her mother "Annie" also came up in our conversation – and we invited her to come sit beside them. She seemed to be younger as well, in her 60's. She was happy to be invited, Jane could hold her hands and felt they were warm. Annie said that her daughter was doing "Just fine."

I invited her guide to join us – and when asked if he was a male, female or light, she saw him as a yellow light with purple streaks running up and down. When asked she said the purple streaks represent deep insight or old consciousness awareness. I asked if he would appear as a male or female and he appeared to her as an older man in a white robe – white hair, blue eyes. When I asked her guide how she was doing, she said "He says, "She could be better."

Since we were standing in the kitchen of a party, I asked her guide if this was a good time to introduce her to her council. It was possible for him to say "No," but he said it was.

I asked Jane if she was "inside or outside" – and at first she said "We're still on the boat." So I asked her guide to "bring her to her council." I pointed out that he knows what I'm talking about even if Jane did not – and she said they were "outside." She could see some trees and the ground was "forest." It's at this point I remembered to turn on my recorder.

Rich: We're with Jane's guide at her council. We're outside with her "council." And first of all, allow me to thank the council for allowing us to come here. How are they arrayed?

Jane: In a line.

So let's go to the council member on the far left. Is that a male, female or light?

A male.

Describe him, age, clothing, whatever you can see.

He's about Seventy. He's wearing a white robe, has white hair.

May I ask you a question, sir?

He says, "Yes."

What's a letter or a name I can use for her address you?

"Dee."

Mr. Dee. Thank you. How is Jane doing?

"Jane is still hurting."

Still hurting over the loss of her husband. I'm sorry.

(Jane nods)

Mr. Dee. What do you represent on her council?

"Strength."

Can you transfer or put some of that strength into our friend here, and give her a feeling of that transfer so she knows she's felt it?

(Nods). I can feel it in the top of my head.

Mr. Dee, correct me but there's no pain that she can't overcome. Please correct me if I'm wrong.

He said "Yes."

How many councils are you on Mr. Dee?

"Many."

Do you represent strength on all those councils?

"Sometimes something else."

If you could introduce us to the person on your left. Is that a male, female or light?

Female. She's also wearing white robes.

Is she younger, older?

She's younger. Dark hair. Her name is the letter R. But now I'm hearing "Arie."

Arie, can I ask you some questions?

She says, "Yes."

How's Jane doing?

She says, "She's doing better."

So that's a little different than Mr. Dee. What do you represent on her council?

"Lightness. Lightening up."

How many councils are you on Miss Arie?

"Not many."

So this is kind of a special relationship between you and Jane. Have you had a lifetime together before?

(Jane nods).

Do you want to show it to Jane? What country are we in?

"France."

And what year comes to mind?

"1918."

What was the purpose of that journey? What did you learn from that lifetime?

She says, "Liberation."

Can you show Jane what she looked like? Was she a boy or girl?

"It was a transition. She was a boy in a previous life becoming a girl in this one."

She was sort of in the middle of that? And so in what city was this?

"Paris."

Any friends in that lifetime now that she knew then?

"Yes. Somebody that she knows now."

Let's ask her friend on the flipside "Joe" to come forward. (Her deceased partner) Joe, do you want to show Jane a life you guys had before? Where was it on the planet?

He says, "We discussed this. Joe and Jane discussed their past lifetime in ancient Persia. This is something we talked about. Jane was like a lowly slave girl and Joe was a prince."

So, let's ask Joe. Was this memory accurate? They had a lifetime together in Persia?

"Yes."

Arie, can you introduce the person on your left?

I'm seeing an older male with white hair, also wearing white.

Can I ask you for a name or a letter we can call you?

The letter "H."

So we have Miss Aria, we have Dee, and we have H. Dee represents strength? Miss Arie you represent light, or lightening. And H, what do you represent?

He says, "Equanimity."

How many councils do you sit on?

"Twenty."

How do you think Jane is doing?

He said, "Fine."

We've gone from "hurting" to "okay" to "fine." Joe, how is she doing?

"Okay."

So what do you guys think about this form of communication? Why did you drag me over to this party so that I can help her talk to you? What is it you want her to observe from this exercise?

"Greater understanding."

And if you can just give her an example of what that is. She doesn't have to say what comes to mind.

(Nods) Okay.

Let me ask, does it include the ability to heal people through story telling?

"Her presence and her work."

I've heard this consistently (about people in the arts). Even in my own journey, my own hypnotherapy session; "Story telling can help people's disposition or health." Laughter can change their disposition. So is that true?

"Yes."

Mr. H? You're helping her with equanimity, to be calm. So is there a spokesperson for this council? Does anyone want to come forward? Or is it one of these three?

"They're all equal."

Who's her spark? The one who you know gets her going creatively?

That is Dee.

Mr. Dee, can you show her an example of something where she didn't really feel like doing it, but you were there to inspire her?

(She nods) "It was grounding. Making a sense of purpose."

Let's ask her guide, can you take her to a place of healing? He knows what I mean, a place that people go to after a tough lifetime to reconnect to their energy. Are we inside or out?

We are inside. It's a room with an altar.

Let's go up to the altar. Take a look at what's on it.

It's funny, there's a kind of candelabra.

Okay, is that a specific religious artifact? Are the candles lit?

(Jane nods) Yes.

What does she do in this room to reconnect to her energy? Does she sit down? Does the energy come to her?

I'm going down in front of the altar, like sort of kneeling.

Can she call that healing light into her? She could do that anywhere, right?

"Correct."

Is she always connected to you, no matter where you are?

"Yes."
*****

I include these two sessions because they were both impromptu – apparently our guides are always available no matter where we are, even in noisy restaurants or at a party.

CHAPTER TWENTY-ONE: A COMPENDIUM OF COUNCILS

PART ONE

Paul Aurand – Hypnotherapist/Author

PAUL AURAND - A VISIT TO THE COUNCIL *(FROM THE BOOK FLIPSIDE: A TOURIST'S GUIDE ON HOW TO NAVIGATE THE AFTERLIFE)*

RICH: Can you describe your own life between life session?

PAUL: It was a Civil War scene, I was in a pile of bodies, not quite dead. And then finally, I left that body and was met by my spirit guide, and pretty quickly was taken to this sort of domed place where the council, the wise beings were, and they were going to review my life with me.

As I approached this building, I thought I was going to go in and be judged. One of the greeters came forward and said "No, no. There's no place for that here, this is not about being judged, there's no place for guilt or shame, that's not the way for you to enter here." I was reassured there's no need to fear I was going to be judged.

Inside, I saw they had robes, I'd describe them as purely energetic and I felt that unconditional love again. They didn't really speak, but rather took me mentally through the experiences of a number of lifetimes. It wasn't like watching a movie or looking at them in a book - they actually put me into those lifetimes, so I could re-experience them from a different perspective.

One in particular was when I was a slave owner. I was by the side of the road and I was whipping my slaves. It was horrifying to see I could have that sort of attitude or mentality. I didn't even consider them to be human; I seemed to care more about my animals. It was very unpleasant. They showed me other lifetimes where I'd been calloused about people's feelings.

Then the council brought me back and said "You're getting much better. The work you're doing now is benefiting people." They gave me the profound experience of reconnecting with the whole, being part of the Creator, part of the universe. An incredible feeling. Then they said "When you judge, when you criticize, when you discount, you separate - this is what causes the separation from the whole." They didn't talk about it as a philosophy, but gave me the experience of being separate again. "When you do this, you diminish the light for everyone." What a profound lesson for me and the world. We have learned from doing this work there are life lessons within each lifetime; we're here to accomplish certain things. It's a school where we learn and grow, but in addition to life lessons, there are soul lessons; lessons we may take many lifetimes to learn."

HOWARD SCHULTZ - THE COUNCIL OF ELDERS (From FLIPSIDE)

A few months later, I arranged for an old friend, a prolific television producer to do a hypnotherapy session with Scott De Tamble (lightbetweenlives.com) The transcript is in the book FLIPSIDE: "The River of Souls." He recalled a lifetime that ended in Dachau, that of a young Jewish girl from Denmark named Helga.

Scott De Tamble: Let's move into that sacred space. How many beings are awaiting us?

HOWARD: There are five. The tallest one is in the middle - it goes short then tallest then taller than short... They look almost like a crown.

How do they appear as individuals?

One is very tall, very thin. Almost like... like one of the trees, but not one of the trees.

Is the tall one the spokesman? Or are they all equal?

He's the leader, but there's a female to his left and she wants to speak too. Everyone else is quiet.

What would the female like to say?

"Welcome home. The journey is far from over. You're doing so well. We miss you, but you must continue on."

What was the life purpose as Helga?

There wasn't enough time to bring enough light, but enough to bring some good.

What is the life purpose now as Howard?

To bring much more light.

What's the point in having it taken away?

Otherwise there's no game. (Laughs). It's too easy the other way.

Is this something he agrees to? That he does himself?

I don't do it myself; it's been arranged though. It was a bad choice to arrange it. But otherwise there would be no challenge.

Let me ask your female elder on your council what's the purpose of having challenges like this?

"It's about patience and understanding, it's to learn about trust and patience."

What was the connection between that past life and this life?

"Be crazy fearless. Fear nothing; be bold."

What about his competitive streak? Why does he hate losing?

"It comes from being human... That's part of the human being. Because where we come from (in the life between lives), there's no winning or losing."

Being here, we enjoy this?

This is the game, yeah.

Is there a pattern to the lives he's lived?

The pattern is always to bring that special something... It's the light - the promise is the light, the bringing of the light. This is his pattern, over and over.

Bring the light? Can you put that in other terms?

It's to bring what is there in this other place (between lives) - to bring to this place. To bring peace and the knowing that "all is well."

About the specific purpose of this lifetime, what's the main life purpose?

To bring light to many people. This is his tool. We've never had this before, to be able to reach so many people.

Does he have specific lessons in this lifetime?

The life of Helga was very shocking, very upsetting; it's like "Let it go, shake it away."

He's still having residue?

It's the source of his doubt. The world can be shocking, horrible and bad. Her life was to show him how bad it could be.

Let's halt this and take him to a place to cleanse him of this darkness and doubt.

The soul river.

Let's go there. Tell me about this place.

This is where one washes the soul.

You all walk in together?

Yes. With the elders. This is... These are the waters to forget. The waters to wash clean.

Let the water cleanse you. Be there with the elders. Stay as long as you need to.

(Lips moving) I'm aware... That (my life as Helga) it burned my soul. That time burned my soul. (He takes a deep breath...)

Let the waters soothe your soul. Rest now. While you're resting, etch this in your mind. Your body and soul can always remember this place. You can return to this place of healing anytime you wish. Take your time; tell me when you're ready.

I can go now.

Did you wash away the trauma? How do you feel?

I've carried that a long time. It's better now.

What's the message you got from that time?

I never knew the darkness could be *so*... It was really dark.

Now you have a taste of that, and you can help others who've experienced dark times.

Now there's no need for doubt.

Is there anything you would like to ask the council? Take your time.

Give me your strength, give me your knowledge. Be my courage.

How do they respond?

"We are here for you. Yes, of course."

Let me ask what he needs to touch that strength and courage, how can he contact you to be able to have that flow through him?

"Don't doubt it; we are there for you." Be bold and fearless.

Any messages from the council for this soul here?

"All this you know." And "You make us laugh." (Chuckles).

I'm sorry to say that Howard passed away some years later while sitting on his favorite beach in Hawaii. He was a good friend, and has shown up often in our research, an excerpt of this interview is in the film "HACKING THE AFTERLIFE." (HackingTheAfterlifeFilm.com)

Howard Schultz – Lighthearted Entertainment

JOEL - THE COUNCIL OF ELDERS

"Joel" is a literary agent. He was a skeptic about this process, but agreed to do a hypnotherapy session with Scott De Tamble. In this case, Scott came to his noisy literary office to do a hypnotherapy session. (Excerpts are in the film FLIPSIDE (FlipsideMyFilm.com) and transcript is in the book FLIPSIDE.)

Scott De Tamble: Let's talk to the council about your current state.

"He needs to imprint the phenomenon that there are past lives and he does have guides, and he does have protection for himself and has council members that will talk to him."

What's the purpose of this session today?

"To experience, to figure if he wants to go further in this field and to also bring as much light and intelligence and love back to his daughter and back to his wife."

Anyone else on the council?

Yes, I see my grandmother. (A pause, while he speaks to her) Okay.

Etch this in your mind, the bright light, and the loving people. Is there somewhere else Frenchie would like to guide you to?

Frenchie (my guide) wants to bring me to a gigantic church with 100 foot ceilings, gold statues, pews made of gold, tremendous choir singing, just the two of us, sitting and listening - the whole thing is for us...

What is this place?

He says "This is your church, this is your synagogue and this is your temple, I just want to show you that all the spiritual things you're doing right... It's your holy place. Your church, temple, synagogue, ashram. We've built it for you."

You've helped build it with your devotions?

My guide Frenchie's leading me to a different place that looks like the Taj Mahal and he says "Come in, this is yours too." (Gestures with his hands) "That's yours and this is yours, you deserve it and you've earned it, it comes with servants and elephants and monkeys and food and wine and fruit and you can have six wives or seven mistresses, or none, and there's children and food and people are happy in this Taj Mahal; it's yours." It's huge.

So you have this as well.

He's got his spirit and his secular; it's been built with your spirit and they're both enormous benefits to you - walk into the church to feel the energy or bring people into the Taj Mahal, give them gold, whatever you want in an endless supply. And Frenchie says, "You can come back here anytime you want, they're never going to go away, they're yours forever."

Awesome. Maybe it's time to rest... Let's have your guide take you somewhere to do that.

We're in Tahiti in a grass hut and I'm on this table and I'm being massaged and oiled and my shoulders are being rubbed and it's just a beautiful Tahitian breeze and it's wonderful and so relaxing and then as soon as they're done I'm going into a deep sleep and relaxing; they've given me something to drink; some kind of relaxing tea.

Let's ask him about the kidney problem you mentioned...

I asked (my doctors) for an operation to fix it, and they wouldn't do it. They said "Let's live with it."

Is there a deeper meaning?

The one that keeps coming up is the memory of the lifetime with a spear in the side - I was running away and they got me.

So what's the message you're supposed to get?

That you can't run away from yourself. That truth is your identity and if you live the truth then anything aberrant or off to the side is going to dissipate. That's the best you can do.

So once again...

"Don't run away from the truth. Because if you run away, we're going to throw another spear at you." It's like saying "Take what belongs to you and don't run away from it." You didn't need to steal the gold, it was yours, you were the son of the King, and it was your gold. Why were you stealing it?"

The spear in the back, you understand it now?

It feels better already.

Okay, keep your church and the Taj Mahal close to your heart... (Etc as Scott talks Joel back to consciousness)."

ROBERT BEER - THE COUNCIL OF ELDERS

Robert has taught at Oxford University, and has been an expert in Nepalese art for decades. This is from an email he sent me describing his session with a Newton trained hypnotherapist in London.

London Hypnotherapist: Let's go to a place of learning.

ROBERT: There are beings here. I have humility and bow before them. They are Elders. They're luminous, white, wearing robes with folds, a little bit like choir boys' robes, pleated. They're radiant white. They wear silver medallions and there are 5 or maybe 6 beings. They're androgynous, but appear as male; in essence, they are who we are, projections of ourselves, our own potentiality. The image I see is like "The Last Supper." They're in a semi-circle, behind a curved panel, a blue light behind. It's a bit like a Sunday school! It's a dome structure made of panels of blue. The curve of the rostrum follows the curve of the dome. The dome is blue, like stained glass within a gold lattice of triangles.

As I look around, I see there are fine rays of light, and the beings have auras like deities have. I can smell roses and jasmine on my hands, the smell of divinity, of sanctity. It's a cathedral of light with Guides, beings, friends.

My daughter Carrina is my main Guide. Her face is radiant with light… They're like icons; they're not in a complete state. I feel overwhelming awe with these presences… too wise and too enlightened to be human. But it's wonderful.

Let's ask for help in healing the sadness we touched on in your current life. (Note: His daughter Carrina passed suddenly.)

It's very healing to have these images of seeing Carrina so joyful and not to have the pain of missing her. She's advanced, but advancement on this level… I'm looking into the philosophy rather than any dogma. She can take human form and will again. My work in this world is to take the dogma out and see from our own experience what will help. Human birth is precious, but I believe we have complete freedom to assume any form. Our Guides are us; we are not separate. We have this incredible capacity to assume responsibility rather than place it on our Guides and Elders, although they embody what we aspire to. I would like to take away from this the ability to help people with bereavement.

Put that message to the Elders.

They say, "You do the best you can already." To pay attention to every human, that's what I'm good at. I can keep my attention on them and inspire them. "Be content with what you've got," is the message.

Artist/Author Robert Beer

From IT'S A WONDERFUL AFTERLIFE VOLUME TWO

In the follow up books to Flipside, I focused on scientists research consciousness outside the brain, as well as other practitioners. While attending a wedding in Connecticut I met a shaman who presided over the wedding, and we had a lively discussion about the research. Later, she shared with me the audio recording of her own session with a Newton Institute trained hypnotherapist. (I was not in attendance.)

Meeting the Council – SHAMAN MIKKI BALOY

Hypnotherapist: What does (your guide) Ezekiel have to say?

MIKKI: "Welcome back, happy to see you." He's sort of poking me a little, like (entering) the press conference. "We know you like to make an entrance, ever the actress."

Do you ever meet with wise beings between-lives?

Yes. The council.

Would you like to go with someone or by yourself to visit them?

I go by myself. I know where they are.

Okay, going there, describe your travel route, what you see along the way.

There's a little foot bridge over the pond, I stop there and look at the view and then continue. There's a white stone pathway, like a white sidewalk. White marble columns, beautiful lawns and trees, there's a building that looks sort of Grecian, pillars and a dome roof. There are pillars that have four corners. From a distance, I'm reminded of the Taj Mahal too – seen from above, apparently there's a window in Chartres, that looks like this – the Rose Window? I don't know – there's a beautiful white stone. There are stairs to the front entrance. Approaching it I feel that this is a special and sacred thing but not in an intimidating way. I don't feel

I need an appointment or that I have to do anything in particular, but I am aware this has importance.

Okay, go ahead inside.

Ah, a beautiful room!

Can you describe it?

Checkered board floor, but beautiful different colored stone, and indoor pool, fountain, almost looks Middle Eastern, hanging plants, beautiful, lush plants, open air, birds are flying in and out of the windows, it's sort of like every culture at once, Grecian Roman pillars, and this Middle Eastern mosaic tile – it's just gorgeous.

How many beings are waiting for you?

Three. I'm being shown an empty chair, too. The fourth is off doing something else.

Is Ezekiel with you or are you alone?

I'm alone. I'm across the pool from them.

Look closely, do see any gender among the members?

A woman and two men.

How are they dressed?

She is very regal, wearing purple robe that's a little more fitted than the others, very stately and tall. The man next to her is sort of short and round, wearing white. Very simple. And the other man is sort of like Obi Wan Kenobi – bearded with a grey robe. They're telling me that the fourth who couldn't be there is some woman – very lively, outgoing woman in light blue.

So you have two males and two females?

Yes, but today just the one.

Do you miss having her at this time? Or do you understand why she's not here?

I understand.

Is one of these elders the chair person?

The woman.

Are they wearing any sort of ornaments?

The one in grey has a gold medallion. It's sort of rectangular but with rounded corners. The (other) one has something smaller I can't quite see, but he has bracelets – and the woman has a similar gold rectangular bracelet – they're sort of embossed or engraved with something I can't quite see.

Can you try to look at little closer at the design? Do you have a sense of the meaning of it?

There's a jewel in the middle, then it looks like a wave cresting. She's saying it's a metaphor for something - like the jewel can't be eroded.

Do you have a sense of what that jewel means? The individual soul? What does it mean to her? To you?

Hm. Yes, it's this soul – the soul is the truth – it's also that there's no problem with the ocean, it's not trying to erode the jewel. It's cleaning it over and over and over again. It's the relationship.

Beautiful. Does the number of your council change after each lifetime?

That fourth woman comes in and out. It's okay, but it's always those four.

Anything different about the surroundings since your last visit?

I think it's more colorful, like they've painted it. She's pointing to the koi – "We've got new fish" (Chuckles).

What's the first thing you hear in your mind when you're addressed?

It's the woman and she says "They're happy I'm there, and she knows why I'm here." She's reminding me that everything led to this point. She's shaking her head "There are no accidents ever." And I've been told this before.

What else does she say?

"That there's nothing they can tell me that I don't already know."

Do they have a certain area of expertise when they question you that relates to your own level of experience?

The one in grey seems to embody the martial arts. He teaches me to be savvy, to protect myself without doing harm. Using skill – discernment, but used (metaphorically) like a Tibetan sword of wisdom.

A sense of aikido?

He really is like Obi Wan – (I'm hearing) that the ("Star Wars") character wasn't accidental. The character was modeled on the sort of archetypal thing that he is – representing mastery. The male guide on the right is about laughter and pleasure, creature comforts, sensuality, he's sort of like Bacchus. Maybe he is Bacchus – he's like Dionysus and all of his ecstatic energies.

The woman?

She's like *Ayahuasca*. She's sort of nodding, saying there's not too much more to say about that.

I like her. So what do your elders say about your progress?

I'm actually doing better than they expected. Like I've skipped ahead a few steps.

This is okay with them?

Yeah. Um, they're saying the combination this time of the body, and the brain, and the spirit, and the circumstances – they're like saying "Yeah, you nailed it."

Shaman/Author Mikki Baloy

MY COUSIN MARGARET

A cousin of mine asked about finding a hypnotherapist near her home state. I recommended Chuck Frank who practices out of Hollywood, Florida. I asked her to make an audio version of the session, as I know Chuck does not – he takes notes instead. However, having an audio version allowed me to transcribe what was said.

CHUCK FRANK: Ask your guide if he can take you to your council now?

Yes, he can do that.

Let me know when you're there.

We're on the outside of it; it's like Roman columns and a round or oblong like pool. It's marble and we're walking barefoot on the marble, just walking to a table which kind of looks like the table in the painting of the "Last Supper," only it's curved. Everyone is behind the table in a few tiers. It looks very real. I'm trying to pretend it's not - but it appears real.

How many behind the table?

Fourteen.

Does one seem to stand out more than the others?

Yeah, but very egalitarian. My little brother is here. Oh my God, he's so handsome. He's very wise. He's very smooth and smiling and relaxed and no anxiety – this is who he really is. He's sitting there, just very handsome, and causal, and smiling like it was nothing. And (like) "I am here to help you."

Stand in front of him and float into him and see what he sees.

(Cries and laughs.) He says "Marge you're a genius," and he's laughing. He says "You're a genius at what you do; you bring out the best in everyone." He's my teacher.

Is he still alive?

No. What we perceived was a miserable life, he had agoraphobia. He's wonderful. My sisters are here – my father, not there. My brother said I can go back anytime and I'm ok with that. He says "Be a genius at what you do, do what you do best, you never have to feel alone again." He's singing "For He's a Jolly Good Fellow" to me. It's so jovial, I love it; it's free and solid. "Thank you."

He's saying "Thank you for bringing me there." They're telling me to thank you (Chuck Frank, the hypnotherapist) and for bringing me home, and now I get to be happy. They're saying "It's just the work of love, it's not serious business; it's just play." Okay, I'm ready to go back, they're shoving me. They're laughing.

Heart connect to the entire council.

Everyone's got their arms around each other, singing "So long, Auf Wiedersehen." I see my grandmother Mimi, oh wait, Rich would want to know – Aunt Anthy and Uncle Ro are here. (Note: Anthy and Ro are my parents) Rich's mom and dad - Rich wanted to know how his mom is doing, so we can tell Rich. She's laughing, she's the loudest laugher!

My grandfather and my grandmother whom I'm named after are here, my grandmother's companion and helper is here, my uncle, my mom's sisters, and Rich's mom Anthy's got her red hair, and they're like drunk happy, not alcohol drunk, but happy -- she's singing, playing piano and Rich's father, my uncle Ro, is saying "We are having a family party."

They're happy?

They are playing bridge, smoking cigarettes, sing irreverent, loud songs. I can see them together in the red brick house that Rich's father designed and built – they're in the North Room, the party room with the piano. I see there's a sign, right in the council, it says "Always a party at the Martinis." (Laughs) Hey Luana's there! Rich's friend Luana - I never met Luana -- But Luana is there, I see her, even though I never met Luana; everyone's there. Silliest group of souls ever.

 Cousin Margaret in Boot Hill, Tombstone

JOJO

Jo is someone I met while living in New York city. A great sense of humor, we had many laughs while I was working for the Charles Grodin show and traipsing around Tibetan shops. A few years ago, while writing the book "IT'S A WONDERFUL AFTERLIFE" volume two, we had lunch together. During the lunch she casually mentioned that she could have an "out of body experience" at will. I began to record our conversation.

RICH: Have you ever had the experience of visiting a group or a place that seemed like it was a council?

JO: Yes, I felt like I went to visit a council. I found myself on this ship and it was round, and everyone was very still. There were two rows of people, maybe 24 altogether, and it felt like a council, or board to me. The colors there were very monochromatic. There were Earthy colors, brown, white, gray, and I saw they had long robes... There was a front row that was seated and the back row that was standing. I was outside their circle watching. I don't remember seeing anyone in the center.

Were they there for you?

I don't think so. I just came upon them. Maybe I was reporting to them. But I wasn't in front of them.

So let's revisit that moment now if we can. Try to step back into yourself there, look around and see if there's one person who is addressing or speaking to you.

(Closes her eyes) There was a man with a dark beard, cleanly shaven, not straggly.

Anything he tried to impart to you?

He said "You've done very well." And "You've come very far; you must rest and rejuvenate in this lifetime."

How can you connect to them on a daily basis?

He said "We are always here and she knows how to connect to us at any time." I heard "She is a giver of light and spreads love to many, many people."

That's important for you to hear, obviously. How can you stay connected?

He said "We are always available for all of you. At any given time."

Now if we could just ask them to give us lottery numbers.

(Laughs) Very funny.

I do get laughs over there frequently. Are there any other messages for the rest of us?

"Open your hearts." (Aside) They said to me that I still don't realize that message."

*****

FROM HACKING THE AFTERLIFE - JENNIFER SHAFFER

As fans of "Backstage Pass to the Flipside" know, Jennifer Shaffer came into my life in an unusual way. She works with law enforcement agencies nationwide on missing person cases in her role as a medium/intuitive, eight years ago we started filming our weekly meetings. That turned into the podcast Hacking the Afterlife. (HackingTheAfterlife.com) But when we first met, I suggested she do a hypnotherapy session with Scott De Tamble, and she let me film it.

SCOTT DE TAMBLE: Jennifer wanted to meet with her council and we have questions to be asked.

JENNIFER: "We're here." (aside) It's so fast.

Describe this council for me.

There are twelve.

How are they arranged?

Mary is one of the 12. She's at the end of the table. On the left end.

I would ask the council, will one of you speak with us today?

One male comes forward, says, "Yes. I will speak."

I have many questions for you. Are you willing to address them?

"Yes. Call me William."

So William, how is Jennifer doing as a soul?

"She is more of a danger to herself; she's like a little kid who scrapes her knees. She has all of the keys, everyone does."

Tell me about the keys that she has.

"She has the keys to all the dimensions, of all the places and the sacraments, the rituals, and their purpose. She gets closest and then goes back to feeling like she's going to die. She's not going to die. No one dies."

I would ask you about Jennifer's psychic abilities in this life.

"She needs to reach farther and not be consumed by how small people think; it's not their fault. Fear is the only thing holding her back because she has been killed many times for speaking." (aside) Interesting. "Her throat hurts, right?"

That's right, William. Tell her about that.

"She has to not feel unconnected to that 7th dimension of what we had to portray. She is connected but is constantly annoying us about not being connected." (Aside: Oh my God).

She's always connected? How can she feel that?

"I stopped making us separate; she has her rituals to feel safe and while she knows that's just to keep her fear down, she should just know that we're here…. We're here to help her, the last thing we want is for her not to hear (us). She is the one holding her fear."

What is the primary lesson in the Jennifer lifetime?

"The primary lesson is to make the other side known." (aside) That's impossible.

What does that mean?

"To acknowledge spirit; she doesn't always acknowledge them. She thinks she has to shut down (after a session). Even if you don't like something, you put that vibrational frequency out. Well, she puts out that she can't do it or that she's afraid, or that she just wants to be by herself; that does not work."

How would you advise her in this?

To just "be." She makes us exhausted and *we don't get tired.* "Exhausting" she says. Good thing we love her.[1]

We have some questions for you today: What is the best way for Jennifer to translate spiritual information?

"She needs to put her guard down first, then she needs to say "It's okay." She needs to treat them as if they're going to tell her their darkest secrets, even though there is no dark. Then she needs to listen.""

How can she put her guard down?

"By putting her heart open. She forgets that the heart is the gateway."

That reaches back to the...

"Yes, she heals hearts. She's vulnerable at first, she's afraid of getting hurt."

What does she need to understand about that?

"She needs to let that go. She needs to know that we're taking care of the frequencies that have caused that pain from her lifetimes. But it's like cleaning up a big mess, it takes many years in her lifetime."

Is there anything she can do to accelerate that process?

"She can be quiet." (Jennifer laughs)

*****

From ARCHITECTURE OF THE AFTERLIFE

Some years ago I got a call from the producer of Art Bell's show to appear as a guest. After he heard me speak on the show he left "Coast to Coast" with George Noory, he wanted me to appear on his radio show. However, it didn't happen. Some years later, I got a call from the same producer, Heather Wade, who had taken over for Art, and was doing his show. He had retired. She asked me to appear on the show.

The following is an excerpted transcript of something that happened live on air.

HEATHER WADE/ ART BELL

(Note: Heather is not familiar with my books or Michael Newton's books. In his research, Newton found that people report to have 3 to 25 people in their "soul group" with the average being around 15. That is – "people who normally incarnate with us from life to life.")

At this moment, we've met Heather's guide – an Asian man who goes by the name "Mr. Chown." (My spelling, could be another one entirely.)

RICH: *(to Heather's guide)* Mr. Chown can you take her to visit her council?

Oh now... this is really weird, really strange – it's like an outdoor area, but it's in space.

How many people are there in this council?

I can count right quick; seems like a dozen beings there.

How are they arrayed?

It's a completed circle and I'm in the middle.

May we talk to the spokesperson for the council?

There's a female with a book; it looks like she's in charge.

Stand in front of her and describe what she looks like.

She also looks Chinese to me – she also has long white hair, she's wearing white clothes that reflect up on to her face... she looks sort of ageless, but I could guess in her 30s.

Go over and offer your hand as if you can take her hand in yours.

Ah...gosh, it's strange because I can feel the crease in her hand where she was holding onto the book. Her hand is soft and she's smiling at me and she's saying "It's been a long time."

Can we ask her name?

Her name? "Chen."

Ms. Chen would you show our friend here the book you're looking at?

Oh. There's my name... there's pictures.

How is your name written? In script? What's the typeface?

This is very strange - it's not in any language I'm familiar with here in the waking world, it's different, looks like it's made up of different characters but I can read it.

Describe what you see inside the book; are there pages and can you turn them?

Yes, there are pages and I can turn the pages.

Please turn to a page Ms. Chen would like you to look at.

Okay, she's opening up the book, it's going back deep into the book. So now, I don't know, it's like three quarters of the way into this book - I'm just guessing - and I see a picture of a house.

Does this house look familiar?

Yeah, it does, looks like the house where I live. Oh my god, (I see) I'm sitting on the porch and now I have white hair, and I'm rocking in this chair and I'm sort of staring out and uh... -ok this is weird it looks like a photograph (in the book) but the picture is moving, I'm in this rocking chair and if I look out, you can see the wind in the trees and everything... it's like a moving photograph.

Ms. Chen, because we're doing this live on the air, would you please give her what message this passage represents? Can you put words in Heather's mind to explain?

"Things seem so large and so immediate.... but things pass, and the pain is not what matters. It's the love that matters. And it's how you talk to each other that matters." And I'm asking (her) for more and she's shaking her head.

Ms. Chen would you take hold of Heather's hand and you mentioned the word love can you give her a sensation in her body so when you mention love she can experience that?

Now she's laughing; she thinks this is really funny. Richard, I've got to tell you – I'm in an air conditioned room and I'm getting this

sensation that feels like when you take Niacin – you get this hot flush that makes you feel you're 5 degrees hotter from the inside out. Then goosebumps all over.

Thank you Miss Chen.

It's not just for me (this is occurring) "Every soul has this." that's my understanding I'm getting... I don't know how to express this, but there is non-verbal information... and "Everybody has this. People who feel that they're alone - are never alone."

Ms. Chen seems like the spokesperson in the group... anything about her appearance?

I see where... that there are certain areas.... her ears and hands and neck have sparkles.

What quality does she represent in terms of your journey?

"Courage."

Was that for a previous lifetime, something Heather was able to overcome?

"That's for this lifetime."

Put into Heather's mind how you think she's doing now ... and if this is important work she is doing on the radio?

"Almost the same answer as before; she didn't want to but now that she's doing this .. Yes. It's a little slow for our taste, but yes."

Interesting answer.

It is so strange; I almost feel as if I'm in two places at once... and so I'm here talking to you on the air and...

Let's ask Miss Chen, is this space you're in now part of our universe?

"When it's time for you, this is where you'll come."

(Note: Part two of this interview was recorded two years later. In the interim her boss Art Bell has passed away and helps with the interview.)

HEATHER: (ON AIR) I'd like to bring Richard Martini back onto the show. Such a gift you have to be able to do this with people to demonstrate it on live radio.

RICH: Well it's not me; this is about people connecting with their loved ones on the flipside.

This is as *woo woo* as I've ever gotten; it's so personal that I can't sit here and say this isn't rehearsed or a performance; it's what's coming through and it doesn't get any more real than this. Art is saying that Rich has established a stronger link... is that correct?

When I say "Look at your council" what do you see?

I find myself the energy body appears to be traveling through a dark area, looks like space, distant points of light; it must be stars.

Are we inside or outside?

We're outside in a sense, there is a table, a half circle table, a group of people there; they seem impatient.

How many do you see in front of you?

Twelve. Six and six.

Art, stay with us; how do you think Heather's doing?

He says "She's keeping the studio clean, I appreciate that – things seem to be working and I'm very proud at what she's done. She's done more than I ever thought you could."

So who wants to speak to us?

He's pointing out Miss Chen at the table – but he says "If you're here you need to speak with David. He's pointing to an older gent. He's towards the right of the table, third from the end. He's wearing loose fitting clothes, not robes, has on a beige shirt, laces up the center of the chest. He has long baggy pants, and he's got beads. He has brown hair and little bit of a beard; not too long.

David is it okay for us to talk to you?

He's very kind but says "I've been waiting." His hands feel very warm and soft, he's very welcoming. He's got blue eyes and shaggy

hair and a four inch beard – he says "He's not trying to have a beard, just not shaving."

What's a quality do you represent on her council?

"The latter part of her spiritual path."

You've been waiting patiently – how is Heather doing?

"There is more to go," he says. And "You got off the path and now your back on, thank goodness. You came to your senses now you're back on track and we need to keep you there.

What was up with this event – this consciousness altering moment? (Heather had told me about falling, waking up on the floor with a broken leg.)

Oh my God, Rich. I'll just say it. He says we did that to her because she needed to learn a lesson. She was thinking about... and this... okay this is going to get into sensitive material, he says "She was contemplating ending her life, and we're not going to let that happen. She doesn't get to make that choice."

For those listening in... it's important to hear that we are never alone. Thank you for sharing that Heather. Allow me to ask, David is everyone tethered to their council?

He says "We're always here, if you can get through to talk to us, we're always here."

What's the most effective way for them to connect with you?

"All you have to do is just quiet the mind - quiet the mind and go deep into your mind you'll find us if you keep looking and asking, you'll find we're right there."

Have you incarnated on the planet?

"Yes, a long time ago."

How many councils to you sit on, David?

"Six."

You've been with her for many lifetimes?

"Nine lives so far; this would be the ninth. She's doing better now, almost slipped off the path in a bad way but we set that right, and now we're pretty sure she's going to do what we set in place..." He's showing me that I agreed to this path "before she came here."

Who put the thought in my head to reach out to heather?

"Art Bell."

Can I ask David, are you familiar with what I'm doing?

"Oh, we know you Richard."

May I ask how? Were you guys sitting around the council water cooler?

"You just keep showing up in councils, they recognize your voice, you've guided so many souls, there are councils members on many different councils, four of my council members are on other councils for other souls, councils for groups of souls, you've talked to so many souls, that now they recognize your voice when they show up."

What's your opinion of what I'm doing?

For the betterment of all the souls, they're all intertwined. There's more to this.. Okay, I'm hearing, "When you are guiding one soul to the right thing, that branches other souls onto the right path for the right thing. There are plans for everyone and when we don't follow them it causes damage, there's a collective spirit and when one soul is not on the proper track it disrupts that field..." (Heather aside) I don't understand that, I'm just passing this on.

David, is this accurate?

He's talking about you Rich; he's saying "You are on your right path and you're helping souls here and over there and that's helping the whole field to be less disturbed. What you are doing is putting souls on the right path." He says, "You're able to help heal souls that are over there that aren't quite sure what to do over there." (Heather aside) I'm getting a warm wave of emotion from the entire council as I say this; they consider you a friend.

*****

CHAPTER TWENTY-TWO – COMPENDIUM OF COUNCILS

PART TWO

Lhasa – earliest statue of Buddha

This interview is from "Architecture of the Afterlife."

INTERVIEW WITH MEDIUM TONY STOCKWELL

This is an excerpt from ARCHITECTURE OF THE AFTERLIFE. Tony is a well respected medium who tours often with James Van Praagh in Europe. Tony was introduced to me through a mutual friend, and I took him for lunch at Paramount studios. During our lunch, I started to ask him questions and then took out my recorder to record those questions and answers.

At some point, Tony's guide "Lunga" (a Tibetan monk) brings him to visit his council. Having traveled in Tibet, having met many Buddhist monks, I've met more than one who appears as someone's guide on the flipside. While Tony is an accomplished medium, he told me that no one had asked him these kinds of questions before. He was not familiar with me or my work at all.

RICH: Lunga, would you take Tony to visit his council? Would you tell me, are we inside or outside?

TONY: Inside. There are eight in a circle.

Let's go around to the eight different people. Approach the first person on your far left. Is this person a male or female?

Female. Young.

What color is her hair? Or what is she wearing?

White.

Does she mind if I ask her some questions? What would Tony call you?

"Mother."

Very good. About how old is mother?

About 20.

Is she wearing any ornament or something around her neck?

Gold.

What does the gold represent to Tony and his spiritual evolvement? What did he earn to gain your participation on his council?

Feels like "tolerance of intolerance."

Thank you, Mother. Next person down the row – is that male or female?

Androgynous. Dark skinned. Green eyes.

Let's ask their name.

Funny thing, but it sounds like "Mira."

Mira... which means "to look; what is he or she wearing?

"It's not important."

Any jewelry?

"Wood. (He holds his shirt, as if holding onto something.) It's a bear carved from wood. A carved bear."

Mira, please tell Tony what that bear represents. What did he do to earn that bear?

(Long pause.) "It goes with bravery and standing up for what you believe in. Courage."

So far, we have tolerance, courage, we've also heard that Tony has earned service, and kindness... let's go to your lead council person. Is it a male or female?

More masculine. Not Earthly.

Is there a name we can use to address him?

It sounds random... but it sounds like Moishe...

Does Moishe have any object on his clothing?

A star... it's small... like on his chest.

What's it made of?

It's light... that moves. It's attached...

What's the sensation you get from touching his hands?

Family.

Take a look at the star... is a pointy, like a symbol, or an actual star?

It's a star... just light.

What does this star represent in terms of spiritual evolvement?

It's a way of accessing a space or an area... we don't go to.

Who's "we?"

I don't know. It's a portal of some kind.

Are we allowed to go there?

(He shakes his head, no.) "It's just... he's not ready."

What does the portal represent? Is that a place that's of higher consciousness from a different realm?

"It's a totally different realm."

Like, if where we are sitting on earth is the 5th realm... and where we're having this conversation where you are is the 7th realm; how far does this portal go to?

"Way higher. It's hard to put it into words. It feels like... it's everything."

All encompassing?

"Everything but... lighter, everything but ... more than."

******

KIMBERLY BABCOCK – from ARCHITECTUE OF THE AFTERLIFE

I was approached by Dr. Elise Medhus about interviewing a medium that she was going to work with. Numerous friends have been to see her, online, on the phone – and always come away amazed.

At this point in the conversation, our first, she says that she's seeing "the archangel Gabriel" as one of her "spirit guides." As I've done before, I try not to address the concept of who someone is seeing, whether it's a famous avatar, or someone they knew in life – I try to ask them the same questions.

RICH: Gabriel can you show Kim her council?

KIM: (Laughs.) He says "Why sure, she's never asked."

Describe the journey.

We're inside. There's a big, long table, there's two people here that I recognize, there are 8 altogether. Quite a few are male.

From left to right, what's the first fellow's name?

There's Gabriel, and then next to him is a man who is telling me his name is Asur...

What quality does he represent in your spiritual evolvement?

It has to do with "protection." It seems my connection with him is to understand and share that there's no need for protection. (Kim listens) So there's no need for protection; to avoid fear.

Rich: So his quality is showing you how to have a lack of fear?

Kim: That there's no need (for people) to protect themselves.

Let's go to the next one. Asur; what's his role in your life?

I see this spelling, A S U R; but he doesn't go by that; he prefers "Zeus."

Zeus, are you the lead member of this council?

There is a person that is but it's not him ... He says "There is a lead person but I'm the one she talks to all the time. One council member represents protection, one is safety, one is a continual support – the need to feel comfort or comforted," he says. They're showing me (my spiritual evolution) like an incarnation from an infant to adult. Almost like going from an infant to who I am now... and there's a big gap in between. I am remembering who I am; (the quality is) like "Remembrance" is the quality I'm getting from him. In order for me to trust myself who I truly am, I have to trust this (process).

Who's next on your council?

There are the two guides that I see all the time (in my work). This one man I've asked for his name many times; and he just wants to use the word "Chief." I see him as a Native American; full head dress on.

May I ask what tribe that represents?

He's saying "Little Foot" or "Black Foot."

(Note: "Blackfoot, also called Blackfeet, North American Indian tribe composed of three closely related bands." *Britannica.*)

Let me ask you Chief – did Kim have a lifetime as a Native American?

(She holds up two fingers)

Two Native American lives? May I ask, who is next to you...

It's my guide "Kristen."

So what quality does Kristen represent on your council?

"Communication."

Who else is here? To your left?

(A long pause. Kim smiles. Shrugs.) It's Mother Mary.

Okay, let's thank her for coming. How does she appear to you?

When she stands, each time we address her, she stands. I can see she is shorter – she is wearing blue. She has on something casual, like a casual dress that's blue. She has dark eyes and her hair is brown... but not dark brown. She said "go a little bit lighter with (the description of) the hair. Not dark brown."

Can I ask you a direct question Mary?

"Ask me a direct question."

Or are people just seeing him as they need to see him and it's not accurate one way or the other?

All I can say is that when something is inaccurate, the energy stops flowing. But as you are speaking, her energy – her energy goes right through me... it just keeps flowing. (Aside) Why is she sprinkling rose petals in front of you as you speak?

No idea. Is this accurate that you serve on other councils?

She says, "Yes." (A pause) She says the rose petals are for safety.

So I don't slip and fall? Or so that I do slip and fall?

No, "for safety."

Mary, can you introduce us to the last person on Kim's council?

Kimberly looks into the distance. She pauses. "That's interesting. He's like this gruff guy... – Arrgh.. Edward."

Is he young or old?

He's feels like a young 50ish; but he's gruff, he's a "toughen up" "charge ahead" kind of guy.

What's he represent?

"Striving, passion..." he's so passionate and he's – not proud, but grounded. That's a really good word to know yourself.

Can we speak to your guides?

(Kim laughs.) There's four females but one is funny. She keeps pointing at you. She keeps pointing at you, your higher self, they're bringing you forward; she's just being playful. She brings this guide forward, this feminine energy, her name sounds like Eleanor.

Nice to meet you Eleanor. Can we ask you some questions?

She's very willing – for what it's worth, when I connect to her the energy feels very high, don't know how else to explain it...

Can you show Kim her soul group – the people she normally incarnates with?

She's showing me like... it's funny she calls it a classroom – a room full of different souls.

How many are here?

Over 20. As we plug into them, I can see them but what Eleanor is saying is that Kim prefers to associate with masculine energy because apparently I carry more of it myself.

If there was a theme for your class or group to work on over many lifetimes is there a theme to what you're doing?

This is so interesting, as she does things, she... as I see Eleanor shift her awareness; it's like I'm looking through her (point of view). She went like this... (lifts her hand) "Stand up everyone, introduce yourselves," and I hear Gabriel – this is the archangel, the angel known as Gabriel. And to answer your questions (about names) the names aren't important, it's important why you're plugging into these vibrations because of how it changes your essence, your soul, like your vibration, has nothing to do with our physical self; when you plug into these – Eleanor is saying you're not one consciousness you're threads of a compilation, and this is who you belong to... the threads you belong to this classroom; they're contributing to the essence of who you are.

Can I ask Gabriel to come forward?

As he comes forward I feel like he's standing at my right, and I feel what's the word? Invincible. It's like I am very tall, like invincible... like nothing can touch or harm me, like a strength not of this world... it's him. He's claiming that.

Are you the same Gabriel that people refer to in history or is the identification a way of explaining frequency?

He responds; "I am Gabriel." That's how he responds to you – he takes my breath away. It's so strong.

I guess my question to you, is are you the same Gabriel that visited Abraham, Mary, or the prophet Mohammed in a cave? Or was that another Gabriel or the same frequency?

Before I can answer, he wants to point out that got a massive rope around his chest and he keeps saying for me to look at it... And he says... "It represents strength." It feels really dry, he's showing me all the threads now, and how they're intertwined. They're close together... and (thus) it is really strong – "You see where it's frayed; it's really weak, that's what you're supposed to teach, tell people to come together because together we're stronger (when together), and when we aren't we're weak." It's taking my breath away.

Okay. Thank you for that. Interesting point, and well said. Kim, is there anyone else in this group we need to speak with?

He says yes (to you) about the story about the cave; he says "Go back to that question."

The question about whether you're the same Gabriel who runs into these people over various time periods.

He keeps saying "Resurrection." I asked him if that's what he meant about (referring to) the cave. He keeps saying "Resurrection." Wow.

Resurrection?

"Yes sir," he says. He keeps giving this over and over; "Resurrection."

Before we go, can you show Kim a place of healing where she can go after this lifetime where they took her to heal? Is there a place for her to heal?

(Tears fall from Kim's eyes). He's showing me. He just shows this room... like we walked down this hall, and it's all white, but the whiteness feels tangible. He's on my left and this is Gabriel leading me, and he's sort of there at this opening and he goes like this (points with her hand) and there is this room... it's like gold inside. There's nothing here, but the walls are gold the walls are the vibration of Kim; not the earthly Kim, but the higher (version of) Kim.

He's talking about... he's talking about the way that you heal others or help others, those words don't really... they don't grasp the depth of what he's saying... (the ways you heal others) are what makes the walls so strong here – that's what is healing for you.

Gabriel is talking about how something might have a stamp of time on it, but it's really not defined by that stamp of time. It's always occurring, it's always in existence, so therefore, that's what upholds this vibrating place, this room that continues to grow.

Is this a room that Kim created?

"Yes."

From her experiences healing people? Is this a construction of things she achieved in her work?

He says "Yes." He says "She'll go and she'll see by running my hands (over the walls), merging with that energy, she'll see both sides of it... so if healing were to occur from someone else, if I did something to make someone else heal, I would experience not just the Kim perspective, but their perspective too and that's why it's so strong – but this is for everybody.

Let me ask, can you give her a sensation of remembering this room now?

She reacts. "Oh." She sighs, begins to cry softly. "He... um. He brought Christ forward."

Oh, our pal Jesus. Can we talk to him a little bit?

(She laughs.) Jesus is like, "Well do we have time to talk to Jesus?"

I'm familiar with talking to him.

He (Gabriel) brought him (Jesus) forward and (Jesus) said "This is her home; she knows her home in me."

Describe what he looks like to you.

Depends basically what I ask for, either emotionally or vibrationally what I'm seeing.

Let's ask for a visual, a physical feature. What's he look like?

He's taller than me, not a whole lot. His hair is like dark brown... his eyes are like a blue green. He's wearing like really plain... (begins to cry) He had me feel the hair on his face.

Jesus, can you step back a few feet? We can't have a conversation if you're going to freak our friend out here. I need to change your clothes to something more casual...

He's wearing a jeans and a tee shirt now! He just did that as you were speaking!

Let her see your tennis shoes please. Let her see that you're a regular person.

He's just so compassionate... "but I'm also just like you," he said. (Points at me.)

You mean like Kim or like me? I know he has a sense of humor.

"Both of you," he said.

I have a question for you that Kim doesn't know the answer to, but you do. Has anyone complained about me writing about you in my book "Hacking the Afterlife" where I have a number of people who remember lifetimes with you?

He says "It brings a level of truth and awareness that is important right now. It is needed."

 Kimberly Babcock – Medium/Author

*****

DR. DREW PINSKY

I was invited onto a podcast by Dr. Drew's wife Susan Pinsky. She had on two mediums, one being my pal Jennifer Shaffer, and she invited me to share their podcast. Just prior to going on air, I ran into Dr. Drew, and said "Hey, the last time we met we talked about this idea of talking to the Flipside. You want to try that?" He said "Sure, I don't believe in it, but I'm open to try."

At this point, Dr. Drew has recalled a lifetime where he was the "Burgermeister" of a city in Germany in the late 1800's (the name he recalled corresponds with the historical record) and I've asked for his "guide to come forward to assist us."

RICH: I want your guide to take Drew by the hand and walk him into his council.

DREW: Council?

He knows what I'm talking about. Are we in a room or outside?

(After a pause) In a room.

About how many people are here?

Twelve.

Take a look at how they are aligned.

Against the wall. (Laughs, as if confused) **I feel like Native Americans are here.**

Let's go to the first person on the far left. What's that person look like?

(Laughs) **Like a female Pilgrim.**

Describe her. What's her name?

She's the only woman in here. She's wearing dark with an apron and wearing this bonnet. *Marie.*

Thanks Marie; can we ask you some questions? Can you put in Drew's mind how you earned your position on his council? What's the that you represent in his journey?

She brings "history."

Ah. Hence the Pilgrim's outfit I'd guess – very clever. Can you take her hand? Describe how she looks. Eyes, hair color?

She has blue eyes, light hair.

What's the emotion you get from holding her hand?

Kindness.

What kind of kindness are we talking about?

Gentle, wise, deliberative.

Marie, how do you feel about what we're doing?

"Everyone thinks this is weird."

Marie, can you give drew a sentence that we need to share with our audience?

"Wisdom is wealth."

Drew, have you ever heard that suggestion before?

No.

(Note: It's a proverb in Swahili; "Wisdom is Wealth." Wikipedia)

Let's go to the next person (on the council).

This feels weird, because he's a Native American.

How is he dressed? Does he have a headdress with feathers?

Yes.

How many feathers in his headdress?

A lot. 90 all the way down his back. Up and then down.

Look carefully at his face. What's the emotion you get looking at him?

I'm having trouble staying with it... "depth?"

Let's take a hold of his hands, sometimes that helps.

No. He doesn't want me to.

Look at the front of his dress, is he wearing any symbols or emblems or jewelry?

Beads... he's making me emotional, that's why I'm having trouble looking at his eyes...

Just try to focus on his beads... can he give us a name or the tribe that he represents?

"Humanity." Is there a tribe by that name?

The Sioux considered everyone in the tribe to be humanity. Everybody who was not in the Sioux was not humanity. Let me ask; can I characterize you as Sioux?

"You could characterize me a Sioux."

Are you Lakota, Dakota or Nakota?

"Nakota."

You've been watching over him for so many lifetimes, do you feel as if Drew is doing a good job?

"He will." He's waving a spear over me. It's ceremonial. It feels like he's doing a blessing. Like some power is being transmitted (to me.)

What's he imparting to you?

(To have) patience and (there's) work to be done.

In your council, the first person gave you "patience," and this counselor is imparting "kindness and patience?"

She said "Wisdom is wealth."

Dr. Drew Pinsky

*****

SCOTT DE TAMBLE

As noted Scott is a very talented hypnotherapist. I often refer to him as a virtuoso. I know that people claim to "have not gone anywhere" with a hypnotherapist, but in all the sessions I've filmed with Scott (dozens) people did "go somewhere." At this point in our friendship, he was asking me what I was up to, and I was trying to describe this process of "asking questions without hypnosis" and calling it "guided meditation." I suggested we might try to do so together. My comments are in italics. Scott's are in bold font.

RICH: Just give us a name for this guy on your council... the person to the far left. What's his name?

SCOTT: The names are going to slow us down.

Have you heard of me or my work?

"We know you."

Is this an appropriate method, shortening the process?

"You're doing what you do." He's just laughing.

What's so danged funny?

He's just laughing at our struggles. They just enjoy watching the antics of us.

Yes, like the flea circus. We get that ... but can you grab Al's hand? What does that feel like?

He doesn't really have hands... but okay. Feels like connecting with a very wise and large intelligence.

Can I ask you some questions? I promise they'll be both pertinent and impertinent.

"That's what we expect."

How many councils do you serve on?

"Thousands."

What would you like to tell Scott, aside from what you tell him every day?

"Have more faith in us and connect with us, even as we're doing now in a flippant way — follow your heart, follow your dreams. Standard stuff."

So can we call this the flippant-side?

"Brilliant."

Along those lines, allowing people to have a normal conversation with you not based or steeped in all the things they normally have to go through to get to you – they can speak to you in any venue, correct?

"Agreed."

Is there any sensation you can impart to Scott that tells him you're there tapping on his shoulder?

"Sure." The feeling is when the wind is in my hair and face...

Look around the Council a bit. How many are there here?

We'll call it nine women and men.

Some are in attendance and some are out?

Yes. There could be seven, eight, ten, eleven; depends.

Those that are not here; are they working?

Not needed.

To the left or right - anyone else want to weigh in on Scott?

There's a woman who looks like Deanna Troi from Star Trek; she's about 50...

A name we can call her?

Call her V. (Scott laughs.) She's wearing a dark jewel-tone dress.

What do you represent for him?

"Passion."

You wanted to speak earlier, what did you want to say?

"He is a very passionate person... he holds it back for whatever reason, but we would like him to explore and express his passions to a greater degree."

Passions toward work? Talent? People?

"Just to feel that passion – doesn't really matter how."

What does it feel like?

Like a lot of energy... happy, kind of bouncy.

So V, have you incarnated before with Scott?

"Yes, but in very ancient times before this civilization; in other worlds, or other dimensions."

Where you with Scott when he was a Commander of ships and people many lives ago?

(Note: This is a reference to a memory Scott shared with me, of a lifetime a long time ago, where he saw himself as leading a war.)

"Not with him, but knew of him."

I know Scott had a memory of leading them into battle; he felt bad because people were lost, but I've spoken to someone else [that he doesn't know in this life] who knew him in that era. And they said that he saved millions of lives. Is that correct?

"Yes, he has gone to war many times. But long ago."

So how come is he not leading people into battle? Or is this another version of that in this life?

"That phase is over; this phase is more about shining light."

You wanted him to be more passionate, or enjoy more passion?

"He already is more passionate, but he needs to allow his passions to be expressed."

What color are V's eyes?

Violet.

How long is her hair?

Dark. Long… to mid-back.

V, have you incarnated in the past? When was the last time you incarnated?

"A million years ago."

What do you miss about being here if anything?

First she says "nothing," but then says "Well, there are pleasures… physical pleasures. Like touching… and eating…"

What would be something you'd remember eating?

"Fruits, like grapes… and drinks, somewhat like wine."

Let me ask you a question that might seem esoteric… about Greek mythology – when they talk about the ancients and Mt. Olympus. Are they talking about their Guides and Councils? Just translating that into words?

"It's a mishmash."

How many other Councils do you serve on, V?

"Hundreds of thousands."

Is this odd for you to have a conversation like this in a café in Santa Monica?

"It's fine. He doesn't always need the long form of ritual."

If you were going to give Scott an image of something that happened in a lifetime that you were the most responsible for, what image what would that be?

She showed me a star and a rocket ship. I've always had a, well, a passion, to explore other dimensions and other places.

Does Scott still travel around deep space even though he's not aware of it?

"Even in this moment."

So some part of his higher consciousness is out there?

"More than one."

Let's pick one that's traveling around.

"He knows of the one that's monitoring in a space station; there is another one that is in a long journey on a ship. It's part of the Service that he belongs to."

Tell me about this Service that he belongs to... is it something new?

"Ancient. It's for a federation that still exists."

Is there a name for this federation?

She says "It comes across as being timeless, but it also was to do with time itself. It's exploring space but also exploring time... not just space travel, but traveling through time."

Let's look around anyone else we need to talk with?

Someone's saying "Jennifer and you are doing good work."

(Note: He's referring to my podcast with Jennifer Shaffer - HackingTheAfterlife.com)

Let's say hello and goodbye to everyone – we bypassed Scott's guide, and walked into his council – Miss V I'd like to know more about you.

She says, "Get in line." My guide says, "We're all cool with this, we know you."

Rich Martini, Jennifer Shaffer and Scott De Tamble

TERESA ANN SESSION – FROM ARCHITECTURE OF THE AFTERLIFE

Teresa (not her real name) is a friend of a friend. She is not a medium or a hypnotherapist. In fact she's about as far removed from the "*woo woo*" world as can be, with a career in law enforcement. We met through a mutual friend and asked if I would take the time to chat with her about an issue that she was having with regard to a boyfriend.

This is one of those sessions that must remain anonymous because of "Teresa's" career and the idea that she would be chatting about a past life with anyone might be detrimental to her career.

In my first chat with her, prior to turning on my tape recorder, she was able to recall a lifetime in Calabria, southern Italy. Her name in that lifetime was Anastasia and she recalled a date of 1432. She remembered the life death of this woman, and when she died, she recalled "returning home" to her friends on the flipside. She was met by her guide – her current grandmother Josephina (who has been with all of her lifetimes.)

I asked Josephina if we could go in to visit with Teresa's council. Teresa said that once inside the council chamber, it reminded her of a scene in "Indiana Jones" when he was below, and all of those judging him were above. (I don't recall that scene, but made a note of that memory.)

As she entered her council she said she saw 5 individuals and when she said "the first individual looked like an alien" I took out my cellphone and begin recording. Again – she's not under hypnosis, I'm not trying to guide her into hypnosis – we are just chatting over lunch and she is "connected" by looking over my shoulder into the distance.

RICH: Okay, I'm recording now to help me transcribe this – (at this point) We are in our friend Teresa's council now and her guide Josephina is still here.

TERESA: She's next to me.

What does your guide look like, how old is she?

She's 26. She has blue eyes, brown hair.

Does she look like you?

Yeah.

What is she wearing?

She's dressed like Dorothy from "The Wizard of Oz." Wearing like a dress that has straps and comes across. It's blue.

How is your guide dressed?

I see her wearing black. Mauve paints and a beige sweater.

Let's go back to our first council member – can you give us your name?

"Lilly."

Can you take hold of her hand? What's that feel like?

Her hands are smooth.

Is there an emotion associated with holding her hand?

It kind of scared me - the look of her hand.

When you're holding her hand does she seem familiar, does she feel distant, what's the emotion?

It feels secure.

Secure. Lilly are you familiar with what I'm doing here in your council chambers?

She said "Yes."

What's a word that represents the reason you're on her council?

"Faith. Faithfulness."

What does that mean? Being true to someone else? Your beliefs?

I'm getting both - I'm getting faithful to people that I love and also having faith in the universe... Having faith in yourself.

Lilly, can I ask a personal question?

"Yeah."

What planet do you normally incarnate on, or have in the past, is it in our universe?

(It's) "In another."

Can you tell us what the environment was like? Did you ever have a lifetime with Teresa on your planet?

I'm getting "No."

Thanks for answering that. It's unusual to meet someone like yourself and I appreciate talking to you. When you describe Lilly, is her face round, angular?

It's oval, and huge, and flat... like she has no wrinkles almost like shark skin.

Her eyes?

They're big like alien eyes. Big... they're her big feature.

Does she have an Iris? Is it all one color?

They're black but I feel like the lid is like a lizard's and comes in from the side.

(Note: This law enforcement agent is not a fan of science fiction, but is a fan of digging for facts. So my asking for specific questions is not something she wouldn't apply to her own work – but at the same time, it's unusual. There's no hypnosis involved; we are sitting in a noisy pizza restaurant in Manhattan Beach.)

Try to take both of Lilly hands in yours. Lilly tell us, how is our friend Teresa doing?

She says "Fine. Keep going."

(Note: At this point Teresa listen, then makes a face - shakes her head. Tears come into her eyes.)

What's happening Lilly?

(Teresa aside) It's like I don't want to hear it.

Say it aloud and we can judge it later – just say it aloud. Let Lilly play her role. What does she say?

"Everything's going to work out."

Is there any advice you can give the planet how to save our planet?

"Love."

Now, can you introduce us to the person next to you on the council?

It's a man. He's wrinkled. Old... like 80; his name is Joe.

Joe, is this odd for you to have one of your charges interview you?

He says "a little."

So I take it you don't know me or have heard about me talking to councils.

He says "No."

I appreciate you talking to us. What's a word that signifies your role here for Teresa?

"Power. Personal power. Recognizing her own power."

Are you available to help her recognize her own power, are you the person who rejuvenates her when she needs it? Do you help rejuvenate her?

He's like "That's what I'm here for..." – but I don't think the rejuvenation is mutual.

How many other councils do you work on Joe?

"I got three."

Lilly?

"Seven."

Joe. Here's a chance to tell our friend Teresa something that can help with her path and journey. What can you say?

"Stay the course."

Should we talk to other council members? Who's in charge?

The one in the middle.

Male? Female, neither or both?

(Laughs) A female who looks like Whoopi Goldberg.

What's a name we can call you?

"Susan. She's 50. Hair is black, has long dreads... she's wearing purple, a magenta purple outfit. She has a hat on but I feel like I'm interposing this from when Whoopi was on star trek."

Susan, this image you're presenting of you on Star Trek – is this so she can be amused by seeing you?

"Yes."

Would you consider yourself a spokesperson for the council?

"Yeah."

What quality do you represent in Teresa's spiritual evolvement?

"I guess laughter. Comedy."

And what's the quality of the person next to you represent?

"Strength again..."

A different strength? Physical?

"Yes."

What about the fifth person at the end – what quality of yours do they represent?

"Quiet calmness."

Okay, let's ask Susan, how is our friend Teresa doing? Anything you want to tell her?

She's laughing at me, like, "This is what you signed up for... she's laughing that I'm here using you..." (to access her) not in a menial way, but she thinks it's comical that I need help.

Let me clarify – you're chuckling because our friend Teresa is using me to address you?

"Yes."

Is this unusual to access you?

"Most people can, they just don't try."

How is it that you're able to do this?

"Through me."

Through you Susan or through Teresa?

"Through *me*."

Why are people able to do this now and why couldn't they before?

"Consciousness."

How has consciousness altered or changed?

"More aware."

I appreciate you guys speaking up with us – any last words you want to give Teresa?

"You got this."

Thank you for stopping to chat with us today.

They said "Oh of course, anytime." They are blowing a kiss en masse, like the panel in The Newlywed Game."

*****

Again, Teresa remains in her position with this law enforcement agency. I appreciate her allowing me to share her interview.

PIECES OF EIGHT FROM ARCHITECTURE OF THE AFTERLIFE

This session is from someone I met many years ago, making a film in Los Angeles. An African American, he's not connected to anything about the flipside per se, but he is part native American, and grew up around the idea of the unseen being part of our lives. We're having lunch at a local restaurant, he's asked what I've been up to, and I suggest I demonstrate it – and take out my cell phone to record it.

At this point in the conversation, he's met his guide "Pearl" and she is showing him how she's been watching over James' (not his real name) entire life.

Rich: Pearl, let's walk James in to visit his council. Can you do that?

JAMES: "**Yeah**."

Are we inside or outside – where are we?

Outside.

How many people are here?

About 20.

How many are members of your council?

13.

How are they arrayed?

Just standing. I'm sitting.

Let's go to the first person on the farthest left.

Female in her 80's. It's my grandma Betty. She's wearing a dress with small little flowers, a flowered reddish orange dress. She still has her tattoos... she was in the Holocaust.

Let me ask you, Betty. How is James doing?

She laughs. "All right."

What is the quality that you represent on James' council?

I'm hearing "happiness and love."

Who's next to her?

My grandfather that I never met – he's wearing a long braid. (Blackfoot). His name is Henry.

Hello Henry. Are you familiar with what I'm doing?

"Very much so."

How can that be?

"I heard about you from my dad." (James aside: that was a weird thing to say.)

Not so weird - thanks for talking with us – James take a hold of Henry's hand. What's that feel like?

Rough. He's a hard working kind of... he's in his 70's.

What's he wearing?

Brown pants, brown shoes, a tan colored shirt.

What word represents your role on his council?

"Protection."

On how many councils do you serve Henry?

"Four."

How about Betty?

"One."

Henry – how do you feel James is doing?

"Better than he thinks."

Pearl are you familiar with his life on another planet?

"Yeah."

How does that relate to this lifetime? Why did you allow James to come here today to see this?

"To get some truth."

Who said that?

Pearl.

What is that, Pearl? You mean as in "The nature of reality?"

"Yes."

How is this new information going to help him with his work and career?

Something's going to happen – I don't know what it is – but it's good.

CHAPTER TWENTY THREE – A COMPENDIUM OF COUNCILS

PART THREE

Last Judgment – Horn players

OLIVIA – FROM ARCHITECTURE OF THE AFTERLIFE

Olivia (not her name) is an actress that I met in a producer's office. He invited me to his office to meet her, because at some point she started talking about dreams and reflections about her spiritual life – and it reminded him of my work. We'd never met, but I just started in by asking some simple questions.

She quickly recalled a lifetime in India, with incredible details that I was able to verify in terms of clothing, dress, the kinds of structures she was seeing. At some point she's referring to the Hindu deity Shiva, whom she is a devotee of in this previous lifetime – and I'm asking him direct questions.

RICH: Shiva, I need your help here, where does she go, does she meet with her guides?

OLIVIA: (Quickly) Yeah, I'm going up to this meeting.. to have a meeting with the.. 12, like a group of 12 and everyone is there they're asking me, "What did you learn...?"

Are we inside or outside?

We're inside, it's like a room.

Describe the room; what do the floors look like?

Very white. Marble. There are big pillars and long chairs.

How is this group arrayed? Are they waiting for you? Are they in a line, standing sitting, in a semi-circle?

There's a long table and they're sitting along the table spread out – one of them is standing on the left end.

Let's go to the guy standing, describe him to me.

He's old, and wise; a wise man. About 65. He has long white beard. He's wearing a long white robe to the floor.

What color are his eyes?

Blue.

May I ask a direct question?

Yes.

What's your name, for the purpose of our conversation?

Michael.

Can you look from Michael's point of view at our friend here Olivia, about how old is she or how does she look?

(Describes Eline) She's uh.. about 35. The same person... I saw earlier in her past life memory. Same as before, long dark hair – she came for this final meeting, she's wearing the same clothes, white, kind of bluish that she had in the hospital.

A sari?

Yes.

Can you hold Michael's hands?

They're hard... Dry skin. (She smiles). He's older. Sometimes they...

I know Olivia doesn't know the answer to this – but Michael, you do – what quality do you represent in her journey?

"Learning."

What do you mean by that?

"Experience."

How do you think she's doing?

"I'm here to help to guide her through life lessons and difficulty she's facing. I'm here to remind her what she's supposed to learn in this life, so she doesn't have to learn them again in the next life."

How is she doing?

She's doing well, in this previous life (in India) she was a little stuck with her parent's pressure, living the life her parents wanted her to live, so she didn't get to learn (much) and then she married and was living the life he wanted her to live."

You mean in her life as Eline in the 1400's?

"Yes, it was a lot of pressure on her."

How do you think she is doing now?

"She's doing good; she's learning a lot of lessons, also, she's went through a lot of difficult tests in her life, examinations."

Correct me if I'm wrong, Michael; Olivia chose this lifetime.

"She wanted to finish the journey she started out. She wants to return to life and finish this and come back to live with them..."

She wants to "finish her life?" You mean this one or the previous one as Eline?

"She wants to finish her lessons."

Going down the row, the word that represents what you're doing on the council. How'd they earn their seat? The person next to you?

"Unity."

Okay, the next?

"Love."

The next?

"Hmm. He's the guy in charge of the others."

Let's go to him for a second.

"This person makes sure that – because sometimes they are very different people, it gets hectic (in here) so this guy is the one who takes care of everyone."

What can we call him?

"Julian."

How's he look?

"Younger. About 30 years old. Blue eyes, short hair. Tall."

Julian, are you sort of the "key person" in this council who herds all the cats to come in here?

"Yes, he's the kind of person who if he sees something is going on that's difficult, he helps. If too much is going on..."

So what's your quality that you represent in Olivia's life?

"Her higher self."

The kind of the person who connects her to... to spirituality?

"Yes."

How do you do that? How do you connect her to spirituality?

"Um... through many sources really, signs... and books – a lot of different sources. He always makes sure she's connected, because sometimes she gets disconnected."

Let me ask a mechanical question. Is it easier to talk to her when she's asleep?

"Yes. I send messages to her by night."

But she doesn't remember them when she wakes up, but her higher self does?

"Yes."

JOSH DAVIDOW – FROM ARCHITECTURE OF THE AFTERLIFE

Josh is a filmmaker whom I met while trekking in India with Robert Thurman. He edited my film "Journey into Tibet with Robert Thurman" and made his own film following Robert around Bhutan. But at this moment, Josh is living in New Zealand and has startled me by revealing he had a near death experience while we were atop Mt. Kailash in Western Tibet. At some point, I walk him back into that memory, meet with his guide and suggest a place to visit.

RICH: Let's visit his council.

JOSH: We're inside; it's like a courtroom built out of white pearl. The walls, the floor is white pearl as well. There are columns; it's a circular room with columns all around.

How many council members are here?

Six; they're in a semicircle.

First person on the left – male or female, neither or both?

It's neither... kind of a... more male.

Is it okay to ask you some questions?

Yeah.

What's your name?

"Sith."

Describe this person to me –

He's sitting down. But if he was standing, he'd be about 6 feet tall. No hair... back eyes.

Sith, can Josh take your hand in his? What's that like?

I feel a kind of dread.

What do his hands feel like?

He kind of seems alien. He's got three sort of fingers – it's like almost like a claw; but very benign looking.

Soft or hard claw?

Soft, kind of mushy.

How are his eyes?

Normal sized – but all pupil; all black.

What's he wearing?

Doesn't look like clothes – looks like the same skin on his hand, like a putty… but it's like a sheeny putty.

Cream colored?

Grey.

Sith – can I ask some direct questions?

"Sure."

Are you familiar with me or the work I'm doing with councils?

"No."

What's one word that represents your quality on Josh's council?

He said "Discipline."

Where are you from Sith? Are you from a planet in our universe?

"Another universe."

Let me ask' has Josh had a lifetime on your planet?

"Yes."

If it's all right put that lifetime in his mind. Where are we?

Inside. (I'm) In a building, seems like a very mechanical, almost like a fertility clinic.

Josh, have you been in building like this one in this lifetime?

No!

Is this where he works? What does Josh look like? Male or female?

Neither – he kind of looks like Sith.

What is Josh's role in this lifetime? Scientist? Doctor?

Yes. He's a doctor. It has to do with fertility.

Are you guys having difficulty with fertility on your planet?

"No."

Is there a problem related to it?

"No."

Do people from your planet come here to Earth?

"Yes."

What can we call your planet?

"Organ."

Oregon? I've been there. (Keeping this light)

(Josh laughs)

Is there a role that Josh has on our planet related to this lifetime? A kind of doctor helping people on this planet?

"You mean Earth? Yes."

What role does Josh play in terms of helping the Earth – is he visited by people from our planet for information?

"Yes. While he's sleeping."

He's not consciously aware of having an event or talking to aliens?

"No."

But you're showing it to him now?

"Yes."

How does the information get passed?

"We experience it while he sleeps."

What's the value of that information back home on your planet?

"To make better people."

To make better people on your planet?

"No. Making better people on Earth."

"It's a cookbook!" Just kidding. So, you're helping alter the consciousness of this planet; is that correct Sith?

"Yeah."

Is it a physical thing? This altering the consciousness of the planet?

"No, it's changing thought patters and habituation –yeah…"

Let's head back to his council. Sith represents "discipline" – let's speak to the person on the council next to him.

It's a woman, she looks about 65. She's blonde, in good shape. She has blue eyes.

What's her name?

"Sonam."

What is she wearing?

Like a white – not a toga – if you saw "Defending Your Life" the film – like that. Her smile is incandescent.

If I may ask; what quality do you represent on his council?

"Beauty." The "beauty presence" in all things.

Sonam, has Josh had a lifetime in Tibet before?

(Note: I ask because Sonam is a typical Tibetan name.)

"Yes."

Could you show that to him – where is he?

"He's on a mountain."

What's he do for a living?

(Josh aside) It looks like I'm always schlepping, Rich. It looks like he's a Sherpa.

Josh is a guy who has chosen lifetimes where he helps people from one place to the next by moving and assisting, is that correct Sonam?

"Yes; he likes to help."

Why did he choose that life?

"He likes to help; he also has trouble standing still."

Sonam and Sith – for both of you; how is Josh doing in this lifetime?

"Pretty good."

Any adjustments he needs to make?

"He needs to stand still."

By standing still do you mean stay calm. Meditate? What's a good way for him to practice that?

"Stand still." It's quite profound what they're saying… I've been moving a lot.

Sonam, Sith, give him a visual of how to do that; stay still.

"He can do that where he is."

Let's talk to your lead counselor.

He's a bald male…kind of boring in my judgement.

(Laughing) Well, I wouldn't say that about my council leader.

He kind of looks like an attorney. His name is M…o…n…t… y.

Would people on this council consider you the lead guy?

"Yeah."

How many councils do you sit on?

"6000."

How about you Sith?

"4800."

Sonam?

"26,342."

Jesus you guys are busy – I appreciate the answer – either that or y'all have a great sense of humor. How about you Monty? Are you familiar with my asking these questions?

"Yes." (Josh aside) They think you're on the right path.

It is a little unusual – usually when people meet their council - they've just died, and they have to go through those emotions. In these sessions, we're visiting briefly, not planning to stay.

"You're like the court reporter."

It does help center people and it does help them with some kind of encouragement. What's a word or emotion that would describe what do you represent in Josh's spiritual journey?

"Equanimity."

Thank you. Other than "slow down" - what does he need to do?

"Find the laughs."

That's pretty valuable. Anyone on this council represent laughter?

"Yes. He's kind of Robin Williams/leprechaun kind of guy."

Let's talk to him for a minute.

He looks like a wild-eyed half leprechaun, half satyr.

Like a gargoyle?

Like a leprechaun torso and head with a horse/pony like legs and attachments.

What's a name we can use for him?

"Skizmack."

Can I call you Skiz for short?

"No. Skizmack."

You represent laughter in Josh's life?

"The lighter side of things."

Has Josh had ever had a lifetime on your planet?

"No."

Can you take us there? Is it here in this universe?

"Somewhere else. In another universe."

Let's look at your family Skizmack; how many are in it?

"About 8 children including himself, a mother and father."

Do they all look like him?

"Kind of."

Skizmack – I'm going to ask you some questions if you don't mind - is your planet the source of our myths about leprechauns?

"No."

But people on your planet have appeared to folks on Earth, correct?

"Yeah."

I'm not saying <u>you</u> in particular are the source of those myths – but someone from your planet showing up on Earth – maybe a whole crew of them having fun?

"Maybe."

Put that in Josh's mind – you guys sound like you might be the source of those stories; am I wrong?

"You're right." It's blurry though. You can't get a direct answer from the guy.

It's not exactly a normal conversation.

(Josh laughs.)

I've talked to folks who've had a lifetime as a fairy... a medium who when she was a little girl, remembered meeting a gargoyle – I interviewed the gargoyle – he said "It's not my fault I scared her as a little girl, most people don't see me…" So Skizmak, I'm just pointing out you're a Leprechaun – so where the heck is the Lucky Charms? Have you heard that one before?

"No." He doesn't know what you're referring to.

Okay, sorry. Let me ask; does your planet look like Ireland?

"A little bit – it's very green, but it's quite dark."

What I'm suggesting is, perhaps an Irishman had a near death event and saw these leprechauns on this planet…

"Yeah, whatever."

I'm observing that most mythological creatures in our history are not from our planet, but they met or saw them in their actual existence.

All I'm getting from him is him saying "Interdimensional travel is very real."

Would the other two council members come forward?

One looks like the father in the TV show "The Brady Bunch." His name is Ennit.

What word or quality do you represent on Josh's council Mr. Ennit?

"Peace."

Did he learn that from a difficult life or were you bringing peace to him?

"He earned it."

Does he want to see that?

"He can examine it. We're inside a cockpit of a plane."

Is this World War I or II?

"Two." He's American. His name is Major Deluca or Deluise - something Italian.

(Note: From a military website with crew listings, Eugene De Luca, 33586632 SGT flew aboard this plane the "Lady Belle.")

Major – what squadron are you in?

"I'm in Mayfair – he's in the Air Force. I'm hearing Mayfair."

Did you die in Europe or Asia?

"In European theater."

Were you shot down?

"Yeah."

Over what country?

"England."

Over Mayfair?

"Yes."

Thank you- what kind of plane were you in?

"A bomber."

Other guys went down with you... Name of your bomber?

"Lady belle."

Was that the Memphis Belle you're referring to? The one in the film?

"No. It's a different plane."

Any reason for Josh to look up your lifetime?

"Not really."

(Note: How accurate are these memories? I'm casually asking a friend over skype to recall something and he suddenly remembers dying in World War II in a bomber. So, I took the time to track down Major Deluca (He was a Sergeant when he arrived in England aboard the "Lady Belle.")

The bomber Lady Belle that Josh has never seen but is remembering.

What did you learn from that lifetime?

"Not to die in fear."

That's an unusual choice for Josh; mostly he's been schlepping – why did you choose a life to fight?

"I thought it was right."

It was an adventure – did you have any kids; a family?

"No."

You had an adventure... if you're going to be on stage 100 times might as well be in a bomber at least once.

"It's similar to other lives – he wanted to help."

Let's go back to Arthur for a second. How much of your conscious energy did you bring to this lifetime? How much of your conscious energy did you bring to Josh's life – to the guy who nearly died on Mt. Kailash?

"26%"

Why did you allow him to have that event on Kailash?

"To change direction. Yeah.... I... (unintelligible) I was talking to my guide. About the change that occurred in Josh. He says, "He's got to figure a way to get the best out of himself. And make the things that are very complex and frightening in their complexity make them... simple."

What's a 1, 2, 3? Is there a particular meditation he should try?

"Teach himself or get himself to a place where he can – teach others to go inside and experience the lightness he and the others have."

 Josh Davidow Filmmaker

SCOTTIE

Scottie is a friend who is a successful actress. She expressed an interest in the research, and we met for lunch in a busy restaurant in Sherman Oaks. Scottie had not read any of my books, but was curious about the process. After a few minutes, we were able to access her guide "Oscar."

RICH: So Oscar, how do you think Scottie is doing in this lifetime?

SCOTTIE: "Pretty good. She's actually trying too hard. (laughs)

Can we visit her council? What's that look like?

"It's a place with lots of feminine energy... sort of like a spa... like a witch's circle. Like a "good witch" circle."

Is this a place for her to recover?

"Yeah."

So, look around this coven. How many people are here?

"There are 8."

Is this her soul group or council?

"Feels like a council."

(Note: If someone mentions a crowd of folks in a room or outside, they're often either a "soul group" or a council. I'm skipping ahead because "Oscar" knows where I'm aiming.)

So, he's taken us to visit the council – are we inside or outside?

Feels like inside, but because of the thick tree overgrowth.

How are these people arrayed?

In a circle. Some are sitting; some are standing.

How about you?

I'm lying down. It feels like (I'm) healing.

Let's pick some council members to talk to – who wants to go first?

Isabelle. She's elegant, gentle, about 50, wearing a flowing blue dress. Big blue rings around her neck.

What do those rings represent?

An expression or emotion.

Take her hands in yours, how do they feel?

Soft.

Any emotion?

Relief.

Can I ask Isabella a direct question? Is that okay?

"Yes."

Are you familiar with what I'm doing?

"Yes."

What am I doing?

"Guiding."

As well as asking questions. Is that annoying?

"It's okay."

How many councils are you on?

"Nine."

Does Scottie know any of the other people you serve with on?

"All of them."

What quality do you represent that you earned this spot on her council?

"Truth."

Is that something Scottie learned during a lifetime?

"She's learning it now."

And next to you?

"Elizabeth." She's golden. She's like 25 (years old).

If you hold her hand, what do you feel?

Radiance.

What's the quality you represent in Scottie's journey?

"Radiance."

(Note: Funny. She answered my question before I could ask it.)

How many councils do you sit on?

"Three."

Is that because of your age – does someone older have more councils?

"Not really, no, I just like to keep it light."

How is Scottie doing?

"She's been through it – she's starting to connect to me, to build up radiance."

Is there anyone on this council that is the spokesperson for your council who wants to come forward?

I feel like a man is here.

What's his name?

Edwin. Looks like Gandalf. Blue eyes. Beard. About 80.

Let me ask is this familiar what I'm doing?

"Yeah." He says, **"Amusing."**

Why do you find it amusing?

"Because it's just... it's important work."

How is Scottie doing?

"She's... funny. She's doing well."

Anything you want to tell her?

"Lighten up."

She needs to lighten up. Is she on the right path?

"Yes."

Anyone else want to come forward and speak to us?

Teresa. She's kind of like "punk."

Teresa what do you want to tell her?

"She needs to dance more. Dance around with life more and dance physically."

How many councils are you on Teresa?

"Five."

Edwin?

"Twelve."

So, Edwin, you are aware of what I'm doing?

"Yes. She's been waiting a long time to do this."

Scottie

*****

MITCHELL – ARCHITECTURE OF THE AFTERLIFE

Mitchell is a writer/producer/director. He's had some great success in television. He's a fan of the research, and is familiar with it. We were having coffee, and I suggested a demonstration. We met in my local cafe; Cafe Luxxe. My questions are *in italics*, replies are in bold. I turn on my cellphone recorder:

To recap, I asked Mitchell if he had a guide, and you saw a woman?

She's willowy, hippie-ish, moderately thin, green eyes, blonde, gray, straight hair.

I'm going to ask her some questions – is that okay?

"Yes."

Did you bring Mitch here today?

She's like "That's why we're here."

What's her name?

She said "Brook." First thing she said.

Is that a metaphor?

"No," she's saying. It's straight up her name.

Brook, how many lifetimes have you been keeping an eye on him?

"I've always been," was her first response.

Okay, that was a trick question. If she's your guide, then it would be all of them. How's he doing?

She's happy. He needs to chill. "Sit by the brook and chill."

(Aha, she is a metaphor!)

You were there when he planned this journey; you and Mitch worked out what he was going to do, kids, etc. Is he on the right path?

"Yes." She's saying "Yeah, for the most part, he's on the right path, following the path."

You want to show him where the path veers?

The metaphor I get is rocks in the river; I've gone around them. I've had rough waters; I've handled them for the most part.

Are these rocks lessons or jewels for Mitch?

She's saying "They're more like an obstacle course – like a river with rapids, you have to maneuver around them, sometimes you tumble and go over them in the water. And sometimes you come up spitting water, I've worked through those stresses."

Is there any time you've been with him Brook, during his lifetime – some incident where you interceded?

She went to ... she's showing my daughter's adoption – she was taken from me and she came back.

(Note: Mitch and his wife adopted a baby girl, and the mother changed her mind at the last moment. And then after a few months, changed her mind again and they adopted her.)

Did you intercede emotionally? Structurally?

She helped the birth mom be okay with that.

Brook let's walk Mitchell in to visit with his council. What comes to mind?

We're outside. It's not really a place, it's like clouds, like in a clouded place...

Outdoors but like in deep space?

Just a floaty cloudy place.

Look around this structure – is there a floor? Or clouds?

We're above the clouds, when you look down you see down to the earth, there's like this classic like council place with five people.

Are they sitting in a row?

Semi-circle.

Go to the first person on your far left.

It's a male. About 70. Sitting. He has a kind face, grayish beard.

If you were going to cast him?

He looks like the actor who played "The most interesting man alive."

What's this counselor's name?

Begins with J. Like Jedidiah or something.

Jedidiah. Is that right? What can we call you?

"Jed's good."

Walk up to him, take hold of his hand; what's that feel like?

Very welcoming, firm but also soft. He does a two hander. The emotion makes me feel like I'm "Okay." That idea of that I'm met with calm. It's also encouraging, supportive, also kind of... to not forget to be on, to stay on the path. It's almost like a proud father.

Let me ask Jed some questions. I'm just curious. How many councils do you sit on?

"Many. More than a 100... countless."

Does Mitchell know any of the people whose councils you sit on?

He's saying "no" –... now he's thinking.

He's got to go through them all! Let me ask what quality you represent that got you a place on his council – your role in his life and journey.

He's saying, "I'm just one of the pillars of support."

You're a guy of support – but correct me if I'm wrong, please. You earned this place or represent something Mitchell learned from one or all of his lifetimes. Is it being a pillar of support? Being a standup guy?

"I'm here because he has something to share, has always had something to share and I'm here to help him support him in that sharing."

Am I familiar to you what I'm doing (talking to councils)?

He says, "In an indirect way, people have attempted to communicate with him (before) but never as directly."

So why is this becoming more prevalent now? Something that used to be sacred or sacrilegious... here we are in a coffee shop just yakking with you. Has there been a shift in consciousness? What's happening?

He's saying it's specific to the recipient, the openness where I'm at. Everyone has a specific reason (why they might access this information).

What's Jed wearing?

Just like casual linen pants and a white linen shirt, open; chest hair.

Let's go to the person next to Jed – is that a male or female?

That person... he's showing me a woman, she's similar to Brook but different. She's in her 70's. Her name is... I'm coming up with Mia.

That's fine. May I call you Mia?

"Sure."

Take her hands – what's that feel like?

It's exciting. I feel like... thrilling. She's communicating a feeling of thrilling.

Is that what you represent? Being thrilled? (She says later "life force.")

"Yeah."

How many councils do you sit on?

"Not as many."

So, Jed was bragging?

(Mitchell laughs) Her response was "not as many as Jeeed."

I like to stir it up with councils I meet. So, Mia how many?

"100's."

That's a lot.

She says, "But compared to Jeeeed...."

Ha. Okay, what do you represent in Mitchell's journey - the thrill or excitement of being alive?

"It's all of it, mindfulness of the moment."

What's she wearing?

She's got some necklace with some amulet... I don't know what it is.

She knows what it is. Describe this amulet – is a creature? A thing?

She's saying, "It's a living stone."

Okay.

"It's a life force. What she's showing me is when she and me experience those moments of excitement; this thing literally pulsates."

Who created that?

It was passed on to her by her ... she's saying, "It was given to her by a counselor."

Cool. Mitch, have you ever heard of such a thing?

"No."

I just wanted to clarify. You're seeing something that is new for you to observe, not part of your consciousness. I've never heard of such a thing, it's new information.

She told me she has a little version of it. (?) By the way the person sitting next to her is an older man; he's telling me "Everyone here is getting their sense of humor from me."

Mia can you put a sensation in Mitch's body? A feeling of this life force stone.

She just did.

Okay, let's talk to the guy next to her.

His name is Henry. He looks like... what would be a Borscht-belt comic in his 50's... loose tie, Rodney Dangerfield kind of a guy...

Henry, how many councils do you sit on?

"Just a few. Between 10 and 20." He's very specific that he's saying he's offered (to sit on councils of) people but he makes discerning choices.

Who makes the offer?

It's not a higher council, it's almost energetic; that's how councils come together.

Henry have you ever had a lifetime on earth?

"Yes, a long time ago." I think he's saying somewhere 3 or 400 years ago.

Were you a funny guy then?

"Yeah."

Funny with your friends? Or for money?

He says "It was both survival, the conditions, but seeing that era that was like.... medieval... It was in the middle east, there was a lot of stone and markets."

Would you call yourself a standup back then?

"I had a light point of view."

Let me ask, how do you think Mitchell doing?

"He was a good choice – he's saying he was a good choice to take on."

What do you represent in terms of Mitchell's spiritual evolvement?

"Humor."

Are you the spokesperson for this council?

"We all speak but that's Jed. (He's the spokesperson) When they need to communicate he's there."

Henry, who's on your left?

It feels like a young girl. She's like 12 years old. Her name is A... Aly.

Nice to meet you Aly; how many councils do you work on?

"Just a few – ten." She's wearing like a sun dress and she has her bike. I feel like she doesn't want to be hanging out – she'd rather be riding her bike.

What's the quality you represent in Mitch's life?

She's saying that (the quality is) "there's more to come."

You represent the future?

"Yeah. When I take her hand, I feel like I'm on my own bike and riding.

I appreciate you coming by to say hello, never met anyone quite like you. Okay, who's next?

Oh... that's my dad.

Is it your dad or someone who looks like him?

It's him. He says, "call me Frank."

What's he wearing?

Casual windbreaker; dressed casually.

Frank this must be a little weird for you – is it?

"No, it's nice." He's saying he talks to me all the time.

Mitchell

STEPH ARNOLD – ARCHITECTURE OF THE AFTERLIFE

Steph Arnold is a successful author; this full transcript is in the book. She wrote a best selling story about her experience dying during childbirth, but predicting the details which saved her life.

RICH: Can we walk her into her council?

STEPH: "Yes."

(Can we visit your council?) Are we inside or outside, describe the journey?

We're standing outside walking on the path, there's a door in the distance, it's a sidewalk path; like an arch…

Is there a building in the distance?

The door is attached to a building. It's white but a little gray. There are no markings on it …One way in, one way out.

What's it look like inside?

Um; it feels like the room is wide open… It feels spacious like if you were looking at a regular classroom – there's like ten feet between each chair. This is bigger.

How about the walls?

A warm white.

How many people are here?

Like 30. Anywhere between 18 and 30. They're kind of stacked.

Let's go to the first row. How many in the first row?

Six. In a line.

Let's go to the first person to your left.

It's a female with black hair and glasses in her late 20's. Like hazel eyes. Wearing like a white tee shirt. Simple tee shirt and a long skirt – like off white.

If you are allowed, reach over and take her hands and describe that.

It's like a friend, an old friend, somebody who's warm and very smart and kind eyes.

What name can we use to speak with you? May we speak to you?

"Yes." Priscilla came to mind.

Thanks. How do you think Steph is doing?

"She's going to be fine."

That's a little different than what Ida said; "struggling."

(Nods) Mm-hmm.

She's doing pretty good?

"Yes. She is."

Priscilla, have you heard of me?

"Yes I have."

How so and put that in Steph's mind.

"Through a dog."

Okay, that's unusual, which dog?

I see like a German shepherd mix.

(Pause. Stunned). Wait. Is this dog part German shepherd and part miniature collie?

"Yes."

Is it... are you saying you know of me via my dog, Sam? How do you know Sam?

I don't know.

Well, Priscilla does.

(Steph laughs) I just am seeing her playing fetch with him.

Just trying to clarify, if you will. Is this my dog Sam or some other German shepherd?

"That's how we know each other; through the dog."

*Is it **my** dog?*

"I believe it is." She's smiling. She's saying, "You don't want to believe what I'm telling you." She's talking to me... that I don't believe it.

Okay, this is a bit odd, but I talked to my dog Sam a month ago with the help of a medium. And Priscilla just described him.

(Note: This is one of those mind freezing moments that sometimes happens during a session. A month earlier, I spoke to my dog, Sam, because I invited him to a session with Jennifer Shaffer, my medium friend who works with law enforcement ("Backstage Pass to the Flipside: Talking to the Afterlife with Jennifer Shaffer.") Sam told Jennifer the details of his passing which included him seeing my brother just prior to dying. These were details I didn't know as I was out of the country at the time. But they occurred 40 years ago. My brother confirmed what Sam told me about his seeing him just before he died. And now – speaking with Steph, whom I had not met prior to this skype session, her council member is telling me that she knows of my work "speaking to councils" through my dog Sam. Who died 40 years ago? Can I just say "Wow!" Mind officially blown.)

Author with his dog Sam circa 1969.

Priscilla, Steph sees you as a friend. Does she know you outside this council?

"No."

How many councils do you sit on?

"About 40."

Any of your charges that Steph might know? That you oversee that Stephanie might know?

Who's alive or who's passed?

Either. If something comes to mind.

No, nothing.

What quality do you represent that allows you to sit on Steph's council?

"Compassion."

Can you introduce us to the person to your left?

It's a male, stiff as a board. He's tall, his torso is very long. He's wearing a vest and a tie. And a white, white shirt, but he's got on a brown tweed vest.

I forgot to ask if Priscilla is wearing jewelry?

A ring with a pearl on it.

What does that pearl represent?

Her mother.

How about this vest guy fellow; what's his name?

"Fred."

Is it okay to ask you questions?

"Yes."

(Note: She seems to take on his persona of aloofness.)

Can you take his hands?

They're rough and they're cold.

What do you represent in her spiritual evolvement?

"Logic."

Have you had any lifetimes with Steph?

"Twice."

Does she want to explore one of them?

"Not right now."

Okay, so is there a person in charge of this council, the spokesperson? Who's that?

There's a woman, almost looks like a character from "Little House on the Prairie." A teacher at the school, old fashioned with buttons up to the neck and a long straight skirt – her name is Mildred.

May I ask how many councils you work with?

"A lot. I've lost count."

Sorry, Fred, how many do you work on?

"Four."

Mildred you have the benefit of all of these lives and lifetimes, this vast knowledge of observing and guiding and it's amazing job you have, and I want to thank you for allowing us to chitchat – have you heard about what I'm doing?

"Yes. They said there's somebody always knocking at the door."

What's the value of what I'm doing?

"Tethering - connecting from one side to the other and showing that there is a line."

That's a beautiful way to put it; we're always tethered to our guides?

"Yes. But it's more like if you imagine Jack in the Beanstalk... the tethering comes from the boundless infinite; there's always a hook into that world that will always be grounded in this world."

What one word would you use to represent her?

"The producer."

Have you been helping her with that?

"Yes."

Thank you. Let's ask everyone, what's the purpose of allowing Steph to see things that would happen in advance? To make her life miserable?

"No, she has the ability to connect."

Is Steph tapping into the matrix? Into consciousness?

"It will soon become clear and it will launch this really high-speed highway."

Stephanie and others are helping people to work on this highway?

"Yes, everyone has this piece (of it.)"

What's the time frame for this highway (connecting us to the flipside) to come into existence? In our lifetime?

"Yes, you're going to see the start of the roller coaster in the next ten years."

So, Mildred – do you have some lottery numbers for me?

"(Steph laughs) "It's the intention behind it that counts."

Is Steph doing what she's supposed to be doing?

"Yes."

And if you could put a sensation in her body somewhere for her so she knows when you're reaching out to her. Can you feel that?

Steph nods.

How was that Steph? Fifteen minutes.

(Steph aside:) How do I know that I didn't make this up?

Because you just said the identical things others say – you'll see it when I include it in a chapter in my next book. You say basically the same things everyone else has said about this journey. If you're not familiar with my books, or with Michael Newton's reports, how could you possibly imagine this place or these people or even the concept that you are tethered to them?

Wait; I know what the gold ID bracelet is! I remember it now; I don't have it anymore. It was a gift my father gave me – and it did

said Steph on it… from my dad. I'll check this jewelry box I have I haven't opened in a while. Amazing.

Steph Arnold Author

******

MATTHEW – ARCHITECTURE OF THE AFTERLIFE

This is an unusual example of me accessing a council on behalf of someone else. In this case, her ex-boyfriend had passed suddenly and while accessing him, I asked her to visit with her council. At some point, the lead council member thinks it's a bad idea and disperses the council. The only time this has happened. Sean is a friend of Matthew's, it's not her real name.

RICH: Can you bring your guide forward? Is that a male, female neither or both?

SEAN: It's a spirit. It's just like a light. Quite close. It's white – like Tinkerbell. Small (she gestures with one hand).

I'd like your guide to manifest as a human so we can talk to you – what do you see?

My guide says "no."

I'm asking your guide directly to manifest as someone we can chat with.

She's a fairy.

Okay don't judge it. About the size of your hand?

Yes.

What's this guide's name?

"Tara."

Describe her. How many wings does she have?

Four. They're like a fly's wings; quite strong.

What color are they?

Clear – translucent. She's a woman. About 4 inches high, she has brown hair, light blue eyes; she's very sweet. (Wearing) Like a fairy outfit... it's green blue...

Like Tinkerbell?

"Yes."

Tara. Can I ask you direct questions and you'll put the answers in her mind?

"Yes."

Have you ever incarnated on our planet?

"No."

In the place you come from does everyone look like you?

"Yes there's a lot."

Tara, I spoke to someone recently who resembled someone like you. Are you aware of this?

"Yes. I am."

Tara are you aware of me?

"Yes."

What's your opinion of what I'm doing?

"Good work."

Next question can you walk our friend in to visit her council?

Into my what?

She knows what I'm talking about.

She says "Yes."

Funny; Tara knows your council but you don't – do you know what I'm talking about Sean?

No, I don't.

I'm just verifying that you don't understand this (idea of a council) but your guide does. Are we inside or outside?

Inside. It's like a white room; everything is very white.

What's it made of? Marble?

Yes. It's clear as a bell white, the ceiling is normal sized; it's very white. It's a very big ceiling – large ceiling; it's flat.

How many people are in here?

There are people walking around; like ten people.

How are they arrayed – in a line, semi-circle?

Walking in front of me. I'm standing at the back.

Let's move forward – ... what do you look like to Tara?

I'm still dressed in the sarong actually.

Let's see if we can talk to your council. How are they arrayed?

Everyone is still walking in front of me...

Tara let's go to the first councilmember on your left.

It's a man. Dressed in Greek clothing – in a white toga. He has a wreath on his head, like a gold wreath. He's 40 maybe. Dark hair, brown hair, brown eyes.

What's a name we can use to call you?

"Simon."

Have you known Simon before or only here?

He seems familiar even though I don't know him.

May I ask; do you know me?

"Yes."

Any comment about this work I'm doing?

"Good work."

Let me ask you Simon – how is our friend doing?

"She's fine."

How many councils do you work on?

"A few. About 20."

What's the one word that represents your role in our friend's journey?

"Good."

What do you mean by that? Doing good, acting good, being good?

"Like (having a) solid foundation."

So the word represents someone who does good is that correct?

"Yes."

Just for context – did she earn that in one lifetime or in many lifetimes?

"Many lifetimes."

Simon, let me ask, in this memory of a lifetime when our friend was married, what (theme) did she need to examine?

"Love."

Why did she choose this current lifetime? What's the connection between this and that one?

"To help him."

And... who else?

"She can help a lot of people."

How so?

"She can get messages. By listening carefully."

Put in her mind's eye how she can help people in the future (in terms of her creativity and work.)

"She just has to listen carefully. Just follow and listen." (Sean aside) I don't know what you're asking.

Simon. Can you introduce her to another person on her council?

He says, "No." (A pause) They're all walking away.

Who's the spokesperson for this council?

There's a woman. Yes, she's quite powerful.

Can you give us a name to converse with you?

"Nora."

Thank you – Nora, am I correct in asking this? You represent the council for our friend here?

"Yes."

Is there something about the questions I'm asking that aren't appropriate?

"Yes." She says "They want to kick us out."

Before we go – are you aware of what I'm doing?

"Yes; she doesn't agree with it."

Okay, let me clarify – you don't agree with it because you don't want to alter Sean's path by showing her what's going to happen next?

"Yes."

I don't want to do that – If I may ask you, what quality do you represent in her spiritual evolvement?

She says "We have to leave. We shouldn't be here. Enough questions."

Okay, before we go, is it true that our friend is always connected to you at all times? Can access you through her heart at all times?

"Yes."

By the way how many councils are you on?

"Hundreds." (Sean aside) They want us to go.

Thank you council for allowing us to come and chat with you...

(Note: I'm a bit like Colombo here – the detective who always asks one more question. We were being told to leave, but I continued to ask questions to clarify why we were being asked to leave.)

Tara can you walk her in to visit with her soul group?

We're outside – like ten people. My friend is there. He looks the same, about the age we saw him earlier.

Anyone else you recognize?

My sister.

How many boys and girls here?

Ten. More men than women.

How does your sister look? She's still on the planet, right?

Yes. She's not really all there.

Tara, correct me if I'm wrong, the reason she's not all there is because only part of her energy is back home, correct?

"Yes."

But when you compare your sister to your friend; she's etheric but he's all there correct?

"Yes."

How many lifetimes have you had with your friend?

"Ten."

Tara, correct me if anything I'm saying is inaccurate; we choose lifetimes with a significant other because we trust them... we have unconditional love for them.

"Yes."

Can you show our friend her life planning session for this current one? Are we inside or outside?

Outside.

Are we with a small or large group?

Smaller group.

Are there any of the people we saw at the council?

"No."

These are the folks helping you plan this (lifetime's) journey – at what point did you say that you would sign up for a lifetime with your friend knowing that he wouldn't stay here long?

"Yes." I somehow say "Yes, I'm happy to do that again."

Can I ask you a simple question?

"Yes."

Why did you ask her to participate in your life? What was the story line you wanted to learn from?

"It's not about money."

(Note: I have no idea what he means by this comment, but I later I discovered that this friend "Mr. Big" was a wealthy person.)

Does she know what that means?

"Yes."

Tara, everyone in this lifetime is just another incarnating soul, and we are all connected, is that correct?

"Yes." (Sean aside) It's funny I keep getting that message over and over again.

What's the purpose of holding onto anger?

"Let it go."

Let me ask your friend this question; "Are you dead?"

"No."

So not only is he still alive, but he's also trying to say "let it go." Is that correct?

"Yes. I had nothing to do with it."

Did you ask everyone in your life to participate in your journey?

"They agreed."

So Tara; why did you allow Sean to access this information?

"Because she has to let go."

Tara is there a sensation you can give our friend to remind her she's always connected to you?

"Yes." It's like a light. Like a little light.

Tara, is this your way of letting her know you're close by?

"Yes."

Also your way of reminding her to let go. Is that correct?

"Yes."

Let me ask your pal, why did you let her reach out to me?

He felt sorry for me that I had these things running around in my head.

How did you find me?

He lived in LA; he knows people you know.

By the way Tara, can I ask you about the planet you're from?

"It's in another universe."

Has anyone come to visit your planet you're aware of? In their sleep?

"Yes. Yes."

So the idea of fairies comes from your planet?

"Yes."

Fairy isn't the right word. What would you call yourself?

"A being."

A light worker?

"Yes."

Okay, thanks everyone!

It's so interesting!

*****

COWBOY DAUGHTER JENNIE from Architecture of the Afterlife

I met a woman at a screening who asked about what I was doing, and I explained it over coffee the next day. As usual, I started asking her questions and then turned on my cell phone. She'd never read any of my books nor knew me at all.

RICH: Can we go and visit her council?

JENNY: "Yes."

Describe it please.

We're inside, it's like a ... okay, looks like the war room in "Game of Thrones." Where Kaleesi would sit around the map table. That room.

How many are here?

Eight. Like I'm in front and they're around – semi circle.

Let's go to the 1st on your left – male or female?

Male.... I recognize him... my friend Duncan. Same age as when he died - no sorry, younger than when he died. Sorry Duncan. Early 70's.

What is your role on her council; what word represents her journey?

"No doubt."

She's been provided that for many lifetimes?

"Yes."

Are you the spokesperson?

"No, just one of the members."

Are you familiar with what I'm doing?

"Yes. "

Who told it to you?

He said he was very... okay... he's saying "he was really closed in this lifetime, so this is...." he's really excited, (to be here) because he was kind of mean around... I mean... he didn't get...

Duncan, you've known her for many lifetimes?

"Yes."

How many councils do you serve on?

He said "ten." He was saying to me this was his first time as a council member on *her* council.

But you're on other councils?

"Yes."

Beatrice, let me ask you what's that thing around your neck (she mentioned earlier)?

It's like diamonds... That's like – a metaphor – it's um... what's coming... The future – and some rubies and emeralds."

The future (for Jennie) is diamonds and gems?

Duncan wanted me to know that the cameras are the connection between us; he gave me a camera and he's showing me that... is our connection.

Is he responding to my question "How do you know me?"

How he got on my council. He felt the connection with me – the connection of the two of us... he's saying he realized when I visited him in the nursing home and he gave me the camera, that was when he realized there was a connection. So when he got to the afterlife, that's how he got onto my council.

Okay, thanks for clarifying that. Duncan, giving her the camera was that a selfless act on your part?

"Yes, ironically one of the first."

So in his life it was hard for him to be selfless but by giving something to you he showed other councils members that he deserved a place on your council?

"Yes."

Duncan who's to your left? Male or female?

Male. It's my grandfather... Frederick.

What is the quality you represent on this council?

"Peace of mind" he says.

Is that something she's working on? "Peace?"

"Yes."

Let me ask are you Frederick, are you familiar with what I'm doing?

"Yes yes yes."

How so?

He said "cooler talk." (Jennie aside: What's that mean?)

What? (I laugh.) I understand it. I often say it during a session – that they know from "hanging around the council water cooler and talking about it."

(Note: Doesn't get much weirder than having a council member refer to a joke you've only made to other council members – and having the person in front of you say "I don't get it.")

I'm just curious Frederick; can you put it in her minds' eye who told you about this?

He says "Jack."'

He thinks I'll know who Jack is? Is it Jack Nicholson?

(Jennie aside) He's still alive right?

He is.

He says, "You would know."

Let me ask; what's the first letter of his last name?

N. He laughed – first thing he said was "Nicholson" and then said to me "Tell him Nelson!" But he actually said "Nicholson" first.

Well that's funny – I am aware of what he means. Let's ask him again – see if he says something different. Who made you aware of my work?

He keeps saying "Jack."

(Note: My friend Luana Anders who facilitates our podcast and who drew me to this work was a lifelong friend of Jack, so it makes sense his "higher self" would know about it through Luana on the flipside.)

Jennie is always tethered to you, correct?

"Yes."

That's the whole point of this exercise, isn't it? We are talking to people you don't consciously know...

Yes, I didn't know him.

But he's connected to you in a profound way. Let's talk to the spokesperson of your council.

Frederick is claiming that role.

Okay, thanks. What do you want her to realize about anyone else on this council?

He says "Not at this time."

You've met a couple and I think that's the most important part of this exercise; to meet a couple. So Frederick how is she doing in terms of her path?

Yeah... he wanted to pick the right word.

Your dad said "great," Beatrice your guide said "well" and Frederic says "meh?"

That's why I want to wait – he's choosing the right word.

(After a pause). So Frederick, how is she doing?

"She's right where she needs to be, right on the cusp," he said.

Thank you sir. That on the cusp comment relates to the future, to Jennie's future, correct?

"Yes."

Those diamonds around Beatrice's neck. So Beatrice - you stuck her in front of me (sat her next to me at a screening) to do what?

(Jennie aside) I know.

What do you know?

"She needs guidance and to understand her power in this life to actually bring forth the manifestation of the prosperity associated with this energetic power."

Correct me if I'm wrong Frederick; prosperity doesn't mean money, does it?

"No; the ability to prosper in this lifetime."

We use it as a term related to money... but it's the energy or prospering?

"Yes, it's very different. I understand that the energetic part of my lesson, he's saying was... the whole point (is) what I'm on the cusp of is.... that going from believing – being not worthy versus worthy."

Thank you Frederick. What's one sentence you want to tell her in terms of her relationship to her mom?

"Just feel worthy."

*****

CHAPTER TWENTY-FOUR – COMPENDIUM OF COUNCILS

Part Four

Simonetta Vespucci - Botticelli

IRIS

Iris is someone I've known since high school. We're old pals, and she became interested in the research. She signed up for a teaching session with Scott De Tamble. I was filming some of the sessions for him. At this point they had run out of teams, and Scott asked me to step in to allow Iris access this information (without hypnosis.) At this point, she's being escorted by "Miss S."

RICH: Can you walk Iris in to visit her council?

IRIS: "It's another place. We traveled at the speed of light. We're outside."

Thank you for allowing me to ask you to do that; what's that experience to travel at the speed of light?

"It's quick."

Like the speed of thought?

"You've gone from a place in deep space to another place. We're in the clouds.

When you're in the clouds can you see down below?

"I can see down below, but up above is blue sky."

How many people are in this council when you look around?

"Like ten."

How are they arrayed?

"In a semicircle."

First I want to thank Miss S for escorting us, and staying with us, if you don't mind. Council may we speak to you?

"Yes."

How far away from you are they?

"A couple of feet. They're over here (gestures) – and I'm sort of over here."

So go to the person on the far left, is that a male, female, neither or both?

"It's a ball of light."

Get as close as you can to it. How large is it?

"Like a volleyball... When you're close it feels good and energetic and warm. It's soothing."

So this ball of light, can I speak to you directly?

"Yes."

Would you do me a favor and manifest as a human so we can converse?

He keeps trying but it goes back into the ball.

What's a name or letter we can address you by?

L. Lila... sounds female, but is not.

Can Iris put her hands around you?

Yes. It feels soothing, feels good, feels like I'm at peace. makes me feel like I'm at peace.

Lila, what quality do you represent in Iris' spiritual evolvement that earned you this place on her council?

"Peace."

Did she earn that in this life or a previous lifetime?

"Previous."

How is Iris doing?

"She needs to pause more."

Is she doing what she set out to do?

"She's getting there."

How many councils do you sit on?

"12."

And the person next to you? Male or female?

Neither. A light again. Navy blue. Lila was white with a gold center.. a white center, looked gold because of the light.

Can we ask you questions? Can you manifest as a person?

Okay – again it's hard, it's flashes in and out. Neither male nor female, has no gender.

What's a name we can address you with?

"Pamash."

Thank you Pamash. When Iris puts her hands around your light what does she feel?

"Compassion."

Is that the quality you possess that earned you a place on her council?

"Yes."

How many do you work on?

"22."

Are you aware of this work?

"Yes I am, Rich."

Is it a good or bad idea?

"It's a good idea, but public awareness is difficult."

I'm not fishing for a compliment, just like to hear different points of view.

"You're a pioneer. It's good. There's no glory in being a pioneer."

Most pioneers wind up on crosses. I always ask for lottery numbers but they never give them. Are you going to be different Pamash?

"It's fate."

Okay, so you're on 22 councils, compassion is your main focus. Who's the comedy guy on your council?

"Well... one is laughter."

Let's have that person stand up.

"Another light. This one is purple – it's Amethyst."

How many councils do you serve on?

"81."

A name to address you?

"Liam."

How do you think Iris doing?

"She laughs a lot."

Let me ask; you represent laughter, on her council, correct?

"Yes."

Laughter makes people heal; is that what her ability is?

"Yes. A lot of healing through humor – a lot of laughter through healing humor."

Who is the lead council member?

"It's Kolabra."

Let me guess. A light?

"Yes."

What color are you?

"I have every color. Not a rainbow, but every color. I reflect all light."

So you're mostly white?

"No, I'm every color, I'm a ball of every color light I'm a prism... I'm reflecting all light."

How many councils do you serve on?

"Thousands."

Is there a word associated with your service on her council? A quality she's earned?

"I'm all qualities."

I understand... all variations of light. When she looks at you what does she see?

"A prism of colors, they're vibrant, they're mesmerizing."

Is there a feeling or emotion associated with them?

"I would say it's every emotion, every feeling; it's everything. I am everything."

So Kolabra, how do you think Iris is going?

"She's here doing what she's supposed to be doing."

It's important to know she's always tethered to you and everyone at the council. Anyone else want to speak up?

"Yes. It's I don't know their name but this light is like a burgundy color and represents "pain.""

What's your role in her journey?

"You need pain to grow. You need pain to grow."

Did she earn your place on her council from previous lifetime?

"Yes, previous ones. We all grow, but she grows through pain. We all grow through pain but she really grows through pain."

How many councils do you sit on?

"Four."

On all of them do you represent pain? I would think they'd be disconcerted when you show up.

"Yes. All emotions are good, there's no good or bad – we're light. Light leads the way. Light leads the way; there's no good, bad, male, female. We exist for growth. All emotions lead to growth. You grow through emotions. Emotions are energy."

So when you work with Iris in terms of pain, how does that work? I understand how laughter works, compassion, courage –how does pain help them grow?

"Through the pain experience they develop memories – these base memories compounded help them see the light. I'm seeing a flash of almost like blood vessels, they're like blood vessels from lifetime to lifetime that like a tree, grow."

So they're always connected like roots.

"Like roots going up but not down. They're growing. In the light."

I want to thank you all for allowing us to speak to you – you have a reason for her to experience this. Does someone want to speak to her about why they allowed her to do this today?

"They have a message for you Rich; I'm getting "keep on the path, that you're going to your council is lighting the way, and you need to listen more – they want you to listen."

What do you want Iris to do?

"We want her to connect with more people. Iris meets a lot of people and this is a way to introduce this work."

Iris – AskIrisLibby.com

*****

UNO'S COUNCIL – FROM "ARCHITECTURE OF THE AFTERLIFE"

"Uno" is a filmmaker who had just returned from India and Nepal where he was making a film about Padmasambhava, the famous Indian pandit who brought Buddhism to Tibet in the 8th century. He said that he "felt compelled" to make the documentary.

RICH: *Who wants to come forward and escort us into Uno's council?*

UNO: It's.. my guide. "I am his intuition since we haven't talked yet."

So how do you manifest in Uno's mind – male, female or both?

"I am neither; I am more of a light. A higher self."

But for purposes of our conversation, if you could manifest as a person, so we can have this conversation I think it would be helpful.

"I am an extraterrestrial actually."

Like a Pleiadian or reptilian?

"Yes. A *"Pleia-dilian."* (Laughs.)

Well we have one Uno – so I'll call you Due. How's that?

"That's funny, why not?"

Are you familiar with the work I'm doing Mr. Due?

"Yes, both through Uno and from being in the realms."

Can we go in to visit Uno's council?

"Yes."

Describe this to me – are we inside or outside?

"Outside. We are in nature on Earth. I see more plants and bushes."

How many individuals are here to speak to us?

"I see about three. Standing."

Let's speak to the person on the far left, what do you see? Male, female? What do they look like?

"Yes, the strongest, he's a reptilian. He's about 6 feet tall. His eyes are brownish, blackish. His skin is kind of gray, brown, green mixture."

What would be a name to use to address you sir?

"Something you can't really say with the human tongue, but we could just say ... K, a, m, l, i, n."

(Note: Kamlin is a Hindu name for cupid or love (Kama is the Hindu God of love.)

Let me ask; Kamlin, how is our friend Uno doing?

"He's had some trouble dealing with the "reptilians" in his family line, so to speak, but he has overcome this aspect very well."

Have you ever incarnated on Earth?

"No, I have never."

So have you and Uno ever incarnated on the same planet together?

"Yes we did many thousands and thousands of years ago."

Where is your planet? Is it in our solar system, universe or another one?

"It's not in this solar system, but near Orion."

Is there a name for your planet?

"You could call it B, a, s, t, r, a, n."

(Note: Bastran is a word that means "to clothe oneself" in Nepalese.)

Can you show Uno what the place is like on Bastran? What's the environment like?

"It's kind of harsh in the human sense... lots of rocks and hot temperatures and we live "under the surface.""

If you could show Uno a place he lived – what does that look like?

"It is in many caverns that we have. There is technology of course, but it's built within cavern structures."

What's the purpose of Uno leaving your planet where all his friends are and incarnating on Earth?

"There are other factors in his sojourn, as people would say, but as far as leaving our planet. It's more... just him coming to earth to try to help."

To help in terms of climate change or in terms of consciousness awareness?

"Yes, more of consciousness awareness, and he the fact that he was reptilian and there's a need for a reptilian energy to come to earth because they know about the reptilians who are influencing others in a negative way."

How many councils do you sit on?

"I sit on five councils."

What quality do you represent on his council?

"I am his strength and power."

Is he wearing any jewelry by the way?

"I wear some jewelry and some clothes." He has a ring; like it goes across his fingers. "It represents something to Uno. It represents his strength as it is... like brass knuckles." (Uno laughs.)

Please introduce us to the person next to you.

There is a female Pleiadian.

How does she look to you?

"She looks human with long, dirty blonde hair."

What do you represent on his council?

"His compassion, warmth and sweetness."

Has Uno ever incarnated on the planet earth near Tibet?

"Yes he has – a few times even."

What would be one of those lifetimes be close to where he visited Tibet?

"Yes, he was close to Samye."

(Note: Samye is outside of Lhasa, and is where the Tibetan King invited Guru Rinpoche to build a Buddhist monastery (the first) in Tibet in the 8th century. Both Uno and I have been there.)

Are you familiar with the work I'm doing talking to councils?

"Yes, you have been talking to many people about councils and trying to help humanity at the same time."

Is this a valid thing to be doing? Is there value to it?

"Yes, of course because these are the kind of things people disbelieve but need to hear the most."

What do you want to tell people of our planet?

"The most important message for humanity right now... is for them to remember what they really are; that is -- a piece of consciousness, that is -- a piece of what you would say is God, or source or what have you; that's the just most important thing for people to know. They are caught up with being a "self" and being "a body.""

Are you always tethered to Uno?

"Yes, we are always connected to him in the relative sense."

Can you help him in times of need?

"Yes, he should use us more often."

How many councils do you sit on?

"I sit on six."

Can you introduce us to the person next to you?

"There is another to my left. It's a male." He looks like a human as well, actually. "I look about 35. My eyes are blue, my hair is blond."

Have you had a lifetime on earth?

"No, but, I am a humanoid."

What quality do you represent on Uno's council?

"I am his intelligence, wisdom and know-how in life."

How many councils do you sit on?

"I sit on six."

Are you familiar with my work and if so how?

"Yes, because you are known to be working and word gets around."

In terms of people on earth who may be listening to this, what do you want to tell people?

"Humanity is in a crisis because they do not know who they are and there is so much that is changing at the moment. And so people really need to get on track as far as... hm - spiritual things I guess you would say, they just need to get off of the material worries and that sort of thing; the same old story really."

You said you are humanoid – yet you haven't incarnated on Earth; where have you incarnated?

"I have not incarnated on earth, but I am incarnated in an area close to the Pleiades."

Are you choosing to manifest as a blond haired blue eye guy to make it easier to communicate with you?

"No, some Pleiadeans can look somewhat like me. There's different bloods going around, you know?"

Were your parents or genetic information from earth at some point?

"No. It's more like the other way around for humanity."

So human DNA came from the Pleiades instead of the other way around. Has Uno ever been visited by people from other planets?

"Many times when he was a child."

Was he aware of this?

"It's been blocked (from his mind) but he knows it's true."

Can you put it in his mind what happened?

"He saw gray aliens at his bed – and they took him away. "

"Due" help us with this memory. These grey people were they friends or strangers?

"Sure, someone he knew but it wasn't for positive reasons necessarily at that moment."

But in terms of his overall lifetimes – these friends of his had shown up to get information from him, correct?

"You could say that."

Almost like Columbus sending people to a distant shore and later his friends show up to say what have you learned?

"Yes, but there are different instances both good and bad."

Well, who can help us with this one? This concept of good and bad. From what I've learned in this research is that concept doesn't exist where you people are, but it exists on the planet because it's polarized.

"Yes, but it's more complicated."

Okay, just pointing out that humans have latched onto this good versus evil, god and Satan concept; it's not in the research. Or am I missing something?

"Yes, evil in that sense does not exist – but there are extra-terrestrials that have their own agendas as well. Of course, Satan doesn't exist and evil could be considered self-interest. It does exist in some form with extra-terrestrials but the higher you go the less there will be."

Correct me if I'm wrong, but once you're human you're not aware of your lifetime on another planet.

"Yes."

So even if someone normally incarnates on another planet - they might be more aggressive but that is something they can change or contain?

"You can choose."

What do you want to tell Uno?

"Uno needs to stay on the same path he's doing with his practices, try to relax and not get too aggressive in his energies as he likes boxing."

I've talked to people who box on the flipside...

"Sure, nothing wrong with it, but Uno doesn't need it right now."

Let's ask his guide to take Uno to a place of healing.

Okay. We're inside. There's a bathtub; kind of like an Egyptian chamber looking place. Bricks and a brick bathtub kind of thing. The bricks are gold.

Is there water in this tub?

"Yes."

Can you put yourself into it?

"Yes."

What impressions come to mind?

"Lots of light; like the water is full of light."

So what is that light composed of?

"Source energy."

Is the water associated with an entity or being?

"Yes, but not in a normal sense – it's pretty close to source."

Since it's a yes, I want to ask this entity some questions.

"Yes, but you might not get normal answers."

Let's ask this light which is close to source; do you represent consciousness?

"I represent all things."

Do we have to do something to experience source?

"Yes, but how could you not, because it's everywhere."

I'm just saying humans need to be reminded; if you want to experience source you start by opening you heart?

"Yes, that's true."

What's a way people can help save the planet from climate change?

"I would tell them just to open their hearts and become more who they are... I know I'm not answering your question."

I heard something similar during an interview "You need to love water, love yourself and then love the earth."

"Yes because then you reconnect with who you really, are so to speak."

Padmasambhava - Britannica

*****

JOANNA – from "ARCHITECTURE OF THE AFTERLIFE"

Joanna (not her real name) is a friend for over 20 years. A successful business woman, she's famous worldwide for her work. We were at a friend's home when she mentioned a "dream" she had as a child – had no idea why it popped into her head, but that she could access everything about it. I suggested we have coffee and discuss the dream. At some point I turned on the cellphone to record the following:

RICH: (Let's ask your guide) Ariel, can you walk her into her council?

JOANNA: "Yes."

Where are we? Inside or outside?

We're inside. It's a big room; they're all in a circle. There are a few; at least ten.

Ariel, I have more questions for you, so if you could hang with us, please. So you are aware ten people? Are you standing or sitting?

I'm standing. And suddenly I'm extremely tired... all of a sudden like weirdly pressured.

Is there a reason for that feeling Ariel?

"No; it's the energy of the room, everyone's energy..." I can feel it.

Let's ask Ariel to lighten this energy. Can you do that?

She nods. "It's lighter, but I'm still tired."

There are ten of them. Male or female, other or light?

Male. There's someone here who has got big gold wings – he's standing.

Well, let's go over to him first. What can we call you?

(Listens) Everyone's got these same sort of names. He says "Josiah."

Josiah; are you familiar with what I'm doing?

"Yes."

How so?

He says "He has a connection to "Jay-man."

(Note: For purposes of conversation instead of using the word Jesus, we decide upon the term Jay-man or Jay-Zeus to make it less formidable or "mind bending.")

So can we ask you Josiah, how is Joanna doing?

"Doing good!"

What quality do you represent on her council?

"Success."

Ah, hence the golden wings. Take a look at him; what's he wearing?

He's got blonde hair and has these magnificent gold wings, up high, huge, halfway open.

Wow. Talk about an entrance.

He says "You have to go sideways to get anywhere."

That's funny. Josiah, how many councils do you work on?

He's saying "five."

And are you the spokesperson for this council or one of the many?

He says "He's high up but not the spokesperson."

You represent success. What message do you want to tell her at this moment?

"That a lot more is coming. More than I think I can even handle... but that I can do it and not get overwhelmed."

Overwhelmed personally?

Work wise – "Don't get overwhelmed."

Josiah says he's aware of my work via Jay Zeus. How did you become aware of it? Just curious.

"It was part of somehow... his is with Jay's grouping on the other side."

Like part of his group? Resonates at the same frequency?

"Yeah."

Cool. So success is coming to our friend, what else do you want to tell her that she can pass along to other people?

He said "There has been a clearing. An easier, bigger path."

For the planet or for her?

Sorry; "for her."

He's on your council after all, and I asked him a question that relates to you.

Hang on. He says "But there is a clearing happening on the earth too."

Thank you Josiah. Who else wants to speak up from her council. The spokesperson for her council, perhaps?

The spokesperson is in a long trench coat and hat something from the 30's. It's dark olivey brown, the hat is dark olive. He's male, has a salt and pepper beard – (Joanna aside:) Everyone's got a beard.

What color are his eyes?

They're like silver – but not the color silver, like white grey. I've never seen that color before.

Can I ask you some direct questions? What's a name we can use for you?

"Noem."

(Note: Noemi means delight.")

Is it weird for you to have someone like our friend here talking to you?

He says "He's been waiting for us."

What quality do you represent in her council?

"Life path." Has anyone said that before?

No, but I've heard quite a few. Makes sense. Like an architect of your lives. How many councils are you on?

Eight. (Joanna aside:) My life path number is 8.

It's also the symbol of infinity... So are you like a life planning kind of person?

"He is _the_ planner."

How do you think Joanna is doing?

"On track."

Why did you guys decide to have this career that she's been so successful at?

"It was decided by the council."

Really? I mean there was a life planning session, they were pitching it, someone pitched it – was that you Josiah? Who pitched that?

"Yeah. Josiah and Ariel pitched it."

Like this is a cool thing for her? To what end?

"To inspire and touch many people not for what we think acting is for. It's all coming now."

I understand – like the millions of people who have seen her perform have captured her frequency on some level – so over there their conscious energy is aware of her?

"Yes, it's now, it's been coming."

That idea that we can become aware we're all connected.

"Mm-hmm."

Who's the comedian on this council?

Noem says "He's hilarious."

So that's you?

He says "Of course; everyone else has beautiful outfits, he's in a trench coat, hat and glasses."

Has anyone on your council had a lifetime on Earth?

He has, in the 1930's, when my mother was born.

Let's take this moment to reflect on how cool this is, we know you're keeping an eye on our pal here, everything's going to be okay. What's that feel like holding their hands?

"Peace."

And that feeling you got from the Jesus – that bolt of unconditional love – that was a powerful feeling. Have you ever had anything like that?

No, I've never had that feeling that I just felt.

So he can help you experience that at any time. Let's ask – how many people beside Joanna does Ariel work with?

Eight thousand.

Okay, that's an interesting answer.

(Note: It's interesting because we were speaking to Ariel who is Joanna's guide, who just happens to be an archangel. I know that sounds odd, but I've met other ones, mostly on councils.)

May I ask, have I met you before?

He says "Yes." (shrugs) He says, "He watches over you too."

Since when? Since the beginning of my journey?

He said "Recently." Were you meditating and somehow you called to him, or one of my guides?

If I can ask him; where did we meet?

He says "On the flipside, when you were separated from your body – you were in another consciousness."

*****

MARIE

This is a friend who speaks French as a native language. She was visiting Santa Monica. Over lunch we took this trip together at Caffe

Luxxe over coffee. This excerpt begins after speaking to her guide. I turn on my recorder.

RICH: *Is it all right to bring her to her council?*

(Marie hesitates:) "He says she's not ready."

Very good. But I am. Why don't we go visit her council for me and she can sit in the back?

MARIE: I'm in front of a table with people.

Okay. That was fast; Sorus said she's not ready but allowed it. Thank you.

"As a human she has the free will to do it without permission."

Okay. I don't want to disrupt her path in any way.

"She's strong she can take it."

I'd like you to participate.

"I'm here."

I just want to say that I'm not going to alter her path in a bad way.

"She cannot go in a bad way." (Marie aside:) He's tough!

Are we inside or outside?

Neither inside nor outside. It's a long table like a banquet table.

How many people?

More than ten sitting down. I'm in front of them standing.

Let's start with the person on the far left, male or female, neither or both?

I see only males. Far left is a male, he's older, but younger than the others.. like 25 maybe... dark black hair, he's far away. Has brown eyes.

Let's go closer to him. Look him in the eye. Let me ask; is it okay to talk to you?

He says "I'm not (the one) supposed to talk." He says we are the ones doing the talking.

What's a name to address him with?

He says "no name that you would understand."

How about a letter?

He says "call me Mo."

Nice to meet you.. and thank you for allowing us to have this conversation. Mr. Mo.

(Marie aside:) They don't laugh. They aren't laughing.

I don't always get laughs, but are you familiar with what I'm doing?

"We know you."

I get the feeling you disapprove of me asking questions. Correct?

"Yes; she has her path."

I won't disrupt her path – we're not going to talk about her future. I'm only going to ask about you.

"She needs to open the doors herself."

Here's my question to you; what quality do you represent on her council?

I hear "Justice."

How many councils do you sit on?

"Three."

How is Marie doing?

"She cannot go wrong."

So then there's nothing to worry about here; thank you Mo. Have you ever had a lifetime on earth?

"Never."

Where do you normally incarnate or did you incarnate?

"That's none of your business." (Marie laughs, shrugs)

If you know me Mo, as you say you do, you know I ask questions. Did you have a lifetime there?

"Yes."

Is it in another galaxy?

"Yes."

Something she would know? That she remembered in a dream?

"We've been there together."

Put that in her mind's eye, without fear or judgment, show her this place – Are we inside or outside?

It's a very cool place. it's like outdoors... like very colorful elements... colors are more vivid, more flashy.

How many people exist on this planet?

"Three million."

Is this planet in another galaxy or in another universe?

"Other universe."

I've heard descriptions of a few so this is not unusual for me.

He says "He knows (that)."

Sorry to be so persistent Mo. What do you call this planet in case I run across it again?

"You cannot know the name, it's a different way to name things. It's not comprehensible to you."

Can you show her what you look like on that planet? Present yourself in front of her – or what does she look like? Did she have arms and legs?

"It's more like etheric, not completely *ghosty*... but a different density and dimension."

Kind of like you can see-through a person?

"Exactly – it's like fluid; there is no legs or walking."

Is it more of a mental planet?

"Yeah, yeah."

Is there a lifetime on that planet?

"Time doesn't exist there" (as you know it.)

So you exist over there now?

"Yes."

So does she exist over there now?

"Yep."

What percentage of her energy is on the planet?

20.

What percentage of her is on our planet?

"Say that again? Her consciousness is with her everywhere. Her entire consciousness is with her on earth."

But in terms of your journey, do people from your planet come to earth?

"All the time."

To gather or pass along information?

I'm hearing "It's a luxury... it's a luxury to have the opportunity to incarnate here. It's elective."

She chose to come here?

It's hard... (to incarnate on Earth) but it's like when you pass this game test, you learn much more on earth than anywhere else, like a condensed form of spirit knowledge.

Mo, can I ask why you've never incarnated on Earth?

"My frequency is a different frequency. I don't need to incarnate."

What's Mo wearing?

All are wearing white, same clothes. Some wear pendants.

Let's go to a person wearing a pendant.

It is a guy in the middle...

Let me ask about the pendant. What's it look like?

A planet. Looks like Saturn with a ring.

What does that represent?

"It doesn't have anything to do with the planets; it has to do with what kind of community or section he is from."

What quality do you represent in her spiritual evolution?

He's like a part of ... he represents "education."

We had Justice, Education, Learning.. What's a letter we can use for you?

It's a sound and not a letter. Life Effff... He's older, has white hair, white beard, dreads like the Celtic guys.

Are you familiar with what I'm doing?

"Yes we know you. You have found a bridge to us. You came through people to us many times."

Is this a good or a bad thing?

"They cannot judge. They cannot do anything."

Well, normally they only talk to folks who have died. This is a bit different.

(Marie aside) It feels like we're interrupting them.

Have you ever incarnated on earth Eff?

"Never."

How many councils are you on?

"Ten."

What's the emotion you're getting while being near him?

He's like "You don't want to fuck with him." (Marie laughs)

Well he is a teacher... it comes in all forms.

"It's not like they "judge your growth," they measure it.. They meet to.. not to judge, but at the end of the day they know how to measure. Not measure progress, but..." He says, "There's no right or wrong; it's a measurement."

Do you not want to talk about your planet Eff?

"No. It's not something you can comprehend."

A planet with water or air?

"It's a different more subtle, even more subtle of density..."

Did you like it there, did you have friends there, people you loved?

(Nods) "It's home."

How did you earn this spot on her council?

"It's work. She earned (my role); consciousness. She knows a lot. It's been a few lifetimes."

Is there a leader of this council?

He's a little bit more kind, has an open face. He's right beside the previous guy.

How old does he appear?

Like in his 70's; he is less closed faced.

What's a letter or word we can use to address him?

"Bee."

Thank you Mr. Bee. Are you familiar with what I'm doing?

"Yes."

Is this a good thing what we're doing, talking to her council?

He showed me... "It's like ... parting the chrysalis and forcing the butterfly out." They're worried or are advising caution about not forcing the being... "Sometimes this work, you need someone to

tone up the muscle first before opening up the doors of the chrysalis – some are curious and some are ready to hear it – the curious people should go first to the readiness place."

Mr. Bee. I know that you know more than I could ever know on this topic, but once a person experiences something it becomes a knowledge based event. So even a person reading this passage may not believe it, but it allows their higher conscious to embrace it.

"They may need more experiences to reach that bridge." He says "It's all part of the cosmic timing." He's agreeing that "it depends." (Marie aside:) He's nicer than the other guy; more soft, but he's strong.

My point is the people who read this chapter who are in their chrysalis stage won't understand it.

"Sometimes there's a shock and the shock is making them lose time more than helping them. ("Lose time" in terms of their spiritual evolvement) Because it's like almost like a handicap, instead of..."

Instead of learning or absorbing it?

He's saying "Slowly and one little window at a time in accessing this understanding or this knowing."

Well, don't some people need to be pushed out of the next to learn to fly?

"That is against cosmic timing. They want you to be aware that (this information) it's not for everyone."

I say it often; this research isn't for everyone. I put that in the books; If it's disconcerting, return it, get a refund. "Not everyone is supposed to know how the play ends."

They are acknowledging that you are cautious with this information. On paper it could help everyone; but it's not for everyone.

Why did you allow her to access this, come into the council today?

"Because she can."

We were told she wasn't ready, but she is?

"She has her free will."

She barged her way in here. Anyone else want to speak up? My I ask why there are no women here?

(Marie aside:) I was looking but I didn't see any.

I've never run across it before – is there a reason for that?

"It's her path."

How often are you connected to her?

"She is always connected to us."

Jesus showing up again! Wow had a conversation with him yesterday – can't believe you showed up the next day.

"I like you," he says.

Ha. I'm putting that on the cover of the next book. "Jesus likes me."

He says "It was not easy to bring down (to Earth) the principle of love" But now what I hear or feel is "My job was to inject or engrain, inscribe the principle of true, real love."

The kind people consider "unconditional love"?

That's not what he says but it's what he means. "Before, we didn't have the principle of love."

There must be some reason you're allowing me to talk about this without an attachment to organized religion. You said once because "it was time."

"They're ready not to leave their religious beliefs... but is time to unravel... to open the rope..."

The rope of religion?

"It was necessary before, we don't need it anymore, so we can unravel and just retain this principle of love."

How can we do that?

"From within... like listen to the heart kind of thing." He says "You cannot force the process; you can encourage it." He says "Pay attention to the ego – be careful of the ego, watch the ego." (Marie aside:) That's not just for you – that's for everyone. That's our roadblock.

I had a dream someone told me to annihilate ego – "vanum populatum." Annihilate things of vanity – the things that are not love.

But he says "Watch out." He says "Understand the complexity... that you don't want to destroy the ego, and get rid of everything that is ego – what remains is sovereign. Honor yourself, which is not only the ego." He's trying to put the words in my mouth... He's talking about vanity – the selfie kind of thing, the vanity of the ego.

Vanity blinds us?

"The superficial layers that cover the essence.... don't forget your essence. That needs to be super powerful, to be sovereign, integrated completely – integral. That's the personality. He recommends a return to your persona, the essence, be as creative as you want to form your essence, from your inner fire, but not from what's around you."

That's interesting, anything else you want to tell our friend?

"To keep watching the balance, because we have to fight this polarity, we have to watch out the duality, the polarity; too much selflessness is not right, too much ego is not right, balance. There's big importance in being... true love means to come from a strong fire within, the essence of a person, loving not because you gave that love to me, but you are generating it. It's important to not kill all the ego – it's finding the right amount of ego to hold onto." (Marie aside:) I think that's for me.

If you can focus on the love within, unconditional love, you can generate that outward?

He says "You can reach this only when you have integrated, when you are integral, full, that comes from acknowledging yourself." He was showing me to go to the reverse of selfie, from inside to the outside world; "find your own power within, not from without."

Like a reverse selfie?

"Yeah, it all comes from within."

So what you project to the world – don't focus on what the world projects onto you, focus on the power you can project... a sense of lover and power and balance?

"Once you love yourself you are able to spread the principle of love."

What else dude? Now that Marie has your frequency in her head she can communicate with you.

"She knows."

What a fun thing we were able to be together in this space.

"Any time dude."

Who said that?

"Jesus."

*****

DR. TAYLOR – ARCHITECTURE OF THE AFTERLIFE

Dr. Taylor is the daughter of two friends of mine. She's got a PhD in her field, and we just happened to be in the same space to grab some coffee. She asked about what I was doing, and the following conversation ensured, recorded on my cell phone. (Dr. Taylor is not her real name.) At this point in the conversation, her guide is answering my questions.

Rich: Can your guide please walk her to her council?

DR. TAYLOR: We're both inside and outside; inside but an outside feel like a green house. There is diffused light – no plants but the feeling of plants. There's just the two of us – and the council.

How are they arrayed?

There are five standing shoulder to shoulder. A mix of men and women.

Thank you council for showing up – from left to right?

They are male, female, male, male, female; left to right.

Let's talk to the first person.

A male.

I'm going to ask him .. can you take his hand, look him in the eye? What's his name?

It's Jonathan!

What is it you've earned to be on her council?

"Patience. She always wants it faster sooner."

What do you tell her?

"To calm down and relax."

Jonathan introduce her to the person on your left.

Her name is Nancy; with brown medium length hair, 55. She's all about excitement, adventure. Living it up.

I heard someone say "Nobody comes to the flipside wishing they held back more." How is our friend doing?

She thinks I'm doing well but should be having more fun. That I should travel more.

Where is she supposed to travel?

Some island in a developing country – like an island retreat with yoga everywhere.

Let's go to the next one over –

A guy ... it's David. He's older.

What's his spiritual evolvement for you?

"Honesty."

How's she doing?

"She's doing better lately."

Don't tell me more I don't want to know. Next person over?

It's Henry! He's younger. He's all about learning.

Education. Who's next?

Desiree; she protects me, looks over me.

Is there anyone on the council that can speak on behalf of the whole council?

Yeah, the first guy – Jonathan.

Let me ask, when we met you, you were teasing us, acting like you barely know her.

"Yes."

Why was that?

"To be safe."

Do you approve, or is this okay what we're doing? Asking questions to councils?

"Yes."

"Why?"

"Because it's time... to listen."

To shift our focus to listen more to people who are guiding us?

"Yes."

And the lottery numbers are...?

Taylor laughs.

Jay, can you tell her why she chose that lifetime on the island, what's the overall theme of her journey?

"Industry."

What's that mean?

"Creating things." On the island she was creating sculptures...

What's the best way for her to share her ideas?

"YouTube!"

Is that what he said?

That's what he said.

Describe it to me – just her talking... about her work?

About something. About something I made or wrote.

She records that and films herself, is she talking directly to camera? Is that helping people?

"Yes. To understand themselves."

What's she talking about; psychology or spirituality?

Psychology that leads to the spiritual.

Let's take her back to the healing place, the garden – show her what that regeneration process is.

I'm sitting, quietly. On the earth. Just sitting cross legged.

What does she do to generate that healing energy?

Meditate – close your eyes and wipe your mind.

Give her a 1, 2, 3 so she can connect.

"Call upon ancestors that care. Ask them to pay attention or help out."

Anything you want to ask them?

"How are they doing?" They said they're doing great.

Any advice for me?

"Yes, keep going!"

And one sentence she could pass along to her clients?

"You are stronger than you think."

*****

RAYLENE – from "ARCHITECTURE OF THE AFTERLIFE"

Raylene Nuanes is a medium who lives in Colorado. I met her through Dr. Elisa Medhus (Channeling Erik) who wanted me to chat with her and see if she was someone she might work with. I'm including her visit to her council.

RICH: I wonder if we can walk Raylene in to visit her council?

RAYLENE: There are five men here; they look like they're from biblical times.

Describe the room for me.

I don't see any doors, just brightness like light, a round table, not lengthy.

There's 5 here... plus you?

Plus me, and my guide Arnold; so seven. I want to call these men "wise men" – they're from biblical times.

Let's go from left to right.

The first is named Paul, then Adam, then Jeremiah, then Mark and Abraham. They're talking to me about decisions that I've got to make – deciding on whether I choose to stay longer.

This was a conversation you had before – we're stepping in on it?

Yes.

Who is the primary spokesperson for this group?

Paul, he's the one you'd call in charge – they all have the same standing... but he would be the main one to speak with.

What does Paul look like?

He needs to shave (laughs). Sorry, he has long hair to about his shoulder – it's brown, he's older, gray coming in. (to Paul:) Sorry.

No reason to apologize for what you see, and he is projecting his image to you.

His hair is long and curly – not tied back. Sort of how Jesus might appear to you. He's wearing one piece of clothing over his chest, what looks like a skirt – he has hairy legs and arms – very hairy.

The clothing is something he made himself. Maybe out of a tree; not clothing we have - feels rough like tree material.

Let's ask him; what is this fabric and why are you wearing it?

He says, "I made it out of wheat, and I'm wearing it because this is the clothing I lived in ...this is the fabric I used for clothing in this time period."

The sash – is there any kind of symbol other than the cloth?

There are rock crystals. He's telling me, "The black ones represent protection, the aqua helps him communicate with God" as he calls it.

Each one of these individuals is here because of you Raylene, and they represent some aspect of you. Let's ask. I'll guess Paul represents something to do with nature.

"Yes. They're talking about representations for all of them – there is "protection" from Paul, Jeremiah shows me "love," that is a kind of love in terms of loving people without judging them... (Unconditional love) Mark is here – he's talking about "communicating with children." He says he's a guide of mine. Abraham helps me "transition from place to place, life to life" – he's a guide as well.

What quality does he represent?

He says "Lessons; there are many of them."

Let me ask them, is this is an unusual thing to be interviewed like this?

He said "They don't often get interviewed – they wish to be a part of this more often, but this is about humans being more open to it." He's thanking you.

Paul, if you could give us insight or guidance – how many times has she been in front of you?

"Hundreds." He says my current lifetime is my last one here. He says "If she chooses to come back she can, but she is an old soul and is living many lives ... she's a therapist, helper on the other side for people that transition."

But if Raylene decides to come back here ... that's her choice?

"Yes."

What you're saying she's reached a point where she doesn't have to come back?

He says "Yes, as everyone has free will. They can come back whenever they want or perhaps as an animal."

I've found it's rare in the research to cross over between animal and human – animals reincarnate as animals in general, is that correct?

He says "That is correct." He is pointing out their school is like ours; "They choose to be animals."

If I wanted to come back as an animal rather than human, how does that work?

"You don't get the pleasure of being by humans, the aquarium you choose to live in. If you decide to return as a dog, or if you want to come down for love, each individual has those experiences they want to experience."

What I've learned is that we only bring about third of our energy.

"Yes." He says "Yes, this is called your higher self."

What is Raylene's higher self-doing?

He's smiling; says, "She gets into trouble, messes with people." (Raylene aside) I like to joke with people over there; but I'm not that way in life!

Like a playful leprechaun? Or a gremlin?

He says "The gremlin creatures are real, and some are manifested; if you have fear - based on these creatures - you can manifest them as well."

I would assume gremlins have their soul group and councils?

"That's correct; there are lower vibrations, some call them "demonic" or those who are stuck that don't realize they've died."

Let's talk about demons for a moment. We don't find that concept of evil in the afterlife research. Could you address that?

He says "That's the world over here (on earth). There is no hell." I'm hearing, "There is no hell and your belief structure is structured around you – if you believe in creatures, lower vibrations, they can exist for you – it's dependent upon your belief structure."

Why is it this information becoming accessible?

He says "Humans are shifting, it's becoming easier to talk to us. The universe is shifting, it's easier to connect to this dimension. By thinking of a person, you're connecting to a conscious level of our soul."

What is that?

"You have an awareness of home, where you come from. You know there's something bigger beyond this body of ours, it's all on a conscious level."

Why is this happening now?

"So humanity can grow. People can learn about the afterlife and spirit dimensions, ET's and other beings from spirit worlds, which helps them grow." He's talking about us helping them on the other side to communicate with us, lowering their vibration to communicate with us. There are a wide range of things happening, meditation, people seeing an image in their head, and accepting that. It's shifting."

Anyone on your council want to tell people something that might be healing?

"Be patient with your spiritual awakening ability, tell people to get books and read. You all have spirit guides and councils, everyone has their own spirit guides, council and family – anyone can call upon us."

(Afterwards, to Raylene) That was wild. Have you ever accessed your council before?

No.

*****

JENNIFER AND TRIXIE – from "ARCHITECTURE OF THE AFTERLIFE"

This session was on Skype, I'm meeting with someone I've never met before, she's an Ivy league graduate (Harvard) who happens to have the skills of a medium. It's our first conversation. At this point in a session, I'm speaking to Jennifer's guide who calls herself "Trixie."

RICH: *Trixie can you walk Jennifer in to visit with her council?*

JENNIFER: We're going – now I'm in this hallway, she's kind of walking ahead of me, and turning around and saying "Hurry up." She's all business.

Describe this hallway.

It's very modest – like a stone... arched... but kind of like 9 or 10 feet tall.

Let's go to where the council is waiting.

It looks like we're in a dome shaped room and it's very dimly lit. I can't tell where the lights are coming from. The ceiling is navy blue – about 30 feet high.

How many people are here?

There's a lot. They're sitting around this semicircular table, facing us, backs to the wall. There's got to be at least... Let me count... there's 16. Sitting around a table like a semicircle.

Trixie can we walk our friend up to the council?

She says, "Sure."

Let's look at the person on the far left. Is that a male female, neither or both?

He doesn't look human, kind of like a creature, kind of green with weird pointy ears that come out the side. Kind of Yoda-like... but scarier looking than Yoda; not very attractive.

Well, let's offer that you may look kind of scary to him as well. Can we go up to him and ask him some questions?

He says, "Yes," but I feel he's hesitant.

Can I ask for a name or letter to address you by?

The name he tells me is "Yerg."

Mr. Yerg. Is he more male or female?

Very male – sorry he reminds me of a troll or animal in some way.

Let's try not to judge that – take his hands in yours. What's the sensation?

Okay. Rough, kind of scaly, kind of cool – fingers are really skinny ... I don't really like touching his hands, can I let go?

Try not to. It's important to make this connection. Look at his eyes. What color are they?

They're kind of yellow with flecks of black, but the irises are reptilian.

Mr. Yerg, I appreciate you talking to us, but if I may – are you familiar with what I'm doing?

He says "I know exactly what you're doing."

Okay; has Jennifer every incarnated on your planet?

"Yes."

Can she take a look at that?

He says "She's seen it before."

But if we can examine that; where is this planet? Is it in our universe or is it in another one?

"This one."

If there was a human word associated where the star system is?

He's saying "signet" – signa?

(Note: There is a star constellation called "Cygna." It's referred to as "Alpha Cygni" (which sounds a bit like Cignet.)

How many planets are in the Cygna star system? A few or just one?

"Many."

If you could put in Jennifer's mind's eye what her existence was like; was there dirt, trees, water?

He's showing me a dream that I had many years ago. I woke up I knew I had traveled somewhere I knew looked beautiful – kind of like Earth except the sky wasn't blue it was pink. The light seemed to come from everywhere in the sky; you could see what looked like moons – he's showing me that's the planet he's from.

How many moons did you see?

Two.

Let me ask, what was the name of this planet?

Its sounds like Chitsnu.

Were people more intelligent than on Earth?

He says it's not a question of intelligence, it's a question of integrity... the development of their integrity was higher.

That's a wonderful answer, thank you.

He says "It's the truth."

Are there many people on the planet who have lived on Chitsnu?

Not many.

Has Jennifer ever been visited by people from your planet?

He says, "Not from here but from other planets."

What quality do you represent in Jennifer's spiritual evolvement?

He says "scathing self-honesty."

The development of integrity. How is she doing in terms of that concept?

"Better and better. She's not there yet."

What is Yerg wearing?

It's a material I've never seen before, looks shimmery but like Kevlar; if you tried to touch it, it would move. It shimmers. It's dark grey with a metallic flecks to it. It's kind of like a robe thing – but I feel like he's armored; (like) he's a badass.

Kind of like a uniform? Is there any animal on our Earth that wears this kind of skin?

He's showing me an armadillo.

So this is armor?

The texture of it – the toughness of it.

Do you serve on any other councils?

"No."

How many of her lifetimes have you been on her council?

Just this one.

So you have earned this position, let's say, earned your participation in this lifetime – is that correct?

"Yes."

Can you introduce her to the person next to you?

A female. She looks interesting, older .. she has this air of royalty or something ...she's nice but not super warm; just kind of regal is the word.

If you could put a name or initial in her mind?

"Kay."

Kay, how many councils do you serve on?

"Six."

Are you aware of what I'm doing, this council questioning?

She says "We're all aware of it."

Am I the only one doing this?

(There are) "Not many, but you're not the only one."

I'm curious. How did you become aware of it?

She says "She can't explain it, they know things that are of importance come to them automatically – not with everything, just with the things they need to know about."

How do you think our friend Jennifer doing?

She says "Marvelous."

Is she wearing any jewelry at all?

Only this weird giant emerald stone ring on her middle finger – a weird ring.

What word or quality of her spiritual development do you represent?

"Discernment."

Let me ask you about that emerald – what does that represent? Is that something Jennifer earned or you earned?

She says "I don't want to talk about my ring – there are more important things to talk about."

Let's ask Trixie – can you tell us about your blue headband? What's that represent?

She says "Defending..." She defended someone or many people; she earned it defending people.

You said there's a jewel in the middle – a gold jewel? What's that represent?

She says, "It's a stone we don't have here on Earth, it represents reaching other beings."

Like a communication device? Does it work like a crystal, amplifying energy?

"No. It allows her to communicate – I don't know if she means "understand" or for us to understand; it somehow enlarges the communication between her and other beings."

So the jewel itself help you to communicate? Does it lower the vibration?

She says "That's one of the things it does."

(Note: I'm asking questions that relate to "communication." As I've heard in other sessions, they have to "lower their frequency" in order to communicate with us.)

Anything you want to tell Jennifer or people in general?

She's saying "She helps me know when I'm getting interference from the other side that I shouldn't be talking to."

"Discernment." Very good. What was your impression when Jennifer was talking to drunken spirits?

She has a funny reaction – she says "Exactly!" and slaps her forehead. It's the first time she's been funny – she's very austere otherwise.

Did you help her with that Kay?

"Yes."

How did you do that? Make her get rid of her homemade Ouija board or close those doors?

(Jennifer laughs.) She says "Jennifer's still using the ("homemade") board I keep telling her to use pen and paper. (Jennifer aside) Someone keeps coming through and saying "pen and paper!" She wants me to graduate to pen and paper.

That's new information for you?

Absolutely.

Should we speak to the lead counselor here?

She stood up. (Jennifer laughs) I don't want to tell you what she looks like; you're going to think this is crazy – as if she's saying "Imagine me as Glenda the good witch." Oh my God; I just figured something out. When I was a kid I was scared witless by the Wizard of Oz. Dorothy, flying monkeys – the only part of that movie I liked was "Good Witch Glenda." She just downloaded this to me.

Take hold of her hands.

They're squishy; like little kids hands. Almost spongy.

Any emotion associated with them?

"Love." She's a very loving person. She loves helping people; that's her big thing, helping, helping; she loves it.

What does "love" mean?

"Trusting." She says "That's it. That's all there is."

Describe her to me.

She's little – like 5 foot 2, teeny little thing. Blonde, just like Glenda in the movie – wavy blonde hair, that crazy crown on and the pink dress... blues eyes. White satin shoes with diamond butterfly buckles on each one, very sparkly.

Shall I call you Glenda?

(Jennifer aside:) She laughs. "Yeah."

How's our friend Jennifer doing? Is she on the right path?

"Very much so." She's looking at me and saying "You'll be exactly where you're supposed to be in ten years." (Jennifer aside:) I mean I couldn't make this up if I tried – this is like crazy town here!

Glenda, show Jennifer what she looks like to you.

Okay, this is weird. I see... I don't see a person, I see light. It's like swirling kind of, looks like clockwise, like a tornado kind of. It's white, whitish but again with sparkles, opalescent glittery sparkles in it... that's how she sees me.

What colors?

Pinkish; maybe like a pale blue, barely blue.

How many councils do you represent Glenda?

She says "Oh so many... Around ten thousand."

What do you think about what I'm doing interviewing councils?

She says "I love what you're doing. It's so important keep doing it, don't stop! You don't realize how important your work is. And how many of us are coming to help you – still coming." She says "You're a threat to some, I know you find that hard to believe – she means to them over there, not Earth people....

Should I worry about starting my car? (Mafia joke)

"No." She says "You have protection around you, trust me you have plenty of protection; don't worry."

Back to you Glenda... have you incarnated somewhere else a long time ago before you started this work as a council member?

I know that sounds weird but she says "I don't remember."

Is there an emotional connection to what you're advising them to do?

She shows me a veterinarian, and using the analogy that "You can't have an emotional connection doing what we do or you wouldn't be able to do it." You know how doctors can't operate on their own kids? She showed me that but she's not showing me a doctor but a veterinarian.... (Jennifer aside:) Maybe she sees me as a pet.

The kind of therapy work, the kind of work that Jennifer is doing, it can help save the planet, is that correct?

"Absolutely," she says.

Anyone else on the council you want her to speak to?

There's one guy she's pointing to... she's pointing to her left. He looks 65; his name is Herman. He stands up, is my height. Wearing something from Renaissance times... like a leather vest, with sleeves. He's got a lot of silver jewelry – rings bracelets. He's kind of channeling the Rolling Stones guitarist Ron Wood.

What quality do you represent on her council?

He says "Looking out for the little guy." He says "Our actions have such ramifications that we have no idea how far into the future and how far they go."

You mean like a stone hitting a pond turning into an avalanche?

I think he took your cue, but he's showing me a snowball as it goes down the mountain and getting bigger and bigger to have more impact. He's showing me ... so I'm kind of a sucker when it comes to animals, I feed everything. I put out food for the birds, then the crows started eating that, then I put out cat food for them and here come the squirrels; it looks like Mutual of Omaha's "Animal Kingdom" in my backyard.

You help one person and the next is helped too. Thank you Herman.

He did a little bow like "It's my pleasure and honor."

Where do want to take her Trixie?

She wants to go to the library.

Do you have your library card on you Trixie?

She says "I am the library card."

Are we inside or outside?

We must have shape shifted or something... because we're inside some structure or building. Like in "Alice in Wonderland," when you get really small.. I can't tell you what this place looks like because it's moving; it's like alive.

It's a building that's alive... are we looking at books? Energetic forms? Monitors?

It looks like kind of small sized blobs of glowing lights in the shape of tennis balls. She says this is how.... and she's pointing at me – this is how she accesses the information. This is weird – I always pictured the library as beautiful books.

Let's take a tennis ball out that has the memory of when Jennifer chose her lifetime, can we do that?

"Yes." She is gesturing her arm open like... "pick one." They're floating – they're tennis ball sized, they're not really physical; it's like light. The outside of it looks like hexagonal mesh.

Trixie help with this. Are these the fractals that contain all of our memories that travel with us from life to life?

She's saying "Yes, yes, yes yes!" Like 100 times; she's saying "Yes, yes, yes!"

So you're saying the Akashic library is the fractals that travel with us from life to life?

"**Yes!**"

These balls of light retain the memories of our previous lifetimes?

"**Yes!**"

Let's go back to looking at it from a macro view – is the energy inside of it moving, bouncing around or is it solid?

It's moving. It's like a honeycomb beehive thing. And if you look at it closely, you can see inside one honeycomb thing that can't be more than a couple of millimeters wide, and you see another one.

You see like a fractal... mathematical constants?

Yes.

Trixie, help her to access a memory from that ball of light.

She's actually squeezing the ball, she's showing me that's what you do – squeeze it to get the download.

Is this an entire lifetime or is this a moment within a lifetime that you've led?

It's a moment. We're on Earth. Oh god, this is more snow.

Is this from Jennifer's current life?

No. We are in the north – like Newfoundland. Not the north pole but way up. We call it Canada, but it wasn't then. I was female. Showing me as a kid maybe 14. Black hair... eyes look almost black, really dark, like your typical Aleutian or Eskimo kid. Big furry Nanook of the north boots.

What's this young girl's name?

I get the letter K, but it's a long name.

So what about this memory does she need to access now?

I was responsible for a lot of the food gathering; she's showing me my dad was killed or not in the picture, and it was my

responsibility to help my mom with the food. The year is 12 something... 1250 - 1260 AD.

Important to see you could be depended upon by others for their survival. You've been a person who's healed and saved people. Is that correct Trixie?

It's to show her how resourceful she is and how she doesn't use it now. She's showing me I had to act like a boy, didn't have time to play with girls because I was too busy with these duties... I had to grow up faster which was hard but good for me to learn.

Was she supposed to remember being more resourceful? To have courage?

She's saying "To know she can take care of herself."

Let's put that memory back into the time frame – anything else she needs to see in this library?

She wants us to go over and meet this little old man who kind of runs the place. She wants us to say hello and to give him a little thanks for taking care of all the ... she calls them "books." He's so cute – just under 5 feet tall. I don't know his age; his face is timeless. He looks human, really old but really young at the same time – I can't describe it; a million years old.

What's his name?

He says "Huey." (Jennifer laughs.) That is so not what I was expecting.

Nice to meet you Huey – can I ask you some questions?

He says "I'd be delighted."

Are you aware of what I'm doing? I know it sounds like I don't believe it.

He says "In general, yes, but he's too busy to pay much attention to the specifics."

That would make sense. Have we spoken before?

He says "Yes – but not in this manner." I don't know what he means.

Like I was filming someone asking you questions and I happened to be in the room at the same time?

"Yes."

(Note: I had a flash of a session with Kelly at the start of this book. I was in her room filming, not asking questions, but there when he answered Kelly's questions. In a subsequent session with medium Jennifer Shaffer, this same Librarian confirmed he's the same. He appears in our podcast "Hacking The Afterlife" as "Five.")

What's your opinion of people talking about a shift in consciousness – what would that mean to you?

The first thing he says "It's been a long time coming; we've been waiting and waiting and waiting."

You mean "we" in terms of humans?

"No, the flipside people." (People over on his side) **He's saying that he "gets more visits now than he used to and he's excited because he didn't have enough company until recently. He likes it; his thing is "the more the merrier."**

Did you choose this job? Or was it given to you?

He says "Both."

I was writing about this today – "What or who is God?" I'm curious what your answer would be?

He's pointing to all the little balls and saying "This is God." (Jennifer aside:) Probably because he's a librarian. He probably has a lot of time to read.

Has your name always been Huey?

He laughs, says "My name is whatever you want it to be."

What do your friends call you?

He's chuckling; "They call me Maestro."

Why does everyone see the library differently?

He says it exists, but not on any kind of plane we can visualize or understand.

You mean it exists etherically, like seeing a rainbow they see it from their perspective?

He says "Yes and no." You and I, Rich, we're physically unable to conjure what it is so we have to put these constructs around it – we see a tv screen or a scroll or a glowing little ball.

That would mean the library is reflexive of the person experiencing it?

"No." He's scratching his head like "How do I explain this?" He says, "There are many dimensions in other dimensions, there are no words to explain to you how this exists." He says, "The best I can tell you is "What you perceive it to be, is as good as what it makes (it be) on our side."

So he's saying "This is beyond words?"

"Yeah: we can't conceptualize it."

Same goes for "God" I suppose. What is it that you want to tell people?

He says "Spread the word about my library because you don't remember anything down there." He's referring to us on Earth. He says "Reading doesn't make you smarter, reading makes you braver." He's using light balls as an analogy; "If we discover what's happened to us, we'll understand we have crazy phobias from stuff that happened in the past; we can learn why we're afraid of spiders or windows and it will make us braver."

What's the best way to access you?

He's saying "You're doing a great job Rich... of learning – he says "Dream time is particularly easy but you have to set the intention before you go to sleep." He says "That's the easiest way, set the intention that you want to come and visit and find these books and with practice you can get here very easily." He's saying "For most people," and he's got this cute little old man look – he's making a sad face – he's saying "They'll never find their way here."

*****

So I'm ending this book on Divine Councils with this visit to a Librarian that was insisted upon by a guide named Trixie, who took us to visit the council, and then insisted we make this side trip to the Akashic library. In one of the interviews with this Librarian that I did via Jennifer Shaffer (search MartiniZone.com for the term "Five" as he used that name to be non-denominational) he was asked if there was a better word to use than Akashic, since it means "invisible" or "etheric" in Sanskrit, and people might be confused about visiting their own. He said "It took humanity this long to understand the word, no point in changing it now." **He's a funny guy.**

He has come up in other sessions with other people – and he refers to himself as the "Head Librarian." I think it's fascinating that he included the Akashic Library in the questions "What or who is God?" It's worth noting that it was Kelly's interview with him that started this book – and that ends this book. I asked him that question in hopes he'd repeat himself "God is beyond the capacity of the human brain to comprehend, it's not physically possible to do so. However you can experience God by opening your heart to everyone and all things."

Which I found to a profound way to explain how anyone can experience God. It's easy to say "Open your heart to everyone and all things" but next to impossible to do. However, conceptually, those that can do so, at least to someone in their lifetime – give unconditional love to – has a "taste of the experience." And interesting that when I asked that question, he pointed to the volumes of information in the Akashic library; "This is God." If we follow that for a moment – and now I'm having a flashback where he came to me in a dream and insisted that I talk about this – if we think about our "vast library of lifetimes" as "God" – or as consciousness, we get a better handle on "what or who God is."

That is – we ourselves are the summation of all the lifetimes we've led. We are part of the vast fabric, medium of consciousness that is throughout all the universes and worlds, that permeates our universe, that is how the fabric of reality is created. And by pointing to these books on the shelf, these "glowing tennis balls" he's pointing out those fractals – the thing that got Trixie so excited when I referenced them – these mathematical fractals that retain all the emotional memories of our lifetimes, is what composes the Akashic library. And further, these tennis balls represent all of our hopes, dreams and memories – all of them, each breath, each thought, each part of our journey.

I'll end our journey on this note about "finding our way home." It's not enough to realize that this whole other world on the flipside exists, it's important to realize that it is part of us, we are connected to our loved ones at all times. They are literally a thought away. On behalf of all the council members I've spoken to, I want to thank them. "So why are you allowing this person to access this information at this point in time?" They answer is often a version of "it's time" or "it's important" or "it's part of the evolution of all societies throughout the universe." Clearly this isn't new information. But clearly it's not common knowledge. Time for it to become so.

SUMMARY - SUMMA THEOLOGIAE MORALIS

In summary; it's a lot to take in. Everyone has a guide? Everyone has a council? I plan my lifetimes in advance with their help? Once one has bypassed the "filters on the brain" anyone can access this same information. (Note: See Dr. Greyson's book AFTER for a chapter of filters on the brain and how they block information "not conducive to survival")

The fun thing about data is that it has to be consistent and reproducible to become data. The suggestion here is that anyone can access this same information if they take the time to do so. That this information has been available since mankind began writing about the experience of being human; but it's been hidden, covered up or otherwise not easy to understand or grasp.

Why access is this information of value if it's not readily available?

Because it eliminates fear of the unknown, it alleviates fear of dying, since the persona doesn't disappear, but moves on to other avenues and journeys. Recently, a friend who passed came through to offer that in his short lifetime he had always been one to "dive in." He had jumped from airplanes, gone scuba diving, was all about experiencing everything he could. Perhaps because he knew his life would be cut short, he was "hell bent" on experiencing as much as he could.

That doesn't mean that everyone should do the same – but it does give context to a shorter life. Some folks know how long they're going to be on the planet, their higher self knows, and they act accordingly. Some are not aware at all why they're on the planet, and act accordingly. However, we all can gain access to information that isn't readily available. We can access our guides, our classmates, our teachers, our council members if we take the time to learn how. They share information on a "need to know basis" – that is, if someone isn't ready to access this information, it won't be forthcoming. If one has signed up for a lifetime that precludes knowing why they did so – they won't be able to. However, when asking council members the reasons for them to "allow me to ask these questions" there are various answers that relate to "Well, it's time" or "all civilizations on all planets eventually get to this point in its existence." Or "People are suffering and they need to understand the process."

All I can do is ask questions and film or record the answers. If the answers were all over the map, or based on a person's belief system, then that's what the data and research would show. But it doesn't. Strangers, friends, people I've never met, people in noisy parties, at restaurants, in café's – in a strict setting, it doesn't matter. People report the same things. They can see or hear their guide, their guides or teachers, or loved one on the flipside who can escort them in to visit with their council. Members are people, beings, enlightened ones who've been watching over us all of our lifetimes. These folks don't just sit on one council – they sit on many. And the roles are various – not everyone has the same makeup or number of folks, but everyone, without exception has people who watch over them. Who are accessible if we take the time and effort to reach out to them.

I have no illusions that this book, this information will change anyone's opinion about how the process works, and I have no illusions that scientists will have an easy time accepting these reports "not done in a clinical setting." But having done this for over ten years, I know the setting has little to do with the information, the information doesn't change, and learning that life goes on can be healing, life enhancing and transformative.

I've had enough people reach out to me on Quora (Hacking the Afterlife forum) where they claim to have had a dream or some kind of vision where they see me on the flipside talking about this information, sometimes in a classroom setting. While I'm not aware of such a thing consciously, I have to allow that it's possible, at the very lease to allow to mean it when I say *"I'll catch you on the flipside."*

And as final summation, here are excerpts from my own visit to my council, which spawned this research.
After a week of filming these mind bending sessions, then President of the Newton Institute, Paul Aurand suggested I try my own session. At

first I was hesitant – after all, can't be reporting something someone is participating in, but because I felt I could easily see if someone was leading me somewhere – I agreed.

I did my first session with Jimmy Quast of Easton Hypnosis in Maryland. "Rayma" is the name I'd given to my guide, whom I'd never consciously met before, but when I saw him, it felt like we were old friends.

My First Trip to a Council

Jimmy Quast: Let's go to the council. Does Rayma come along on this trip?

(Pause) Richard: He's there with me. He says "You're on." (Like an actor going onstage.)

What's this like?

Beautiful room; beautiful in a light sense. A radiant room, radiant place.

The energy, what's that like?

Very peaceful... (Laughs) I feel like it's a little bit of a performance.

By whom?

By me, but because they're used to my sort of antics, everybody's in a good mood. Eight people that I can see. There might be more...

What do they look like?

Non-denominational... sort of just lights.

Not flashy?

No, rich hues of purple and a little bit of red tinge over there. Just purple with a tinge of vermillion... (Seeing a woman cloaked in a purple light, but a few streaks of bright red shining within).

What's the red mean to you?

Fierce... warrior... fierce person. I've got green here, but it's a purple green... What's the color called... chartreuse?

Just checking again, how do you look to them?

That dark blue (color) with maybe a little, I want to say, purple.

It is what it is?

And... I'm asking them my questions.

(NOTE: I'd read it was helpful for the hypnosis session to bring a list of questions that might be answered. I had no clue I would get this far in my own session, but the night before, I quickly jotted down some questions one might ask God if they had the chance.)

Rich: They're saying... "Yes." (Laughs.) "Yes, you were a monk in Tibet, not so long ago."

Jimmy: Something that you want to pause and go look at it?

(Seeing a monastery, the dirt floors, carrying a butter lamp) It was in a monastery that was an old tradition of Buddhism, closer to the older dogmatic point of view. Nyingma? (One of the older Buddhist sects in Tibet.) They're reminding me this monastery was not as rich in tradition. The reason I was there was to learn patience (laughs) because the teachers were not very bright and I felt I knew more than they did. That particular life, as a Tibetan monk, was to learn patience.

Is there a pattern with you and patience?

Through eternity. They're also taking me back to my other question. the vanum populatum question; it was a dream that came to me and it was me (my higher self) speaking to me, part of my energy that's back there (between lives), speaking to me in Latin..

And those words...? (Reading what I've written on his notepad.)

"Vanum populatum."

Does the meaning of that deepen now that you...?

They're all amused by the cleverness of me speaking in Latin to myself, knowing I (in this life) don't speak Latin, never studied Latin, would write it down because it was unusual, and then knowing I would look it up (on the internet) and find the Latin translation. Knowing that only by my forcing myself to examine these words as a puzzle, would I come to embrace or understand them. As if just saying "Destroy the Ego," or "Annihilate Vanity" wouldn't help me get it - I had to Google it in order to understand it. And knowing the concept was the same I'd learned in Tibetan philosophy about stripping away the ego. What they're saying to me is "If you heard it as a phrase you would have dismissed it, but because you heard it in another language, you gave it depth."

Ok. I'm asking them another of question... I'm asking them about a project I'm working on right now, and the question I'm asking them is, "Is this important to focus on?" and they're hesitant to respond, in the desire to not direct me where I may already be going..

They are saying to me "You know the answer, why are you bothering us with the question?" But the answer is -- that this person I'm writing about had a tremendous amount of influence, energy-wise, on the planet, and that's why it's important to tell their story. Whether it gets made or not is not important, but the focus on the person and the energy is...

*****

When I returned home to Los Angeles, I asked Paul Aurand who he would recommend on the West Coast to help me with further research and he recommended Scott De Tamble (LightBetweenLives.com). I reached out to Scott and began filming sessions. At some point he suggested that I do another one.

I thought it would be a great opportunity to see what was different. Maybe I had made up the memory of being a Lakota medicine man?

(As reported in FLIPSIDE). When we began the six hour session, as Scott "counted me down" I stopped him; "It's weird. It's like I've walked back through a garden gate that I left open. I'm already there, I'm back where I was two years ago."

Two years of earth time had gone by, and a few seconds of time on the flipside. At some point we did a "second visit to my council."

Second Visit to my council:

Scott De Tamble: Rich wants to know about his council. Can you describe the scene?

I'm in my guide Rayma's conscious mind – I'm looking at myself, Richard standing in front of his council, like the last time we were here and seeing it from my guide's point of view. I'm seeing myself, Richard standing in front of the council, eager and shy, clever and funny, but maybe too much in his head thinking he's clever and funny.

The council finds him amusing. But they've known him a long time, we've been here a few times, and he's always entertaining. They appreciate him, because you don't get a lot of entertainment up here and the idea of having someone with his sense of humor is refreshing...

Scott: How many members in the council?

Eleven. Eight up front. 3 alternates hovering behind.

Does the council number change?

Yes. With age. (By that I meant experience)

Let's go to a council visit before the lifetime as a Lakota Medicine man. (Which I learned during the earlier session with Jimmy Quast.) How many council members are there?

Seven. Richard has picked up one more since then. I'm trying to look at this 8th council member from his most recent journey.

Let's ask Rayma (my guide.)

Rayma's saying "It's a healing person on the council; somebody connected to Luana and her healing class. I'm also getting there are 8 in front now, the three people behind are people he knows, but they're hidden so he can't see them - Luana might be in there, back row of the council."

Who is in the council?

(Identifying the various members by their roles) "From left to right; Healer, Teacher, Orator, Energy of Art; as in Artistry, Painting, Theater and all that. What is that? Four? Then comes Courage, five. Humor or the energy of humor, of comedy."

All male?

"We have a mixture. Humor is male, a kindly face, I've known him forever. The last one is Music. Then an energy transfer specialist. Someone who specializes in the transference of energy from one entity to another. These are all abilities Richard has access to. By the way, comedy and tragedy are the same thing. I'm hearing this again, it's faster between your ears and your lips with comedy, but tragedy has the same affect in terms of energy. Making people laugh is a quicker way to heal them, but people experiencing tragedy through your art is another way to heal them, it just takes longer - not any better, not any worse."

Not any deeper?

"No, when you're talking about energy repair in somebody that's damaged and you have the ability to make them laugh, you have an instant repair. It's like a flat tire that gets inflated instantly. When you repair somebody by showing them the damage, they cry and go through a catharsis, it takes a little bit longer, but the repair is the same. It's just laughter is a faster way of healing people. As they say, "Dying is easy, comedy is hard.""

I'll ask for a piece of advice in his life today.

"To consider what Sacred Energy means, what energy might be sacred. If you can phrase it in that way, you don't have to lose your sense of humor, but you can examine things from a different point of view. Try to allow for the Sacred more in your life. Not in terms of the church, but in terms of your honoring and paying homage to the energy within."

Can you give an example?

"It has to do with when you're about to create something. When you go to say a prayer, you put yourself in a position of prayer. You might go to a church and kneel down and go through all the accoutrements to get to the prayer and the effectiveness of the prayer is stronger because you've focused your energy into that moment. You can say a prayer anywhere, driving a car, people pray all the time - when they're on a roller coaster, "Ah! Don't kill me!" When you allow yourself to have the focus to make it Sacred, it allows you to become more connected to the prayer. If your working environment is cacophony and you're figuring "I'll fix this later," you haven't put yourself in the Sacred, in that church like atmosphere; Equipoise. The tip; bring the Sacred into your life on a daily basis, and within your relationships. There's something very miraculous about being with whoever you are with on the planet. Find the sacred in that, instead of the profane."

Let's give Richard a last chance to see if he has any questions for his guide.

(From Richard's point of view) This has been such a vast revelation of knowledge I feel like a child walking into a candy store with a million pieces of candy, "What am I supposed to do with all this?" "Oh, it's your job to pass this along to the rest of the planet." I'd like to pay homage to everybody assisting and to Scott for taking us on this journey. As well as to pay homage to Rayma and others who generously showed up to help make sense of what I'm saying. I'm speaking out loud and my brain repeatedly tries to question it, so thanks to Richard for allowing me to speak spontaneously. It's not easy, because his mind is always editing. Just to say with great awe and inspiration and praise, thank everyone for sharing this special wisdom and knowledge and let's hope I'm capable of fashioning it in such a way to benefit others. That is why we're here - to help others on the planet, to find their true selves and overcome obstacles, emotionally and energetically."

I'd like to ask his guide to show Rich a final message today.

"Just showing Richard what Sacred Art means and giving him a visual so when he's in a space where he tries to create, he'll connect to that. If you follow the Sacred in your art, it'll come out and whether it wins awards or not, isn't important, what is important is the energy."

"if you make something beautiful, it doesn't matter whether anyone sees it or not."

"It's the energy of creation; you turn it into existence and it reverberates throughout the Universe."

So that's what he needs to focus on. Creating the sacred?

"Creating Sacred art. Please remind him."

So here we are – a decade after these visits to my own council to examining trips to councils without hypnosis. What have I learned? "Try to allow for more Sacred in one's life."

And to quote Robin Williams from the flipside;

"Love love."

AUTHOR'S THANKS and BIO

To my wife and kids who have put up with me for *so long*. To Sherry for sharing her dreams, to Olivia for sharing her experiences, to RJ for recalling so much about a previous lifetime that it's mind bending.

To my pal "Kelly" for sharing her experiences with me, to all of you folks who allowed me to use pseudonyms for your council adventures. To Michael the film director, the translator from Argentina, the Minister from New Hampshire and his wife. The money analyst in Switzerland. All contributed greatly. To Robert Thurman for putting me on this journey, for Jennifer Shaffer for being so good at what you do, Scott De Tamble for showing me how it's done, to Paul Aurand, Pete Smith, Michael Newton and the crew at the Newton Institute. To Kearie, Benedict, Coco, Devin, Elise, Julia, Margaret, Romke, Yannik, Mario B, Will, Michael L, Mr. Myers, Janet, Simon, Hao, Lillian, Mirella, Andrew, Iris L and Cathy, Raylene, Chanda B, Scottie, Uno, Tracey, Marie, Howard, Laurie, Mitchell, Jessica, the many Jennifers in my life. You all know who you are.

Also the members of IANDS who introduced me to the research at the University of Virginia, Dr. Greyson, Dr. Tucker, Ed and Emily Kelly via Cheryl Birch. To Dr. Brian Weiss for continuing his research, as well as the Newton Institute, and to Dr. Wambach for leaving behind such a clear record of your work. To Akila W, thank you and don't forget me in your Nobel speech. Joel Gotler, whose memory of being stabbed in the back by his father with a spear thrown at his chariot led to the cure of a lifelong kidney issue – on camera in Hacking The Afterlife Film.

To my parents Anthy and Ro, who continue to assist me from the flipside, my brother Jeffry who has just left the planet, brothers Charlie and Robbie who continue the family traditions. Thanks to those who've supported the ongoing research for "Hacking the Afterlife" – from Quora, from the internet, those who visit RichMartini.com and follow the links to leave something to help cover costs. A million thanks. And to all these Council Members, who graciously allowed me to ask impertinent, yet important questions; thank you!

Bio: Chicago native, author and award-winning filmmaker Richard Martini has written and/or directed 9 theatrical feature films. "Flipside" was his debut non-fiction book on a topic. The documentaries

"Flipside" and "Talking to Bill Paxton" "Hacking the Afterlife" are distributed by Gaia TV and Amazon Prime.

Has written for "Variety" "Premiere" and "Inc.com" His books include "Flipside: A Tourist's Guide to the Afterlife" "It's a Wonderful Afterlife: Further Adventures in the Flipside volumes one and two" "Hacking the Afterlife" have all have been to #1 in their genres in kindle at Amazon after his appearances on "Coast to Coast" radio with George Noory. "Backstage Pass to the Flipside: Talking to the Afterlife with Jennifer Shaffer 3" and "Architecture of the Afterlife" "Tuning Into the Afterlife" are available online or via major online book outlets. This is his 10th book.

For more information: *RichMartini.com - MartiniZone.com* on YouTube. Podcast: *HackingTheAfterlife.com.* Author photo by Grammy award winning Russ Titelman.

My council. For Broski Jefferson. 3/6/45 – 4/29/22